TURKISH FOREIGN POLICY
1943-1945

SMALL STATE DIPLOMACY AND
GREAT POWER POLITICS

Prepared under the auspices of
the Center for International Studies
New York University

A list of other Studies in Peaceful Change
appears at the back of the book

TURKISH
FOREIGN POLICY
1943-1945

SMALL STATE DIPLOMACY AND
GREAT POWER POLITICS

BY EDWARD WEISBAND

PRINCETON UNIVERSITY
PRESS

L.C. Card: 72-7801

ISBN: 0-691-05653-6

Publication of this book has been aided by
a grant from the Whitney Darrow Publication Reserve
Fund of Princeton University Press

This book has been composed in Linotype Baskerville

Printed in the United States of America by
Princeton University Press

To My Mother

ACKNOWLEDGMENTS

MANY individuals generously contributed time and knowledge during the course of this study.

Professor Christina Phelps Harris, Department of Political Science of Stanford University, initially interested me in Turkish foreign policy. Professors Jan Triska and Robert C. North, codirectors of Stanford University's Institute of Political Studies, first introduced me to the intricacies of foreign-policy analysis.

Professor Ahmet Şükrü Esmer, the doyen of Turkish scholars in the field of foreign affairs, clarified several difficult problems as did Professor Fahir Armaoğlu, the former dean of Siyasal Bilgiler Fakültesi (the Political Science Faculty of the University of Ankara). Professor A. Suat Bilge, the incumbent Turkish Minister of Justice and Professor of International Law and Political Science at the University of Ankara, provided valuable insights as did Professors Mehmet Gönlübol and Halûk Ülman, both of the Siyasal Bilgiler Fakültesi. I wish also to thank Professor Enver Ziya Karal, a member of the Faculty of Language, History and Geography at the University of Ankara, for many enlightening hours.

As for diplomats and government officials, Zeki Kuneralp, at present the Turkish Ambassador in London, and the late Cevat Açıkalın, Secretary-General of the Turkish Foreign Ministry during the period about to be reviewed and a lifetime senator in the Grand National Assembly, were profoundly helpful. Feridun Cemal Erkin, former Turkish Foreign Minister and Deputy Assistant Secretary-General of the Foreign Ministry during the war, and Selim Sarper, Turkish Ambassador to Moscow in the period between 1943 and 1945, provided useful information.

Tevfik Erim, a distinguished Turkish International civil servant, was helpful in discussing the personal relationships among Turkish statesmen in the 1930's and 1940's. I would

vii

also like to express appreciation to Kâzım Özalp, the former chairman of the Parliamentary Group of the Republican People's Party and to Uluğ İğdemir, the President of the Turkish Historical Association, for sharing their rare understanding of Turkey's political institutions, personalities, and policies with me.

Ahmet Emin Yalman, who at almost ninety years of age is the dean of journalism in Turkey, conveyed the dramatic flavor of life and politics in Ankara during the Second World War. In this connection, Madame Irena Sokolnickia, wife of the Polish Ambassador to Turkey during World War II, who was the dean of the diplomatic corps in Ankara during the war, also deserves thanks.

These acknowledgments would not be complete without mentioning Mr. and Mrs. Şeyhullah Turan. I shall always cherish their many kindnesses. I must also express my gratitude to Semih and Betty Üstün. Semih must surely be among the best Turkish language instructors in the United States. He and Betty made the study of Turkish nothing less than sheer fun.

I would like to take this opportunity to thank Margaret A. Wormser for her care, patience, and efficiency in performing secretarial services. I would also like to thank Phyllis B. Goldberg for her efforts during the preparation of this book.

I would also like to acknowledge the assistance of the late Lord Swinton, director of the United Kingdom Commercial Corporation during the war.

Professors Dankwart A. Rustow and Kemal Karpat provided important insights. My sincere thanks also go to Professors Walter Weiker and George Liska as well as Harry N. Howard for their penetrating suggestions.

The Menemencioğlu family, including Nevin Menemencioğlu, Turgut Menemencioğlu, and Mrs. Nermin Streater, kindly allowed me to refer to the unpublished memoir of Numan Menemencioğlu. Mrs. Streater and Ambassador Turgut Menemencioğlu also provided invaluable insights into the person and policies of their extraordinary uncle.

ACKNOWLEDGMENTS

This study could hardly have been completed in its present form without their assistance.

I would also like to thank former President İsmet İnönü. This great leader who has done so much to guide Turkey's political destiny kindly consented to answer a whole battery of questions.

I would like to acknowledge Ü. Halûk Bayülken, at the time of writing Turkish Foreign Minister, for his friendship and encouragement. He has contributed much to this study.

My friend and former teacher, Professor Majid Khadduri of the School of Advanced International Studies of The Johns Hopkins University deserves special mention. It was, after all, his original suggestion that I pursue this study. Throughout the many years of preparation he has been a constant source of edification, insight, and knowledge. His place among the great scholars to have studied the Middle East is secure, and I am deeply grateful to have been his student.

To Professor Thomas M. Franck, Professor of International Law, School of Law, New York University, goes my everlasting appreciation. This study, like many others published under the auspices of the Peaceful Change Series of the Center for International Studies of New York University, stands as a testament to his inspiring leadership as Director of the Center. It was his firm conviction that the worlds of academic teaching and policy-making could be brought together in an interdisciplinary graduate teaching program where students and faculty would work together as colleagues on problems of pressing national and international concern that provided precisely the right kind of environment in which to complete this study. Those privileged to work with him benefited not only from his characteristically incisive criticism but from his sense of the dignity and joy of true but relevant scholarship. I am only too happy to have this opportunity to acknowledge my intellectual indebtedness.

CONTENTS

Acknowledgments   vii

Introduction   3
The Analytical Framework: The Operational Code of
   Turkish Foreign Policy
The Impact of Kemalism on the Ideology of Turkish
   Foreign Policy: The Priority of Peace,
   Sovereignty, and National Development over
   Expansionist-Revisionism
The Second Principle in the Operational Code of
   Turkish Foreign Policy: Russia as Primary
   Threat to the Security of the Republic

PART I. INSIDE TURKEY DURING THE WAR

I. The Policy-Making Process   33
   İsmet İnönü and The Constants of Turkish
      Foreign Policy
   Numan Menemencioğlu and the Ministry of
      Foreign Affairs
   The Council of Ministers
   The Grand National Assembly and the
      Parliamentary Group of the CHP
   The Turkish Historical Society

II. The Press and Public Opinion in Turkey   72
   The Press in Turkey During the War
   Public Opinion in Turkey During the War

III. A Brief Analysis of the Economic Picture   88
   The Scourge of Inflation
   Repressive Domestic Measures
   Turkey's Economic Dependence on Germany
   The Attempt to Break Loose from Germany
   The Anglo-American Preemptive Purchasing Program
   The Issue of Chromite and the Turkish Reaction
   The Result of Tough Turkish Bargaining

xi

PART II. TURKISH NEUTRALITY FROM CASABLANCA TO THE
CAIRO CONFERENCE: THE WARTIME STRATEGY

IV. Allied Ascendancy Begins: The Conference
at Casablanca 119
The Casablanca Meeting
The Casablanca Agreement and Its Consequences
The Doctrine of Unconditional Surrender

V. The Conference at Adana: A Meeting of
Misunderstandings 133
The Adana Talks
The Ambiguous Aftermath of Adana

VI. Operation Footdrag 146
The British Play Their Hand with Russia and Turkey
The Turks Drag Their Feet
Churchill Plays His Trump
The Turkish Escape and Supply Route

VII. Pressure on Turkey Mounts: Meetings of
Foreign Ministers 167
The Moscow Conference: The Russians Try to Force
Turkey into the War
Menemencioğlu and Eden at Cairo: The British
Play the Russian Hand
The New Turkish Strategy: A Tactical Shift

VIII. Pressures on Turkey at the Summit:
Meetings of Heads of Government 192
The First Cairo Conference: A Brief Handshake
The Tehran Conference: The Soviet Reversal
The Second Cairo Conference: İnönü Confronts
Roosevelt and Churchill

PART III. TURKEY'S EFFORTS TO CONTAIN ALLIED VICTORY

IX. A Time of Estrangement 219
The Deterioration of Anglo-Turkish Relations
Menemencioğlu Approaches the Russians

X. The Shift in Internal Policy 230
The *Varlık Vergisi*
The Pan-Turanian Question
Pan-Turanian Elements
Pan-Turanist Partisans in Government and
Their Influence on Decision-Making

XI. Realignment of Turkish Foreign Policy 257
The Cessation of Chromite Deliveries to Germany
Menemencioğlu's Resignation and the Closure of the
Straits to Axis Warships
Severance of Relations with Germany

XII. Turkey Between Emerging Spheres 274
Allied Victories during the Summer and Fall of 1944
Soviet Occupation of Bulgaria and the Reaction
in Turkey
The British Occupation of Greece: A Time of
Tribulation
The Churchill-Stalin Meeting of October 1944 and
the Decision to Establish Spheres of Influence

XIII. The Search for Postwar Security 295
The Dumbarton Oaks Conference
The Crimea Conference: The Ending of War
The Turkish Declaration of War
The Soviet Note of March 19, 1945
The San Francisco Conference: The Turkish Perspective

XIV. A Historical Note: The Predicted Soviet
Demands on Turkey 315

XV. Conclusion: Summary Analysis 319

Bibliography 335

Index 361

INTRODUCTION

INTRODUCTION

THE ANALYTICAL FRAMEWORK: THE OPERATIONAL CODE OF TURKISH FOREIGN POLICY

Turkish policy-makers, as they led their nation through the mine fields of wartime diplomacy, were guided by two principles. The first was the priority of peace, sovereignty, and national development over all expansionist-revisionist aims of foreign policy; the second was that the Soviet Union represented the primary threat to the security of the republic.[1] The ruling elite in Ankara, whatever their individual differences, fully accepted these principles and for all their tactical flexibility, remained rigidly, sometimes stubbornly, within the parameters established by them.

The priority of peace over expansionism and the primacy of the threat posed by the Soviet Union point to certain fundamental concerns that had confronted a long succession of Turkish and Ottoman policy-makers. Their evolution was different in the sense that the priority of peace came into being only this century with the Kemalist Revolution, whereas the perception of Russia as the main enemy had emerged during the course of three hundred years of history. But during the period under review, both served as ideological guides in foreign policy decision-making; together they constituted the operational code behind Turkish diplomacy.[2]

[1] The author wishes to thank Ü. Halûk Bayülken, at the time of writing Turkish Foreign Minister, for sharing many insights concerning the ideological foundations of Turkish foreign policy; Mr. Bayülken should not, however, be held responsible for the use I have made or failed to make of his comments.

[2] The priority of peace and Russia as central enemy comprised ideological norms in that they derived from the "manner or the content of thinking characteristic of an individual, group, or culture" and

This code, given the character of these two norms, was not without its inner contradictions. The priority of peace, for example, was noninterventionist in implication. By adhering to it, Turkish leaders rejected adventurist policies that threatened to bring Turkey into the war. Neither the glitter of new lands, nor the luster of potential glory, not even feelings of moral obligation toward the British, their only formal Great Power ally in the war, prompted them to assume a more forward diplomatic posture. The Soviet Union was one of the belligerents, however, and the Turks could not simply regard the fray with a sense of non-involved disinterest. On the contrary, the fact that their traditional "archenemy" was engaged in battle often made interventionist policies seem necessary to national defense. In the shifting strategic circumstances of the war, Turkish policy-makers, as so often in the past, identified the security of their nation with the containment of Russia. In their view, the Communist Revolution had done nothing to modify Czarist dreams of territorial expansion. On the contrary, communist ideology, certainly the Leninism and Stalinism given expression by Soviet leadership since 1917, seemed to them to openly encourage the pretensions of the Czars in this regard. They were hard put to conceive of any difference between traditional Russia and the Soviet Union insofar as territorial ambitions were concerned. To the Turks, Soviet policy toward them was still a matter of Russian design. This despite the rapprochement between the Kemalist and Bolshevik governments. To the extent that the Cold War involved perceptions of territorial conflict, Turkish

---

reflected "the integrated assertions, theories, and aims that constitute a sociopolitical program" of a society, as in *Webster's Third New International Dictionary*. The term "operational code" refers in the present context to the principles regarded by Turkish policy-makers as basic to and necessary for effective action in the field of world politics; also see Nathan Leites, *The Operational Code of the Politburo* (New York: McGraw-Hill Book Co., 1951).

leaders were thus among the first set of policy-making elites to have envisioned its broad outlines and possible rise.

Consequently, Turkish neutrality, although a policy of self-abnegation, was interventionist in that it tried to work toward the creation of a balance of power between the belligerent coalitions. On account of the partnership of the Soviet Union, Turkish officials tended to believe that a total victory on the part of the Allies could not guarantee Turkish sovereignty. They thus became determined to try to influence the direction of the postwar settlement toward an equilibrium among the Great Powers that would accomplish what the Turks assumed they could not do alone, limit Soviet expansionism. The Turkish operational code, therefore, consisted of two principles each of which suggested the advisability of opposing diplomatic positions, a neutrality that was noninvolved and one that was "activist" in purpose if not in style. In part, this is a study of how and in what ways Turkish policy-makers resolved these inconsistencies in the context of the system-transforming diplomacy of 1943-1945.

Essentially, the book is divided into two parts. The first analyzes the policy-making process inside Ankara and assesses the relative influence of individual leaders and institutions within society. Different members of the policy-making elite tended to emphasize different aspects of the operational code on the basis of role or personal history. These will be outlined. Domestic pressures, moreover, were not equally supportive of the two major operative guides to policy-making. Certain internal elements elevated different norms, the most important of these being the Pan-Turanian movement and various economic interest groups. A description of these along with an evaluation of their impact upon Turkish diplomacy will also be presented.[3] The purpose of

[3] Please note that the main discussion of the Pan-Turanian movement is found in Part II, Chap. x, below. Although it may be read in conjunction with Part I, it was placed within the context of historical

Part I, therefore, is to describe the domestic sources of Turkish foreign policy.

The second half of this study analyzes Turkish diplomacy as it responded to the exigencies of war and the imminent defeat of the Axis. To keep Turkey true to the norms of the operational code, Turkish officials employed a full range of diplomatic tactics and maneuvers. Their position at Adana in February 1943, for example, or their posture during the Cairo Conferences of late 1943, or the Turkish shifts in domestic and diplomatic policies in 1944, represent tactical applications of the operational code. Part II portrays these policies and attempts to analyze their impact during the historical period that saw the end of the Second World War but also witnessed the rise of the Cold War.

Although Turkish policy-makers unanimously concurred on the substance of their operational code, disagreements occasionally arose concerning emphasis as well as timing. The most important of these culminated in İnönü's relieving Numan Menemencioğlu of his portfolio as Foreign Minister. This will also be discussed in Part II since it reveals how conflicts develop in foreign policy decision-making even when the ideological assumptions being operationally applied are fully accepted by the officials involved.

That Turkish policy-makers responded to Great Power political pressure by employing a manipulative diplomatic strategy has already been suggested. Although forged in concrete circumstances, this strategy provides an opportunity for insight into the general nature of small state diplomacy. The concluding chapter of this book illustrates this.

Since the basic operational code behind Turkish foreign policy was ideological in nature and reflective of certain historical events and considerations, the remainder of this introduction consists of a brief history of their origins.

---

developments during 1944 in order to emphasize the diplomatic character of İnönü's suppression of the movement.

The Impact of Kemalism on the Ideology of Turkish Foreign Policy: The Priority of Peace, Sovereignty, and National Development over Expansionist-Revisionism

Of the great socio-political revolutions in the history of the modern state, including the French, the Marxist-Leninist, and the Maoist, the Kemalist Revolution in Turkey represents the only one that has produced an ideology of peace, sovereignty, and national development over that of militant revisionism. The obvious reason for this is that Turkey, after its war for independence, recouped only a fraction of its resources. Consequently its power base simply did not permit it to entertain such illusions. Perhaps, too, for this reason the impact of the Kemalist Revolution on societies other than Turkey has been minimal, at least in comparison to these other revolutions. The extent to which Atatürk and his transformation of Turkish society serve as a model of development in many other countries, especially predominantly Muslim ones like Pakistan, Malaysia, or Indonesia, should not be overlooked, however. In any event, Kemalism stands alone among revolutionary ideologies in its emphasis upon domestic reform as opposed to foreign revisionism. According to Kemalism, Turkey, in its relations with the rest of the world, was to seek recognition as a sovereign entity, commerce on the basis of comparative advantage, and to seek to enjoy the full benefits of comity and peace. The slogan "peace at home, peace abroad,"[4] signified

---

[4] For other references, see Lord (John Patrick Douglas Balfour) Kinross, *Atatürk: A Biography of Mustafa Kemal, Father of Modern Turkey* (New York: William Morrow and Co., 1965), p. 458; Ferenc A. Váli, *Bridge Across the Bosporus: The Foreign Policy of Turkey* (Baltimore: The Johns Hopkins Press, 1971), pp. 54-55. For a supplementary treatment of the ideological bases of Turkish foreign policy, see Kemal H. Karpat's essay in his edited collection, *Political and Social Thought in the Contemporary Middle East* (London: Pall Mall Press, 1968), pp. 297-305. A more general description is available in Suna Kili's *Kemalism* (İstanbul: Robert College Publications, 1970).

Atatürk's rejection of the pursuit of power and glory as distinct from security.[5] With the one exception of the Sanjak of Alexandretta, now the province of Iskenderun that was forcibly ceded to Turkey in 1939,[6] Turkish foreign policy since the founding of the republic on October 29, 1923 has remained true to the nonrevisionist norms of Kemalist ideology.

There is nothing in the annals of the Turks nor even in the personal history of Mustafa Kemal that could have led one to predict in 1923, however, that the priority of peace and national development would be so central to the ideology of the new Turkish state. Atatürk had been a soldier throughout his mature life; he had acquired preeminent authority in 1923 by galvanizing his people to fight against the incursions of the Greeks and, by implication, the British. His generation were the heirs to the imperial history of the Ottoman dynasty that was rooted in the militant Islamic traditions of the *Jihād* or Holy War.[7] Atatürk countered whatever pulls these ties may have had in a charismatic *volte-face*. As Bernard Lewis comments, "Renouncing all foreign ambitions and all pan-Turkish, pan-Ottoman, or pan-Islamic ideologies, he deliberately limited his actions

[5] This is not to suggest that Atatürk rejected the role of force in international politics. Rather, he emphasized the importance of security or in William T. R. Fox's terminology, "the power not to be coerced" as opposed to domination or "the power to coerce"; see William T. R. Fox, *The Super-Powers* (New York: Harcourt, Brace & Co., 1944); also consult Arnold Wolfers, "The Role of Power and the Role of Indifference," in his collection, *Discord and Collaboration: Essays on International Politics* (Baltimore: The Johns Hopkins Press, 1962), pp. 81-102.

[6] The author has traced this episode in a monograph entitled, "The Sanjak of Alexandretta 1920-1939: A Case Study," in R. Bayly Winder (ed.), *Near Eastern Round Table 1967-1968* (New York: New York University Press for the Near East Center and the Center for International Studies, 1969), pp. 156-224.

[7] See Majid Khadduri's classic description, *War and Peace in the Law of Islam* (Baltimore: The Johns Hopkins Press, 1955), esp. Book II, "The Law of War: the Jihād," pp. 51-137.

8

and aspirations to the national territory of Turkey as defined by treaty, and devoted the rest of his life to the grim, laborious, and unglamorous task of reconstruction."[8] His was a revolution that was truly revolutionary in that it can only be properly appreciated through recognition of the extent to which it reversed the ideological patterns of the past.[9] Atatürk transformed the ideological norms of Turkish foreign policy through a socio-political program that restructured society. Completely aware of the influence of domestic forces over foreign-policy behavior, he stated in 1927, "What particularly interests foreign policy and upon which it is founded is the internal organization of the State. Thus it is necessary that the foreign policy should agree with the internal organization."[10] The radical alteration of the ideologi-

[8] Bernard Lewis, *The Emergence of Modern Turkey* (New York: Oxford University Press, 1961), p. 250; this book remains one of the great interpretations of Turkish history available in English.

[9] For an interesting analysis of Atatürk's leadership role in transforming Turkish society, see Dankwart A. Rustow's "Atatürk's Political Leadership," in Winder, *Near Eastern Round Table*, pp. 143-55; for a fuller exposition, see Dankwart A. Rustow, "Atatürk as Founder of a State," in an edited collection by the same author, *Philosophers and Kings* (New York: George Braziller, 1970), pp. 208-47. Rustow, *ibid.*, p. 214, suggests that the central tenet in Kemalist ideology was national sovereignty; for Atatürk the Turks had a right and a duty to maintain a nation-state that "possessed complete independence"; Rustow, *ibid.*, p. 216, also argues that Atatürk stressed "the primacy of foreign over domestic policy." This contradicts the assertion here that Atatürk, after the establishment of sovereign Turkey, was primarily concerned with the problems of domestic development. The gap between the two positions is narrowed, however, insofar as Rustow and the present author do agree upon the role of two corollary propositions in Kemalist ideology stemming from the "central tenet." In Rustow's words, 1) "Rights can be effectively asserted only through one's own force, not vicariously through someone else's"; 2) "Force must back Right, but no rights must be claimed beyond what force can hold." In this Rustow seems to be suggesting a point basic to the present analysis, that Kemalism rejected all forms of revisionist expansionism and foreign adventurism.

[10] From Mustafa Kemal Atatürk, *A Speech Delivered by Ghazi Mus-*

9

cal norms of foreign policy therefore occurred as part of a process involving the near total reconstitution of the values and institutions of society. The priority of peace, sovereignty, and national development over expansionism was inextricably tied to the process of Westernization and secularization through which Atatürk reshaped Turkey and which affected the lives of every Turkish citizen. To violate the principle establishing the priority of peace over revisionism, therefore, was to fly in the face of the entire fabric of social order created by the Kemalist Revolution, and for this reason, Turkish policy-makers were so deeply committed to it.

The normative standards of peace, sovereignty, and national development over those of expansionism became operative in Turkish foreign policy through the two methods used by Atatürk to create a Turkish nation-state: secularization and Westernization. Through the pedagogy of secularization and Westernization, Atatürk demonstrated how to cement nation with state. Prior to the Kemalist movement, no notion that combined Turkish ethnicity with territoriality had existed. The political implications of nationality had been so completely destroyed by the universalist pretensions of Islamic-Ottoman orthodoxy that the very concept of a single Turkish people comprising a delimited territorial state only came into being with Atatürk. Out of this Kemalist marriage of people with territory, the ideological norms of a foreign policy appropriate to the nation-state were born. A major principle was the priority of national development and peace over imperial adventurism. To understand the genesis of the ideological norms of Turk-

tafa Kemal, President of the Turkish Republic, October 1927 (Leipzig: K. F. Koehler, 1929), p. 657; also see Váli, *Bridge Across the Bosporus,* p. 55. Rustow, "Atatürk's Political Leadership," p. 148, describes this as a "speech to end all speeches" in that it took six days to deliver to a captive audience. It has come to represent the official account of the founding of the Turkish republic.

ish foreign policy, therefore, it becomes necessary to describe the role of secularization and Westernization.

The process of secularization, first of all, was the way chosen by Atatürk of bringing the Turkish people back to their essential Turkishness. Secularization, in a Kemalist context, meant more than the destruction of the political and social authority of Islamic orthodoxy. It referred to a transformation of both the personal and collective bases of identity.

During the Ottoman period, social ascription was based almost exclusively on religious values. Until the nineteenth century, the term "Ottoman" carried neither ethnic nor national connotations. It referred to the mélange of people that had accepted the teachings of the prophet Muḥammad and were governed by the dynasty founded by Osman I. The ideology of Ottoman theocracy, therefore, conceived of nationality and citizenship solely in terms of affiliation with Islam and loyalty to the Ottoman Sultan.[11] Individuals, for example, were categorized either into Muslim, a member of the brotherhood of faith, or *Ḥarbī*, the hostile infidel, or finally the *Dhimmī*, the protected infidel who by treaty agreement with the Sublime Porte usually lived unmolested

[11] F. H. Hinsley in his *Sovereignty* (New York: Basic Books, 1966), esp. pp. 49-52, analyzes why the theocratic premises of Islamic tradition prevented the rise of even the concept of sovereignty. He writes, "God was thus absolute in the Caliphal community, and neither the nature of His power nor the nature of that community, the community of all the faithful, was technically conceivable in sovereignty terms. Such a hierarchy of authority was similarly incompatible, as incompatible as were the actual conditions, with the development of the idea of sovereignty within any of the various societies of which Islam or any of the Caliphates was made up." Lewis also analyzes the incompatibility of Islamic orthodoxy with the concept of sovereignty. For his illuminating discussion of the evolution of a concept of patriotism in Turkish culture, see Lewis, *Emergence of Modern Turkey*, Chap. x, "Community and Nation," pp. 317-55. Niyazi Berkes, the student and translator of the works of Ziya Gökalp, has also written on the subject in *The Development of Secularism in Turkey* (Montreal: McGill University Press, 1964).

in a separate community or *millet* within the empire.[12] For the Muslim, the *Ḥarbī* were objects of proselytization and were to be subjugated, if all else failed, by means of the *Jihād*. The universe of peoples were divided into two houses, the *Dār al-Islam*, the House of Islam, and the *Dār al-Ḥarb*, the House of War. It was the collective responsibility of the Muslim community to strive to expand the House of Islam until the lands of the infidel had been completely absorbed.[13] A chosen agency to achieve this was the House of Osman.

The Kemalist sponsorship of secularization was primarily designed to replace such conceptions, that had long ago ceased to reflect realistic possibilities, with those of Turkism. Although the Turks had been the predominant influence in the Ottoman Empire, as manifested among other things by the fact that their language had been the *lingua franca* of the empire, their perceptions of themselves as a people had not occurred in a manner permitting the rise of a nationalist ideology until the 1850's. During the latter half of the nineteenth century this gradually changed for a combination of reasons, the challenge of other nationalisms both within and outside the empire and the influence of Turcology inspired in part from the West, for example.[14] Gradually, there grew the realization that Turkishness could mean more than the attributes of personal style; that it could provide the cultural basis for collective identity. Kemalist secularization, by crushing the hold of Pan-Islamic and Ottomanist ideologies, represents the culmination of this trend. It thus represents the process through which nationalism was allowed to take root in the hearts and minds of the Turkish people. Henceforth, they would regard themselves as a distinct nation with their own social heritage and historical tradition.

[12] For further discussion, see Khadduri, *War and Peace*, pp. 162-201.
[13] *Ibid.*, pp. 55-73.
[14] For further analysis, see Lewis, *Emergence of Modern Turkey*, pp. 339ff.

The Turkism of Atatürk, however, was designed to
achieve more than the rise of cultural nationalism. Its purpose was the creation of a Turkish state. It rejected all forms
of vague nationalism in favor of one based on the Western
notion of statehood. Westernization meant many things to
Atatürk, including the modernization of Turkey's infrastructure, but first and foremost it meant the creation of an
independent territorially defined Turkey.

This idea, seemingly so commonplace, constituted a total
break with the past. The need to Westernize had, of course,
been apparent to Ottoman reformers for decades and, in
retrospect, the reforms they instituted represent major mile-
stones in the history of the Ottoman Empire. The purpose
of these reforms, however, was to revitalize the empire without altering it politically. Their's was thus a dual mission
of Westernizing the empire sufficiently so as to maintain it
as a viable political entity while, at the same time, preserving the empire's pristine qualities as an amalgam of many
peoples ruled autocratically by the Ottoman Sultans. They
were doomed to failure. Generation after generation of
Ottoman reformers tried but failed to achieve a balance
between these two increasingly incompatible goals. A brief
account tells the tale and illustrates how fundamentally
different the Kemalist notion of Westernization was from
all interpretations that previously had received any attention in the empire.

Sultan Selim III's attempt in 1792 to create a new military order, the Nizam-ı Cedid, by crushing the Janissary
corps, or the great reforms of Mahmud II between 1826 and
1839, were designed with the purpose of reforming the empire but solely in order to preserve it.[15] So, too, were most

15 In regard to the Nizam-ı Cedid, see *ibid.*, pp. 56ff, 70-71, 73-74;
also, Şerif Mardin, *The Genesis of Young Ottoman Thought: A Study
in the Modernization of Turkish Political Ideas* (Princeton, N. J.:
Princeton University Press, 1962), pp. 145, 217; in regard to the reforms
of Mahmud II, see Lewis, *Emergence of Modern Turkey*, pp. 75ff; also,
Mardin, *Genesis of Young Ottoman Thought*, esp. pp. 149-55; for a

of the reforms of the period of the Tanzimat.[16] The famous Imperial Rescript of the Rose Chamber (Gülhane Hatt-ı Hümâyunu) that marks the beginning of the Tanzimat on November 3, 1839, and the Illustrious Rescript (Hatt-ı Hümâyun) of February 18, 1856, did introduce many real Western social and legal innovations but never to the extent of challenging either the absolutist or the universalist assumptions behind Ottoman rule. Not until the rise of the Young Ottoman movement in the 1860's, led among others by the great literary figure Namık Kemal, did such conceptions as representative government or fatherland begin to take hold in the Ottoman Empire. But for even as progressive a thinker as Namık Kemal, the usefulness of Western political ideology depended primarily on the extent to which it pointed the way toward the revitalization of Ottoman society through the creation of a Pan-Islamic state. A devout Muslim, he held out the dream of a Pan-Islamic Ottoman state in which a parliamentary government would eliminate the absolutism of the Sultanate, a proposition for which he was exiled.[17] It was this issue of absolutism that separated many of the Young Ottomans from the men who had led the reforms of the Tanzimat while remaining loyal to the Sultan. Although the Young Ottoman advocacy of constitutionalism and parliamentary practice often resulted in arrest or banishment, they in no way were seeking to undermine the political structure of Ottoman unity with its

---

fuller description in English of the end of the Janissaries, see Howard A. Reed, "The Destruction of the Janissaries by Mahmud II in June 1826" (Princeton University, unpublished Ph.D. dissertation, 1951).

[16] *Tanzimat* means "regulations," but when referring to the historical period of its name it is taken to mean "Reorganization."

[17] This great literary figure has received much attention; the most satisfactory interpretations available in English are again those of Lewis and Mardin. It might be noted that Namık Kemal was the grandfather of Numan Menemencioğlu, Turkish Foreign Minister 1942-1944, who figures prominently in the events discussed in the major body of this study.

patchwork of nationalities. On the contrary, many of the Young Ottomans railed against the Tanzimat reformers for their failure, as they perceived it, to protect the empire from the weakening impact of a hybrid Westernization that permitted autocratic rule but diluted cultural integrity. It was in part for these reasons that they were so critical of the experiment in constitutional practice conducted in 1876 by Midhat Paşa when it did occur.

The Constitution of December 23, 1876, represents, in a certain sense, a culmination of the reforms attempted in the tradition of the Tanzimat.[18] It was certainly the last. Designed to save both the empire and the emperor, it was paradoxically but understandably attacked from both the Left and the Right, either for doing too little or too much. It offended the sensibilities of the more conservative elements in that it threatened to impose parliamentary liberalism over the rule of the Sultan. The Young Ottoman reformers, including Ziya Paşa and Namık Kemal, condemned it for introducing only the trappings of a parliamentary system without challenging the political status quo. In any event the constitution was short lived. For the Sultan, it never represented anything more than a diplomatic device with which to try to obtain leverage in European diplomatic circles.[19] The shadow of his repression would hang

[18] This episode has been the subject of study; see Robert Devereux, *The First Ottoman Constitutional Period: A Study of the Midhat Constitution and Parliament* (Baltimore: The Johns Hopkins Press, 1963).

[19] Abdülhamid, in asking Midhat Paşa to proclaim a constitution, was acting primarily to gain diplomatic leverage with the West against Russia. This is demonstrated by a concurrence of events. In the autumn of 1876, Russia was preparing to initiate a war against the Ottoman regime over Bosnia, Serbia, and Bulgaria. The Disraeli Cabinet attempted to head off the outbreak of hostilities by convening a conference of the involved parties in İstanbul. That Abdülhamid, in asking Midhat Paşa to become Grand Vezir, was acting primarily with a view to the international political situation is dramatized by the fact that he did so on December 11, only one day before the conference officially began. The actual promulgation of the constitution took place two weeks later on December 23, 1876, while the conference was still in

over the empire until the Young Turk Revolution of 1908.

During his long reign, Abdülhamid II attempted to preserve the empire by blending reactionary government with administrative, legal, and educational reform. In so doing, he struck his own balance between Westernization and imperialism. The combination failed. Technical reforms,[20] although desirable in themselves, did not satisfy increasing demands for political change. The result was the emergence of a formally organized political opposition.

This opposition soon became divided into different groups, each emphasizing varying degrees of Islamicism, liberal Ottomanism, and, for the first time, Turkism. Their aims, however, were similar in that they all sought to preserve the empire. Ideological and programmatic differences revolved almost exclusively around questions concerning the means that would politically change the empire while keeping it intact. One such group, the League for Private Initiative and Decentralization, for example, sought to transform the empire into a decentralized Ottoman state. Its leader, Prince Sabaheddin, a nephew of Abdülhamid II whose father Damad Mahmud Celaleddin Paşa had defected to Paris in December 1899, envisioned the rise of a constitutional monarchy that would rule over a loose federation of nationalities.[21] It was, of course, another group, the Committee on Union and Progress, that engineered the famous Young Turk Revolution in 1908 and finally deposed the Sultan one year later.

With the rise of the Young Turks came the ill-begotten

---

progress. When the conference failed to avoid war after four weeks of deliberations, the Sultan waited only two more weeks to banish Midhat Paşa.

[20] The Sultan promoted the construction of a telegraphic network, one such reform, in order to enhance his centralized control over the provinces. The existence of such a system, however, proved to be a great resource for Mustafa Kemal during the early days of the Kemalist resistance movement.

[21] See Lewis, *Emergence of Modern Turkey*, pp. 197-99.

dream of an empire ruled by Turks and devoted to Turkish cultural domination.[22] At first, there were those in the Young Turk movement who were less truculent in their attitudes toward other nationalities living within the empire, but the powerful wing represented by the Committee on Union and Progress became increasingly supremacist. Once in power, it brutally suppressed the separatist goals of the Bulgarian, Armenian nationalities. The rise of Turkism or *Türkçülük*,[23] to use Ziya Gökalp's word, through the Committee on Union and Progress, therefore, in no way effaced the imperial traditions of the Ottoman past. The ruling triumvirate, comprised of Enver Paşa, Cemal Paşa, and Talat Paşa, was as dedicated to the empire as Abdülhamid. They, too, fostered administrative and legal reform but this time in behalf of the Turkification of society instead of in the name of Ottoman control. For the suppressed the difference was slight. The Young Turks, moreover, were driven by Pan-Turanian dreams. Enver Paşa particularly coveted the emergence of a state that would embrace all Turks, including the millions living in Russia. Even Ziya Gökalp, the intellectual who did so much to formulate the basic doctrines of Turkism, was in 1911 propagandizing Pan-Turanism.[24] When the bug of nationalism finally bit

[22] See E. E. Ramsaur, *The Young Turks: Prelude to the Revolution of 1908* (Princeton, N.J.: Princeton University Press, 1957); for an early critical account of the movement, see Salih Keramet Bey, "The Young Turk Movement," in Eliot Grinnel Mears (ed.), *Modern Turkey* (New York: The Macmillan Co., 1924), pp. 476-90.

[23] See Elaine Diana Smith, *Turkey: Origins of the Kemalist Movement and the Government of the Grand National Assembly 1919-1923* (Washington, D.C.: Judd and Detweiler, 1959), p. 50.

[24] See Lewis, *Emergence of Modern Turkey*, p. 345. For further materials on the person and thoughts of this figure who is generally regarded as the intellectual leader of the Kemalist movement, see Ziya Gökalp, *Türkçülüğün Esasları* (*The Foundations of Turkism*) (Ankara: Matbuat ve İstihbarat Matbaası, 1923); Uriel Heyd, *Foundations of Turkish Nationalism: The Life and Teachings of Ziya Gökalp* (London: Luzac and Co., 1950); Niyazi Berkes, "Ziya Gökalp, His Contribu-

the Turkish people, therefore, its venom continued to be associated with the maintenance of the empire. Kemalism, however, was its antidote.

The notion of a Turkish state appears only with the rise of the Kemalist movement. Through the charisma of Mustafa Kemal, the Turkish nation developed a sense of patriotism that substituted loyalty to a homeland for the specious aims of imperial rule. Kemalism thus inspired the Turkish people for the first time to conceive of themselves as comprising the population of a state. During the period between May 19, 1919, when Mustafa Kemal landed at Samsun to take lead of the resistance movement, and the adoption of the basic constitution on April 20, 1924, not only was the republic established but the very idea of Turkey (*Türkiye*) was born.

Atatürk's Anatolianism, derived from his understanding of Western notions of the state, was a key to his success. Anatolia had been the traditional homeland of the Turks for centuries. Atatürk transformed previously Romantic forms of Turkism by emphasizing Anatolia as the true land of the Turks. This glorification of Anatolia, symbolized by the transference of the capital to Ankara on October 14, 1923, was not the action of a reactionary movement tending to parochialism. For Atatürk, Anatolianism represented an ideological commitment that would help Westernize his people by transforming them into a state. Just as secularization was designed to strengthen Turkism, Westernization was at first primarily designed to facilitate the emergence of a state.

The new Turkey that would arise from the flaccid heap of the Ottoman Empire would thus be founded upon the presumptive right of the Turkish people as a nation to sovereign control over the land that they had so long inhabited. This right to national sovereignty was affirmed one way or

---

tion to Turkish Nationalism," *Middle East Journal*, VIII (Autumn 1954), 375-90; also, Enver Behnan Şapolyo, *Ziya Gökalp* (İstanbul: Güven Basımevi, 1943).

another throughout all phases of the Kemalist struggle for independence: in the resolutions passed during the Erzurum Conference, July 23 to August 17, 1919,[25] in the declaration passed by the Sivas Congress on September 9, 1919,[26] in the Amasya Protocol,[27] in the famous National Pact (*Millî Misak*) of January 28, 1920,[28] in many of the first decrees of the Turkish Government after the establishment of the Grand National Assembly April 23, 1920, including the Law of Fundamental Organization, January 20, 1921.[29] As the first of the founding Nine Principles (*Dokuz Umde*) of the Republican People's Party issued on April 1, 1923, states, "Sovereignty belongs unconditionally to the nation."[30] This statement, a blend of Turkism and Anatolianism, reflects the ideological unification of nation and state. It also represents the process of Westernization and points to the Kemalist identification of sovereignty with the renunciation of all imperial pretensions. Henceforth statehood automatically implied noninterventionism or, as suggested above, the priority of peace, sovereignty, and national development over expansionist-revisionism.

Unlike so many states founded in this century that had to fight for independence against colonialism, Turkey won its sovereignty by disavowing its own colonialist past. Although the Turks, too, had to defeat in battle a number of enemies that were attempting to dissemble their homeland, they, as part of their originating national experience, renounced all desire to control the destinies of other peoples which for them was a major departure. The glory of the Turkish nation would no longer be defined by its influence over other peoples but by their social development within set bounda-

---

[25] Smith, *Turkey*, p. 17; for another account of the entire period, see Kinross, *Atatürk*, pp. 163-363.

[26] Smith, *Turkey*, pp. 19-22.   [27] *Ibid.*, pp. 23-24.

[28] *Ibid.*, p. 25; Smith provides the text, *ibid.*, pp. 153-55; also see Lewis, *Emergence of Modern Turkey*, pp. 243-45; also Mears, *Modern Turkey*, pp. 629-31.

[29] Smith, *Turkey*, p. 48.   [30] *Ibid.*, p. 160.

ries. If sovereignty meant keeping "Turkey for the Turks," it also meant the renunciation of foreign adventures and, to the extent possible, an end to ideological antipathies between Turkey and the rest of the world. Turkish foreign policy was not to be Utopian in the sense that it ignored the realities of power relations among states.[31] "Realist" pursuits, however, were to reflect an emphasis upon economic and security interests. Self-aggrandizement through the forced possession of more territory or the domination of other peoples became permanently proscribed.

The Kemalist imprint of Westernization, therefore, left more than a belief in the right of the Turkish people to territorial independence; it bestowed upon the Turkish nation and their leaders that succeeded the great Gazi, a deep commitment to the primacy of peace, sovereignty, and national development over all forms of adventurism. This ideological norm, which comprised the first tenet of the operational code behind Turkish foreign policy, helped to define the limits of interventionism beyond which Turkish policy-makers during wartime would not go, no matter what the threat or enticement. This holds especially true of İsmet İnönü, who had been at Atatürk's side throughout the formative years of the republic and had remained steadfastly loyal to its Kemalist traditions.

The Second Principle in the Operational Code of Turkish Foreign Policy: Russia as Primary Threat to the Security of the Republic

The wars between the Ottoman Empire and Czarist Russia, as is commonly recognized, played a central role in the prehistories of Turkey and the Soviet Union. Since the seventeenth century, Russia's expansionist policies in Rumelia, in the Balkans, in the Crimea, and throughout all of Transcaucasia had helped it to become the "archenemy" in Ottoman eyes. A succession of major defeats at Russian hands,

---

[31] See Váli, *Bridge Across the Bosporus*, p. 55.

moreover, had consistently confronted the Sublime Porte with the reality of its declining power.[32] It was Nicholas I, for example, who coined the phrase "the sick man of Europe" when proposing to the British Government in 1844 that the Ottoman Empire be partitioned. Generation after generation of Turks have been called upon to fight Russian armies in order to defend the ever shrinking territory of the empire. The scars, at the outbreak of World War II, still ran deep.

Revealing in this regard are conversations held in 1934 between Atatürk and General Douglas MacArthur. The Gazi predicted that a major war would break out in Europe around 1940 and that Germany would succeed in occupying all of Europe except Britain and the Soviet Union. Atatürk also declared that the "real victors" would be the Soviets.

> We Turks, as Russia's close neighbor and the nation which has fought more wars against her than any other country, are following closely the course of events there, and see the danger stripped of all camouflage. . . . The Bolsheviks have now reached a point at which they constitute the greatest threat not only to Europe but to all Asia.[33]

This statement, uttered during a period of comparatively tranquil relations between the governments in Moscow and Ankara, reflects the second ideological principle that comprised the operational code behind Turkish foreign policy during the war: the primary threat to the security of the republic was Soviet Russia.

[32] Much, of course, has been written on the history of the Eastern Question and the Russo-Ottoman rivalry. Smith, *Turkey*, pp. 129-50, provides a useful bibliography that lists most of the standard works on Ottoman history as does Lewis, *Emergence of Modern Turkey*, pp. 481-95. Of particular relevance to the present treatment is Váli, *Bridge Across the Bosporus*, Chap. I, "From Empire to Nation-State," pp. 1-41, and Chap. v, "The USSR, the Straits, and the Balkans," esp. pp. 165-73.

[33] As cited in Kinross, *Atatürk*, p. 464.

Turkish policy-makers during World War II viewed events on the battlefield primarily with this norm in mind. Losses and victories suffered or achieved by either Great Power coalition were assessed primarily in terms of what the consequences would be to the accretion of Soviet power. Turkish officials assumed that if ever they permitted a reasonable pretext to occur, the Russians would jump at the opportunity created by it in order to occupy Turkey or, at the very least, to fortify the Straits. They set out to prevent this while, at the same time, doing everything prudently within their power to strengthen the hand of the countervailing powers, Britain and the United States, but also Germany. Thus policy-makers in Ankara tended to perceive the belligerent coalitions in terms other than that of "Ally" and "Axis." The Soviet Union represented the major enemy, and whatever form the resolution of conflict eventually took, it had to contain Soviet power and Russian ambitions. This perspective, the very principle identifying the Soviet Union as the primary threat in the war, emerged in the course of the many confrontations between the two societies. Since the founding of the republic, Turkish policy-makers, as evidenced by Atatürk's remark above, have assumed that the many wars with Russia have given them a special insight into the patterns of Russian foreign policy. These wars, thirteen in all when listed together, present an outline of the foreign relations of the Ottoman Empire. Such a sketch also traces the emergence of the second principle in the Turkish operational code.

The first Russo-Ottoman war began in 1676 at the instigation of the Grand Vizier, Kara Mustafa. Turkish losses were considerable and a truce, among the first the conditions of which were not determined solely by the Sublime Porte, was negotiated on January 8, 1681.[34] The Ottomans suffered another defeat some two years later, this time at the hands of

[34] The Treaty of Sivatorok, signed between Austria and the empire in November 1606, was the first occasion where the Sublime Porte accepted a negotiated truce rather than one "dictated" by the Sultan.

the Polish hero, Jan Sobieski, outside the walls of Vienna, and the consequent alliance among the royal houses of Russia, Austria, and Poland, among others, marks the beginning of the decline of the empire.

Between 1696 and 1700, the Russians and the Austrians defeated the Ottomans once again. Several treaties signed at Karlowitz in 1699 settled temporarily the disputes between the Ottoman emperor and Austria, Poland, and Venice, but to the decided disadvantage of the former. The Ottoman Empire lost all of Transylvania as well as the rest of Hungary and Poland. The Treaty of Karlowitz represents the first occasion in which a full-fledged peace pact had been signed by the Porte. Prior to this, it had agreed only to temporary armistices in the Holy War against the infidel.

The disintegration of the military capacity of the empire was not altogether precipitous, however. The next engagement between the Ottomans and Peter the Great witnessed a victory for the Turks on the river Pruth and even a somewhat magnanimous armistice agreement toward the Russians in July 1711.[35]

The decade of the 1720's saw the theater of war shift to the Caspian region. Since neither the Ottomans nor the Russians could muster preemptive force, a spheres of influence agreement was arranged in 1724. During the following ten years the Russians made significant advances in the development of their military capabilities, while the Janissary establishment was beginning to show real signs of disintegration despite efforts at military reform led by the Grand Vizier Damad İbrahim Paşa. During the Russo-Ottoman War of 1735-1739, the Russians under the command of B. C. Münnich dealt the Ottoman Empire a decisive defeat in the Crimea in August 1736. Remarkably, the Ottomans succeeded in pushing Russian and Austrian forces back across the Danube during 1737-1738. The Treaty of Belgrade final-

[35] The text of this treaty is conveniently found in Jacob C. Hurewitz, *Diplomacy in the Near and Middle East: A Documentary Record* (2 vols.; Princeton, N.J.: D. Van Nostrand & Co., 1956), I, 39-40.

ly signed in September 1739 left the Sublime Porte in a relatively strong position given the previous defeats, but with the strategically located Ottoman fortress at Azov demolished.[36]

The sixth major war between the empire and Russia occurred thirty years later, between 1768 and 1774, in part as a result of the machinations of Catherine II. This confrontation, involving Ottoman defeats in Bessarabia and the Crimea, ended with the capacity of the empire to function as an autonomous power in European politics severely impaired. The Treaty of Küçük Kaynarca (July 21, 1774) was the most humiliating the Sublime Porte had ever been forced to sign.[37] Tatar populations were granted their independence; large provinces in Rumelia were ceded to Russia; the Ottoman emperor was required to pay an indemnity to the Czar who received the honorific title of Padishah; the right of Russia to protect Christians inside the Ottoman Empire was established.[38] Finally, the Russians were enabled to assert a long-desired presence in the Black Sea and thereby, as Hurewitz writes, "stirred the ambitions of the Tsarist regime for control of the straits."[39] After this treaty the Sublime Porte was no longer considered to be a political force in European diplomacy. Its influence derived from weakness and occasional British concern over the consequences to the European balance of power of a partitioning of the empire. The Treaty of Küçük Kaynarca therefore represents the first manifestation of the so-called Eastern Question.

Seven more wars were waged between the Ottoman Empire and Russia in the 130-year period between 1787 and 1917, almost one for every twenty years. The outcomes were unrelievedly dismal for the empire. The Treaty of Isaşi

[36] For text, see *ibid.*, pp. 47-51.   [37] *Ibid.*, pp. 54-61.

[38] What also contributed to the enmity between the Russians and the Ottomans was the ideological rivalry created by their conceptions of themselves as protectors of a major religious faith. This is manifested in this provision.

[39] *Ibid.*, p. 54.

(January 9, 1792) that ended the War of 1787-1791 confirmed the Russian hold over the regions surrounding the Danube and Dniester rivers. The Treaty of Bucharest (signed on May 28, 1812) which ended the War of 1806-1812 ceded Bessarabia to the Russians and granted independence to the Serbs. By the terms of the Treaty of Adrianople (September 14, 1829) which brought the War of 1828-1829 to a close, the Russians brought their frontier to the eastern shores of the Black Sea and obtained undisputed control over the entire Caucasus.

By 1831, the Sublime Porte had become so weak that an Egyptian army under the command of İbrahim Paşa, the son of Muḥammed Ali, actually defeated Ottoman forces at Konya. The Sublime Porte in desperation turned to Russia for help. The Russians landed on the Asian side of the Bosphorus in order to protect the Ottoman capital against the Egyptian army that was threatening it. Under the terms of the Treaty of Hünkâr İskelesi (July 8, 1833), the Sultan entered into a defense pact with the Czar, promising to consult with the head of the Russian Government on issues concerning mutual security and peace. The Sublime Porte also agreed to close the Dardanelles to the warships of non-riparian powers.[40]

The Crimean War of 1853-1856 found the Ottomans receiving the outside help of other powers, but this time against Russia. Britain and France, later Sardinia and more importantly Austria, sought to limit the extent to which Russia would dictate its terms of peace with the Sultan. The provisions of the Treaty of Paris (March 30, 1856), in which Russia abjured its right to protect Christians living in the Ottoman Empire as well as its right to sole control over the Danubian provinces, reflect the intervention by these countries.[41]

By the time the War of 1877-1878 broke out, the Ottomans had lost the support of the British, French, and Aus-

40 *Ibid.*, pp. 105-106.   41 *Ibid.*, pp. 153-56.

trian governments, however, in part as the result of cruel repressions leveled against a number of subject peoples, particularly the Bulgarians. Consequently, the Great Powers refused to assist the Sublime Porte until hostilities ceased. The war ended in a rout for the Ottomans with the Russians taking Adrianople on January 20, 1878, and marching on Constantinople as far as the Çatalca lines. The terms of peace contained in the Treaty of San Stefano, signed on March 3, 1878, reflect the overwhelming victory of Russian forces. The provinces of Kars, Ardahan, and Bayazıt (Doğubayazıt Kazası) were ceded to Russia while Rumania and Serbia received independence. Bulgaria became, for the first time, a separate entity although not yet independent. The Great Powers, appalled by these terms, sought to modify them at the Congress of Berlin, called at the behest of Chancellor Bismarck. In a treaty signed on July 13, 1878,[42] the Sanjak of Bayazıt was returned to Turkey and the territory of Bulgaria was reduced. The Sublime Porte, for its part, agreed to institute reforms designed to improve the lot of the subject peoples still remaining under Ottoman authority.

The reforms subsequently attempted by the Sublime Porte especially in Rumelia were hardly sufficient to satisfy the nationalistic spirit running rampant after the turn of the century. The result was the First Balkan War (1912-1913) which saw the rise of Serbian, Bulgarian, as well as Greek Christians against the Ottoman Sultan. Although not a Russo-Turkish war as such, the revolutionaries were openly supported by Russia. After a series of battles, the Turks were once again forced back to the Çatalca lines when a truce in the fighting was arranged. An exploratory conference of representatives of the Great Powers, held in London in December 1912 under the chairmanship of Sir Edward Grey, ceded Macedonia and western Thrace to the Balkan allies. Adrianople or Edirne was handed over to Bulgaria. On January 22, 1913, the Turkish Government presented

---

[42] *Ibid.*, pp. 187-91.

these terms to an assembly of Ottoman notables who agreed to them. A coup the following day led by Enver Paşa, however, prevented the formal acceptance of the cession of Edirne to Bulgaria with the result that on February 3, 1913, hostilities resumed. The Great Powers, particularly England, intervened to insist that the Balkan Allies begin negotiations on the basis of terms agreed to in London. This, in effect, brought the war to an end in May 1913. Within a matter of weeks, however, the so-called Second Balkan War broke out among the Allies themselves. The Turks, seizing the opportunity, took Edirne. The peace treaty of September 29, 1913, with Bulgaria and of March 14, 1914, with Serbia finally established the Meriç (Maritsa) River as the border with Bulgaria and confirmed Turkish possession of Edirne.

The final Russo-Turkish war was, of course, the First World War. The Young Turks, anxious to return the empire to its former glory and driven by anti-Russian feelings, formed a fateful alliance with Germany. On September 9, 1914, they declared the capitulations abolished. On October 29, they attacked the Russian fleet in the Black Sea with two German warships, the *Goeben* and the *Breslau*. Russia no sooner had declared war on November 4, when Enver Paşa, substituting Pan-Turanian delusions for military strategy, led the entire Ninth Turkish army to brutal defeat in the frozen climes of the Trans-Caucasian Mountains. In contrast, a series of brilliant Russian offenses, also in the Caucasus, led by General Nikolai Yudenich found Russian forces overrunning Turkish positions at Erzurum and, later, at Erzincan. Only Mustafa Kemal, commanding the Sixteenth army, succeeded in stopping them with impressive operations west of Lake Van.

It is thus perhaps one of the great ironies of history that the Russian Government was the first to recognize the Kemalist regime as the legitimate government of the new Turkey. Once Atatürk had become head of the new Turkey, he sought and achieved a modus vivendi with the new revolutionary government of the Soviet Union. The reason seems clear enough. Concurrent revolutions brought Lenin and Mustafa Kemal strangely together during their early years of rule while both were primarily engaged in the consolidation of their internal power. The first official diplomatic undertaking of the Kemalist Government was Bekir Sami Bey's mission to Moscow in 1920 designed to win arms, money, and other forms of support from the Bolshevik Government. The Kemalist movement, moreover, was not without resources of its own. Given the civil war still raging inside Russia in 1920-1921, and the threat of foreign intervention, the Turks realized that the Russians would be pleased to receive offers to refrain from inciting Turkish elements within Russian territory and to provide secure southern boundaries. As a result there were a series of agreements between the two governments during the period between 1920 and 1925, the most important of which were embodied in the Treaty of Alexandropol or Leninikan (December 3, 1920),[43] the Treaty of Friendship (March 16, 1921),[44] and the Turko-Soviet Treaty of Neutrality and Nonaggression (December 17, 1925).[45] The impact of these treaties, however, and the accommodations they presumably represent, were never sufficient to diminish the intensity of the traditional Turkish image of the Russians and their expansionist designs.[46]

[43] See the discussion in Kinross, *Atatürk*, pp. 240-45 and that of Váli, *Bridge Across the Bosporus*, p. 19.

[44] This treaty included a provision that confirmed Turkish possession of the provinces of Kars and Ardahan. Article 1 also sets forth a doctrine of nonintervention in that the contracting parties agreed not to recognize any peace treaty or other pact "imposed upon the other against its will"; for text, see Hurewitz, *Diplomacy in the Near and Middle East*, II, 95-97.

[45] *Ibid.*, pp. 142-43. This treaty involved formal commitments by both parties to remain neutral in times of conflict involving the other and to "abstain from aggression."

[46] Karl W. Deutsch and Richard L. Merritt, "Effects of Events on National and International Images," in Herbert C. Kelman (ed.), *Inter-

The impact of these two ideological norms was to influence Turkish perceptions of available foreign-policy options in such a way that they attached national security to the creation of a Great Power balance of power after the war. Since Turkey would not engage in foreign adventures but could not protect itself adequately against any major power that might, the only path open to it seemed to lie in the direction of systemic equilibrium. The checks and balances of such a system, the Turks concluded, might achieve what they could not accomplish alone: the maintenance of a high degree of autonomy for all small states including Turkey. As we shall see, this goal of establishing a balance of power after the war, especially between Germany and Soviet Russia, became uppermost in their strategic reasoning. To their horror, however, as far as they could tell, this was not true either of the British or the Americans.

---

national Behavior: A Social-Psychological Analysis (New York: Holt, Rinehart and Winston, 1965), pp. 132-87, at p. 144, point to the resilience of the Russo-Turkish mirror image by way of demonstrating how events tend to reinforce cultural or political images. They write, "Present-day Turkish government messages about national policy, such as preparedness against Russia . . . merely are apt to reinforce traditional attitudes that may stem more directly from the policies of earlier Turkish governments between 1853-1918, not to mention numerous Turkish-Russian military clashes during the seventeenth and eighteenth centuries. In this sense the traditional beliefs of peasants resemble a savings account of memories: memories of current policies of past generations seem to accumulate, sometimes with interest, until they become the traditional peasant folk belief of later generations."

PART I
INSIDE TURKEY DURING
THE WAR

ONE

THE POLICY-MAKING PROCESS

DURING the war years, the foreign policy of Turkey was one of neutrality, and the content of that policy, with its broad consistencies and pragmatic shifts was primarily the work of one man: İsmet İnönü. In molding state policy, İnönü was not alone, however. He regularly consulted a small foreign-policy "establishment" which extended through the Cabinet or Council of Ministers (Bakanlar Kurulu), the party and the parliament (Türkiye Büyük Millet Meclisi—TBMM), and included a number of individuals in the press and such organizations as the Turkish Historical Society (Türk Tarih Kurumu—TTK). Most important among those relied upon by İnönü in regard to foreign policy decision-making was Minister for Foreign Affairs 1942-1944, Numan Menemencioğlu.

İSMET İNÖNÜ AND THE CONSTANTS OF TURKISH FOREIGN POLICY

The predominant factor behind all public policy in Turkey during the period under review was the influence of İsmet İnönü.[1] Between 1943 and 1946, the distance, in

[1] Many key figures active during the period of the Seventh Assembly testify to this fact; among those interviewed by the author, Professor Ahmet Şükrü Esmer, Cavit Oral, and Kâzım Özalp were most illuminating on the role played by İnönü during wartime. Professor A. Suat Bilge, when interviewed in Ankara, April 25, 1966, was the head of the legal department of the Turkish Foreign Ministry and Professor of Political Science and Law on the Political Science Faculty (Siyasal Bilgiler Fakültesi) of the University of Ankara; he subscribes to this view as does Fahir H. Armaoğlu, former Dean of the Political Science Faculty and at present head of the Institute of International Relations (Dış Münasebetler Enstitüsü) of the University of Ankara. The author

terms of status and influence, between the President on the
one hand and the Prime Minister and Secretary-General of
the Cumhuriyet Halk Partisi (CHP) on the other increased
considerably. As Frederick Frey succinctly observes, "Put
epigrammatically, İnönü had no İnönü!"[2] In other words,
İnönü fully controlled the instruments of government. He
exercised control with authority granted to him as Chief of
State as well as with the powers he acquired as leader of the
party in a single-party political system. "The rudder of the
Turkish ship of state," as İnönü's biographer Şevket
Süreyya Aydemir remarks, "was completely in the hands of
İnönü—with all that this implies."[3]

This holds true in the realm of foreign affairs. İnönü did
not attempt to attend equally to all areas of governmental
policy. He, like all policy-makers at this level, found it necessary to select certain priority issues. Although a soldier by
training and a highly successful administrator, İnönü devoted the greatest proportion of his time and energy to

is also indebted to Professor Enver Ziya Karal, one of Turkey's eminent
historians and a member of the Turkish Historical Society during the
war, for his interesting reflections on İnönü as a foreign policy decision-
maker. Reference will be made below to these interviews as well as to
relevant written material; for a detailed description of the life and
career of İsmet İnönü before the war, see Alaettin İbrahim Gövsa,
Türk Meşhurları Ansiklopedisi (*Encyclopedia of Famous Turks*) (İstan-
bul: Yedigün Neşriyatı, 1946), pp. 188-90; Kadri Kemal Kop (ed.),
Millî Şef İnönü'nün: Hitabe, Beyanat ve Mesajları (*National Leader
İsmet İnönü: Addresses, Declaration and Messages*) (Ankara: Recep
Ulusoğlu Basımevi, 1941); Şakir Ziya Soku, *İsmet İnönü: Hususî, Askerî,
Siyasî Hayatı* (*İsmet İnönü: His Private, Military and Political Life*)
(İstanbul: Ülkü Basımevi, 1939); Yusuf Ziya Ortaç, *İsmet İnönü: 1884-
1932* (İstanbul: n.p., 1946).

[2] Frederick W. Frey, *The Turkish Political Elite* (Cambridge: The
Massachusetts Institute of Technology Press, 1965), p. 235.

[3] Şevket Süreyya Aydemir, *İkinci Adam: İsmet İnönü 1938-1950* (*The
Second Man: İsmet İnönü 1938-1950*) (İstanbul: Remzi Kitabevi, 1967),
II, 153; Zeki Kuneralp, the Turkish diplomat, told the author that
İnönü "completely controlled the political situation in Ankara during
the war." (In a personal interview, London, September 8, 1969.)

foreign affairs and, to an extent, "allowed the government to take care of itself."[4] In various instances he paid particular attention to developments outside the realm of foreign policy. For example, he personally maintained tight control over the press and other forms of mass media; he directed the administration of martial law through his Minister of Defense, Ali Rıza Artunkal, and carefully watched the progress of the *Varlık Vergisi* or tax on wealth which was levied at the end of 1942.[5] But foreign policy was, for the most part, İnönü's prime concern in this period.

There is much evidence for this. Feridun Cemal Erkin, at this time the Deputy Assistant Secretary-General of the Foreign Ministry, recalls having five or six weekly sessions with the President in which İnönü established the guidelines for that week's decisions.[6] One of Cevat Açıkalın's first innovations upon becoming Secretary-General of the Ministry for Foreign Affairs, furthermore, was to institute a practice whereby all diplomatic correspondence and cablegrams were transmitted immediately to İnönü.[7] This procedure enabled the President to be apprised of diplomatic messages and intelligence reports as soon as they were received. İnönü could thus keep abreast of developments as easily as Menemencioğlu or other officials at the Foreign Ministry. İnönü concedes that these procedures greatly facilitated his management of foreign affairs.[8] Reports and

[4] The quotation is from a personal interview with former President İsmet İnönü in his home in Ankara on September 21, 1966; for a statement on İnönü's training as a soldier and career as an administrator, see e.g., Aydemir, *The Second Man*, p. 210.

[5] These issues will be discussed below.

[6] Personal interview with Feridun Cemal Erkin, Ankara, June 16, 1966.

[7] The author was privileged to have many conversations with Cevat Açıkalın during the summer and early autumn of 1966; quotations and citations referring to personal interviews with Senator Açıkalın are all from this period.

[8] Personal interviews with former President İsmet İnönü, Ankara, September 21 and September 22, 1966.

recommendations from his ambassadors in the field represent, parenthetically, the single source of information upon which İnönü claims to have most relied in decision-making.

To understand Turkish foreign policy during the period under review, therefore, one must outline those constant elements or considerations which İnönü brought to bear as he guided Turkey's course during the war. At the top of any such list is his well-known innate sense of caution. İnönü claims to have conducted foreign relations according to what he describes as the first principle of military strategy, the need to be prudent. "The one cardinal principle in setting foreign policy which I followed throughout the war was that an early mistake is hard to make up."[9] Consequently, Turkey, under İnönü, was always prepared to enter the war—but only under certain conditions set by him. He ruled out from the first rash actions or bold initiatives which could have deliberately involved Turkey in the fray.[10]

This element in İnönü's make-up, although it may have succeeded in keeping the war from being fought on Turkish territory, did not save the former President from severe criticism during the war or since. In answer to the question as to what was Turkish policy during the war, Nadir Nadi, for example, states, "We [Nadi and a clique of friends in the Turkish press] used to kid about our administration, calling it a 'banana regime,' meaning that it was whatever you made of it."[11] Later, much criticism fell upon İnönü

[9] Personal interview with İsmet İnönü, September 21, 1966.

[10] Both İnönü and Açıkalın testified to this but much supporting evidence is found in İnönü's speeches delivered every November 1 throughout the war; consult Hasan Âli Yücel (ed.), *İnönü'nün Söylev ve Demeçleri* (*İnönü's Speeches and Declarations*), Vol. I (İstanbul: Millî Eğitim Basımevi, 1946). İnönü made a particularly interesting comment in his November 1, 1942 address when he stated that it was becoming increasingly more difficult to pursue this well-known policy "as everybody is becoming more and more irritated"; *ibid.*, p. 369.

[11] Nadir Nadi, *Perde Aralığından* (*Through an Opening in the Curtain*) (İstanbul: Cumhuriyet Yayınları, 1964), p. 22; Tekin Erer in a

on the grounds that his prudence destroyed the manliness of the Turkish nation.[12] Others, outside Turkey, have since described Turkish foreign policy during the war as "timid"[13] or "pusillanimous."[14] But İnönü remains convinced that his application of prudence to foreign policy decision-making during wartime spared Turkey considerable damage and much grief.[15] Public sentiment at the time seems to have substantially agreed. İnönü received a position paper prepared by the Turkish Foreign Ministry in March 1943, indicating that all segments of the population, including the army, were opposed to his taking a more aggressive stand, specifically, one which could lead to war.[16]

Turkish neutrality, then, as guided by İnönü, was essentially a policy of waiting.[17] The philosophy of prudence as applied by İnönü caused him to develop a specific style of decision-making, one which moved day by day. Aydemir pointed to this phenomenon when he wrote that İnönü,

---

critical examination of the İnönü regime entitled *Yasakçılar* (*Prohibitionists*) (İstanbul: Toker Matbassı, 1964), p. 72, writes: "Turkey was an ally of democratic nations in those days [during the Second World War], but it was governed by a national leader [*Millî Şef*]. In other words, it would drift in the direction of whichever side would win and say 'I am with You.'"

[12] Aydemir, *The Second Man*, p. 135; Nadi, who is generally highly critical of İnönü in his book discounts this particular criticism as being "weird accusations," *Opening in the Curtain*, p. 37.

[13] Professor William H. Medlicott, for example, in a personal interview in his office at the London School of Economics and Political Science, London, March 10, 1966; Professor Medlicott is the author of *The Economic Blockade*, Vols. I and II (London: Longmans Green & Co., 1952-59).

[14] George E. Kirk, "Turkey," in *The War and the Neutrals*, ed. Arnold and Veronica M. Toynbee (London: Oxford University Press for the Royal Institute of International Relations, 1956), pp. 345-66 at p. 365.

[15] Personal interview with former President İnönü in Çankaya, September 21, 1966

[16] Turkish public opinion during the war is discussed below.

[17] The author is indebted to Professor A. Suat Bilge for the phrase *neutralité d'attente*.

during the war, was always struggling to gain time through an attentiveness that evaluated events from hour to hour.[18] As İnönü himself once cautioned, "Let us first live through the evening, let us first live through the morning, and not by years, months or weeks."[19]

This is not to suggest that İnönü failed to imbue Turkish foreign policy with definition or purpose. On the contrary, he brought to bear in policy-making a deep sense of conviction. The fact that he prudently worked day to day does not mean that he possessed no long-term objectives. On the contrary, he operated with a commitment to one basic proposition: the preservation of Turkey for the Turks.[20] Ever since Atatürk's revolution had taken root in Turkey, the touchstone of Turkish foreign policy had been the inviolability of Turkey, the right of Turks to determine their destiny on their own land.[21] During the war, İnönü regarded this right and the preservation of Turkish boundaries as the basic tenets and principal objectives of Turkish foreign policy. Atatürk was the one to instruct his people

[18] Aydemir, *The Second Man*, pp. 157-58.

[19] *Ibid.*, for an elaboration on the theme of prudence in bargaining written by İnönü, see "Negotiations and the National Interest," in James T. Shotwell (ed.), *Perspectives in Peace (1910-1960)* (New York: Frederick A. Praeger for the Carnegie Endowment for International Peace, 1960), pp. 135-49.

[20] Personal interview with former President İnönü; also, İsmet İnönü, *Ten Eventful Years: 1938-1947* (New York: Turkish Information Office, 1948); İsmet İnönü, "La Neutralité Turque au cours de la Deuxieme Guerre Mondiale" ("Turkish Neutrality during the Second World War"), *Dictionnaire Diplomatique Internationale*, Vol. IV, published under the direction of A. F. Frangulis (Paris: Académie Diplomatique Internationale, 1957).

[21] Professor Enver Ziya Karal emphasized the importance of this in our conversation in his home in Ankara, May 2, 1966; Professor Karal has, of course, written widely on this subject, e.g., *Türkiye Cumhuriyeti Tarihi: 1918-1944 (History of the Turkish Republic: 1918-1944)* (İstanbul: Millî Eğitim Basımevi, 1945); John Kingsley Birge also mentions this as being an underlying principle of Turkish foreign policy; see his "Turkey Between Two Wars," *Foreign Policy Reports*, XX (November 1, 1944), 194-207 at p. 195.

on the territorial basis of the modern state during their transition from an imperial power to a sovereign entity, but it was İnönü who convinced Lord Curzon at Lausanne in 1923 that Turkish territorial integrity could not be transgressed except at great cost to the violator.[22] He seems to have convinced Mussolini and Hitler of this as well. This deserves special attention.

İnönü began to fear Mussolini's Italy long before he feared the threat created by Nazi Germany; it was Mussolini, not Hitler, who first threatened Turkish boundaries. After the Italian campaign against Ethiopia in 1935, İnönü became apprehensive that Mussolini might attempt to annex the fertile region of Antalya, something Mussolini repeatedly indicated he wanted to do.[23] On the other hand, the desire of the German people to be reunited by annexing the Saar seemed quite comprehensible in 1935.[24] İnönü's attitude changed once the Germans invaded Eastern Europe and the Balkans; the Sudetenland was one thing, Poland and Bulgaria another.[25] Throughout the war, more-

[22] For an account of how İnönü handled the British at the conference in Lausanne, written in Turkish and published during the war, consult Ali Naci Karacan, *Lozan Konferansı ve İsmet Paşa* (*The Lausanne Conference and İsmet Paşa* (İstanbul: Maarif Matbaası, 1943); for an account almost as favorable as Karacan's, written in English, consult Roderic H. Davison, "Turkish Diplomacy from Mudros to Lausanne," in Gordon A. Craig and Felix Gilbert (eds.), *The Diplomats: 1919-1939* (Princeton, N.J.: Princeton University Press, 1953), pp. 172-209; also Kinross, *Atatürk*, pp. 354-63.

[23] Aydemir, *The Second Man*, p. 111; also Anthony Eden, *Facing The Dictators* (London: Cassell, 1962), pp. 320-21.

[24] Professor Enver Ziya Karal suggested this in our meeting of May 2, 1966.

[25] Cevat Açıkalın emphasized the significance of the effect Germany's invasion of Poland and Bulgaria had upon İnönü; consult *İnönü's Speeches and Declarations*, p. 358, where İnönü describes the independence of the Balkan nations as one of the basic foundations of Turkish foreign policy; Ahmet Şükrü Esmer's "Türk Diplomasisi" ("Turkish Diplomacy"), *Yeni Türkiye* (*The New Turkey*) (İstanbul: Nebioğlu Yayınevi, 1959), p. 86, emphasizes the deep sympathy for the Poles in Ankara throughout the war.

over, especially during the period of Axis ascendancy, İnönü never hesitated to inform the Germans, or the Italians, that Turkey would not peaceably tolerate an encroachment on its territory, that Turkey would respond to the fullest against any invasion.

Nor did this fail to have an effect in Berlin. Ribbentrop on one occasion instructed von Papen, for example, that all pressure against Turkey was to remain completely diplomatic since the War Command felt certain that it possessed insufficient force for an invasion of Turkey.[26] İnönü's constancy regarding the inviolability of Turkish territory may also help to explain the substance of Hitler's letter to him, March 3, 1941. This letter, transmitted while German troops were in the process of occupying Bulgaria, conveyed assurances that the occupation of Bulgaria in no way threatened Turkey.[27] Hitler informed İnönü that he was taking the precaution of keeping his forces sixty kilometers from the Turkish border so that no doubt would be cast

[26] Lothar Krecker, *Deutschland und die Turkei im Zweiten Weltkrieg* (*Germany and Turkey in the Second World War*) (Frankfurt am Main: Frankfurter Wissenschaftliche Beitrage Vittorio Klostermann, 1964), p. 225.

[27] A copy of this letter can be found in *ibid.*, appendix; also United States, Department of State, *Documents on German Foreign Policy 1918-1945, The War Years*, Series D, XII (Washington, D.C.: United States Government Printing Office, 1962), 201-203; entire series henceforth referred to as *Docs.Ger.F.P.*; Hitler's letter to İnönü, reads, "I have . . . ordered that German troop divisions marching into Bulgaria remain so far away from Turkish borders that no stray shots . . . will be fired." For İnönü's letter of reply, *Docs.Ger.F.P.*, Series D, XII, 286-87. In an annual address on November 1, 1941, before the *TBMM*, İnönü described the implications of Hitler's letter in the following way: "It can be said that our relations with Germany underwent their severest test during their Balkan movements. . . . Hitler, who had then observed and understood our concern and worry expressed his friendship in a private letter to me. My reply to him through the consent of the government and our subsequent correspondence created the atmosphere of mutual confidence which resulted in the Turkish-German treaty of June 18, 1941"; see *İnönü's Speeches and Declarations*, pp. 358-59.

upon Germany's intention to leave Turkish borders alone.[28] This letter, therefore, can be said to represent Hitler's acknowledgment of İnönü's determination to preserve the identity of Turkish boundaries.

In return, Hitler attempted to exact a price; Turkey must do nothing openly destructive toward Germany. Hitler's threats of consequent reprisals in his letter of March 1941 served to heighten in İnönü's eyes the importance of prudence. Indeed, for the duration of the war, İnönü and Hitler both consistently disavowed initiatives toward the other's country that could have led to open conflict.[29] Each

[28] Despite these assurances, the Turks took the precaution of destroying the bridges across the Meriç (Maritza) River that flows between Turkey and Bulgaria; see Türkkaya Ataöv, *Turkish Foreign Policy: 1939-1945* (Ankara: Ankara Üniversitesi Siyasal Bilgiler Fakültesi Yayınları, No. 197-79, 1965), p. 89; Cevat Açıkalın, "Turkey's International Relations," *International Relations*, Vol. XXIII, No. 4 (October 1947), 477-91 at p. 484. It might be noted that railroad traffic was not completely stopped between Bulgaria and Turkey during the war; chrome shipments, for example, were delivered to Germany via this route in 1943; see William Arthur Helseth, "Turkey and the United States: 1784-1945" (Washington, D.C.: Foreign Service Institute, 1957, mimeo.), p. 136; Turkey entered into a nonaggression agreement with Bulgaria on February 17, 1941, a few weeks before Germany invaded it. Menemencioğlu resented the fact that the British and American governments interpreted this arrangement to mean that Turkey had washed its hands of what happened in Bulgaria thus opening up the path for a German thrust through Bulgaria to Greece; the ambassador in Turkey (MacMurray) to the Secretary of State, Ankara, February 2, 1941, United States, Department of State, *Foreign Relations of the United States: Diplomatic Papers*, 1941, I (Washington, D.C.: United States Government Printing Office, 1958), 287-89; entire series henceforth referred to as *Foreign Relations*.

[29] This tacit agreement was later formalized in a Treaty of Territorial Integrity and Friendship between Germany and Turkey, signed June 18, 1941, only four days before the Germans invaded Soviet Russia. The treaty contained a commitment on the part of the two signatories "to respect each other's territorial inviolability and integrity and to abstain from any kind of direct or indirect action against each other"; a Turkish translation of this treaty can be found in İsmail

restrained the other by restraining himself first. They calculated that what each country could force the other to do
was less important than what they hoped the other would
not do. Each country chose a number of negative initiatives,
the Turkish refusal to allow the British to construct air-

Soysal, *Türkiye'nin Dış Münasebetleriyle ilgili Başlıca Siyasî Anlaşmaları* (*Turkey's Main Political Agreements Related to its Foreign Policy*) (Ankara: Türkiye İş Bankası Kültür Yayınları [and the] Türk
Tarih Kurumu Basımevi, 1965), p. 291; it is entitled "Türk-Alman
Saldırmazlık Analaşması"; the Russians published the correspondence
leading up to the signing of this treaty; Arkhivnoe Upravlenie Ministerstva Inostrannikh Diel Soiuza SSR. Dokumenti Ministerstva Inostrannikh Diel Germanii, Vipusk II, *Germanskaia Politika v. Turtsii (1941-
1943)*, OGIZ-Gospolitizdat, 1946; the Russians did so somewhat for the
purpose of embarrassing Turkey politically when they were beginning
to exert diplomatic pressure for a revised regime of the Straits; this collection was translated into French by Madeleine and Michel Eristov
and was published under the title, *Documents Secrets du Ministre des
Affaires Étrangers d'Allemagne* (Paris: Éditions Paul Dupont, 1946);
in July 1968, a Turkish edition of these documents was published in
İstanbul under the title, *İkinci Dünya Savaşının Gizli Belgeleri: Almanya'nın Türkiye Politikası—Almanya Dışişleri Bakanlığı Arşivinden
1941-1943* (*Secret Documents of the Second World War: The Turkish
Policy of Germany—from the Archives of the German Foreign Ministry
1941-1943*) (İstanbul: May Yayınları, 1968); henceforth referred to as
Secret Documents; for references to this treaty, consult *Secret Documents*, documents 1-9, pp. 13-35; a copy in English of the text of the
treaty can be found in Great Britain, *British and Foreign State Papers*,
His Majesty's Stationery Office, Vol. 144, pp. 816-17; also, *Docs.Ger.F.P.*,
Series D, XIII, 1,051; for a fuller analysis of the diplomatic period surrounding the signing of the treaty, consult Ataöv, *Turkish Foreign Policy*, p. 93; Rıfkı Salim Burçak, *Türk-Rus-İngiliz Münasebetleri: 1791-
1941* (*Turkish-Russian-English Relations: 1791-1941*) (İstanbul: Aydınlık Matbaası, 1946), p. 127, refers to the treaty; also consult Franz von
Papen, *Memoirs* (New York: E. P. Dutton and Co., 1953), pp. 477-79;
Professor Ahmet Şükrü Esmer in his account emphasizes that the Turks
succeeded in forcing the Germans to accept a statement in the text of
the agreement which indicated that "existing commitments," meaning
the Turkish Treaty of Mutual Assistance with Great Britain, were in no
way abrogated. Esmer also suggests that the United States was much
more offended by this treaty than the British and as a result ceased all
shipments of aid for a month; see Ahmet Şükrü Esmer and Oral Sander,

bases, for example, to avoid the one positive initiative both feared—attack from the other side.

İnönü, therefore, guided Turkish foreign policy during the war with a view to preserving Turkey's territorial integrity—as little interested in gaining ground as in losing some. This is doubly significant. If İnönü regarded Turkey as inviolable, he also accepted the converse. Firmly unwilling to cede one iota of Turkish territory, he was vehemently opposed to the forced cession of any other nation's lands. This applied to Russia as well. From the first days of German victory over Stalinist Russia to the end of 1942, German diplomacy failed to tempt İnönü into assuming a more favorable position toward Germany by holding out the bait of provinces ceded from the Soviet Union.[30] İnönü's resistance to adventurist or irredentist notions, as we shall see, severely limited the influence of the Pan-Turanian movement over Turkish foreign policy at this time.[31]

Turkey's acquiring territory from Russia was hardly a genuine problem, however. Much more pressing was the

"İkinci Dünya Savaşında Türk Dış Politikası" ("Turkish Foreign Policy during the Second World War"), *Olaylarla Türk Dış Politikası: 1919-1965 (Turkish Foreign Policy with Events)*, prepared by the members of the Institute of Foreign Relations of the Political Science Faculty of the University of Ankara (Ankara: Dışişleri Bakanlığı Matbaası, 1968), pp. 126-71 at p. 145; henceforth referred to as *Turkish Foreign Policy*.

[30] This is an important point and will be discussed below; for now let it suffice to refer to Ali Fuad Erden, *İsmet İnönü* (İstanbul: Burhanettin Erenler Matbaası, 1952), p. 214; General Ali Fuad Erden visited the Russian theater of war behind German lines in 1941 as a guest of the German Government and returned to Ankara to report that "all that was left of Russia was its snow" (interview with Professor Ahmet Şükrü Esmer in Ankara, April 20, 1966). Erden, who strongly supported Turkey's assuming a more positive attitude toward the Axis, writes that İnönü remained "cold and unshakable like a rock of granite" in the face of all attempts to make him decide for any reason whatsoever to join Germany.

[31] Professor Ahmet Şükrü Esmer, personal interview, Ankara, May 11, 1966; this will be discussed further below.

possibility that the Soviet Union might seek to annex Turkish land. To be sure, this was one of İnönü's central concerns. Although when he acceded to the Presidency, Turkey and the Soviet Union had undergone a period of nearly twenty years of unprecedented good will, İnönü's personal experience had taught him to be wary of Russian ambitions. İnönü, for example, had traveled to the Soviet Union in 1930, at a time when Turkish foreign policy was attempting to establish closer relations with the Western Powers but without offending Russia.[32] When he returned, İnönü presented the following analysis to Atatürk before a caucus of the Parliamentary Group of the CHP: the Russians felt isolated particularly by the West and, as a result, were obsessed by what they believed to be the insecurity of their western borders. They desired and would continue to seek friendly relations with Turkey provided that the Turks refrained from actions which seemed calculated to put pressure upon Russia from the east. The Russians wanted their eastern front to be quiet in order to gain time to secure their borders in the west. As soon as they came to regard their western boundaries as safe, "they will no longer care to be friends with us," İnönü advised. Once the Soviets felt no longer threatened by the Western Powers, they would become more aggressive in the east and quite possibly toward Turkey as well. For that reason, İnönü wanted the Soviets never to feel too secure in the west. During April and May 1939, when British and French diplomats were exploring the possibility of a Turkish-British-French-Soviet alliance, İnönü, in the words of Sir Alexander Cadogan,

[32] Mehmet Gönlübol and Cem Sar, *Atatürk ve Türkiye'nin Dış Politikası: 1919-1938 (Atatürk and the Foreign Policy of Turkey: 1919-1938)* (İstanbul: Millî Eğitim Basımevi, 1963), pp. 106-107; for their history of Turkish foreign policy before the war also consult "Türk Dış Politikası: 1919-1938 Yılları Arasında" ("Turkish Foreign Policy: Between the Years 1919-1938"), in *Turkish Foreign Policy*, pp. 5-125; their discussion of the Lausanne Conference is found on pp. 47-55, see above, n. 22.

"insisted on the necessity of Russian participation in hostilities on the ground that it would be disastrous if the Russian Army alone were left intact at the end of a European war." Russian insecurity in the west was Turkey's best protection. That protection would be removed if ever a war in Western Europe created a path for Russian dominance. İnönü predicted in 1930 that this could not in any case occur for at least 25 years. Russia was eventually implicated in the war, as İnönü had hoped; its incipient victory over German forces in 1943, however, made it seem as if the Soviets were about to become completely secure in the west twelve years earlier than İnönü had anticipated.[33]

This perspective of his on Soviet policies may help to explain the severity of Turkey's reaction to Stalin's suggestion at the end of 1941 that the British and the Russians give to Turkey certain areas held by Greece. İnönü feared that perhaps Stalin was planning to annex parts of Turkey in the east. In short, if the one constant that guided İnönü's hand during the Second World War was the preservation of Turkey's territorial integrity, the variable which he perceived to most threaten it was the political ambition of the Soviet Union.[34] During the period of German ascendancy, İnönü did not hesitate to make his apprehensions clear to British and American diplomats. His first official conversation with U.S. Ambassador Laurence A. Steinhardt, upon the latter's presentation of credentials, dealt largely with the question of Soviet influence in the postwar world. Despite the fact that German forces were advancing rapidly toward Stalingrad, the Turkish President warned Steinhardt that if Russia defeated Germany, Soviet imperialism

[33] Aydemir, *The Second Man*, p. 108; Cadogan's report in Great Britain, Foreign Office. *Documents on British Foreign Policy 1919-1939*, E. L. Woodward and Rohan Butler (eds.), Third Series, 1939, v (London: His Majesty's Stationery Office, 1952), p. 452; henceforth referred to as *Docs.Brit.F.P.*

[34] This conclusion was validated in personal talks with former President İsmet İnönü and Cevat Açıkalın.

45

would attempt to "over-run" Europe and the Middle East. İnönü let it be known that he was concerned that Russia, if ever in a position to do so, would take possession of the Straits.[35]

During the war, İnönü brought to his side men of similar conviction. In formulating decisions as well as in executing them, İnönü relied heavily upon a number of subordinates. Since they were well versed in world affairs and politics, İnönü granted his advisers a considerable degree of power and allowed them to function, if not independently, then at least freely. Yet in analyzing the role played by these men, we must be careful to keep the following in mind: the freedom to make and implement foreign policy was a gift from İnönü and can be understood only in the context of his domination over Turkish politics during the period under review.[36] Among those who served in a decision-making capacity as a result of İnönü's discretion, the most important was Numan Menemencioğlu.

NUMAN MENEMENCIOĞLU AND THE MINISTRY OF FOREIGN AFFAIRS

Numan Rıfat Menemencioğlu, a deeply complex individual, a lawyer by training but a diplomat by natural inclination, became Turkey's Minister for Foreign Affairs in August 1942 and served in that capacity until his resigna-

[35] Steinhardt's appointment as Ambassador to Turkey was first announced on January 7, 1942. He had been serving as U.S. Ambassador in Moscow and replaced John Van Antwerp MacMurray. Steinhardt presented his credentials on March 10, 1942, which served as the occasion for his conversation with President İnönü; *Foreign Relations,* 1942, IV, 683.

[36] Nadir Nadi goes so far as to write, "He [İnönü] wanted to run the government up to its last detail singlehandedly. It was heard often that he would bypass the concerned ministers, or even the Prime Minister, to give orders to general secretaries and general directors . . ."; see *Opening in the Curtain,* pp. 185-86.

tion in June 1944.[37] The grandson of Namık Kemal, Menemencioğlu was born the second son of Refet Paşa who represented the province of Menemen in the First Assembly.[38]
Educated in Lausanne, Switzerland, he entered the Foreign
Ministry in 1914. After the War of Independence, he rose
through the ranks, and his unusual brilliance quickly won
Atatürk's respect. In 1933 he became the Secretary-General
of the Foreign Ministry. More an intellectual than a politician, more adept at manipulating ideas than people,
Numan Menemencioğlu deeply enjoyed the study and practice of foreign policy.[39] He writes of his appointment as

[37] The author is especially grateful to Mrs. Nermin Streater, niece of
Numan Menemencioğlu and the sister of Turgut Menemencioğlu as
well as Cevat Açıkalın and Madame Irene Sokolnickia for their descrip-
tions of and insight into the personality and character of Numan
Menemencioğlu; Mrs. Streater, who is the daughter of Muvaffak
Menemencioğlu, the director of the *Anadolu Ajansı* (Anatolian News
Agency) during the years 1927 to 1944 and the older brother of Numan
Menemencioğlu, was in Ankara throughout the war and knew Numan
Menemencioğlu intimately well during this phase of his life; Madame
Irene Sokolnickia, the wife of Michel Sokolnicki, who was Polish Am-
bassador to Turkey during the war and dean of the diplomatic corps
in Ankara for this period, also met often with İnönü and Menemenci-
oğlu. The author interviewed Madame Sokolnickia in Ankara during
July and August 1966; Mrs. Streater was interviewed in London, August
7, August 21, and September 5, 1969.

[38] A short description of the life and career of Numan Menemencioğlu can be found in *Encyclopedia of Famous Turks*, p. 252.

[39] Zeki Kuneralp, former Secretary-General of the Turkish Foreign
Ministry and at the time of writing Turkish Ambassador in London
has said, "Menemencioğlu was not a politician but an intellectual who
deeply loved the Foreign Ministry"; in a personal interview with the
author, London, September 8, 1969. Sir Hughe Knatchbull-Hugessen,
British Ambassador to Turkey during the war, told the author, "I have
never met a mind so quick or cultivated as Numan [Menemencioğlu's]";
in a personal interview, Barham, England, March 1966. French Ambassador René Massigli has written, "There was always an intellectual
pleasure of rare quality during a compact conversation with Numan
Bey [Menemencioğlu]; pliancy of language, delicacy of analysis, ingenu-
ity of hypothesis and subtlety of juridical argumentation, contributed

Foreign Minister, "I did not have to do an apprenticeship for this position; for thirteen years I had found myself at the head of the services of the Ministry and on account of this in the midst of directing the foreign policy of Turkey. My responsibility had now simply taken a different form."[40] Indeed, it can be said that as years went by the Ministry for Foreign Affairs became the center of his life.

By the time Menemencioğlu became Foreign Minister in 1942, he had already done much to mold the Ministry's personnel. Upon attaining the position of Secretary-General, he had immediately begun to improve the caliber of people in the diplomatic service and Foreign Ministry. Men such as Abdullah Zeki Polar, Muharrem Nuri Birgi, the chief and assistant chief respectively of the Ministry's first political bureau; Nurretin Vergin, the head of the second political bureau; Şadi Kavur, Menemencioğlu's private secretary; Turgut Menemencioğlu, the *chef de cabinet* to the Secretary-General of the Foreign Ministry; Kadri Rizan, head of the office of protocol; Fatin Rüştü Zorlu, in 1944 a young consul-general in Beirut were all protégés of Menemencioğlu.[41] Intent upon educating them for their

equally to enrich his statements"; see Massigli's *La Turquie Devant La Guerre: Mission à Ankara 1939-1940* (*Turkey Before the War: Mission to Ankara 1939-1940*) (Paris: Librairie Plon, 1964), p. 282.

[40] The author wishes to express appreciation to Madame Nevin Menemencioğlu, the adopted daughter of Numan Menemencioğlu, for her kind permission to refer to the unpublished manuscript of the memoirs of Numan Menemencioğlu which he entitled, "Les Détroits vus de la Mediterranée: Aperçus, Études, Souvenirs" ("The Straits Seen from the Mediterranean: Glimpses, Studies, Memories"). This manuscript, written in French while Menemencioğlu was serving as Turkish Ambassador in Paris, covers his experiences and outlines his thoughts during the time he was Foreign Minister as well as the period immediately before and after this. The present study represents the first occasion where permission has been granted in Turkey or elsewhere to consult this work; the specific citation above is found on p. 267 of the manuscript; henceforth referred to as *Menemencioğlu Manuscript*.

[41] For a complete listing of the officers in the Turkish Ministry for

work in the Ministry, Menemencioğlu would regularly hold seminars at his home or office during which he would examine them on their reactions to various problems or situations.

Eventually, Menemencioğlu became "quite tyrannical" in protecting his control of the Ministry.[42] The heart or

Foreign Affairs and its diplomatic corps, see Türkiye Cumhuriyeti Başbakanlık. Basın ve Yayın Umum Müdürlüğü Yayınları, *Devlet Yıllığı: 1944-1945* (*The State Yearbook*) (Ankara: Devlet Matbaası, 1945), pp. 137-42; *Almanach de Gotha: Annuaire Genéalogique, Diplomatique et Statistique* (*Almanac of Gotha: Genealogical, Diplomatic and Statistical Yearbook*) (Gotha: Justus Perthes, 1944), pp. 1,122-133. Dankwart A. Rustow attributes the development of a professional diplomatic service to Tevfik Rüştü Aras, Turkish Foreign Minister, 1925-1938, in "Foreign Policy of The Turkish Republic," in Roy C. Macridis (ed.), *Foreign Policy in World Politics* (Englewood Cliffs, N.J.: Prentice-Hall, Inc., 1959), pp. 295-322 at p. 316. Aras did play an important role in developing a properly trained diplomatic corps, but by 1936 he had actually come to resent the extent to which Menemencioğlu had taken over the Ministry. Menemencioğlu did not respect Aras' judgment or personal integrity and supported İnönü in late 1938 when the latter dropped Aras from the Cabinet. The final break between Menemencioğlu and Aras came in 1937 when they disagreed over Turkish participation in the Nyon Conference. On that occasion, Aras urged that Turkey accept the British and French invitations to attend, while Menemencioğlu, along with İnönü, urged greater caution. In any event, Menemencioğlu played a more significant role and deserves greater credit than Aras for the growth of a well-trained diplomatic corps in Turkey during the 1930's.

The author wishes to thank Mr. Tevfik K. Erim for his many insights into the personal relations of the chief officers of the Turkish Ministry for Foreign Affairs during the period before the war; Mr. Erim, a former member of the Turkish diplomatic corps, also served for many years in the Secretariat of the League of Nations; he had studied law in Lausanne, Switzerland at the same time as Menemencioğlu and knew him and Tevfik Rüştü Aras well; interviewed in London, March 3, 1966. For concise histories of this period, consult *Turkish Foreign Policy*, pp. 104-108; Burçak, *Turkish-Russian-English Relations*, pp. 63-64; Nihat Erim, "The Development of the Anglo-Turkish Alliance," *Asiatic Review*, XLII (October 1946), 347-51. Tevfik K. Erim and Nihat Erim Kocaeli are not related.

[42] Mrs. Nermin Streater in a personal interview.

49

"workbench"[43] of the Ministry was its three political bureaus which handled different regions of the world. The first political bureau took charge of Western Europe, France, England, Germany, the United States, and the rest of North America; the second political bureau was responsible for Eastern Europe, the Balkans, Greece, and the Soviet Union. The third political bureau, directed by Şeyfullah Esin, handled Middle Eastern and Far Eastern affairs. Menemencioğlu actively directed these offices and regarded them very much as his domaine.[44] Although difficult to substantiate, it is not difficult to suppose that given İnönü's own personal interest in foreign affairs, this among many other factors eventually prompted İnönü to request Menemencioğlu's resignation as Foreign Minister. In any case, İnönü respected Menemencioğlu's judgment and his ability to negotiate adroitly: "Numan knew his art, was quick and could react shrewdly to situations as they developed."[45]

Equal in importance to Menemencioğlu's tight control over the Ministry of Foreign Affairs is the position he held in relation to his peers on the Council of Ministers. They generally regarded him as the *primes inter pares*. In this vein Frederick Frey suggests that during this period the Foreign Minister "moved to the apex of the ministerial pyramid."[46] Menemencioğlu's relation to the rest of the

[43] Cevat Açıkalın coined the phrase cited above while describing the machinery of the Ministry of Foreign Affairs to the author.

[44] Cevat Açıkalın, Turgut Menemencioğlu, and Mrs. Streater agree on this.

[45] Former President İsmet İnönü in a personal interview with the author.

[46] Frey, *The Turkish Political Elite*, p. 265; Nimet Arzık, in a scathing diatribe directed against the person and policies of İsmet İnönü, *Bitmeyen Kavga: İsmet İnönü* (*Unending Quarrel: İsmet İnönü*) (Ankara: Kurtuluş Matbaası, 1966), writes of Menemencioğlu, "Before becoming a Minister he was Secretary-General of the Ministry of Foreign Affairs . . . for a long time. Even then his words and his name were mentioned more often than the best ministers . . . ," p. 66. Arzık

Turkish Cabinet is demonstrated by the fact that his office
became the unofficial daily meeting place for certain key
officials from other ministries. Every morning at 9 A.M.,
Prime Minister Şükrü Saracoğlu would begin his official day
with a meeting with Menemencioğlu in the office of the
Foreign Minister. This allowed them to present a united
front to the world and enabled them to coordinate their
activities. Other ministers would also attend. Cevat Açıkalın, who usually was present, recalls the central role
played by Menemencioğlu in all these discussions.[47]

Much controversy exists over the policies pursued during
the war by Menemencioğlu. No less a person than Anthony
Eden became convinced before the end of the war that
Menemencioğlu was indeed favorably predisposed to the
Axis cause.[48] Two things can be said now in this regard.
First, Menemencioğlu's primary aim as Foreign Minister
was to keep Turkey out of the war. He, like İnönü, feared
that no matter on what side Turkey fought, it would be
devastated, perhaps even occupied. Menemencioğlu succinctly described the rationale behind his determination
when he declared, "The objective of our foreign policy is
to protect our self-determination to the end. I am certain
that if we entered the war, our self-determination will be
destroyed, and there would not be the slightest gain for my
country."[49] On another occasion, Menemencioğlu declared,

---

recalls Menemencioğlu addressing other members of the Cabinet in
peremptory fashion.

[47] Cevat Açıkalın remembers the mock rage of a foreign diplomat
who had received identical answers to a particularly delicate question
from President İnönü, Numan Menemencioğlu, Prime Minister Şükrü
Saracoğlu and, finally, from Açıkalın himself all in the same day. "How
do you do it?" the diplomat asked Açıkalın. "That is the secret of our
kitchen," Açıkalın replied.

[48] Personal interview with Sir Hughe Knatchbull-Hugessen, Barham,
England, 1966.

[49] Ambassador in Ankara (von Papen) to Foreign Ministry in Berlin,
Therapia, July 13, 1943, *Captured Files*, German Embassy in Ankara,

"We are egoists and fight exclusively for ourselves."[50]
Menemencioğlu believed that Turkey had everything to
lose and nothing to gain in the war; it sought no territory,
no radical revision of its international position. Turkey's
only compensation for entering the war, Menemencioğlu
believed, would be to serve as a battleground for the Great
Powers.

This leads to a second point. Menemencioğlu's reading
of history had convinced him that the self-determination of
small nations was best protected by a balance of power
among the Great Powers. He saw nothing inherently wrong
in a policy that maintained an alliance with Great Britain
and a friendship pact with Nazi Germany. They were both
aspects of Turkey's "active neutrality," a neutrality that
sought to protect Turkey while preventing either the Soviet
Union or Nazi Germany from becoming inordinately
strong.[51] Menemencioğlu once declared, "We therefore wish
this war was not to end with a total defeat either on the
one side or on the other. . . . Turkey's interest is in the
direction of a negotiated peace."[52] Both these countries,
Menemencioğlu thought, shared the same kinds of aggressive designs upon the smaller states; each would only be
held in check by the other. Menemencioğlu shared İnönü's
concern during the period of the "phony war," that the war
would be fought with Russia remaining on the side lines,
neutral and untouched. In a similar vein, Menemencioğlu
deeply feared what might happen should Germany's ambi-

National Archives, Washington, D.C., Micro-copy, Serial T-120, Roll
2618, Frames E 364726/2-E 364726/5; henceforth all unpublished German Embassy documents will be referred to as *Captured Files*, NA.
. . . This is confirmed by Mrs. Nermin Streater, London, September 5,
1969.

[50] Memorandum by the Ambassador in Turkey (von Papen), Ankara,
March 28, 1941, *Docs.Ger.F.P.*, Series D, XII, 411.

[51] This phrase was coined by Menemencioğlu; see *Secret Documents*,
p. 96.

[52] *Docs.Ger.F.P.*, XII, 411.

tion go unchecked. While German ascendancy was still at its peak, he declared, "We do not want much to do with the new order [Third Reich]. For us, every state has its right to independence and its own existence. Too little is known about the aims of the new order propagated by the Axis."[53] By the same token, Menemencioğlu believed that it would be inadvisable for Turkey to become too much the creature of any one large state. During the period of German ascendancy and before the war, Menemencioğlu did much to prevent Turkey from becoming too dependent, economically or militarily, upon Germany. It was he who informed Ribbentrop in 1938 that Turkey wished to pursue a neutralist policy, meaning that Turkey would cease to purchase the bulk of its military equipment from Germany and would begin to model its air force after the R.A.F.[54] Menemencioğlu's reluctance to allow Turkey to become too dependent upon any one of the Great Powers, and his conviction that a balance of power among the great states was a small power's best protection also led him to warn the British about eliminating Germany as a force in European politics. He told Eden, "If you win the war and want to destroy Germany, then a tremendous abyss will open in Europe, a whirlpool into which we, Turkey, will also be swept."[55] As Russia's victories over Germany increased, Menemencioğlu's fears that Germany would no longer serve to check

[53] For Menemencioğlu's concern that the Soviet Union would not be forced to fight in the war, *Docs.Brit.F.P.*, v, 399; for his fear relating to Germany, *Docs.Ger.F.P.*, xii, 411.

[54] Ataöv, *Turkish Foreign Policy*, p. 9.

[55] *Docs.Ger.F.P.*, xii, 411; Raymond Lacoste writes that the Turks perceived the peril of allowing Russia to become too powerful in the heart of Europe with greater "acuity" than the British Ambassador in Moscow, Sir Stafford Cripps, who proposed in early 1942 that the Russians permanently occupy Berlin; *La Russie Soviétique et la Question D'Orient: La Poussée Soviétique vers les Mers Chauds—Mediterranée et Golfe Persique* (Soviet Russia and the Eastern Question: The Soviet Push Toward Warm Waters—the Persian Gulf and the Mediterranean) (Paris: Les Éditions Internationales, 1946), p. 78.

Russian ambitions also became greater. "The basic principle of our policy has always been to have a strong Germany in the center of Europe."[56] This brought him into conflict with British policy, especially when it sought to enlist Turkey's help in what Menemencioğlu perceived to be the establishment of Soviet domination over Europe. "The English know this," he declared, "for we have proved by our policy that although we are allied [to Britain] we will not let ourselves be misused in any way for the advantage of any third power [the Soviet Union]."[57] In short, Menemencioğlu was not guided by what he regarded as false sentimentality. If İnönü brought a prudent style to bear in foreign policy decision-making, Menemencioğlu exercised a strict pragmatic realism. "In politics," he once said, "let us not speak of sentiment, old friendships, and brotherhoods in arms, but of . . . actual interests. . . ." This he did with passionate intensity.

THE COUNCIL OF MINISTERS

Recurrent ill health prompted Menemencioğlu in 1943 to appoint Cevat Açıkalın as Secretary-General of the Foreign Ministry and to bring him back from Moscow where he had

---

[56] *Docs.Ger.F.P.*, XII, 411; Menemencioğlu, like other Turkish statesmen, harbored an instinctive distrust of the Soviet Union and would occasionally reveal this in the company of British and American officials. In November 1941, for example, a Russian submarine sank a small Turkish ship in the Black Sea near the Bulgarian coast. The Turkish Government decided not to protest the incident but Menemencioğlu gave his opinion to the American Ambassador. "He [Menemencioğlu] expressed with unwonted heat," MacMurray reported, "his conviction that although Russia is, under [the] circumstances, making common cause with such democracies as [the] United States and Great Britain she can never be expected to share their political concepts or rid herself of innate political viciousness"; the Ambassador in Turkey (MacMurray) to the Secretary of State, Ankara, November 24, 1941, *Foreign Relations*, 1941, I, 334.

[57] *Docs.Ger.F.P.*, XII, 411.

been serving as ambassador.[58] Açıkalın had studied in Switzerland with Menemencioğlu and, although they were not close at this time, they soon established a firm friendship. By 1943, Menemencioğlu had come to regard Açıkalın as one of his trusted friends and colleagues.[59] Açıkalın's judgment of Menemencioğlu parallels that of İnönü: "a craftsman, a brilliant negotiator, an astute bargainer."[60]

Cevat Açıkalın, therefore, played a role in decision-making during the period examined and deserves special mention. When he returned from Moscow to become Secretary-General, March 1943, he had completed 23 years of service in the diplomatic corps of the Foreign Ministry. Married to the sister of Atatürk's divorced wife, he, like Menemencioğlu, won the favor of Atatürk while still a young man. Although always junior to Menemencioğlu, he played a particularly important role as Secretary-General not only because of his friendship with the Foreign Minister, but on account of İnönü's personal trust in him: "Cevat Açıkalın was always close and useful to me."[61] While in Moscow, Açıkalın came to fear that the Russians might attempt to transform the Turkish entry into the war into an excuse to establish themselves militarily in Turkey.[62] Although not a policy-maker in the sense that he could act independently of İnönü or Menemencioğlu, he took part in most major policy decisions between 1943 and 1946 and can be described as being influential.

Şükrü Saracoğlu also played a role in foreign policy decision-making during the period of Allied ascendancy. Prime Minister since August 1942, a long-time friend of Menemencioğlu, he had served as Foreign Minister in the Cabinet of Refik Saydam during the period of German

[58] Cevat Açıkalın in a personal interview.
[59] Mrs. Nermin Streater in a personal interview, August 21, 1969.
[60] Cevat Açıkalın in a personal interview.
[61] Former President İsmet İnönü in a personal interview, Ankara, September 21, 1966.
[62] İnönü and Açıkalın both confirm this.

ascendancy.[63] In that capacity he had suffered considerable abuse in Moscow where he went for nearly a month, September 26-October 17, 1939, to try to forge an agreement with the Soviet Russia suddenly allied to Nazi Germany.[64]

[63] A brief sketch of Şükrü Saracoğlu's career can be found in *Encyclopedia of Famous Turks*, pp. 345-46.

[64] Much has been written on Saracoğlu's frustrating but significant journey to the Soviet Union; for Turkish reactions at the time, Yunus Nadi, "Türkiye ve Rusya" ("Turkey and Russia"), *Cumhuriyet*, October 19, 1939; Asım Us, "Türk-Rus Münasebetleri" ("Turkish-Russian Relations"), *Vakit*, October 19, 1939; most revealing is Hüseyin Cahit Yalçın, "Türk-Rus Müzakereleri" ("Turkish-Russian Relations"), *Yeni Sabah*, October 19, 1939; for İnönü's comments before the TBMM, see *İnönü's Speeches and Declarations*, pp. 341-42; Molotov subsequently denied making strenuous demands on Turkey; cf. V. M. Molotov, *Foreign Policy of the Soviet Union* (Moscow: Foreign Language Publishing House, 1939), Report by the Chairman of the Council of People's Commissars of the U.S.S.R. and People's Commissar of Foreign Affairs at the Extraordinary Fifth Session of the Supreme Soviet of the U.S.S.R., October 31, 1939, esp. pp. 14-15; V. M. Molotov, *Soviet Peace Policy* (London: Lawrence and Wishart, 1941), pp. 42-43. For fuller analyses, Feridun Cemal Erkin, *Les Relations Turco-Soviétiques et La Question Des Détroits* (*Turkish-Russian Relations and the Question of the Straits*) (Ankara: Başnur Matbaası, 1968), pp. 160-179; *Turkish Foreign Policy*, pp. 129-32; Burçak, *Turkish-Russian-English Relations*, pp. 98-99; Ataöv, *Turkish Foreign Policy*, pp. 56-60; Harry N. Howard, "Germany, The Soviet Union, and Turkey During World War II," United States, Department of State, *Bulletin*, July 18, 1948, pp. 63-78 at pp. 65-66; George E. Kirk, "Turkey: The U.S.S.R. and the Middle East, 1939-1945," in *The Middle East in the War*, ed. George E. Kirk (London: Oxford University Press for the Royal Institute of International Relations, 1952), pp. 443-67 at pp. 444-45; Rustow, "Foreign Policy of the Turkish Republic," pp. 302-303; Necmettin Sadak, "Turkey Faces the Soviets," *Foreign Affairs*, xxvii (April 1949), 449-61 at p. 453; Annette Baker Fox, "Turkey: Neutral Ally," *The Power of Small States: Diplomacy in World War II* (Chicago: The University of Chicago Press, 1959), pp. 10-42 at p. 14.

On this occasion, Molotov demanded that the Turks close the Straits and recognize the Nazi-Soviet partition of Poland; Molotov also spoke of a Balkan bloc under Russian-German control. While Saracoğlu was in Moscow, Ribbentrop arrived completely unannounced to the Turkish delegation and Saracoğlu was kept waiting while Molotov and Ribbentrop bargained. Most accounts agree that this encounter marks

His failure at this time to establish an understanding with
the Russians, and Molotov's bluster which bordered on insult, deeply colored this man's perceptions of Russian postwar aims. Saracoğlu carried the portfolios of both Foreign
Minister and Prime Minister for three months after Menemencioğlu resigned.

The influence of the other members of the Council of
Ministers in regard to foreign policy decision-making was

---

the end of friendly Turkish-Russian relations and the beginning of
revised anxieties in Ankara concerning the imperialist aspirations of the
Soviet Union. Ambassador MacMurray, however, reported that the
Turks were first "disillusioned" by Russia's entering into an alliance
with Nazi Germany which the Turks perceived as a "blow in the face";
the Ambassador in Turkey (MacMurray) to President Roosevelt, Ankara, November 9, 1939, *Foreign Relations*, 1940, I, 446; Elizabeth
Wiskemann points out that Hitler attempted to justify in Mussolini's
eyes the German-Russian agreement on the grounds that it would ensure a "modification of the attitude of Turkey"; *The Rome-Berlin
Axis: A History of the Relations Between Hitler and Mussolini* (London: Oxford University Press, 1949), p. 166; it might also be noted that
one day before the Nazi-Soviet Pact was signed, August 22, 1939, Hitler
told his military generals "Since Kemal's death, Turkey has been ruled
by small minds, unsteady, weak men," International Military Tribunal,
Office of Chief of Counsel for Prosecution of Axis Criminality. *Nazi
Conspiracy and Aggression* (Washington, D.C.: United States Government Printing Office, 1947), III, 583. David Dallin claims that during
August and September 1943 the Kremlin tried to avoid conveying the
impression that it wanted an open break with the Turks and made
an effort to give Saracoğlu a "friendly" farewell; *Soviet Russia's Foreign
Policy* (New Haven: Yale University Press, 1943), p. 110; one of the
more interesting accounts of this entire period is René Massigli's; Massigli describes the atmosphere in Ankara during Saracoğlu's visit to
Moscow, *Turkey Before the War*, pp. 273-92; he suggests that Menemencioğlu blamed the rise of Russia's renewed interest in obtaining
control over the Straits upon "the breaking of Hitler's wave," p. 283;
for text of the treaty of nonaggression between Germany and Russia,
Docs.Ger.F.P., Series D, VII, 245-47; for fuller documentation, United
States, Department of State, *Nazi-Soviet Relations 1939-1940: Documents from the Archives of the German Foreign Office*, Raymond
James Sontag and James Stuart Beddie (eds.) (Washington, D.C.:
United States Government Printing Office, 1948), esp. pp. 1-78.

highly circumscribed. In terms of status and influence, the Ministers of Finance and Interior followed the Minister for Foreign Affairs in the "ministerial parade"[65] during the period of the Seventh Assembly, 1943-1946. Fuat Ağralı and Nurullah Esat Sümer both occupied the position of Minister of Finance during the period under review. Recep Peker, Minister of the Interior, August 17, 1942 to May 25, 1943, advocated a more militantly pro-Axis policy.[66] He was succeeded by Hilmi Uran[67] who, along with Ali Rıza Artunkal,[68] the Minister of Defense, and Hasan Âli Yücel,[69]

[65] Frey, The Turkish Political Elite, p. 265; U.S. Ambassador Steinhardt described Saracoğlu's Cabinet as "outstandingly pro-American and pro-British" which was an oversimplification; the Ambassador in Turkey (Steinhardt) to the Secretary of State, Ankara, July 17, 1942, Foreign Relations, 1942, IV, 727.

[66] Professor Ahmet Şükrü Esmer, personal interview, Ankara, May 11, 1966; Uluğ İğdemir, the incumbent president of the Türk Tarih Kurumu (Turkish Historical Society), personal interview, Ankara, May 20, 1966; and Kâzım Özalp, personal interview, İstanbul, September 27, 1966. They all testify to the fact that Recep Peker advocated Turkey's coming into the war on the Axis side; Walter F. Weiker, "The Free Party of 1930 in Turkey," unpublished Ph.D. dissertation submitted to the Department of Politics, Princeton University, 1962, discusses Peker's career in the period before the war, while Kemal H. Karpat, Turkey's Politics: The Transition to a Multi-Party System (Princeton, N.J.: Princeton University Press, 1959) discusses his career after the war; Karpat writes of Peker, "He was known to be a defender of the one-party system and of strong leadership, opposed to compromise and inclined to use force even in cases when differences of opinion could have been solved with a minimum of diplomacy" (p. 170).

[67] Hilmi Uran has written an interesting account of his experience during wartime, e.g., Hatıralarım (Memoirs) (Ankara: Ayyıldız Matbaası, 1959).

[68] Artunkal served as Minister of Defense throughout the period of the Seventh Assembly, 1943-1946, the last individual, as Professor Frederick Frey observes, to serve a full Assembly term in office; The Turkish Political Elite, p. 291.

[69] Yücel, who edited İnönü's Speeches and Declarations, came under particularly heavy fire from Rightist elements in Turkey for his role in suppressing the Pan-Turanian movement during the war; he is also the author of Hürriyet Gene Hürriyet (Freedom, Again Freedom)

Minister of Education and especially close to İnönü, was instrumental in crushing the activities of the Pan-Turanian movement after May 1944. The well-known General Ali Fuat Cebesoy served as Minister of Communications during much of the war. Like Peker, he is said to have regarded the Second World War as Turkey's opportunity to destroy the power of the Soviet Union.[70] Unlike Peker, however, he was not staunchly pro-Axis.[71]

Finally, one more name should be mentioned, that of Hasan Saka. Although not as important in the context of this history as Numan Menemencioğlu, Hasan Saka succeeded Menemencioğlu as Foreign Minister on September 15, 1944, and represented Turkey at the San Francisco Conference. He came to this post in some measure as a result of the distinguished role he played as liaison between the executive and legislative branches in matters dealing with foreign policy.[72] Let us turn now to the role played by the

---

(Ankara: Türk Tarih Kurumu Basımevi, 1960). Kemal Karpat reports that he was able to find no evidence to support rumors circulating in Ankara during the war to the effect that Şükrü Saracoğlu actually had begun to support the racists and extreme nationalists as a way of combatting Yücel, who, supported by Leftist intellectuals, was attempting to become Prime Minister; *Turkey's Politics*, p. 265, n. 39. It is true, however, that Yücel was associated with the Left in Turkey, although never, as has been alleged, with communist elements.

[70] Professor A. Ş. Esmer, Uluğ İğdemir, and Kâzım Özalp described the attitudes of General Ali Fuat Cebesoy as being, above all, anti-Russian, in personal interviews as listed above, n. 61.

[71] Some evidence of his views is found in Ali Fuat Cebesoy, *Gl. Ali Fuat Cebesoy'un Siyasî Hatıraları* (*General Ali Fuat Cebesoy's Political Memoirs*) (İstanbul: Vatan Neşriyatı, 1957). Ahmet Emin Yalman, who describes Recep Peker, for example, as a "totalitarian personality," categorically denies that Ali Fuat Cebesoy was of the same character. Cebesoy deeply feared the Russians, Yalman reports, but was not pro-Axis and certainly was not influenced by Pan-Turanian ideas; personal interview, London, September, 1969.

[72] Kâzım Özalp, personal interview, İstanbul, September 27, 1966; for a brief account of Hasan Saka's life and career, see *Encyclopedia of Famous Turks*, p. 341.

Assembly in setting foreign policy during the latter part of the war.

THE GRAND NATIONAL ASSEMBLY AND THE
PARLIAMENTARY GROUP OF THE CHP

The fact that İsmet İnönü dominated Ankara's political environment should not suggest that he set himself above the Assembly. On the contrary, he made it a regular practice to communicate with the members of the Grand National Assembly. "People think of me as possessing supreme authority during the war," İnönü has said by way of denying it. "I wielded only a spiritual or guiding influence and always had to submit proposals to the Grand National Assembly."[73] It behooves us, therefore, to discuss the Assembly, its relationship to foreign policy-making during the war, the deputies who played a particularly crucial role, and the operations of the so-called Parliamentary or Party Group of the CHP.

Under Article 4 of the Turkish Constitution of 1924, the sovereignty of the Turkish Republic rested in the hands of the people of the nation who delegated their authority to the Grand National Assembly.[74] The Assembly in turn bestowed its authority upon the President of the Republic who had to be elected by the members of the Assembly from among their own number. The President appointed the

[73] Personal interview with former President İsmet İnönü, Ankara, September 22, 1966.

[74] The Turkish Constitution of 1924 is available in Bülent Tanor and Taner Beygo (eds.), *Türk Anayasaları* (*Turkish Constitutions*) (İstanbul: Filiz Kitabevi, 1964), pp. 105-106; also A. Şeref Gözübüyük and Suna Kili (eds.), *Türk Anayasa Metinleri* (*Turkish Constitutional Texts*) (Ankara Üniversitesi Siyasal Bilgiler Fakültesi İdarî İlimler Enstitüsü Yayın, No. 2) (Ankara: Ajans-Türk Matbaası, 1957), pp. 101-23; for an introduction to this document, Edward C. Smith, "Debates on the Turkish Constitution of 1924," *Ankara Üniversitesi Siyasal Bilgiler Fakültesi Dergisi*, XIII (September 1958), 82-130; all references here to the Constitution of 1924 are from the Tanor and Beygo collection.

Prime Minister from among the deputies in the Assembly; he also had to approve of the Prime Minister's selection of ministers and could preside at will over meetings of the Council of Ministers.[75] The Assembly, therefore, exercised its authority through the President and the Ministerial Council. Beneath this basic structure, however, was the reality of politics. Despite several attempts to develop a dual-party system in Turkey, the CHP existed alone. It alone provided access to political power, it alone influenced government policy. As early as 1923 a practice developed in which a parliamentary group of the CHP was formed for the purpose of coordinating the policies of the government with the party.[76] By the time war broke out, responsibility for approving state policy had shifted from the Assembly as such to the Parliamentary Group (Meclis Gurubu) of the CHP.[77] As A. C. Edwards observed, "a kind of dual parliament" existed in Ankara.[78]

This was particularly convenient during wartime. The debates in the Assembly had to be, by customary practice, open and public, whereas caucuses of the Parliamentary Group were held *in camera*. The formal meetings of the Assembly, held Mondays, Wednesdays, and Fridays, could therefore be perfunctory, revealing what the government

[75] For Articles 4, 5, 6, and 7 of the Constitution of 1924, Tanor and Beygo, *Turkish Constitutions*, pp. 105-106; also consult Frey, *The Turkish Political Elite*, p. 9. The important thing to note here is that despite the separation of government into legislative and executive branches, there was no formal separation of power as is the case with the American system of government.

[76] *Ibid.*, p. 11; for a discussion of party and government control, *ibid.*, pp. 303-304.

[77] Mümtaz Soysal, *Dış Politika ve Parlamento: Dış Politika Alanındaki Yasama-Yürütme İlişkileri Üzerinde Karşılaştırmalı Bir İnceleme (Foreign Policy and the Parliament: A Comparative Analysis of the Legislative-Executive Relations in the Field of Foreign Politics)* (Ankara: Ankara Üniversitesi Siyasal Bilgiler Fakültesi Yayınları, No. 183-165, 1964), pp. 104-105.

[78] A. C. Edwards, "Impact of the War on Turkey," *International Affairs*, XXII (July 1946), 389-401 at p. 393.

wanted and reflecting unanimity.[79] The genuine parliamentary work—taking stands and forging consensus, reviewing policies of the Council of Ministers, debating decisions, and constructing new legislation—was to be secretly discharged during sessions of the Parliamentary Group which regularly met on Tuesdays. Fuat Sirmen, Minister of Economics for most of the war, has indicated that government ministers were often apprehensive about the questioning they might receive during a caucus of the Parliamentary Group; on occasion they might emerge exhausted or even dismissed from office.[80] In any case, the Council of Ministers received direction during the Tuesday sessions of the Parliamentary Group and kept in close contact with the key members of the Parliamentary Group throughout the week.[81] It is this that particularly interests us here.

What emerges from an examination of the relationship between the executive and legislative branches in regard to foreign policy decision-making is that the power as well as the authority to commit Turkey to a policy decision shifted far in favor of the executive; debates in the Parliamentary Group, alive as they may have been, essentially served the purpose of fulfilling what has been described as the "lyrical function" of parliament.[82] Menemencioğlu and to a lesser extent, Saracoğlu, presented decisions before the Assembly not strictly for approval, which they could almost count on anyway, but in order to legitimize decisions. In seeking such legitimacy, in opening up foreign-policy issues to ques-

[79] M. Soysal, *Foreign Policy and the Parliament*, p. 114; Soysal in part bases his discussion here on an interview with Fuat Sirmen, the incumbent President of the Grand National Assembly.

[80] *Ibid.*, also Hilmi Uran, *Memoirs*, p. 342.

[81] *Ibid.*; also Tahsin Bekir Balta, *Türkiyede Yasama-Yürütme Münasebeti (Legislative-Executive Relations in Turkey)* (Ankara: Ankara Üniversitesi Siyasal Bilgiler Fakültesi Yayınları, No. 100-82, İdarî İlimler Enstitüsü Yayınları, No. 9, 1960), p. 45.

[82] The concept of the "lyrical function" was originally suggested to me by Professor Harry Eckstein of Princeton University.

tions and debate, İnönü, who by law could not participate in these discussions or vote in the Assembly, preserved the fundamental machinery set up by the Constitution of 1924.[83]

In their capacities as deputies in the Assembly and as members of the Parliamentary Group of the CHP, the vast majority of officials in the legislative branch of government were content to allow İnönü and his subordinates to set foreign policy. Cavit Oral, a member of the Assembly and Parliamentary Group at this time, has suggested that Menemencioğlu and other officials on the Council of Ministers would present policies for discussion, but usually only after the key decisions had already been taken.[84] There was never any possibility of the Group rejecting a decision taken by İnönü or Menemencioğlu. Oral suggests, however, that debate on issues having to do with foreign policy allowed the members of the Group to speak their minds for or against the policies of the Council of Ministers. It also permitted them to question Menemencioğlu, Saracoğlu, or other ministers intensively, and to satisfy themselves that the government had considered all the various contingencies relating to a particular problem. The end result was that the İnönü Government succeeded in creating a consensus, which it might already have, but which might not have been as freely given. Further evidence supports Oral's testimony. Pro-

---

[83] Article 32 of the Constitution of 1924 states, "as long as the President occupies the position of the President of the Republic, he cannot participate in the Assembly debates and cannot vote"; see Tanor and Beygo, *Turkish Constitutions*, p. 110; the President's assumed right to direct the conduct of foreign affairs was constitutionally granted only by a symbolic authorization: "The President will appoint the political representatives ambassadors of the Turkish Republic to foreign countries and will receive the political representatives of the foreign countries" (Article 37), as in Tanor and Beygo, p. 111.

[84] Personal interview with Cavit Oral, Ankara, June 5, 1966; Cavit Oral, a deputy in the Seventh Assembly, was active in discussions dealing with foreign policy during the period under review.

fessor Mümtaz Soysal found that İnönü's November 1 addresses, for example, set forth the general guidelines for discussions in the Parliamentary Group throughout the remainder of the year.[85] He also suggests that the motion passed by the Assembly on May 11, 1945, expressing the gratitude of the deputies to President İnönü for his conduct of foreign affairs, represents a prime example of the extent to which the Assembly acted as a rubberstamp of the Council of Ministers in regard to foreign-policy issues. Finally, both Professors Esmer and Armaoğlu have suggested that the committee on foreign affairs in the Assembly was not important either in terms of personal status or in terms of its influence over policy. It was essentially a committee that consistently followed the line set by the government, that is, İnönü.[86] In short, there seems to have been a circular flow: the Assembly bestowed its authority upon the President to act in its and the republic's name; İnönü, in turn, sought the Assembly's approval of foreign-policy decisions; the Assembly reconvened as the Parliamentary Group before real debate took place; when it did, it invariably approved of the government's policies.

Yet one must be careful not to ignore the influence exerted by certain key officials of the Parliamentary Group in regard to foreign policy. İnönü claims that he felt the necessity of touching base with a number of individuals in the CHP and the Assembly before coming to any decision on a policy question.[87] One of the most important of these men,

[85] M. Soysal, *Foreign Policy and the Parliament*, p. 105.

[86] Personal interview with Professor Ahmet Şükrü Esmer, Ankara, May 11, 1966. During the war, Professor Esmer was an assistant editor of the official CHP newspaper *Ulus*, a deputy and a member of the committee on foreign affairs in the Assembly; Professor Fahir H. Armaoğlu, at the time of the interview, April 20, 1966, in Ankara, was the head of the Dış Münasebetler Enstitüsü, the Institute of International Relations of the Political Science Faculty of the University of Ankara.

[87] Personal interview with the former President, Ankara, September 21, 1966.

during the period of German ascendancy, was Ali Fethi Okyar. İnönü paid particular attention to Okyar's recommendations. Professor A. Suat Bilge, in a personal interview with the author, has gone so far as to suggest that "the only person İnönü ever really did listen to regarding foreign policy was Fethi Okyar." Although this clearly tends to exaggerate the role played by Okyar before or during the outbreak of war, Okyar was the one who succeeded in convincing İnönü that Turkey had to align itself with Britain before war began. A former ambassador to London and Minister of Justice in the Saydam Cabinet, Okyar felt certain that Britain would win the war and urged that Turkey sign a defense agreement with it. The Tripartite Agreement of Mutual Defense signed between Turkey, France, and Britain, October 19, 1939, was, to a considerable extent, the result of Fethi Okyar's influence.[88]

[88] Two days after Saracoğlu returned from Moscow, the Treaty of Mutual Assistance between Turkey, Britain, and France was signed in Ankara. This treaty, which provided the contractual basis of the Anglo-Turkish alliance during the war, was quite specific in regard to the conditions under which Turkey was obligated to come to the assistance of Britain and France; Turkey would assist Britain and France in the event that an act of aggression by a European power led to war in the Mediterranean in which both Britain and France were involved; Turkey would also come to the assistance of Britain and France if they became involved in hostilities in defense of Greece or Romania; in return, Britain and France promised to come to Turkey's aid should it be attacked or in any other way threatened by a war in the Mediterranean area. Turkey under this treaty was therefore under no obligation to assist Britain or France militarily unless war came to the Mediterranean, which, as it turned out, it quickly did. The treaty, which was to remain in effect for fifteen years included a *caveat*, Protocol No. 2, which stated that nothing undertaken in the treaty could oblige Turkey to take any action threatening to involve it in armed hostilities with the Soviet Union. For a copy of the original document in English, Great Britain, Foreign Office, *British and Foreign State Papers*, Treaty of Mutual Assistance between His Majesty in respect of the United Kingdom, the President of the French Republic, and the President of the Turkish Republic, Ankara, October 19, 1939, Cmd. 6165, Treaty Series No. 4, *House of Commons Sessional Papers*, Vol. XII (London:

Of all the men outside his immediate circle of ministers, the individual who İnönü, by his own admission to the author, most highly valued during the war was Kâzım Özalp. A distinguished military officer, a Minister of Defense for seven sessions of the Assembly,[89] Kâzım Özalp was, during the war, the head of the Parliamentary Group of the CHP. In this capacity, he served as the main go-between between İnönü, the Council of Ministers, and the members of the Parliamentary Group.[90] Most legislation pertaining to matters of foreign policy presented before the Assembly as well as the debates on foreign-policy questions in the Parliamentary Group were handled and, in some instances, managed by Kâzım Özalp.[91] Özalp admits to having been primarily concerned with the "Russian menace" during the war and suggests that "avoidance of war with the Soviet Union at all costs" was the "guiding principle" of Turkish foreign policy throughout the war but "especially after the Germans began to lose in the Crimea."[92]

His Majesty's Stationery Office, 1940); for a copy in French, Erkin, *Turkish-Russian Relations*, pp. 484-87; a copy in Turkish of the Türk-Fransız-İngiliz "Üçlü İttifakı" is conveniently available in İ. Soysal, *Turkey's Main Political Agreements*, pp. 283-89. Britain and France also pledged in a separate special agreement to grant Turkey £23 million of credit for war materials, a gold loan of £15 million and a credit allowance of £31 million for commercial goods; see Ataöv, *Turkish Foreign Policy*, pp. 60-62; for an interesting account of the role played by Fethi Okyar in defending the Anglo-Turkish alignment based on British documents, see *ibid.*, p. 39, and *Docs.Brit.F.P.*, vi, 74.

[89] Kâzım Özalp held the position of Minister of Defense for a longer period than anyone else; cf., Frey, *The Turkish Political Elite*, p. 291.

[90] Özalp suggested in a personal interview that Faik Öztrak, who also held the position of CHP Meclis Gurubu Başkan Vekili during the period under review, was less interested in military questions and foreign policy than in domestic issues.

[91] Personal interview with General Kâzım Özalp, İstanbul, September 27, 1966.

[92] Cavit Oral and former President İnönü concur in this.

We have already suggested that debates in the Parliamentary Group of the CHP, insofar as questions of foreign policy were concerned, performed an essentially lyrical function. They allowed members to express points of view openly and permitted the government to take a sounding of the feelings and attitudes in the legislature. But these debates, acrimonious as they sometimes could be, rarely, if ever, succeeded in changing the direction of policies set by İnönü and Menemencioğlu. This further points out the highly limited role played by the general membership of the Assembly and Parliamentary Group at this time. For the most part, they chose either to assume no role at all in foreign policy decision-making or were, in a manner of speaking, under İnönü's thumb. But having said this, we must also be careful not to underestimate the importance of this lyrical function. Neither İnönü nor Menemencioğlu ignored the importance of a free exchange of views in obtaining consent to their policies. Nor should we conclude that these discussions were entirely academic in spite of the fact that the strongest legislative opposition could only take the form of acquiescence. İnönü regularly sought the views and thoughts of the Parliamentary Group because this enabled him to sound out the general feeling in the country.[93] The members of the Parliamentary Group can be said to have had an influence on policy-making insofar as they were able to influence İnönü by making it clear what the nation would or would not accept.

In this context, two other individuals might be men-

[93] Professor Mümtaz Soysal notes that İnönü in his capacity of leader of the opposition complained that the government was not consulting the members of the Assembly in regard to foreign policy; Soysal quotes İnönü as having stated in July 1950, ". . . when the war rang Turkey's doorbell . . . the CHP consulted the Assembly even on the matter of cutting our financial relations with Germany," *Foreign Policy and the Parliament*, p. 106; this justification of his own record is correct to the extent that İnönü did use the Parliamentary Group as a sounding board for the reactions of the country to his own policies.

67

tioned: Ali Râna Tarhan and Hasan Saka. Both did take an active part in Parliamentary Group and Assembly debates. A casual perusal through the records of the Grand National Assembly during the period under review will demonstrate how actively Ali Râna Tarhan participated in the legislative discussions of the time. Tarhan was called upon to comment on most pieces of major legislation, such as the *Varlık Vergisi*, the severance of diplomatic relations with Germany, the declaration of war on Germany, and the treaty formulated at the San Francisco Conference. Tarhan's position as Vice-President of the 21-man Independent Group (Müstakil Group) of the CHP made it seem important that he approve of the government's policies.[94] With the death of the Liberal Republican Party, the need for an opposition party remained. In 1939, the Independent Group was formed by the CHP to act, as Frey observes, "as an obvious—though rather fictitious—opposition."[95] Tarhan was the unofficial leader of this fictitious opposition and thus his comments on foreign-policy issues became a major element in the performance of the lyrical function assigned to the legislative branch. But Tarhan's remarks brought no new, let alone, opposing views on foreign-policy questions. Professor Soysal correctly observes that it is virtually "impossible to find differences" in the positions taken by Tarhan and the regular members of the CHP.[96] Tarhan did, however, occasionally point to some of the key ideas and thoughts arising out of the debates in the Parliamentary Group.[97] But officially, İnönü remained the head of the

[94] For a brilliant discussion of the structure and activity of contemporary political parties in Turkey, Tarık Z. Tunaya, *Türkiyede Siyasî Partiler 1859-1952 (Political Parties in Turkey)* (İstanbul: Doğan Kardeş Yayınları, 1952), pp. 540-748; Tunaya notes that the parliamentary activities of the Independent Group became "more intensive" during 1943, p. 563.

[95] Frey, *The Turkish Political Elite*, p. 344.

[96] M. Soysal, *Foreign Policy and the Parliament*, p. 116.

[97] Tunaya, *Political Parties in Turkey*, p. 563.

THE POLICY-MAKING PROCESS

Independent Group and Tarhan, "took orders from him" as the then Minister of Interior, Hilmi Uran, put it.[98]

We have already referred to Hasan Saka's role as liaison. But it is important in the present context to mention that Saka did not travel between two equal branches of government. On the contrary, his role sometimes devolved into one devoted to compelling a legislator's compliance.[99]

One last qualification: it is neither correct nor fair to conclude that İnönü sought to or succeeded in suppressing all dissent. Individuals such as General Kâzım Karabekir, Refet Bele, Yusuf Hikmet Bayur,[100] Recep Peker, Şükrü Sökmensüer, Rasih Kaplan, M. Ş. Esendal, Şinasi Devrin, Faik Öztrak, and Şemsettin Günaltay, to name but a few, expressed opinions not necessarily in conformity with the government policy. Some would have preferred to see a more aggressive and less prudent policy; some wanted to take advantage of Germany's invasion of the Soviet Union and urged that Turkey enter the war on the side of the Axis.[101] İnönü permitted such dissent to exist as long as it did not extend beyond certain limits and threaten his own policies. He allowed divergence, but only to the extent that

[98] Uran, *Memoirs*, p. 344; also Frey, *The Turkish Political Elite*, p. 345. Karpat, *Turkey's Politics*, p. 117, n. 53.

[99] See, e.g., Kâzım Nami Duru, *Cumhuriyet Devri Hatıralarım (My Memoirs of the Republican Era)* (İstanbul: Sucuoğlu Matbaası, 1958), pp. 61-62; Duru, a deputy in the Assembly during the war, claims he received severe treatment at the hands of Hasan Saka.

[100] Yusuf Hikmet Bayur published a book during the war on Turkish foreign policy entitled, *Türkiye Devletinin Dış Siyasası (Foreign Policy of the Turkish Government)* (İstanbul: İstanbul Üniversitesi Yayınları, No. 59, 1942).

[101] For the official listing of the names of the deputies elected to the Grand National Assembly in the March 1943 elections, Türkiye Büyük Millet Meclis (TBMM), *Zabıt Ceridesi (Tutanak Dergisi) (The Proceedings of the Turkish Grand National Assembly)*, Cilt 1, İçtima 1, Devre VII (Vol. 1, First Session, Seventh Assembly) (Ankara: Türkiye Büyük Millet Meclisi Basımevi, 1943), pp. 4-6; henceforth referred to as *T.B.M.M. Zabıt Ceridesi*.

it did not create a genuine bloc of political opposition or, more relevantly, lead to unfortunate political repercussions abroad.

THE TURKISH HISTORICAL SOCIETY

İnönü, moreover, had another way of keeping in touch with the more articulate elements of the public. He would invite the Executive Council of the Türk Tarih Kurumu (Turkish Historical Society) to his home in Ankara for an informal gathering.[102] "We did not realize it at the time," Enver Ziya Karal, a member of the governing board during the war has reflected, "but İnönü would gently ply us with questions—do you think we ought to get into the war?—things like that, often in jest."[103] Sometimes the members of the Council would enter into long discussions in which İnönü would say nothing. Individuals would advocate specific policy choices. Most of the members of the TTK advised İnönü after 1943 that Turkey should stay out of the war. At an earlier stage in the war, however, one member advocated entering the war on the Axis side. Karal remembers İnönü mocking one member for wanting "to push Turkish boundaries back to the Vienna wall." The overwhelming sentiment in the TTK, however, was pro-Allied, says Karal. On the other hand, he adds, Russian victories were "troubling" to most members. The members of the Executive Council of the Türk Tarih Kurumu, 1940-1945 were: Şemsettin Günaltay, the President of the Association, Uluğ İğdemir, Secretary of the Executive Council, Afet İnan, Enver Ziya

[102] One of the more prominent nongovernmental organizations in Turkey during the war, the Türk Tarih Kurumu (TTK) is a semi-autonomous body with the Faculty of Languages, History and Geography of the University of Ankara. It has its own by-laws and regulations and as Uluğ İğdemir, its current president emphasizes, it was during the war and remains today "an independent research organization devoted to scholarship."

[103] In a personal interview with Professor Enver Ziya Karal, Ankara, 1966.

Karal, Şevket Aziz Kansu, Ismail Hakkı Uzunçarşılı, and Hamit Ongünsu.[104] These individuals served as a sort of presidential brain trust for İnönü during the war. But the most important nongovernmental source of fresh opinions and advice came from the press corps in Turkey. Here, too, however, İnönü exercised the prerogatives of censor.[105]

[104] With only seven seats on the Executive Council of the TTK, it is considered an honor for a scholar to be invited to sit on it.

[105] There were others, of course, who were intent upon influencing Turkish public opinion. Nazi and communist underground agents attempted to convince the Turks that their greatest threat lay with the successes of the other. They did this by attempting to create the illusion that Nazi or communist agents were gaining inordinate influence in Turkey and had therefore to be resisted. The Turks were aware of this. A brief prepared for the President of Turkey in March 1943 reported, for example, that German agents in Turkey were themselves "engendering communist activity." Nazi elements hoped to play on Turkish fears of the Soviet Union. "The Turkish regime is thus supposed to become aware of the fact that there is a communist threat." This report also suggested that Nazi agents were actually attempting to "convert a few young Turkish intellectuals to communism." "The purpose of this," the brief continued, "is to force Turkey into taking repressive measures which would earn Soviet enmity for Turkey." But the Turkish *aide-mémoire* included some doubts. Local communist activity could have been Soviet-engendered. "Investigation continues and the President is urged to keep an open mind," the report cautioned; Ambassador in Ankara (von Papen) to Foreign Ministry in Berlin, Ankara, March 31, 1943, *Captured Files*, NA, T-120, Roll 2618, Frame E364579.

TWO

THE PRESS AND PUBLIC OPINION
IN TURKEY

THE PRESS IN TURKEY DURING THE WAR

A MAJOR source of insight into the heart and mind of Turkey can be found in the editorial comments of its press. Throughout the war, the press mirrored Turkey's reactions to the tugs and pulls which were besetting it. Turkish editorials did this from a wide field of perspectives ranging from pro-Axis through pro-Soviet viewpoints.

During the war, however, the Turkish Government carefully maintained strict control over what was published in the press. A number of laws and press regulations granted it wide powers in this regard.[1] Among the most important was press law No. 1,881 which imposed fines and jail sentences upon writers who published articles designed "to disrupt public confidence in the State, or in one or a few of the officials of the State."[2] Nadir Nadi suggests that newspaper editorialists emphasized world affairs in their writings

[1] For a general collection of the laws governing the press in Turkey during the war, Türkiye Cumhuriyeti Başvekâlet. Basın ve Yayın Umum Müdürlüğü, *Basın ve Yayınla İlgili: Kanun, Kararname, Nizamname, Talimatname ve Tamimler* (*Laws, Decisions, Rules, Instructions and Declarations Concerning Press and Publications*) (Ankara: Başvekâlet Devlet Matbaası, 1944).

[2] Türkiye Cumhuriyeti Başbakanlık. *Son Değişikliklere Göre Matbuat Kanunu* (*Press Law with Recent Modifications*) (Ankara: Basın ve Yayın Umum Müdürlüğü Yayınları, No. 15, 1946), pp. 446-64; the regulation cited above is from Section 11, Article 34, paragraph (A) of the press law and is at p. 455; Article 35, paragraph (G) states "Publications concerning issues related to the security of the state and publications concerning measures taken for the security of the state are forbidden," p. 456.

because "criticizing the national leader [İnönü], the government, and the CHP was strictly forbidden."[3] The allegation here is to some extent false; many of Turkey's major publicists were personally interested in foreign affairs. But it is true that newspapers were occasionally shut down for criticizing the government. "It became fashionable to close down newspapers by telephone and to keep them closed for months,"[4] Nadi writes in referring to İnönü's control over the press. He suggests that editorial opinions were kept under surveillance of the General Directorate of Press and Publications and that the Directorate was particularly concerned that the press give no offense either to the Soviet Union or the Axis.[5] Selim Sarper, the Director of the General Directorate of Press and Publications until 1943, has confirmed that his office carefully scrutinized newspapers with a view to avoiding politically offensive articles in the future.[6] The very fact that publicists like Nadi, Yalman, and Sertel, however, were able to examine foreign-policy issues critically while the war was still raging indicates that the restrictions, severe as they may have been, were never entirely stifling. On the contrary, the degree of freedom granted to the press permitted a wide enough range of critical comment to warrant reference to it here.

In 1943, 131 newspapers and 172 periodicals were being published in Turkey.[7] The reading public in Turkey was

[3] Nadi, *Opening in the Curtain*, pp. 21-22.

[4] *Ibid.*, p. 183.

[5] *Ibid.*, p. 41, also pp. 183-84; for the law governing the General Directorate of Press and Publications and especially its relationship to the Foreign Ministry, Sadi Kıyak (ed.), *Dışişleri Bakanlığı Mevzuatı ve Yayınla İlgili Hükümler* (*Rulings Concerning the Press and Publications and the Foreign Ministry*) (Ankara: Başbakanlık Devlet Matbaası, 1947), esp., Law: Kanun No. 4475, "Basın ve Yayın Umum Müdürlüğü Teşkilât, Vazife ve Memurları Hakkında Kanun" ("Law Concerning the Organization, the Function and the Personnel of the General Directorate of Press and Publications, passed July 23, 1943"), pp. 429-45.

[6] In a personal interview, Ankara, July 21, 1966.

[7] Server İskit, *Türkiyede Matbuat İdareleri ve Politikaları* (*Press*

small, however, and the attentive public, those individuals who were not in positions of policy-making but who maintained an active interest in public policy, was miniscule.[8] The total estimated circulation of İstanbul's largest newspaper, for example, was 16,000. During the period between 1943 and 1945, there were eleven major newspapers being published in İstanbul and Ankara. In descending order of circulation, they were:

Cumhuriyet	16,000
Ulus	12,000
Tan	12,000
Yeni Sabah	10,000
Akşam	10,000
Son Posta	10,000
Vatan	7,000
Tasvir-i Efkâr	6,000
Son Telgraf	4,000
İkdam	4,000
Vakit	4,000[9]

Directives and Policies in Turkey) (Ankara: Basın ve Yayın Umum Müdürlüğü Yayınları, 1943), p. 361; İskit refers to press laws No. 1,881 and No. 4,475 along with press law No. 3,837 as being the laws that "determine the relations of the Republican Government with the Press," at pp. 363-64.

[8] The term "attentive public" is borrowed here from the two men who coined it, Gabriel A. Almond and James A. Rosenau; see Almond's *The American People and Foreign Policy* (New York: Frederick A. Praeger, 1960), esp. p. 151 and Rosenau's *Public Opinion and Foreign Policy: An Operational Formulation* (New York: Random House, 1961), pp. 39-41.

[9] Great Britain. Royal Institute of International Affairs, Foreign Research and Press Service. *Review of the Foreign Press*, Series B, Allied Governments, European Neutrals, Southeastern Europe and the Near East (Oxford: Balliol College), No. 177, p. 142; after July 14, 1943, Great Britain. Foreign Office, Research Department, Series N, The Near and Middle East (London: His Majesty's Stationery Office). This publication prepared successively during the war by the Royal Institute of International Relations and the Research and Intelligence Department

Later in 1943, the editor of *Yeni Sabah* revived the newspaper, *Tanin*, which had ceased publication for nearly fifteen years, raising the number of major newspapers to an even dozen.

The news agency that served all these newspapers was the same: the Anadolu Ajansı (Anatolian News Agency). It was founded on April 6, 1920, by Atatürk for the purpose of spreading news about the Kemalist Revolution.[10] The Anadolu Ajansı became a corporation on March 1, 1925, and extended its news coverage by becoming affiliated with a number of foreign news agencies. In November 1944, İnönü asked Muvaffak Menemencioğlu, the older brother of Numan Menemencioğlu and Director of the Anadolu Ajansı since 1927, to resign. During Menemencioğlu's incumbency, coverage in general suffered from a lack of correspondents abroad and from limited access to foreign news services. This prompted Ahmet Şükrü Esmer to make a number of criticisms. Writing in *Ulus*, November 1, 1944, Esmer conceded that the Anadolu Ajansı had become almost totally dependent upon foreign news agencies.[11] Esmer called this a misleading practice since it disseminated its information under its own initials, "A.A." Esmer urged that

---

of the Foreign Office, Whitehall, compiled and translated the editorial positions and statements made in the foreign press and published them weekly throughout the war. Occasionally it analyzed the positions taken or policies advocated in the press; henceforth referred to as the *Review*.

[10] See, Füruzan Hüsrev Tokın, *Basın Ansiklopedisi* (*Press Encyclopedia*) (İstanbul: n.p., 1963), pp. 13-14; this is a useful guide to the histories of many of Turkey's major newspapers as well as to the lives and careers of its main publicists; although largely factual, it is sometimes biased in favor of the Justice Party in Turkey; henceforth referred to as *Press Encyclopedia*. For another review of the Turkish press, Lutfy Levonian, *The Turkish Press: 1932-1936* (Beirut: n.p., 1937); for a review of the Turkish press in Bulgaria, Âdem Ruhi Karagöz, *Bulgaristan Türk Basını: 1879-1945* (*Turkish Press in Bulgaria: 1879-1945*) (İstanbul: Üniversite Matbaası, 1945); for other listings, Karpat, *Turkey's Politics*, p. 74, n. 127.

[11] *Ulus*, November 1, 1943.

the Anadolu Ajansı expand its coverage by sending correspondents to foreign countries and, in any case, to begin
the practice of specifying sources of information. Esmer's
criticisms suggest the tremendous limitations under which
all Turkish newspapers operated during the war. The Anadolu Ajansı was the major source of information servicing
the Turkish press at this time. At times, the press was forbidden to obtain news directly from foreign news agencies.
Given the dependence on foreign news services of the Anadolu Ajansı, the news received by the Turkish press was
often second hand. Even when Turkish newspapers were
allowed to use foreign news agencies, the wire services, especially those of the Allies, failed to provide adequate news
coverage. This tended to enhance the effectiveness of the
Transkontinent Press, the German news agency headed by
Fritz Fiala.[12]

Nadir Nadi asserts that there were no distinct groupings
in the press representing Right, Left, or Center movements
or ideologies. "One could see signatures dedicated to opposite beliefs in every newspaper," he writes.[13] He suggests that
following the announcement of the May 12, 1939 declaration of Anglo-Turkish solidarity, all the newspapers began
to "compete with each other in condemning Mussolini and
Hitler." Upon the German invasion of the Soviet Union,
however, most newspapers hired a retired general to explain
the "technical" aspects of the war.[14] Nadi writes, "These
generals, the majority of whom were pro-German, would
say that it was a matter of a day before the Germans would
take such and such a city, and then when their estimates
would turn out wrong, they would try to explain why the
situation turned out to be this way rather than that. . . ."[15]
Nadi's claim that there were no significant differences
among Turkish newspapers during the war, that they all

[12] Personal interview with Leo D. Hochstetter, London, September 8,
1969, see below, n. 28.
[13] Nadi, *Opening in the Curtain*, p. 37.
[14] *Ibid.*, p. 123.   [15] *Ibid.*

had some pro-Axis members on their staffs, that none maintained a consistent political commitment, tends to erase the important differences which certainly did exist among the newspapers published during the war. Most of these papers were under the direction and control of distinct personalities, men with different loyalties and convictions who often presented contrasting analyses of policies and events.

First in importance was *Ulus*, the official newspaper of the CHP.[16] Under the direction of İnönü's trusted friend, Falih Rıfkı Atay,[17] this newspaper mirrored the policies of the government. Atay and *Ulus* were İnönü's other voices. The foreign editor of *Ulus* during the war was Ahmet Şükrü Esmer.[18] A man of somewhat less stature during the war than Atay, Esmer was close to the inner councils of foreign policy decision-making within the government, and to the extent they existed, within the Parliamentary Group of the CHP.[19] Special note must be granted to his editorial comments.

Nadir Nadi's own newspaper, *Cumhuriyet*,[20] founded by his father Yunus Nadi Abalıoğlu,[21] May 7, 1924, is generally regarded as having favored the Axis during the war. Nadir Nadi attempts to defend his father and the editorial policy of *Cumhuriyet* by justifying his pro-German editorials on the grounds of political realism and Turkish national

---

[16] *Press Encyclopedia*, p. 125.

[17] *Ibid.*, p. 20; Nadi writes that Atay was "sincerely attached to İnönü. He was held on a pedestal, since he was considered the head writer of not just the Party but of the government," *Opening in the Curtain*, p. 171.

[18] *Press Encyclopedia*, p. 54.

[19] Esmer held a seat in the Assembly as did many other journalists including Atay, Yalçın, and Nadi.

[20] *Ibid.*, p. 45.

[21] For Yunus Nadi's long and notable career, *ibid.* An outline of Nadir Nadi's career is at p. 41; an interesting account of Yunus Nadi's career can also be found in Tekin Erer's, *Basında Kavgalar* (*Press Quarrels*) (İstanbul: Rek-Tur Kitap Servisi Yayınları, 1965), pp. 23-24; Erer also discusses Nadir Nadi and his brother Doğan; he refers to Nadir Nadi as an "ambitious socialist," at pp. 75-76.

77

interests.[22] He states that his editorials of July 30 and July 31, 1940, for example, in which he warned that Germany was a major force to be reckoned with, were designed to aid the government's policy of neutrality. His purpose was to shift the balance of Turkish public opinion from a blind dedication to the Allies to a position between the two warring camps. His July 31st editorial, Nadi claims, attempted to discount the possibility of any one nation ever dominating all of Europe. "Hegemony of a single nation is a myth," he declared, arguing that it was a myth perpetrated by those who were trying to create fear of Germany in Turkey out of sympathy for Great Britain.[23] This was not written to defend Germany, Nadi insists, but was published in order to reinforce the climate of neutrality. On August 12, 1940, the government, however, suspended the publication of *Cumhuriyet* until November 9, 1940.[24] By Nadi's own admission, İnönü and the then Prime Minister, Refik Saydam, perceived this and other editorials written in a similar vein to be outside the boundaries they had set for the public expression of views. Nadi quotes İnönü as having said, "These guys want to give me the business. Close down the paper."[25]

Despite Nadi's protestations to the contrary, evidence suggests that Yunus Nadi and *Cumhuriyet* were committed to favoring German interests during the war. For one thing, writers such as Peyami Safa, Muharrem Feyzi Togay, the foreign news editor of *Cumhuriyet*, and General Hüseyin Hüsnü Emir Erkilet, who remained on the staff of *Cumhuriyet* during most of the war, were definitely men of pro-Axis sympathies.[26] Furthermore, Yunus Nadi, owner of

[22] Nadi, *Opening in the Curtain*, pp. 89-94.

[23] Nadir Nadi, "Tek Devlet Hegemonyası bir Hayâldır" ("Single state hegemony is a myth"), *Cumhuriyet*, July 31, 1940; also Erer, *Press Quarrels*, pp. 77-79.

[24] Nadi describes the personal role played by Selim Sarper at this time, *Opening in the Curtain*, p. 99.

[25] *Ibid.*, p. 101.

[26] Nadi confides that Peyami Safa was "staunchly pro-Nazi in foreign policy" and that Hitler's defeat "crushed him," *ibid.*, p. 104; for Safa's

Cumhuriyet until his death in Switzerland on June 28, 1945, was kind to the Axis apparently for commercial reasons.[27] Fritz Fiala, Chief of Transkontinent Press and one of the important agents working for German intelligence in Turkey during the war, testified to this effect in September 1944, when he defected to the West. George W. H. Britt, General Representative of the United States Office of War Information, received a memorandum, dated September 2, 1944, from his field representative, Leo Hochstetter, outlining the information provided by Fiala under interrogation. Britt sent a copy of the Hochstetter report to the American Ambassador in Turkey with the reservation that there was no "guarantee as to the reliability of these things, only to the fact of Fiala having said them." The memorandum is to be found among Ambassador Steinhardt's personal papers in the Library of Congress.[28] Fiala alleged that *Cumhuriyet* was being supported by the German underground.[29] Fiala admits that *Cumhuriyet* and

---

career, *Press Encyclopedia*, p. 97. Nadi refers to Erkilet, who will be discussed in greater depth below, as being pro-German, *Opening in the Curtain*, p. 123. Feyzi Togay, as Nadi admits, "was rabidly and unobjectively anti-Russian on account of his having to leave Russia and seek asylum in Turkey in 1917," *ibid.*, pp. 103-104; a Kazan Turk, Togay was among those named by the government in May 1944 as being part of the Pan-Turanian conspiracy.

[27] The author wishes to enter the disclaimer here that the evidence for this remains largely circumstantial.

[28] United States. Library of Congress, Manuscript Division. *Papers of Laurence A. Steinhardt*, Box 45, "Memorandum," Leo Hochstetter to General Representative (W. H. Britt), United States Office of War Information, İstanbul, September 6, 1944; henceforth referred to as the Hochstetter Memorandum.

[29] Leo Hochstetter in a personal interview with the author, London, September 8, 1969, stated that he was able to substantiate Fiala's allegations during the war. Hochstetter claims that American intelligence proved beyond doubt that Yunus Nadi and Ziyad Ebuzziya received paper newsprint at cut-rate prices from the Germans in payment for their pro-Axis policies. Hochstetter suggests that this was the only form of payment either ever received from the Germans.

Tasvir-i Efkâr received a substantial subsidy in the form of newsprint at a greatly reduced price. He asserted, however, that no direct bribes were given to the Nadis or the Ebuzziyas, adding that they, along with Peyami Safa and others of his ilk, needed no bribing since they were Turanists and Racists.[30] Ahmet Emin Yalman further alleges that Nadi used "his influence as a deputy in the Grand National Assembly for a whole series of war-profiting activities."[31] Nadir Nadi does not directly disavow these allegations; on the contrary, when he relates how *Cumhuriyet* was closed in 1940, he suggests that even İnönü believed them to be true. On August 7, 1940, İnönü was returning to Ankara by train and was greeted at the railroad station by a large party which included Yunus Nadi. İnönü asked Nadi to remain until the greeting party had left. Then İnönü turned to Nadi and declared, "I cannot tolerate political writings for commercial purposes." In response to Nadi's remonstrances, İnönü repeated, "I definitely cannot tolerate it."[32] Whether Yunus Nadi favored the Axis cause for financial purposes or for other reasons, an examination of the editorial opinions of *Cumhuriyet* reveals a pro-German bias which only shifted months after the tide in the war had turned.

Tasvir-i Efkâr,[33] a publication with a long and illustrious history, owned and managed by Ziyad Ebuzziya,[34] was as Fiala also alleges, definitely pro-Axis in 1943. Ali İhsan Sâbis, a man distinctly pro-Nazi, was its director of publications. Peyami Safa also contributed pieces to it. It was closed

[30] The Hochstetter Memorandum.

[31] In a personal interview with the author, İstanbul, 1966: Yalman and Yunus Nadi engaged in a vitriolic quarrel in 1937 in which Yalman accused Nadi of being fascist and Nadi countered by suggesting that Yalman had written brochures about historical materialism as conceived by Karl Marx and Engels; Erer, *Press Quarrels*, pp. 27-30.

[32] Nadi, *Opening in the Curtain*, pp. 98-99; the farthest Nadi goes by way of denying that his father received preferential treatment from the Germans during the war is to assert that his father did not die a wealthy man, p. 199.

[33] *Press Encyclopedia*, pp. 115-17.   [34] *Ibid.*, p. 52.

down during the war, but reopened in 1945 under the name *Tasvir*.

The one newspaper with the most consistent ideological position during the war, however, was not on the Right of the political spectrum but on the Left, namely, *Tan*.[35] Founded in İstanbul in 1934, *Tan*, as Tekin Erer suggests, "defended socialism and democracy" and thus became the "rival" of "Turkish, nationalist and conservative *Cumhuriyet*."[36] Although Halil Lûtfi Dördüncü, Zekeriya Sertel, Ahmet Emin Yalman, and Rifat Yalman were the original founders of *Tan*, editorial policy of the publication in 1943 was completely in the hands of Sertel and his wife, Sabiha. As the war progressed, Sabiha Sertel succeeded in converting Zekeriya Sertel's socialist philosophy into an outright commitment to Soviet Communism.[37] *Tan* was destroyed by anti-communist students in a riot on December 4, 1945, and both Sertels defected to the Soviet Union.

Between the ideological extremes represented by *Cumhuriyet* and *Tasvir-i Efkâr* on the one hand, and *Tan*, on the other, was *Akşam*.[38] Founded in 1918 as a daily evening newspaper by Kâzım Şinasi Dersan, Ali Naci Karacan, and Necmettin Sadak, this paper was close to *Ulus* in editorial policy. At one point, Falih Rıfkı Atay served on its editorial board. Throughout the war, *Akşam* like *Ulus*, maintained a cautious pro-Allied editorial position which sometimes found it necessary to criticize Allied policy but always from the point of view of one who was a friend.[39]

---

[35] *Ibid.*, p. 114.

[36] Erer, *Press Quarrels*, p. 23; Nadi states that *Tan* under the Sertels was the only newspaper in Turkey "more or less totally dedicated to a systematic leftist policy," *Opening in the Curtain*, p. 37.

[37] Ahmet Emin Yalman, in a personal interview with the author, London, September 8, 1969, explained that Zekeriya Sertel was a "weak man" who came under the influence of a "fanatical wife."

[38] *Press Encyclopedia*, p. 11.

[39] In 1947, Necmettin Sadak, *Akşam*'s director of publications and chief editorialist, became Turkish Foreign Minister. It should, therefore, be mentioned that Fritz Fiala alleged that Sadak received funds

Among the most eminent publicists in Turkey during the war was Hüseyin Cahit Yalçın.[40] Solidly sympathetic to the Allied cause, he deeply distrusted the Soviet Union.[41] This produced certain conflicts which, as his alternating periods of satisfaction and disaffection with Allied policies reveal, Yalçın found difficult to resolve. For example, he often sug-

from the German underground during the war. The Hochstetter Memorandum states, "To Fiala's knowledge only one major Turkish journalist was bribed but in an indirect form also. He stated that Necmettin Sadak, editor of *Akşam*, had been given a Mercedes automobile and that his wife on several occasions was the beneficiary of expensive furs and other finery. On a few occasions also a couple of Sadak's Bezique gambling debts were picked up through covering checks." Ahmet Emin Yalman corroborates Fiala's testimony and suggests that Sadak never printed pro-Axis material because he was "cautious." The fact that Sadak was not publishing pro-German material, although he was reputedly supposed to do so, allegedly came to the attention of von Papen. The Hochstetter Memorandum continues, "Fiala related an amusing conversation that took place between Sadak and von Papen. It seems that despite these material overtures for Sadak's favors, the latter had been writing some anti-German editorials. When confronted with this by von Papen, Sadak is said to have explained: 'Rest assured, Mon Excéllence, the Turkish public does not read my editorials. I spread the German point of view personally among my friends who are influential.' To this von Papen replied: 'Herr Sadak, the Reich is not interested in this type of corruption.'" On October 10, 1966, the author attempted to verify this story in a telephone call to Franz von Papen. The former German Ambassador refused to comment, however, and on October 14 wrote in a letter to the author that Turks were all "old friends." The important fact remains that *Akşam* did indeed generally pursue a pro-Allied editorial policy during the war. Leo Hochstetter, finally, says that he was never able to confirm or discount Fiala's testimony regarding Necmettin Sadak. (Personal interview, London, September 8, 1969.)

[40] For a full treatment of the life and works of Yalçın, Suat Hizarcı (ed.) *Hüseyin Cahit Yalçın* (İstanbul: Varlık Yayınları, No. 550, 1957); also *Press Encyclopedia*, p. 129. Erer's *Press Quarrels* describes Yalçın's fear of the threat posed by Nazi Germany, p. 89.

[41] As we shall see, a representative of the Soviet Union would actually suggest that one of the steps Turkey could take in order to improve its relations with Russia would be not to send Yalçın to the San Francisco Conference.

gested that British and American statesmen were not fully comprehending the dangers posed by victorious Russia, but this did not prevent him from urging that Turkey honor its alliance with Britain by coming into the war.[42] During the period of German ascendancy, Yalçın wrote for *Yeni Sabah*, a paper founded in 1938 by Cemaleddin Saracoğlu and under the direction of Reşat Mahmut and Tevfik Erol. In 1943, however, he reopened *Tanin*.[43]

Yalçın was not alone in his willingness to embrace unpopular causes. Ahmet Emin Yalman was often willing to do so.[44] Yalman told the author that "since close friends fully controlled *Vatan*,[45] I felt completely free to take whatever risks I wanted. I wrote and said what I pleased."[46] Yalman states categorically that İnönü and Saracoğlu closed down his paper because of his criticisms of the *Varlık Vergisi*, the tax on wealth that was imposed in Turkey on November 11, 1942.[47]

There were other figures in the press who deserve passing

[42] As will be shown, many of those who opposed Turkish entry into the war did so out of fear that the Soviet Union might otherwise be tempted to invade Turkish territory. Yalçın alone feared the Soviet Union and yet urged that Turkey fight in the war.

[43] *Press Encyclopedia*, pp. 114-15; Yalçın first published *Tanin* in 1908 along with Tevfik Fikret and Hüseyin Kâzım. At this time such men as Ahmet Emin Yalman, Falih Rıfkı Atay, Asım Us, and Halil L. Dördüncü worked for it. *Tanin* was closed down in 1912 by the Sultan. In 1919 Yalçın was exiled to Malta by the British. Upon his return to Turkey in 1922, Yalçın again began to publish *Tanin*. Atatürk closed it in 1928, however, because Yalçın disagreed with several of the major Kemalist reforms including the abolition of the Caliphate and language reform. It was only upon Atatürk's death that Yalçın reentered public life. When he was vilified by the other members of the press for his position on Turkish entry into the war, Yalçın had long known the ardors of being in opposition to the political mainstream. For a brief sketch of the history of *Yeni Sabah, ibid.*, p. 131.

[44] *Ibid.*, p. 130.

[45] *Ibid.*, p. 128; at the time of his dispute with Yunus Nadi, Yalman was an editor of *Tan*.

[46] In a personal interview, İstanbul, September 11, 1966.

[47] In a personal interview, London, September 8, 1969.

mention. Abidin Daver, nicknamed the "civil admiral" by other members of the press for his interest in naval military affairs,[48] was the editor of *İkdam*[49] during the war. In 1943, the *Review of the Foreign Press* wrote that "*İkdam* is far from supporting the Axis, but not nearly so outspoken in its condemnation of Axis policy . . . as others."[50] Asım Us[51] equally merits note as the owner of and principal writer in the İstanbul daily *Vakit*. In general, *Vakit*[52] assumed a moderate or middle-of-the-road editorial philosophy. The other two major newspapers in Turkey during the war were *Son Posta* and *Son Telgraf*. *Son Posta*,[53] founded in 1930 by Halil L. Dördüncü, Ekrem Uşaklıgil, Zekeriya Sertel, and Selim Ragıp Emeç, quickly established a reputation for being opposed to the CHP.[54] On account of its harsh criticisms, the paper was often shut down both before and during the war. It is, therefore, of relative unimportance here. This also applies to *Son Telgraf*. Although its owner and head writer, Etem İzzet Benice,[55] had once served as the foreign affairs editor of *Ulus*, this newspaper's editorials during the war proved generally to be of minor interest here.

There were a number of foreign-language publications, mostly pro-Axis propaganda organs in French or German. The three most important of these were the *Türkische Post*, *İstanbul*, and *Beyoğlu*. The *Türkische Post*, a publication subsidized by German funds and under the direction of Ali İhsan Sâbis, was read by the large German community in Ankara during the war.[56] It was forced to suspend publication by a decision of the Council of Ministers, February 18, 1944. *İstanbul*, on the other hand, was not financially supported by interests outside of Turkey. The oldest on-going newspaper in Turkey, celebrating its 76th anniversary in

[48] *Press Encyclopedia*, p. 5.   [49] *Ibid.*, p. 74.
[50] *Review*, Series N, No. 8, p. 54.   [51] *Press Encyclopedia*, p. 125.
[52] *Ibid.*, p. 127.   [53] *Ibid.*, p. 108.
[54] *Ibid.*   [55] *Ibid.*, p. 42.
[56] The *Türkische Post* will be discussed in greater length below.

April 1943, *İstanbul* completely reversed its editorial policy after the tide had turned in the war.[57] Prior to the Allied occupation of southern France, *İstanbul* had supported the Vichy Government. As a result, it fell out of sympathy with the majority of French citizens in Turkey who opposed collaboration. The full occupation of France and the activities of General Giraud in North Africa, however, along with financial pressures, led to a "change of heart."[58] After April 1943, *İstanbul* presented the news in a pro-Allied fashion. *Beyoğlu*, a publication owned largely by Italian interests but published in French, featured subjects of economic interest. There was finally, one foreign-language publication in Turkey which was pro-communist, *La Türquie*. Owned by the Baykurt family, *La Türquie* was generally guided both by the intellectual propositions of philosophical Marxism and a political commitment to the Soviet Union.[59] Its offices were destroyed by rioting students in December 1945 along with *Tan*.

PUBLIC OPINION IN TURKEY DURING THE WAR

These twelve newspapers attempted to influence the public, and, therefore, some attention should be given to the opinions held in Turkey during the war. Two attitudes predominated: an unwillingness to enter the war and a general distrust of Soviet Russia.

A position paper prepared by the Turkish Foreign Ministry for President İnönü in March 1943, for example, underlined the predominant antiwar feeling throughout the country.

Every layer of the population, even the army which in each state is most anxious for war, is opposed to war.

[57] *Review*, Series B, No. 182, p. 224.
[58] *Ibid.*
[59] The author's analysis; also confirmed by Leo D. Hochstetter in a personal interview, London, September 8, 1969.

Every Turk has understood, today, that Turkey has nothing to gain by entering the war, and that she would enter the field of battle only to protect her own sovereignty, that entry unprovoked by an actual attack or threat against our freedom could only bring our land still more misery, hunger, illness, yes even death and destruction.[60]

A memorandum found in the private papers of Michel and Irena Sokolnicki describes Turkish public opinion in much the same fashion.[61]

If Turks were firmly opposed to fighting in the war, they regarded the Soviet Union as Turkey's main threat. What is interesting about Turkish attitudes toward the Soviet Union during the war is how little the twenty years of good Soviet-Turkish relations seemed to affect the traditionally held Turkish image of a hostile and aggressive Soviet Union.[62] Daniel Lerner's investigation, for example, found that although 80 per cent of the Turks questioned expressed an opinion on the Soviet Union, only 2 per cent based these opinions on current information rather than on the "traditional stock of Turkish folklore."[63] Lerner suggests that Turkish public opinion was much more guided by events that occurred in the eighteenth and nineteenth centuries

[60] Ambassador in Ankara (von Papen) to Foreign Ministry in Berlin, Ankara, April 15, 1943, *Captured Files*, NA, T-120, Roll 2618, Frames E364561-E364569.

[61] Referred to with the permission of Madame Irena Sokolnickia, this memorandum is dated October 15, 1942, and emphasizes the extent to which Turks were opposed to coming into the war.

[62] Ahmet Şükrü Esmer, A. Suat Bilge, Uluğ İğdemir, Enver Ziya Karal, Cevat, Açıkalın, Feridun Cemal Erkin, and former President İsmet İnönü, in personal interviews, all testify to the fact that the interwar period of good Soviet-Turkish relations did little to transform the traditional image in Turkey of an antagonistic Russia.

[63] Daniel Lerner, *The Passing of Traditional Society* (New York: The Free Press of Glencoe, 1958), p. 140; Lerner's study was undertaken well after the war had ended, but given the nature of his findings, one can assume that they held true of Turkish public opinion during the war as well.

than during the twentieth. Feridun Cemal Erkin corroborated this when he wrote, "Thirteen wars in the space of three centuries had given the Turks an infallible scent for the danger and the menace of the Russians."[64] This applies to urban students as well as the peasantry. The destruction of *Tan* represents a spontaneous act of contempt by students toward the Sertels whom they had come to recognize as pro-Soviet partisans.

Throughout the war, finally, economic shortages, hoarding, black marketeering, and consequent strong governmental reaction created an overall sense of demoralization and resentment in Turkey. This will be discussed in greater detail in the economic survey below.

[64] Erkin, *Turkish-Russian Relations*, p. 230.

THREE

A BRIEF ANALYSIS OF THE
ECONOMIC PICTURE

TURKISH wartime foreign policy was heavily influenced by economic considerations and restraints. İnönü, Menemencioğlu, and Saracoğlu, along with officials such as Fuat Ağralı and Nurullah Esat Sümer, were all carefully attuned to the threatening economic situation that arose out of the exigencies of the day. Turkey remained out of the war but could not avoid its chronic ailments, commodity shortages, inflation, and the like. Turkish policy-makers, especially Menemencioğlu, sought to keep the effects of such debilities to a minimum by exploiting the few economic advantages Turkey possessed to the fullest through negotiation.[1] His hard bargaining exasperated both Allied and Axis negotiators alike. As W. H. Medlicott suggests, "tough bargaining" was to Menemencioğlu and to other Turkish statesmen as well, the sign of "highest patriotism."[2] The labors of Turkish statesmen in this regard did not go unrewarded. The Turks received increasingly higher prices for their exported goods which resulted in a comparatively favorable economic situation at the end of the war.[3] In the minds of Turkish statesmen, therefore, the question was how to reap the greatest profit without jeopardizing their fundamental political relationships. This chapter is a brief description of the economic situation in Turkey during the war and the trade and fiscal policies which the Turks pursued in order to deal with it.

[1] Medlicott, *The Economic Blockade*, I, 274.   [2] *Ibid.*, p. 269.

[3] Great Britain. Export Promotion Department. E. R. Lingeman, *Turkey: Economic and Commercial Conditions in Turkey* (London: His Majesty's Stationery Office, 1948), p. 43; henceforth referred to as *Economic and Commercial Conditions.*

THE ECONOMIC PICTURE

THE SCOURGE OF INFLATION

Turkey, a land mass of approximately 300,000 square miles with an estimated population in 1940 of 17,869,901 people, was predominantly rural at the time of the war.[4] Roughly 70 per cent of the population was agriculturally employed despite the fact that only 10 per cent of the land was actually cultivated.[5] Methods of farming remained basically primitive, although agricultural products constituted 91 per cent of Turkish exports between 1935 and 1945 and brought in 70 per cent of the national revenues.[6]

Price levels in Turkey were artificially high even before war broke out and became increasingly so after 1940. A highly inadequate infrastructure made travel and communication difficult and led to exorbitant transportation costs.[7] A fledgling home industry suffered from high production costs and exacted equally excessive prices.[8] Turkey, until the beginning of the war, thus found it more economically feasible to import finished products than to try to manufacture them domestically. Once war actually disrupted trade,

[4] United States, Department of Commerce, Bureau of Foreign and Domestic Commerce. S. Goldberg, "Turkey: Basic Economic Position and Recent Changes," *International Reference Service*, Vol. I, No. 9 (April 1941), 1-4 at p. 1.

[5] Banque de Paris et des Pays-Bas. Étude No. 638. "Situation Économique et Financière de la Turquie" (Paris: mimeo, 1947), p. 4; henceforth referred to as "Situation Économique."

[6] *Ibid.*; for a complete survey of agricultural statistics during the war years, Türkiye Cumhuriyeti Başvekâlet. İstatistik Umum Müdürlüğü, *Ziraî İstatistik Özetleri 1936-1956 (Résumés of Agricultural Statistics)* (Ankara, 1957). Most divisions of the Central Statistical Office have published vital statistics for the war period. Consult Türkiye Cumhuriyeti Başvekâlet. İstatistik Umum Müdürlüğü, *İstatistik Özetleri (Statistical Résumés: Millî Eğitim 1932-1952 (Public Education 1932-1952)* (Ankara, 1953), *Nüfus Sayımları 1927-1950 (Population Census 1927-1950)* (Ankara, 1951). Professor Alexander Melamid of New York University, who has referred to these materials, cautions against accepting them on face value since he discovered many discrepancies on numerous occasions. (In a personal interview, New York, September 24, 1969.)

[7] *Economic and Commercial Conditions*, p. 28.

[8] *Ibid.*

89

however, Turkey became racked with import shortages. This led to even higher prices. The need, furthermore, to maintain a large standing army during the war, resulted in heavy defense expenditures which in turn accelerated the movement upward of the inflationary spiral.[9] The fancy prices offered by the Allies and the Axis for certain Turkish products ironically worsened the predicament by creating a situation in which "too much money chased too few goods."[10] Poor harvests in 1941 and 1942, especially of wheat, necessitated the rationing of even staple foods. Improperly applied governmental controls failed to prevent the prices for these commodities from soaring as well.[11]

During the war the official rate of exchange remained constant at 1 dollar = 1.80 Turkish lira. The actual purchasing power of the lira, however, decreased in leaps and bounds. In relation to other major currencies the Turkish lira at the end of the war was worth only 30 to 70 per cent of its prewar value.[12] In relation to gold, the Turkish lira decreased in value by 233 per cent, a loss two to three times greater than that suffered by English, American, or Swiss money.[13] Insofar as its domestic purchasing power was concerned, the value of Turkish money dropped 254 per cent

[9] The budgetary expenditure for defense equaled more than half of the total of Turkish governmental expenditures in 1943; "Situation Économique," p. 40; total expenditures went from 270 million lira in 1939 to nearly 550 million lira in 1944; Nadi, *Opening in the Curtain*, p. 183.

[10] *Economic and Commercial Conditions*, p. 28; also "Situation Économique," p. 37.

[11] For a general description of the inflationary situation, Aydemir, *The Second Man*, pp. 226-27; Aydemir also describes the inadequacy of government controls at the beginning of the war. He and Şükrü Sökmensüer were asked to submit a report, which they did, outlining some of the main problems and suggesting possible solutions; *ibid.*, pp. 221-22; also, Nadi, *Opening in the Curtain*, p. 176.

[12] Servet Tarhan, *La Monnaie Turque Pendant La Deuxième Guerre Mondiale (Turkish Money During the Second World War)* (Neuchâtel: Imprimerie H. Messeiller, 1952), p. 132.

[13] *Ibid.*

on account of the rise in the cost of living and 344 per cent according to the rise in wholesale prices.[14]

The wholesale price for food of plant origin rose, for example, to a level of 424.9 in 1942 from a base of 100 in 1938.[15] By the following year, 1943, the level reached was 894.5. The years 1944 and 1945 witnessed a tapering off with the level of wholesale prices for the former averaging at 539.4 and the latter at 595.9. Food of animal origin followed the same statistical curve. Again using the year 1938 as the base of 100, prices for this line of commodities reached the level of 386.6 in 1942, 752.8 in 1943, 520.9 and 492.1 in 1944 and 1945 respectively. Wholesale prices of industrial raw materials and partly finished goods rose steadily throughout the war.[16] Perhaps even more graphic are the figures reflecting the rise in the cost of living. In 1942 the wholesale cost of food and beverages in Ankara was at the level of 262.1 above the base of 100 for the year 1938. By 1943, this level attained a peak of 400.6 and underwent only small decreases in 1944 and 1945.[17] Fuel and lighting material followed a slightly different pattern, 141.2 in 1942, 197.6 in 1943, 229.3 in 1944, and 227.2 in 1945.[18] Clothing reached a level of 508.0 in 1943 and remained above 500 for the duration of the war.[19] The rise in the wholesale cost of living in Ankara during the war years averaged 220.9 in 1942, 322.0 in 1943, 330.1 in 1944, and 333.1 in 1945.[20] These figures are generally reflective of the rise in the cost of living throughout the country. Prices in İstanbul actually reached slightly higher levels than those in Ankara.[21]

Retail prices followed suit and hit the consumer with prohibitive costs.[22] The cost per kilogram of bread in Ankara,

[14] Ibid.

[15] Türkiye Cumhuriyeti Başvekâlet. İstatistik Genel Müdürlüğü, Small Statistical Abstract of Turkey 1942-1946 (Ankara, 1947), p. 409; henceforth referred to as Small Statistical Abstract.

[16] Ibid.　　　　[17] Ibid.　　　　[18] Ibid.

[19] Ibid.　　　　[20] Ibid.　　　　[21] Ibid.

[22] Ibid., pp. 411-12.

for example, was 12 *kuruş* (100 *kuruş* to a *lira*) in 1941, 25 in 1942, 41 in 1943, 32 in 1944, and 33 in 1945. The cost of bread in Trabzon rose from 14 *kuruş* per kilogram in 1941 to 70 *kuruş* per kilogram in 1943.[23] Although official figures put the cost of bread in İstanbul at 26 *kuruş* per kilogram in 1942, one account reported that bread was selling for as much as 60 *kuruş* per kilogram on the black market in İstanbul.[24] The costs of beef, mutton, cube sugar, olive oil, and rice also became staggering as the war progressed. The price of beef in Ankara rose from 39 *kuruş* per kilogram in 1941 to 129 in 1944, while in İstanbul prices jumped from 46 *kuruş* in 1941 to 182 in 1944.[25] Similarly, the price of cube sugar went from 50 *kuruş*[26] per kilogram to 345.[27] Olive oil cost 85 *kuruş* in 1941 but 250 *kuruş* in 1944.[28] The mutton that cost 56 *kuruş* in 1941 cost 176 in 1944, while the rice that sold for 38 *kuruş* per kilogram in 1941 sold for 149 *kuruş* in 1943.[29]

Repressive Domestic Measures

The total effect was devastating. As İsmet İnönü declared on November 1, 1944, "Our main concern within the country during the last years has been the nutrition difficulties and the harms of inflation."[30] His government set out to remedy the situation early in the war through a series of domestic and external measures. The external measures

[23] Karpat notes that farming in the Black Sea region is divided into small plots and consists mostly of corn and tobacco. In 1948, the Bureau of Soil Products could not supply this region with wheat since it had sold considerable quantities to buyers abroad. This created bitter resentment; cf., Karpat, *Turkey's Politics*, p. 104, n. 18.

[24] *Review*, Series B, No. 163, p. 598; also Aydemir, *The Second Man*, p. 203.

[25] *Small Statistical Abstract*, pp. 412-13.

[26] In 1941.   [27] In 1943; *ibid.*, p. 413.

[28] In Ankara; *ibid.*, pp. 416-17.

[29] Figures for mutton and rice are for Ankara; *ibid.*, pp. 417-18, 423.

[30] *İnönü's Speeches and Declarations*, p. 317.

consisting essentially of trade policies, as we shall see, on the whole benefited the Turkish economy. The domestic measures, however, involved various forms of repression which the citizenry, especially the peasants, resented. This resentment eventually led to İnönü's political demise.

The most important of the domestic measures taken by the Turkish Government during the war was the Law of National Defense, the *Milli Korunma Kanunu,* passed by the Grand National Assembly on January 18, 1940.[31] In certain realms, the government did not hesitate to exercise the prerogatives granted to it under the law. In order to solve its manpower shortage, for example, the government undertook to impose compulsory industrial work upon peasants. At the discretion of local officials, men who had not been abducted into the military service could be forced to work in strategic industries, specifically the mines, for a year and at low wages.[32] This produced "widespread discontent among the peasants."[33]

Assignments of industrial work, however, primarily affected peasants living near the centers of mining. The de-

[31] Chapter 5, Article 86 of the 1924 constitution stated that "In case of war, or in case of strong and actual movements against the country and the Republic, the executive ministerial council may declare martial law for a period not to exceed one month. The law will be immediately submitted to the Assembly for approval. The Assembly can extend or shorten the period of the martial law"; Tanor and Beygo, *Turkish Constitutions,* p. 120. Since only the Assembly can approve an extension of martial law, the government repeatedly had to submit requests for this purpose; see, e.g., *T.B.M.M. Zabıt Ceridesi,* Seventh Assembly, May 28, 1943, I, 314-15; also Seventh Assembly, June 26, 1944, II, 133. İnönü described the law in 1941 as a way of preventing "the harmful effects" of war; *İnönü's Speeches and Declarations,* p. 362.

[32] Karpat, *Turkey's Politics,* p. 91, n. 28; Karpat suggests that Minister of Economics Fuat Sirmen justified the works laws on the grounds that such labor merely substituted for military service. Karpat, *ibid.,* p. 91, n. 29, cites Hikmet Bayur, however, who argued that these laborers had important work to do on their farms, for the most part had already served in the military, and, in any case, were forced to work for minimal wages.

[33] *Ibid.*

crees of the Bureau of Soil Products (*Toprak Mahsulleri Ofisi*) affected greater numbers. One such ordinance of the Bureau of Soil Products required that peasants sell their crops to it well below market prices. Peasants also had to meet specific quotas set by the Bureau. These quotas typically took away a peasant's entire harvest leaving only what was required for his and his family's sustenance.[34] The purpose of these regulations was to reduce the possibility of widespread hoarding and starvation by ensuring an equitable distribution of food and by keeping the costs of food, particularly bread, low. These policies were misguided, however, and to some extent encouraged the ills they were designed to prevent or cure. The peasants began to hoard their produce with even greater tenacity, and certain rich landowners were able to reap enormous profits by selling their produce on the black market. This often required the cooperation of officials within the Bureau of Soil Products who received appropriate payment from the landowners. Several newspaper reports in 1943 publicized the degree to which corruption was running rampant in the Bureau.[35]

The measures which affected and offended the greatest number of Turks, however, came in the realm of taxation. The system in Turkey during the war of taxing gross earnings led to gross inequities. Whereas wage and salary earners paid the exact amount due to the government, large private entrepreneurs, whose number rapidly increased during the war, were able to pay comparatively little by shielding their earnings.[36] This led to the accumulation of a disproportionately large amount of capital in the hands of a few war profiteers.[37] Such men did not hesitate to spend this money openly and thus increase the inflationary pressure on the lira. İnönü declared on November 1, 1942, that

[34] *Ibid.*, p. 104, esp. n. 17.
[35] See, e.g., *Cumhuriyet*, March 2, 6, 1943 and *Tasvir-i Efkâr*, March 4, 1943.
[36] Karpat, *Turkey's Politics*, p. 92, n. 30.
[37] *Ibid.*, p. 93, n. 32.

The wheeler-dealer, the farm lords, the greedy oppor-
tunist merchant . . . and a few politicians, who think of
all the crises as big opportunities for their political ambitions and who work for [who knows] what foreign nation,
are arrogantly trying to undermine the entire life of a
great nation.[38]

İnönü went on to suggest that it would be comparatively
easy to eliminate these evils. This proved not to be the
case.[39] Tax policy in Turkey fostered an inequitable distribution of wealth throughout the war and failed to curb
inflation. The Tax on Wealth (*Varlık Vergisi*) and the Tax
on Soil Products (*Toprak Mahsulleri Vergisi*) together
taxed selected minorities and the peasants without ever
attacking inflation.[40] The yields which accrued as a result
of these two taxes were never removed from circulation but
reentered the money market immediately.[41] As deflationary
measures, therefore, they were ineffective; as social institutions, they were corrupt. Karpat concludes, "The 'invisible'
accumulation of capital in certain hands, and its squander-
ing . . . was indeed so striking at the end of the second
World War as to become a source of complaint in the National Assembly."[42]

TURKEY'S ECONOMIC DEPENDENCE ON GERMANY

Turkey's economic predicament and its shortages during
the war were created by its prior dependence upon Germany. The imminence of war had prompted Turkish statesmen to risk the inconveniences of temporary economic dis-
equilibrium in order to achieve closer economic ties with
Great Britain, the United States, and France.

German-Turkish trade relations between 1930 and 1945,
with the peaks and depressions, follow a pattern which re-

38 *İnönü's Speeches and Declarations*, p. 371.
39 Karpat, *Turkey's Politics*, p. 92, n. 30.
40 Tarhan, *Turkish Money*, pp. 134-35.
41 *Ibid.*   42 Karpat, *Turkey's Politics*, p. 93.

sembles that of undulating waves. In 1931, for example, Germany received 10.7 per cent of Turkey's total exports and produced some 21.3 per cent of Turkey's imports.[43] Five years later, in 1936, Turkey exported a full 51 per cent of its total exports to Germany;[44] perhaps even more significantly, 45.1 per cent of its total imports came from Germany.[45] In 1938, 46.9 per cent of Turkey's total imports originated from Germany as opposed to 11.2 per cent from Britain and 10.4 per cent from the United States.[46] Export figures for the same year reveal an even more startling contrast: whereas 42.9 per cent of Turkey's total exports had gone to Germany, a mere 3.4 per cent had gone to Britain. The United States received slightly more, 12.2 per cent of Turkey's total exports.[47] Germany, prior to the war, was Turkey's major source of such indispensable items as constructional iron and steel, finished copper, vehicles and engines of all kinds, heavy machinery, tires and other rubber products, glass, newsprint, and pharmaceuticals.[48] Turkey in return exported much of its perishable agricultural produce to Germany.

In 1942 Barbara Ward observed ". . . it is no coincidence that the curve of Turkey's foreign trade has on the whole followed the variations in her foreign relations."[49] During the phase of Turkish foreign policy denoted by the Mutual

---

[43] League of Nations. General Study Conference on Economic Policies in Relation to World Peace. Hazım Atıf Kuyucak, *Memorandum on Exchange Control in Turkey* (Paris: International Institute of International Cooperation, 1939), unpaginated, Table xv.

[44] *Ibid.*; the actual value of these commodities came to approximately 60 million Turkish liras.

[45] *Ibid.*; this amounted to 41 Turkish liras worth of goods.

[46] *Ibid.*   [47] *Ibid.*

[48] *Economic and Commercial Conditions*, Appendix 19, pp. 173ff.

[49] Barbara Ward, *Turkey* (London: Oxford University Press, 1942), p. 91; this is also the general thesis of Yuluğ Tekin Kurat, *Ikinci Dünya Savaşında Türk-Alman Ticaretindeki İktisadi Siyasat (A Survey of Economic Policy in Turkish-German Trade Relations During The Second World War)* (Ankara: Türk Tarih Kurumu Basımevi, 1961).

Defense Treaty with Britain and France, October 19, 1939, Turkish trade with Germany dropped heavily. In 1940, 8 million Turkish liras worth of German imports flowed into Turkey constituting a mere 11.7 per cent of the total.[50] This was the case the following year when German imports reaching Turkey comprised 11.9 per cent of Turkey's total imports.[51] Export figures are equally revealing. In 1940, Turkish exports to Germany were valued at 9 million Turkish liras and constituted only 8.6 per cent of the total value of goods exported by Turkey.[52] Turkish exports to Germany picked up in 1941 with 26 million Turkish liras worth of commodities going to Germany, that is, 21.8 per cent of the total amount exported.[53] The real jump, however, came over the next three years which almost returned Germany to its former position of eminence. In 1943, Germany provided 37.7 per cent of imports into Turkey and received 23.7 per cent of its exports.[54] Imports from Germany dropped slightly in 1944 reaching only 30.4 per cent of the total, but exports to Germany comprised 78.2 per cent of the total.[55] The latter figure is especially remark-

[50] Türkiye Cumhuriyeti Başbakanlık. İstatistik Umum Müdürlüğü, *İstatistik Yıllığı 1942-1945* (*Statistical Yearbook 1942-1945*), Vol. 15 (Ankara, 1946), pp. 349-51; figures are found in a table with the heading *Başlıca Memleketlere Göre İthalat ve İhracat Kıymetleri* (*Value of Imported Goods and Exported Goods by Principal Countries*); also, International Bank for Reconstruction and Development, Loan Department, Eastern Division, "Statistical Tables on Turkey" (Washington, D.C.: mimeo, 1947), Table 50, p. 58.

[51] *Ibid.*

[52] *Ibid.* It might be further noted that Italy was the country that at first took Germany's place as "principal supplier" and "destination" for Turkish goods. Italian-Turkish trade dropped quickly in 1941, when the war in the Mediterranean disrupted trade routes; U.S. Department of Commerce, Bureau of Foreign and Domestic Commerce, "Effect of War on Turkey's Foreign Trade," *Foreign Commerce Weekly*, December 13, 1941, pp. 4-5 at p. 5.

[53] *Ibid.*; for a breakdown by commodities, *Economic and Commercial Conditions*, Appendix 24, pp. 204ff.

[54] *Ibid.*   [55] *Ibid.*

able since Turkey severed economic relations with Germany early in the year. This can be explained by the fact that the Germans were offering to pay exorbitant prices for Turkish goods, that German control over Turkish trade routes prevented Turkish goods from going elsewhere and, finally, that the Turkish Government was determined to abide by its agreements with Germany in 1940 regarding the amount of trade that was to flow between the two countries. The drop in the wave came in 1945 when trade between Turkey and Germany was reduced to almost nil.

Germany's high level of trade with Turkey before the war had not come about by chance.[56] It had been the result of Hjalmar Schacht's so-called "New Plan" for German economic ascendancy.[57] When Schacht became head of the Ministry of Economics on August 2, 1934, he almost imme-

[56] It had come about as a result of determined efforts by Germany. For full analyses of German economic policy and warfare, Cleona Lewis, *Nazi Europe and World Trade* (Washington, D.C.: The Brookings Institution, 1941), and N. Montchiloff, *Ten Years of Controlled Trade in South-Eastern Europe* (Cambridge, England: Cambridge University Press, 1944). Montchiloff served as Bulgarian Ambassador in London prior to the Nazi occupation of that country. E. R. Lingeman places the blame for Turkey's prewar dependence on Germany on its "failure to compete"; see *Economic and Commercial Conditions*, p. 177. For a survey of Turkish legislation concerning exchange control, Kuyucak, *Memorandum on Exchange Control*, Appendix, Table XIII. Despite governmental efforts to the contrary, the Turks had found it impossible before the war to produce finished products that could compete in the world market. Thus they fell prey to the temptations created by German willingness to pay prices well above world levels for agricultural products.

[57] Hjalmar Schacht, *Account Settled*, Edward Fitzgerald (trans.) (London: Weidenfeld and Nicholson, 1949). Schacht describes the reasoning which prompted him to devise the "new plan" as follows: "If a country has insufficient foreign exchange to permit it to buy what it needs . . . then the question of cheapness ceases to be of interest. . . . Might it not . . . be possible to find countries which would be willing to sell their goods not against payment in their own currency, but against some other condition? This other consideration in our case could only be German goods"; see pp. 78-83.

diately instituted a process of payment through accounts. By this system, in Schacht's words, "Foreign countries selling goods to us [Germany] would have the amount of our purchases credited to their account in German currency and with this they could then buy anything they wanted in Germany."[58] The advantage of this process from the point of view of Turkey as well as Germany was that it obviated the necessity of using scarce foreign exchange currencies to purchase commodities abroad.[59] Turkey, anxious to sell its raw materials and agricultural products, Germany, happy to sell its finished products and not fall deeper into debt in terms of the international money market, regarded this barter scheme as a way of spending without cost.[60]

[58] *Ibid.*, p. 81; John C. deWilde, "The German Economic Dilemma," *Foreign Policy Reports*, Vol. XIII, No. 1 (March 15, 1937), 2-16 at p. 6, pointed out that barter under the New Plan took place indirectly. "Under a system of private clearing, foreign exporters have been paid in Aski marks and allowed to sell these so-called Aski marks (*Auslaendersonderkonten für Inlandszahlungen*) to importers wishing to buy additional goods in Germany." As deWilde also suggests, this indirect form of barter was highly successful in promoting German trade with Latin America as well as in southeastern Europe. For a full description of German prewar trade policy in relation to southeastern Europe, John C. deWilde, "German Trade Drive in Southeastern Europe," *Foreign Policy Reports*, Vol. XII, No. 17 (November 15, 1936), 214-20.

[59] *Ibid.*, p. 215.

[60] The cost to both countries was real, however. Germany was forced to buy goods not from sources offering the best deal but from countries that would purchase German products. Thus, as deWilde wrote, the system of clearing accounts "completely diverted German trade from its natural and most economic channels"; see "The German Economic Dilemma," p. 6. The cost of raw materials to Germany also soared, and Germany became increasingly the slave of its own clearing accounts. This was its "economic dilemma." For a concise analysis of the strategic relationship between the raw products in southeastern Europe and German requirements in wartime, Basil Davidson, "Can Germany Live on the Balkans?" *Free Europe*, December 29, 1939, pp. 67-69; for a complete survey of Turkish trade during the war, including that with Germany, Türkiye Cumhuriyeti Başvekâlet, İstatistik Umum Müdürlüğü, *Dış Ticaret 1938-1952 (Foreign Trade 1939-1952)* (Ankara, 1953).

In 1939, Turkish policy-makers began to fear that they had allowed Turkey to become too economically dependent upon Germany and that this might threaten their political maneuverability. On December 14, 1939, Şükrü Saracoğlu stated,

> There is still another truth which requires that, in order that a country may have an independent national policy, the greater part of its foreign trade must not be directed towards a single country. To however small an extent foreign trade becomes the monopoly of a single country, it is very difficult to pursue an independent national policy, even if this country should be an ally. When national policy, the aim of which is independence, and national trade, the object of which is profit, can no longer go side by side, national trade must make a sacrifice.[61]

If Turkey was to break away from trade with Germany, it had to do so in a way that would minimize the sacrifices. The Turks lost no time in placing the burden upon the British.

[61] As quoted by Helseth, *Turkey and the United States*, p. 133; Helseth's reference is to U.S. Department of State Dispatch No. 1343 from Ankara dated January 29, 1940, file reference 662.6731/116; in the negotiations preceding the October 19, 1939 treaty, the Turks emphasized their desire to be free of German control; see, e.g., Viscount Halifax to Sir Knatchbull-Hugessen, Foreign Office, August 2, 1939, *Docs.Brit.F.P.*, VI, 567-68; Halifax informed the British Ambassador to Turkey that Rüştü Aras had told him that before Turkey could "reconcile her foreign policy of co-operation with Great Britain and France with her internal policy," the democratic powers would have to assist Turkey economically. On the following day, Knatchbull-Hugessen informed Halifax that a "feeling of disappointment and disillusionment" was growing in Turkey and that the Turks were coming to believe that the British did not intend to help them along these lines sufficiently"; *Docs.Brit.F.P.*, VI, 574-75.

THE ATTEMPT TO BREAK LOOSE FROM GERMANY

When the Turkish commercial payments agreement with Germany expired on August 31, 1939, the Turkish Government refused to agree to extend it until Turkey's commercial relationships were defined with Britain and France. The financial accord attached to the Anglo-French-Turkish tripartite agreement of October 19, 1939, was designed to clear the way for closer trade relations among the three countries.[62] The British indeed had anticipated that it would be easy to negotiate agreement regarding trade policies with the Turks when they agreed to the generous financial terms contained in the pact of October 19, 1939. The most important outstanding question in this regard was that in relation to the export of chromite. Negotiations began almost immediately after October 19. The Turks insisted that the British agree to purchase 200,000 tons of chromite per year for the next two years.[63] In return, they would agree not to deliver any chromite to Germany. The British eventually agreed, but by that time the Turks had added a new condition. On November 16, 1939, the Turkish Ambassador in London informed the British Government that Turkey's promise not to sell chromite to Germany was contingent upon whether Britain purchased Turkish figs, hazel nuts, raisins, and tobacco. This was resented in London where it was felt that the Western Allies "had done quite well for the Turks."[64] British concern was heightened by the fact that they realized it was impossible for them to purchase enough Turkish goods so as to enable the Turks

[62] For a more complete description of this treaty, see above, Chap. I, n. 88.

[63] With a view to protecting their security, the Turks had also insisted upon the inclusion of a "suspense clause" which provided that the treaty would not come into effect until the British had supplied them with military equipment sufficient to enable them to guard the Thracian border of Turkey; Medlicott, *The Economic Blockade*, I, 273.

[64] *Ibid.*

to eliminate Germany from the Turkish market. The Turks, moreover, insisted that shipments of chromite would go to Germany as long as they had surplus produce awaiting export. With negotiations deadlocked, Menemencioğlu journeyed to London and Paris.[65]

In London, Menemencioğlu continued to insist that the British purchase 2 million pounds sterling worth of Turkish farm commodities. The Germans, he argued, refused to accept any such goods unless the Turks agreed to sell them chromite. If the British wished to prevent Turkish chromite from going to Germany, then they had to provide a market for Turkey's perishable raw products. Menemencioğlu refused to allow the negotiations to proceed until some agreement could be found regarding the purchase of dried fruit. "It would have been possible to call M. Menemencioğlu's bluff by refusing the dried fruit agreement," W. H. Medlicott writes, "but it was not quite certain that he was bluffing."[66] The British accepted Menemencioğlu's demands. Menemencioğlu left immediately for Paris, however, where he surprisingly received support against the British. Upon his return in mid-December to London, Menemencioğlu presented a new demand to the effect that the British Government agree to buy Turkish chromite not for two years but for twenty. The British refused. An agreement, which included the French, was eventually signed on January 8, 1940, however.[67] The British promised to buy Turkish dried fruit until the end of the export season following the cessation of hostilities providing that this did not obligate them beyond the 1942-1943 export season. The British also agreed

[65] Medlicott, *ibid.*, p. 274, states that Menemencioğlu at this time was to prove to be "a resourceful and at times exasperating negotiator."

[66] *Ibid.*, pp. 274-75.

[67] For the British-French-Turkish agreements of January 8, 1940, League of Nations, *Treaty Series*, Vol. 200, No. 4689, pp. 177-89. These arrangements were signed in Paris. The exact title of the main agreements are "An Arrangement relating to the credit of 25 million pounds sterling at 4 per cent" and "An Arrangement relating to the Loan of 15 million pounds sterling at 3 per cent"; see also Chap. 1, n. 88, above.

to purchase 50,000 tons of chromite for each of the following two years and received an option on that mined in 1943. As we shall see, they would soon regret their rejection of Menemencioğlu's proposal to place Turkey's chromite in British hands for the following twenty years.

Turkish negotiations with the Axis had not ceased while Menemencioğlu was away from Ankara. Upon his return, the British were informed that Turkey had agreed to distribute German goods held in Turkish warehouses and to export approximately 5 million Turkish liras worth of Turkish goods including cotton, sesame seed, hazel nuts, tobacco, and most important from the point of view of German economic viability, olive oil, to Germany.[68] It became ever more evident to the British that the Turkish Government was unwilling to agree on a war trade agreement cutting all commercial traffic between Germany and Turkey.[69]

Indeed, after the January 8, 1940 agreement, Turkish diplomacy continued to play the Axis and the Allies against each other. In February 1940 the Turks presented a list of commodity requirements to the British which they wanted before they would consider the cessation of trade with Germany.[70] At the same time, they made similar demands on the Germans, emphasizing their need for trucks, spare parts, guns, plant facilities, locomotives, and railway materials.[71] On July 25, 1940, a commercial agreement finally was signed between Germany and Turkey.[72] This declared that approximately 21 million Turkish liras worth of German commodities would be exported to Turkey. The Germans were to deliver 39 locomotives, equipment for the Sivas cement factory, spare parts, pharmaceuticals, etc. The

[68] Helseth, *Turkey and the United States*, p. 134; also *ibid.*, pp. 267-77. Helseth observes that the Turks informed the British of these negotiations in advance but failed to mention that the agreement would include olive oil.

[69] Medlicott, *The Economic Blockade*, I, 277.

[70] *Ibid.*

[71] Helseth, *Turkey and the United States*, p. 134.

[72] *Ibid.*

Turks were to supply Germany with a full variety of farm commodities, including mohair and olive oil.[73] Such items were high on the list of strategic materials which the British were trying to prevent the Germans from receiving.

One year after the German-Turkish commercial agreement had been in effect, however, German goods valued at only 9 million Turkish liras had been delivered to Turkey.[74] This created an even more pressing need in Turkey for arms and machinery. Germany, for its part, was beginning to eye Turkish chromite with even greater hunger. Consequently, upon the conclusion of the German-Turkish Treaty of Friendship, June 18, 1941, it was announced that Karl Clodius, head of German trade negotiations, would travel to Ankara in September to clarify the situation.[75] Negotiations centering on the issue of deliveries of chromite to Germany lasted until October 9, 1941, when the so-called "Clodius agreement" was signed in Ankara.[76] The Turks

[73] Under the terms of this agreement, one-third of the commodities to be shipped to Germany from Turkey consisted of tobacco.

[74] Helseth, *Turkey and the United States*, p. 135.

[75] For the nature of the discussions between Clodius and Menemencioğlu at this time, see the Deputy Director of the Economic Policy Department (Clodius) to the Foreign Ministry, Ankara, September 26, 1941, *Docs.Ger.F.P.*, XII, 566-68. Menemencioğlu insisted that Turkey's hands were tied in regard to chromite, since the Turks had agreed to deliver ore only to the British until January 15, 1939. The Turkish Foreign Minister urged, however, that Germany enter into an agreement with them. "I never heard Numan [Menemencioğlu] insist on any question in such urging, almost begging, terms," Clodius wrote.

[76] The Clodius agreement actually consisted of the German-Turkish Commercial Agreement and the Payments Agreement, both of which were signed in Ankara on October 9, 1944; for the exchanges relating to these agreements, *ibid.*, pp. 626-27; for the exact text of these agreements, Germany, *Reichgezetzblatt*, Vol. II, No. 42, 1941. "Regelung Des Wareuverkehrs" ("Regulation of Commercial Transactions"), October 9, 1941 (Berlin: Office of German Government Publications, 1941), pp. 375-80; the Turkish text under the title, "Türkiye ile Almanya Arasında Ticarî Mübadelelerin Tanzimi Hakkında 9 Ekim 1941 Tarihli Anlaşma" can be found in Türkiye Cumhuriyeti Başbakanlık. Neşriyat

agreed to ship 45,000 tons of chromite to Germany between January 15, 1943 and March 31, 1943—that is, during the three months immediately after the expiration of the British option. If Germany delivered 18 million Turkish liras worth of military equipment, Turkey would send an additional 45,000 tons of chromite to Germany in 1943, and 90,000 tons during 1944.[77] This agreement did not please the Germans, since they had hoped to induce the Turks to deliver chromite to them immediately.[78] The agreement vexed the British as much, however. It seemed as if the Turks were allowing themselves to become economically dependent on German favors once again. The British and the Americans set out to prevent this.

The Anglo-American Preemptive Purchasing Program

Early in 1940, Prime Minister Churchill asked Philip Swinton to set up the United Kingdom Commercial Corporation (U.K.C.C.) to spearhead the Allies' attempt to prevent strategically valuable imports from reaching the Axis through preemptive buying. Under this program, the British successfully purchased the following amounts of Turkish commodities (in metric tons) in 1941:

---

ve Müdevvenat Genel Müdürlüğü, *Düstur*, Üçüncü Tertip, Vol. 23 (Ankara: Devlet Matbaası, 1942), pp. 93-103 (Office of the Prime Minister of the Turkish Republic. General Directorate of Press and Publications, *Code of Laws*, Third Format . . .); henceforth referred to as *Düstur*.

[77] Medlicott, *The Economic Blockade*, II, 527, conveniently contains a concise description of the terms and implications of the Clodius agreement.

[78] Clodius' immediate subordinate in Ankara, Hans Anton Kroll, admitted that he was "surprised by the Turkish attitude." He later stated that "in almost 6 years of working with the Turks I have found that they are skillful enough to find a loophole in any treaty instrument . . ."; see Minister Kroll to Ministerial Director Wiehl, Therapia, October 13, 1941, *Docs.Ger.F.P.*, XIII, 645-47.

Chromite	151,066
Mohair	3,350
Olive oil	5,091
Valonia	5,000
Valex	1,000
Cottonseed cake	1,622
Cottonseed oil	8,000
Linseed cake	124
Sesame-seed cake	132½[79]

The Americans in 1942 joined the British in their efforts to take Turkish goods off the open market by establishing the United States Commercial Corporation (U.S.C.C.).[80]

Yet the program, from the point of view of preventing crucial Turkish commodities from reaching Germany, largely failed. The Turks scrupulously abided by the Clodius agreement. Turkish exports to the Axis countries in 1943,

[79] Medlicott, *The Economic Blockade*, I, 610.

[80] The British and American agencies operated quite differently in Ankara despite the mutuality of their aims. The Americans, anxious to acquire as much Turkish goods as possible, often made purchases without the consent of the Turkish Ministry of Economics. The British refrained from doing such in order not to offend the Turkish Government. The Americans also hired Turks to conduct their bidding for goods, whereas the British tended not to in fear that they would be cheated; *ibid.*, II, 246-47. This British reluctance, however, seems to have generated considerable resentment. A memorandum in the private papers of Michel and Irena Sokolnicki dated October 15, 1942, observed that "the U.K.C.C. was never able to win the liking and respect of the Turkish businessman because it insisted and still insists on not cooperating and not making use of Turkish organs"; reprinted with the kind permission of Mrs. Irena Sokolnickia. David L. Gordon and Royden Dangerfield, *The Hidden Weapon: The Story of Economic Warfare* (New York: Harper & Bros., 1947), p. 123, criticize both agencies and suggest that the reason why the preemptive purchasing program was more successful in Spain than in Turkey "almost certainly lay in the Allied scattered attack on a large number of commodities." Lord Swinton's (Philip Cunliffe-Lictes), *I Remember* (London: Hutchinson and Co., 1948) contains a glowing account of the success of the U.K.C.C. particularly in regard to Turkey; see esp. pp. 164-70.

for example, were in the following amounts (in metric tons):

Chromite	46,783
Oil seeds	17,942
Fish	17,597
Tanning materials	13,756
Cotton	10,247
Pig iron	9,508
Copper	7,384
Dried fruits	6,445
Skins	2,894
Vegetable oils	2,068
Cotton waste	1,554
Mohair	1,438
Iron and steel ingots	966[81]

The Turks determinedly insisted upon living up to their economic agreements with both sides. Germany would receive the goods promised to it, as would the Allies. Whereas the Turks refused to supply chromite to Germany before 1943, they also refused to grant export licenses to Allied agents that would make the full delivery of promised amounts of goods to Germany impossible. This was tacitly confirmed on April 18, 1943, by the signing of the second Clodius agreement.[82] "Clearly," Professor Medlicott reflects, "the Turks had seen to it that all the goods most needed by the Germans would be reserved for them."[83] The Turks were thus prepared to reserve large amounts of goods for

[81] Medlicott, *The Economic Blockade*, II, 540-41.

[82] The second Clodius agreement called for the export to Germany of Turkish wool and valonia; for the exact text of the second Clodius agreement, Germany, *Reichgezetzblatt*, Vol. II, No. 29, 1943, "Abkommen Zur Regelung Des Warenverkehrs Zwischen Deutschland und Turkei." ("Treaty for the Regulation of Commercial Transactions between Germany and Turkey"), April 18, 1943 (Berlin: Office of German Government Publications, 1943), pp. 355-58.

[83] Medlicott, *The Economic Blockade*, II, 535.

export to Germany. By the terms of the second Clodius agreement, Turkey agreed to supply Germany with 40 million Turkish liras worth of strategically valuable goods within fourteen months of the signing of the treaty, that is, until May 31, 1944.

Menemencioğlu, along with İnönü, was behind this policy of observing the letter of these contractual arrangements.[84] There were several reasons why they believed it to be in Turkish interests first to enter into a series of economic arrangements with Germany as well as the Allies and second to live up to the terms of these agreements, whatever the reactions of the other side. As mentioned before, the British were not in a position to supply Turkey with all the goods it needed. Germany, however, could only be induced to supply such materials if it could get what it needed in return. Thus Menemencioğlu seems to have used Turkish strategic goods as bait to attract German supplies. This policy also served the purpose of deterring Germany from trying to take possession of or destroy Turkey's capacity to mine its ore deposits. Finally, it helped to maintain the prices of Turkish goods.[85] Thus the Turks were perfectly content to sell to the British and Americans amounts of materials and goods beyond that promised to Germany, but did not allow the preemptive purchases of the Allies to eat away or eliminate German quotas.[86] The one thing the Turks did do was

[84] Menemencioğlu was in charge of and conducted most high-level economic and commercial negotiations during the war.

[85] Professor Ahmet Şükrü Esmer, Cevat Açıkalın, and Zeki Kuneralp in personal interviews with the author. The *Menemencioğlu Manuscript* confirms this analysis.

[86] Lewis V. Thomas and Richard N. Frye, *The United States and Turkey and Iran* (Cambridge: Harvard University Press, 1951), p. 93; these authors have argued that "insofar as she dared, Turkey gradually moved to deny the Axis powers access to vital materials"; David L. Gordon and Royden Dangerfield, *The Hidden Weapon*, p. 123, are much closer to the truth when they suggest that the principal reason why the Allied program of preemption failed "was the Turkish policy of allocating many of the most important products between the bel-

to allow the British and the Americans to buy Turkish goods at high prices, prices that had been forced upward by German willingness to pay exorbitant amounts for certain Turkish commodities.[87] It can be said, therefore, that during the period between the first Clodius agreement and the severance of Turkey's economic relations with Germany in April 1944, German failure to deliver the goods it had promised Turkey was a more important factor in preventing Turkish goods from going to Germany than the Anglo-American program of preemptive purchases. The negotia-

---

ligerents." Medlicott, in *The Economic Blockade*, concludes that as of 1943 ". . . the Turks had so adjusted the allocations to the Allies as to retain sufficient quantities to meet their present and possible future commitments to the Axis" (II, 532). These commitments, as we have seen, were quite generous, although, it must be repeated, they in no way pleased German officials at the time.

[87] This is not to suggest that the preemptive purchasing power was totally unimportant. This program, along with the grants made under the Lend-Lease Act, enabled Turkey to remain viable diplomatically as well as economically. If the preemptive purchasing program is to be considered in this light as a form of Allied economic aid to Turkey during the war, then it may indeed be considered a success in the sense that it helped to maintain Turkish independence. This independence, however, led to the failure of the program in regard to its primary task. For a listing of the amount of equipment and commodities assigned and delivered to Turkey under the lend-lease program, Helseth, *Turkey and the United States*, p. 138; United States, Department of State, *Twenty-Third Report to Congress on Lend-Lease Operations*, Publication No. 2707 (Washington, D.C.: United States Government Printing Office, 1945), pp. 15-16. The total amount of defense aid extended by the United States under the Lend-Lease Act was in the vicinity of 43 million; see *ibid.*, n. 51; also, the U.S. President, Message from the President of the United States transmitting the *Thirty-Sixth Report to Congress on Lend-Lease Operations for the Year Ending December 31, 1954* (Washington, D.C.: United States Government Printing Office, 1955); for a general description of lend-lease operations, United States, Office of Military History, Department of the Army, Richard M. Leighton and Robert W. Coakley, *Global Logistics and Strategy 1940-1943*, Vol. IV (Washington, D.C.: United States Government Printing Office, 1955), 522ff.

tions during the war over chromite, as well as other goods including copper, mohair, hemp, flax, valonia, and cotton, amply illustrate this.

THE ISSUE OF CHROMITE AND THE TURKISH REACTION

Of all the goods and commodities in Turkey's possession, the most valuable during the war was chromite. As one author put it, "Chromium is to modern industry as yeast is to bread; only a little is required, but without it there is no bread."[88] In 1939 Turkey produced 16.4 per cent of the world's chromite, approximately 190,000 tons.[89] Production

[88] Arthur Kemp, "Chromium: A Strategic Material," *Harvard Business Review* (Winter 1942), pp. 199-212 at p. 199. Kemp notes that the U.S. Army and Navy Munitions Board classified chromium along with six other metals, antimony, manganese, mercury, nickel, tin, and tungsten, as being of strategic value. For a full discussion, Brooks Emeny, *The Strategy of Raw Material: A Study of America in Peace and War* (New York: The Macmillan Co., 1944). In order to avoid confusion, the terms "chrome," "chromium," and "chromite" should be differentiated. Chromite is an ore with chemical composition of Fe $(CrO_2)^2$ from which chromium and chrome are derived. Chromium is an alloy used in the manufacture of steel and can be combined with other elements to produce a variety of chemical combinations many of which are useful industrially. Two such combinations are chromium acetate and chromium chloride which are used for tanning purposes. Chrome is a yellow pigment derived from lead chromate. The negotiations between Turkey and the belligerents during the war concerned crude chromite, not chromium or chrome as is sometimes suggested.

[89] Ona K. D. Ringwood and Louis E. Frechtling, "World Production of Selected Strategic Materials," *Foreign Policy Reports*, XVIII (June 15, 1942), 90-96 at p. 92; for a complete listing of the world's production before 1940, *ibid.*, p. 205; for a detailed study of the entire mineral industry in Turkey, including a description of the nature and location of chromite deposits in Turkey, see United States, Department of the Interior, Bureau of Mines, Lotfallah Nahai, "The Mineral Industry of Turkey," *Information Circular 7855* (Washington, D.C.: United States Government Printing Office, 1958), esp. pp. 79-96; for an earlier analysis of the growing importance of Turkish chromite, see United States, Department of the Interior, Bureau of Mines, Robert L. Ridgeway, "Shifts in Sources of Chromite Supply," *Information Circular 6886* (Washing-

levels continued at this high rate throughout the war. Turkish mined production of chromite during the war years was as follows in metric tons:

1939	183,300
1940	169,800
1941	135,700
1942	116,300
1943	154,500
1944	182,100
1945	148,100[90]

This led both belligerent sides, desperately in need of chrome, to place inordinate pressures upon the Turks to grant major proportions of ore to them. Turkey, in effect, was thus required to walk a tightrope.[91]

The task of walking this tightrope fell primarily upon Menemencioğlu. During his visit to London in December 1939, it will be recalled, he had offered the British an option to buy all Turkish chromite for the next twenty years,

---

ton, D.C.: United States Government Printing Office, 1936). Ridgeway emphasizes the high-grade quality of Turkish chromite. For an account of how Turkey went about developing its capacity to mine chromite in the early days of the republic, H. von Engelmann, "Turkey Extending Railroads to Develop Chrome Resources," *Engineering and Mining Journal,* June 29, 1929, pp. 1,037-38.

[90] These figures are reprinted from Nahai, *Information Circular 7855,* p. 10; for an exact breakdown of production figures by region, Etibank, Conjuncture and Statistics Department, *Statistics of Etibank Mining Exploitations 1941-1951* (Ankara, 1954). Etibank, a government-sponsored enterprise founded in 1935 under Turkish public law 3460, is essentially designed to promote mineral exploration and production through subsidies to other banks and private firms. For a fuller analysis, see Etibank, "Principal Characteristics of Governmental Economic Institutions to which Etibank Belongs" (Ankara: mimeo., 1949).

[91] Zeki Kuneralp has suggested that its possession of chrome was "an embarrassment" to Turkey during the war. Turkish leaders thus had to walk a "tightrope among the conflicting demands of the belligerents." (In a personal interview with the author, London, February 24, 1965.)

which would have simplified matters. To its subsequent regret, the British Foreign Office rejected this proposal. Menemencioğlu then negotiated the Clodius arrangement calling for the delivery of a maximum of 90,000 tons of chromite in 1943 and a maximum of 45,000 tons in 1944. Whether or not Germany received such amounts depended upon the fulfillment of its commitment to supply Turkey with specified amounts of goods, materials, and equipment. In October 1942, the British and to a lesser extent the Americans began efforts to prevent Turkish chromite from going to Germany. Although Menemencioğlu was willing to assure the Allies that deliveries would not be made until the 18 million liras worth of German war equipment had been received, he steadfastly refused to allow the British to have export licenses which would have reduced Turkey's capacity to supply Germany with the agreed amounts.[92] The British, having made this "the acid test"[93] and the "touchstone of Turkey's attitude toward the Allies,"[94] became incensed. Medlicott notes, "The Ministry [for Economic Warfare] remarked indignantly that the Turks had 'at last come into the open and revealed the full extent of their duplicity.' "[95]

[92] There are many instances where Menemencioğlu explicitly refused Allied requests for licenses to export chromite. The Chargé in Turkey (Kelley) to the Secretary of State, Ankara, October 16, 1942; on October 21, 1942, Menemencioğlu informed Kelley specifically that Germany had "priority" over the 45,000 tons of chromite promised it by his agreement with Clodius; *Foreign Relations*, 1942, IV, 758-62; also *ibid.*, 762-63.

[93] The Ambassador in the United Kingdom (Winant) to the Secretary of State, London, September 18, 1942, *ibid.*, pp. 745-46.

[94] The Chargé in Turkey (Kelley) to the Secretary of State, October 5, 1942, *ibid.*, pp. 753-54.

[95] Medlicott, *The Economic Blockade*, II, 528; in the face of Turkish determination to deliver to Germany the chromite promised it in 1941, the British and the Americans reacted differently. The British were angered but hesitated until April 1944 to threaten the Turks with reprisals for fear of antagonizing them further. The Americans assumed an equally resentful attitude but attempted to thwart Turkish plans

As in the cases of the other commodities listed in the Allied preemption program, the limitation on deliveries of chromite from Turkey to Germany was the result of Germany's failure to live up to its side of the bargain rather than the result of British efforts. By March 31, 1943, Germany had only shipped a fraction of the 18 million Turkish liras worth of arms, and consequently did not receive the full 45,000 tons of chromite that the Turks had reserved for it. Only 1,000 tons of Turkish chromite were shipped to Germany between January 15 and March 31, 1943.[96] The second Clodius agreement, however, granted the Germans a period of grace ending December 31, 1943, for delivery of the war materials. After June 1943, trade picked up rapidly and the Germans saw to it that Turkey received its war equipment. The Turks followed suit and by the end of the year, exports of Turkish chromite to Germany for the year had reached the figure of 46,783 tons.[97] This rapid increase, as we shall see later, stirred the British and the Americans to issue a series of remonstrances against the Turkish Government.[98] The immediate Turkish reaction was to justify their actions on the grounds that Germany was receiving only what it was due to receive under the terms of the first Clodius agreement. In April 1944, however, the Turkish Government acceded to Allied demands and severed economic ties with Germany.

Annette Baker Fox, after discussing these negotiations, concludes, "While the military balance remained even be-

even at the risk of creating further difficulties with the Turkish Government. As Thomas K. Finletter, then Acting Chief of the Division of Defense Materials in the Department of State, wrote, "It looks hopeless but we have to try," *Foreign Relations*, 1942, IV, 775. Ahmet Şükrü Esmer informed the author that this was the issue which caused the most serious friction during the war between the Turkish and American governments. (In a personal interview, Ankara, May 11, 1966.)

[96] Medlicott, *The Economic Blockade*, II, 531.

[97] *Ibid*. In 1943, Turkish exports of chromite totaled 80,828 tons; see Nahai, *Information Circular 7855*, p. 11.

[98] These events will be discussed further below.

tween the opposing powers, Turkey demonstrated that an alliance with one side need not impede a small state from exploiting the bargaining power lying in its possession of a near monopoly over a strategic raw material."[99] This account would not be complete without mention of the fact that on May 19, 1943, the British Government agreed to purchase Turkish chromite at the dazzling rate of 270 shillings per ton for the period between January 8, 1943 and December 31, 1944. In 1940, the British had considered 140 shillings per ton to be high. By mid-May 1943, however, the British matched the price being offered the Turks by the Germans.[100]

THE RESULT OF TOUGH TURKISH BARGAINING

Menemencioğlu's efforts as a tightrope walker enabled Turkey to face the postwar period in fair economic shape. Turkey's balance of trade, for example, was in its favor at the beginning of the war and remarkably remained so throughout. In 1939, Turkey's trade balance was on the order of 2 million pounds sterling; in 1946, the trade balance in Turkey's favor surpassed the 24 million pound mark.[101] These balances were the direct result of the ever-increasing prices Turkey was able to receive for its exports. To be sure, Turkey's state debt more than doubled during the six years of war.[102] In terms of the debts incurred by other nations, however, this increase was relatively "moderate."[103] Moreover, as A. C. Edwards points out, Turkey's national debt in 1946 was serviced by 20 per cent of the government's annual expenditures, also a moderate proportion, comparatively speaking.[104] But the success or failure of Turkey's wartime

[99] Fox, *The Power of Small States*, p. 20.
[100] Medlicott, *The Economic Blockade*, II, 528-30.
[101] *Economic and Commercial Conditions*, p. 43.
[102] *Ibid.*
[103] Edwards, "Impact of the War on Turkey," p. 389.
[104] *Ibid.*; for a listing of all budgetary expenditures of the Turkish

policy cannot be measured in economic terms. To attempt such an assessment, we must turn to Turkish foreign policy in regard to political and military questions.

---

government during the war, see Türkiye Cumhuriyeti. Maliye Tetkik Kurulu (Financial Research Committee), *Yıllık Bütçe Giderleri 1924-1948 (Annual Budget Expenditures 1924-1948)* (İstanbul: Millî Eğitim Basımevi, 1948).

PART II
TURKISH NEUTRALITY FROM CASABLANCA TO THE CAIRO CONFERENCE: THE WARTIME STRATEGY

FOUR

ALLIED ASCENDANCY BEGINS: THE CONFERENCE AT CASABLANCA

THE CASABLANCA MEETING

AT THE end of 1942 and during the beginning of 1943, two events heralded eventual Allied victory: the defeat of Rommel's forces in North Africa and the breaking of the siege at Stalingrad.[1] By mid-January 1943, Anglo-American victory in North Africa seemed assured while, in the East, Russian forces had succeeded in pinning General von Paulus' army down along the Don River and were driving in for the final assault.

These developments presented the American and British military staffs with a welter of new problems involving questions of priority, timing, and long-range planning— questions ultimately political in nature. It was this that induced the President and the Prime Minister to meet in Casablanca at this time, January 12-25, 1943.[2]

The President fervently hoped that Stalin would join them at Casablanca. On three separate occasions, he had

[1] Winston S. Churchill, *The Second World War*, Vol. IV, *The Hinge of Fate* (Boston: Houghton Mifflin Co., 1950), 583-85, 600-603. Menemencioğlu perceived these two events as signifying the turn of the tide; Menemencioğlu in the *Menemencioğlu Manuscript*, p. 268, calls them "the break in the clouds." Erkin, *Turkish-Russian Relations*, p. 217, suggests that Turkish leaders realized that the change in Allied fortunes had made the conference at Casablanca necessary.

[2] For Churchill's description of the discussions leading up to the Casablanca conference, *The Hinge of Fate*, Chap. 13, "Our Need to Meet," pp. 660-73; for a general account of the events leading up to the conference, Herbert Feis, *Churchill, Roosevelt, Stalin: The War They Waged and the Peace They Sought* (Princeton, N.J.: Princeton University Press, 1957), pp. 97-102.

written to the Soviet leader urging him to come to meet them. Stalin, at the time, however, was busy directing the pincer movements that destroyed the Sixth army of the Third Reich or, at least, used this as an excuse not to come to the conference. "Things are so hot now," Stalin notified Roosevelt, "it would be impossible for me to be absent for even one day."[3] Churchill was secretly pleased by this refusal of Stalin's. He shared Roosevelt's desire to meet with the Soviet leader but wanted to do so after the Combined Chiefs of Staff had been able to agree on Anglo-American strategy.[4]

Churchill arrived at Anfa, a suburb a few miles outside of Casablanca, on January 12; Roosevelt arrived two days later. The center of the conference was the Anfa Hotel, a spacious structure that housed both the British and American staffs. A number of villas surrounding the hotel were reserved for the President, the Prime Minister, General Giraud, and, in the event he should come to Casablanca, General de Gaulle. The entire enclave was sealed off by American troops who, for security reasons, also assumed the responsibility for serving the guests, each one of whom as Robert Murphy comments was "of the highest rank or influence in his respective field."[5] Meetings were held in two rooms. The military officials—including George C. Marshall, Admiral Ernest J. King, Henry H. (Hap) Arnold, Mark W. Clark, Albert C. Wedemeyer and for the British, Admiral of the Fleet Sir Dudley Pound, Sir John Dill, General Alan Brooke, the British Chief of Staff, Air Chief Marshal Charles Portal, Sir Harold Alexander, Hastings Ismay, Lord (Louis) Mountbatten, and Lord Leathers—set up shop in the banquet hall of the Anfa Hotel, while their

[3] *Ibid.*, p. 100.

[4] Churchill, *The Hinge of Fate*, p. 662; *ibid.*, p. 99.

[5] Robert Murphy, *Diplomat Among Warriors* (New York: Doubleday and Co., 1964), p. 189. At the time, Murphy was serving as President Roosevelt's representative in North Africa.

civilian chiefs met in the living room of Roosevelt's sumptuous villa.[6]

The members of the British and American delegations, although gladdened by their common victory over Axis forces, were at odds over future strategy[7] when they met at Casablanca. Churchill, on his part, had formulated "an ambitious plan"[8] designed to maintain the momentum of victory: continue the American reinforcement of the British Isles in preparation for a cross-Channel attack against German forces in northern France; begin to mount a campaign in the Mediterranean that would eventually eliminate Italy as an active belligerent; create the necessary circumstances for bringing Turkey into the war.[9] So much did Churchill want the Americans to accept his proposals that he took special care to instruct his subordinates not to impose themselves too forcefully upon them but to take time "like the dropping of water on stone."[10]

[6] *Ibid.* For a complete listing of the principal participants at the major international conferences, United States, Department of the Army, Office of the Chief of Military History, Maurice Matloff, *Strategic Planning for Coalition Warfare 1943-1944* (Washington, D.C.: United States Government Printing Office, 1959), Appendix C, pp. 546-49; henceforth referred to as *Strategic Planning.*

[7] Trumbull Higgins, *Soft Underbelly: The Anglo-American Controversy over the Italian Campaign 1939-1940* (New York: The Macmillan Co., 1968), pp. 45-50; Feis, *Churchill, Roosevelt, Stalin,* pp. 105-108.

[8] *Strategic Planning,* p. 65.

[9] For Churchill's description of the Casablanca Conference, *The Hinge of Fate,* Chap. 15, pp. 574-695.

[10] Murphy, *Diplomat Among Warriors,* p. 191; in order to ensure their success, says Murphy, the British rigged up "a six-thousand-ton ship, converted into a reference library . . . crammed with all the essential files from the war office and had a complete staff of file clerks." With "such thoughtful preparation," Murphy concludes, American acceptance of British proposals was "inevitable." Churchill, *The Hinge of Fate,* p. 678, on the contrary, suggests that there was essential agreement among the Combined Chiefs of Staff and that disagreement was between the Chiefs and Joint Planners which cut through national divisions. These disagreements raised more serious questions, however,

As for the Americans, they were "divided and frustrated" when they arrived at Casablanca, plagued by too many alternatives, none of which appeared wholly acceptable.[11] On the one hand, they favored a continued troop build-up of American forces in the British Isles. On the other, they felt that it would be disadvantageous to keep great numbers of troops idle in the many months before the cross-Channel attack. Admiral King and General Arnold consequently were attracted to Churchill's plans regarding the Mediterranean. General Marshall, however, vehemently resisted, afraid that the Prime Minister's recommended course of action would involve them all in "interminable operations" in the Mediterranean and, as a result, indefinitely delay the opening of the Second Front.[12] Marshall reacted in a similar fashion to Churchill's stated desire to create the circumstances favorable for Turkish entry into the war.

Bringing Turkey into the war was central to Churchill's plans as evidenced by the fact that his initial reaction after the first successes of the Allied campaign in North Africa dealt with such a possibility. In a note to the British Chief of Staff, November 18, 1942, Churchill called for "a supreme and prolonged effort" to induce the Turks to enter the

---

than Churchill seems to suggest. Lord Mountbatten, a major figure on the Joint Planning Staff, disagreed with Sir Alan Brooke, Chief of Staff of British Imperial Forces, on the issue of invading Sicily. If Italy, for example, were to be attacked, then Sardinia, not Sicily, should be invaded, he argued. Alan Brooke, along with Churchill, afraid to arouse American resistance to all British plans for the Mediterranean theater, held out for Sicily as being the only "Mediterranean target available to the British within a context of American approval"; Higgins, *Soft Underbelly*, p. 50. Thus, the disagreements between the Chiefs and the Joint Planning Staff did reflect deeper divisions which broke down along national lines. Churchill and Alan Brooke, for example, after the Casablanca Conference, continued to regard the invasion of Sicily as the first stage in an attack against Italy, whereas the Americans tended to regard it as the Allied stopping place in the Mediterranean.

[11] Feis, *Churchill, Roosevelt, Stalin*, p. 98.

[12] *Ibid.*, p. 106.

war.[13] Churchill delineated the necessary steps: offer Turkey a tripartite Allied guarantee of territorial integrity; equip Turkey militarily; urge Russia to develop its strength on its southern flank so that the Turks would not have to fear an attack by the Axis. One day earlier, November 24, he advised Stalin of his position. Stalin later agreed that it would be "most desirable" to have Turkey in the war.[14] At Casablanca, therefore, Churchill spared no effort to convince the Americans that it was advisable to use Turkey as a base of operations and to build up Turkish defenses in the Mediterranean. Here, again, he met with Marshall's strong opposition.

Eventually, the Americans accepted "the principle of preparing the way for Turkey's active participation" in the war.[15] They also agreed to British proposals for an invasion of Sicily. On the other hand, the office of COSSAC, the Chief of Staff to the Supreme Allied Commander, was established and charged with the responsibility for planning the cross-Channel attack. The Casablanca Agreement, therefore, included elements that each side at the conference had wanted. The Americans and the British undoubtedly left the conference with a clearer conception of where they were going than when they had arrived. They remained as intent as ever, however, on pursuing their individual objectives—in different directions if necessary.

The Casablanca Agreement and Its Consequences

An agreement which did emerge in the course of the discussions between Churchill and Roosevelt was the so-called Casablanca Agreement. The Prime Minister convinced the President to allow the British "to play the hand with the

---

[13] Churchill, *The Hinge of Fate*, p. 697.

[14] *Ibid.*, pp. 698-99.

[15] *Strategic Planning*, p. 65; also, Feis, *Churchill, Roosevelt, Stalin*, pp. 105-107.

Turks,"[16] arguing that Turkey fell within Britain's traditional sphere of interest and that, besides, "most of the troops which would be involved in reinforcing Turkey would be British. . . ."[17]

The President's agreement to this position actually accorded with his earlier tendency to let the British take the lead for the Allies in Turkey. As early as March 1941, the British Ambassador in Washington had surprised Cordell Hull by informing him that the President favored sending all lend-lease materials consigned to Turkey through the offices of the United Kingdom.[18]

Although he had let the earlier incident pass, Hull was deeply distressed by evidence that at the Casablanca Conference Roosevelt had given away even more to the British. His new fears were aroused by Eden who, during his visit to Washington in March 1943, conveyed the impression that the President had recognized Britain's primary role in relation to Turkey and had explicitly agreed to British handling of all Allied interests in Turkey as well as that of control over the flow of goods.[19] Wallace Murray, a State Department adviser on political affairs, wrote that if this proved to be the case, "there would be . . . no need for maintaining an American Embassy at Ankara, nor any necessity for the presence in Washington of a Turkish Embassy."[20]

[16] Two phrases "play the cards" and "play the hand" were used synonymously in relation to the so-called Casablanca Agreement. Cordell Hull, *The Memoirs of Cordell Hull* (New York: The Macmillan Co., 1948), II, 1,365, somewhat bitterly notes that "play the cards was one of Churchill's favorite phrases."

[17] Combined Chiefs of Staff Minutes, January 18, 1943, *Foreign Relations, The Conferences at Washington, 1941-1942, and Casablanca, 1943*, p. 634.

[18] Hull, *Memoirs*, p. 1,365.

[19] Feis, *Churchill, Roosevelt, Stalin*, pp. 119-26, discusses Eden's visit to Washington; also, Earl of Avon (Anthony Eden), *The Reckoning: The Memoirs of Anthony Eden* (Boston: Houghton Mifflin Co., 1965), pp. 430-42.

[20] Memorandum of Conversation, by the Adviser on Political Rela-

Hull was frustrated in his efforts to see the Casablanca Agreement. "The President," writes Admiral William D. Leahy, "had directed me not to divulge any information about the conference without his specific approval in each instance."[21] As a result, there was "no copy available" for Hull who turned for information to the British Embassy.[22] Mr. Michael Wright, British First Secretary, confirmed Hull's apprehensions by informing Murray ". . . that the British Foreign Office understood that at Casablanca the President had given the Prime Minister primary responsibility for 'playing the cards' with Turkey."[23] Hull continued his remonstrances.

On July 16, the President relented and Admiral Leahy sent a copy of the agreement to the Secretary. It, in part, reads as follows:

a). Agreed that Turkey lies within a theater of British responsibility, and that all matters connected with Turkey should be handled by the British in the same way that all matters connected with China are handled by the United States.[24]

This agreement, signed January 20 at the 63rd meeting of the Combined Chiefs of Staff, includes a final report which

---

tions (Murray), Washington, D.C., July 12, 1943, *Foreign Relations*, 1943, IV, 1,068-69.

[21] William D. Leahy, *I Was There* (New York: McGraw-Hill Book Co., 1950), p. 173.

[22] Hull, *Memoirs*, p. 1,367; also Wallace Murray on July 2, 1943, reported to the Secretary of State that the British Embassy, through the agency of Mr. Michael Wright, informed the State Department that "no copy was available for us"; *Foreign Relations*, 1943, IV, 1,065-66.

[23] The Secretary of State to the British Ambassador (Halifax), Washington, D.C., July 10, 1943, *ibid.*, p. 1,067.

[24] Admiral William D. Leahy, Chief of Staff to the Commander-in-Chief of the Army and Navy, to the Secretary of State, Washington, D.C., July 16, 1943, *ibid.*, pp. 1,069-70.

also indicated that the President and Prime Minister had
". . . agreed upon the administrative measures necessary to
give effect to the decision that all matters connected with
Turkey shall be handled by the British."[25] Hull quickly at-
tempted to reassert American independence with regard to
Turkey. In messages to the British Embassy and to the Joint
Chiefs of Staff, Hull declared that the American mission in
Ankara reserved the right to act autonomously in its deal-
ings with the Turkish Government. Hull wrote Leahy on
July 22, 1943, that

> The minutes confirm the Department's understanding
> . . . that nothing agreed upon at Casablanca limits in any
> way the full independence of action of the American
> Government in its political and economic relations with
> Turkey.[26]

The implications of the Casablanca Agreement were clear
to those in charge of supplying munitions and lend-lease,
however. On January 22, 1943, only two days after the Casablanca Agreement, the Combined Secretariat of the Munitions Assignments Board issued a memorandum to the Office
of the Lend-Lease Administration stating that, as a result
of the Casablanca Agreement, the British would be responsible for "framing and presenting . . . all bids for equipment
for Turkey."[27] The "onward despatch" or delivery of equipment to Turkey was henceforth to be a "command function" of the British command in the Middle East.

Upon the receipt of this directive, representatives of the
U.S. War Department informed the Turkish Embassy on
January 29 that in the future British military authorities
were to present Turkish bids for military equipment before
the Munitions Assignments Board. This news was a "stun-

[25] *Ibid.* [26] Hull, *Memoirs*, p. 1,368.
[27] Memorandum by the Combined Secretariat of the Munitions Assignments Board, Washington, D.C., January 22, 1943, *Foreign Relations*, 1943, IV, 1,090.

ning blow"[28] and a "tremendous shock" to the Turks.[29] The Turkish military attaché voiced the suspicion that the decision to allow the British to "retain control" of the flow of lend-lease goods to Turkey, "had resulted from a commitment by Great Britain to 'another Ally' (Russia) to keep Turkey weak."[30] The Turkish air attaché stated that "the Turkish Government should immediately inform the British and American Governments that Turkey henceforth desired no assistance from either the United States or Great Britain."[31] When Dean Acheson, at this time Assistant Secretary of State, heard of the Turkish reaction, he inquired why it had been necessary to "break the news to the Turks."[32] Acheson was told by his subordinates that it had been made inevitable by the decision of the Combined Chiefs that discontinued certain previous kinds of collaboration with the Turks.

The specific dispute eventually became quiescent. A procedure was instituted soon after the inflamed meeting on January 29 which allowed Turkish officials to consult with American representatives concerning bids submitted on their behalf by the British. The British, however, continued to "play the hand" with the Turks until the end of the war. Yet far from stinting on supplies, as the Turks had feared, they proved willing to supply Turkey with more equipment than its infrastructure could handle or its policy of neutrality warranted, perhaps even more than the Turks wanted.

Nevertheless, Turkish officials continued to prefer to deal

[28] Memorandum of Telephone Conversation [with Mr. Richard May of the Lend-Lease Administration] by Mr. George V. Allen of the Division of Near Eastern Affairs, Washington, D.C., January 29, 1943, *ibid.*, pp. 1,090-92.

[29] *Ibid.*

[30] *Ibid.*, Cemal Aydınalp was the Turkish military attaché.

[31] *Ibid.*, Tekin Arıburun was the air attaché.

[32] Memorandum by the Chief of the Division of Near Eastern Affairs ([Paul H.] Alling) to the Assistant Secretary of State (Acheson), Washington, D.C., January 29, 1943, *ibid.*, pp. 1,092-93.

directly with the Americans. George V. Allen on March 16, 1943, in a general review of the Turkish scene, wrote:

> From time to time . . . Turkish officials have indicated their preference for dealing directly with us . . . they would know where they stood much better . . . would know precisely to whom they were indebted, and would have more control. . . .[33]

Allen advised his superiors at State that the Turkish Government was beginning to despair that the United States was losing interest. This created a "dampened enthusiasm" over Allied victories on their part, he observed. The reluctance of the United States to deal directly with Turkey, except through the British, left Turkish leaders uncomfortably uncertain as to what extent or in precisely what ways the United States would support, protect or, if necessary, defend them.

The implications of the Casablanca Agreement, especially the repercussions of the January 22 directive of the Munitions Assignments Board, were felt in Ankara to have a profound meaning. It was certainly not merely a question of goods assigned to Turkey being accredited to one account rather than another. At stake, in Turkish thinking, was nothing less than the role American policy-makers intended to play in southeastern Europe. Roosevelt had accepted Churchill's argument, that the British should "play the hand with the Turks," as if the question were merely a matter of mutual British and American convenience. The British would function in Turkey as the Americans were doing vis-à-vis China. To Turks, no such equation was desirable. Turkish policy-makers wanted an American presence in southeastern Europe.[34] This was due to their fear that Russia would attempt to "Bolshevize" Europe after the war. Any arrangement that seemed designed to cut Ankara off

[33] Memorandum by Mr. George V. Allen of the Division of Near Eastern Affairs, Washington, D.C., March 16, 1943, *ibid.*, pp. 1,099-100.
[34] Cevat Açıkalın in a personal interview with the author.

from Washington or that seemed to remove Washington from direct responsibility toward Turkey troubled Turkish statesmen.[35]

Their reaction to the Casablanca Agreement was also the result of long historical experience. In Menemencioğlu's mind, for example, it awakened memories of the days when the Ottoman Empire was "the sick man of Europe."[36] Any suggestion that Turkey was to be included in the sphere of influence of a single European power deeply offended him.[37] This was true of all leading Turkish officials. Their experience with the British occupation during the First World War had hardly prepared them for a filial relationship now.

On July 13, 1943, Menemencioğlu made his reaction to the Casablanca Agreement clear to von Papen. Asked by the German Ambassador whether he thought the Allies had placed Turkey within the British sphere, the Turkish Foreign Minister replied, first of all, that "this was completely so." "Turkey," he continued, "is exclusively within the British sphere of influence, while Russia is exclusively within the American sphere of interest."[38] Menemencioğlu accurately described the Casablanca Agreement which required all U.S. military equipment and other materials destined for Turkey to be registered with and transferred by the British. Menemencioğlu's resentment then became

[35] Former President İsmet İnönü and Cevat Açıkalın in personal interviews with the author.

[36] Mrs. Nermin Streater in a personal interview with the author.

[37] Turgut Menemencioğlu, personal correspondence with the author, September 30, 1969. His Excellency Turgut Menemencioğlu is at the time of writing Turkish Ambassador to the Central Treaty Organization (CENTO); during the war, as already mentioned, he served as *chef de cabinet* to the Secretary-General of the Turkish Foreign Ministry. George V. Allen in his memorandum of March 16, 1943 (*Foreign Relations*, 1943, IV, 1,099) commented, "An additional reason for the Turkish attitude was undoubtedly a feeling that they were being treated more or less as a British colony or protectorate."

[38] Ambassador in Ankara (von Papen) to Foreign Ministry in Berlin, Therapia, July 13, 1943, *Captured Files*, NA, T-120, Roll 2618, Frames E364726/3-E364726/4.

manifest. He stated that he had replied to U.S. Ambassador Steinhardt's complaint that Turkish officials had publicly thanked Britain for a grain shipment which had come primarily from America by saying, "The British kick me every day to account to them for these 62,000 tons."[39] Menemencioğlu requested that Steinhardt put his complaint in a letter. "Of course," the Turkish Foreign Minister concluded, "the letter never arrived."

The Casablanca Agreement seemed to Turkish leaders, therefore, to suggest two things: first, a gradual American withdrawal from the Turkish sphere and second, the reassertion of Britain's right to act as a colonial power. Menemencioğlu's hope that relations among states in Europe would be held in equilibrium through a balance of power after the war seemed thereby threatened. But the significance of the Casablanca Agreement in all probability would not have been as great in Turkish eyes had it not also been for the doctrine of unconditional surrender.

THE DOCTRINE OF UNCONDITIONAL SURRENDER

Roosevelt's announcement on January 24 that unconditional surrender was the only basis on which the Germans could negotiate for peace came as a shock to Turkish leaders. They perceived the doctrine to assume the eradication of Germany as a power in Europe. The Turks followed the proposition to what seemed to be its logical implications— if Germany were completely annihilated, the Russians would conclude that they were free to dominate Europe.

Feridun Cemal Erkin has suggested that at this time, "It was the established fervent conviction of the Turks that the existence of a strong Germany was an ineluctable necessity for Europe's peace and equilibrium."[40] Turkish leaders perceived the politics of unconditional surrender to entail disastrous consequences. It would reinforce the German will

[39] *Ibid.*   [40] Erkin, *Turkish-Russian Relations*, p. 222.

130

to resist and thus would become "an obstacle to a cessation of hostilities at a time when it might still be possible to halt the Russian advance in the direction of central Europe."[41] Turkish statesmen were thus also aware of how the doctrine of unconditional surrender could alter the demarcation of zones. At Adana and throughout subsequent months, Turkish policy-makers repeatedly warned Allied officials that "the line where Soviet forces . . . would meet Allied armies . . . in invaded Germany would determine the boundary between free Europe and that part of Europe that would be compelled to be Sovietized."[42] Turkish leaders hastened to advise the Allies that "it was vital to the free world that this demarcation be situated as far to the East as possible."[43] As far as Turkish statesmen could tell, however, the Western Allies were refusing to heed their advice. On one occasion Menemencioğlu complained, "I have been knocking myself out to make them [the British and Americans] understand that before they destroy Germany's military potential, which is the only thing that can resist the Russian avalanche, they are already at war with the Russians."[44]

Gradually, Turks began to reason that Britain's inability to heed good advice was the result of its unwillingness to do so. Turkish leaders, who at this time resented Britain for seeming to act paternalistically, feared the British were planning to renounce responsibility toward Turkey in favor of the Russians.[45] Turkish leaders suspected that the British had entered into a secret arrangement giving the Russians a free hand in Turkey on condition that Stalin would fight to the end. In this event, Turkey would be left alone

[41] *Ibid.*, p. 220.   [42] *Ibid.*, p. 221.   [43] *Ibid.*

[44] Ambassador in Ankara (von Papen) to Foreign Ministry in Berlin, Therapia, August 18, 1943, *Captured Files*, NA, T-120, Roll 2618, Frame E364526. Turkish newspapers reacted circumspectly to the announcement of unconditional surrender, but none except *Tan*, January 29, 1943, reacted favorably.

[45] Former President İsmet İnönü in a personal interview with the author.

to face the Soviet Union.[46] The announcement of the doctrine of unconditional surrender seemed to forecast this development.

To Turks, therefore, in Erkin's words, "The doctrine of unconditional surrender was the greatest mistake of Allied policy."[47] It "fanaticized" the war. And "in purporting to regulate the fate of Germany, it in fact regulated the fate of the whole of Europe."[48] Turkish leaders thus perceived themselves as facing a dangerous new situation after Casablanca. The Allies had decided that Germany's power was to be destroyed by "unconditional surrender." Russia was clearly in the ascendant and, with Germany vanquished, would face no countervailing Continental force to restrict its appetite for Eastern Europe. The British seemed either unwilling or unable to sense this danger, but, rather, were working in close collaboration with the Russians to speed this outcome and, if possible, to force the Turks, by entry into the war against Germany, to help dig their own grave. As for America, it seemed less interested and more remote to the Turkish leaders than ever. In the midst of these thoughts, the Turks learned that Prime Minister Churchill was planning to come to Turkey.

[46] Cevat Açıkalın in a personal interview with the author.
[47] Feridun Cemal Erkin in a personal interview with the author.
[48] Erkin, *Turkish-Russian Relations*, p. 219.

FIVE

THE CONFERENCE AT ADANA:
A MEETING OF MISUNDERSTANDINGS

THE ADANA TALKS

CHURCHILL had been emboldened by American acceptance of British plans to invade Sicily. He thus decided to pursue his plans to bring Turkey into the war, the "key" to his strategy in the Mediterranean, by visiting with Turkish statesmen.[1] Churchill's War Cabinet did not take kindly to this. They informed the Prime Minister, "Our experience in 1941 was that a promise extracted from them [the Turks] in Cyprus was promptly gone back on in Ankara. We do not want you to court either a rebuff or a failure."[2] Eden recalls that "it was the Turkish part of the business which troubled me. I did not think that we should get any results in that stubborn quarter."[3] Churchill proved unrelenting "and we yielded," Eden states, "with . . . 'the poor comfort that we have had the best of the argument and shall suffer the worst of the consequences.' "[4]

President İnönü has testified that he went to Adana to meet Prime Minister Churchill with two purposes in mind: to warn Churchill about Russian postwar intentions and to obtain an increase in British deliveries of war materials and armament.[5] Although İnönü still feared a German attack, his real concern at Adana was the threat posed by Russia

---

[1] Churchill, *The Hinge of Fate*, p. 696; Churchill writes, "President Roosevelt and I had long sought to open a new route to Russia and to strike as at Germany's southern flank. Turkey was the key to all such plans."

[2] Eden, *The Reckoning*, p. 421.   [3] *Ibid.*

[4] *Ibid.*

[5] Former President İsmet İnönü in a personal interview with the author.

and what the British intended to do about it.[6] This was true of the entire Turkish delegation. Saracoğlu's experience during his fateful visit to Moscow in 1939 prompted him to seize the opportunity to act as a "strong speaker."[7] Had not Prime Minister Churchill himself "expressed the view that Russia might become imperialistic," Saracoğlu asked. This possibility "made it necessary for Turkey to be very prudent." What would guarantee Turkey's integrity after an Allied victory? Saracoğlu declared that he was "looking for something more real" than an international security organization. "All Europe was full of Slavs and Communists. All the defeated countries would become Bolshevik and Slav if Germany was beaten."[8] Erkin, like his superior, also felt these concerns. Before going to Adana, Erkin is reported to have said, "England and America will someday be grateful to Germany for having sacrificed its best youth to defend Europe against the Bolshevik menace."[9] Erkin later emphasized the fact that the Turkish delegation feared that the Russians wanted them to enter the war unprepared so that they would be softened up for a Russian invasion. The Turks had come to suspect this on the basis of the Polish experience. The example of Poland illustrated in a most tragic way the assertion that "the Russians would do their best to exploit any Turkish weakness resulting from the miseries of war."[10]

[6] Former President İsmet İnönü in a personal interview with the author; also, Aydemir, *The Second Man*, p. 134.

[7] The quoted phrase is Aydemir's; *ibid.*

[8] Churchill, *The Hinge of Fate*, pp. 709-11; Erkin, *Turkish-Russian Relations*, p. 224, also writes that during the talks at Adana, Prime Minister Saracoğlu repeatedly warned Churchill of Soviet imperial intentions toward the Straits, the Balkans, and Eastern Europe and that this "was causing great anxiety in Ankara." Erkin cites Saracoğlu as having said, "The defeat of Germany would leave a tragic vacuum which would make all the vanquished countries easy prey to communism."

[9] Embassy in Ankara to Foreign Ministry in Berlin, Ankara, January 6, 1943, *Captured Files*, NA, T-120, Roll 2618, Frame E364556.

[10] Erkin, *Turkish-Russian Relations*, p. 226; Turkish fears that the

Such arguments were hardly what the buoyant Prime Minister had come to Adana to hear and discuss. He immediately attempted to reassure his hosts. "Things did not always turn out as bad as was expected," he said.[11] "I would not be a friend of Russia if she imitated Germany. If she did so, we would arrange the best possible combination against her, and I would not hesitate to say so to Stalin."[12] Churchill had made it clear in his opening remarks that he was acting as spokesman for the Allied coalition. His trip to Adana had the backing of both the United States and the Soviet Union. The Russian victory at Stalingrad had marked the turning point in Allied fortunes. What Stalin wanted the Turks to do could not be shrugged off by Ankara. "I know," Churchill concluded, "that Premier Stalin is most anxious to see Turkey well armed and ready to defend itself against aggression."[13] Aydemir has correctly suggested that Churchill should have known that "Turkish statesmen would not take these reassurances seriously."[14]

Churchill had traveled to Adana to hasten the defeat of Germany, and he did not hesitate to press the role Turkey was to play against the Axis. A situation might arise, Churchill reasoned, where Turkey would have to defend itself from a German thrust to the East. This would become probable if its need for oil and other minerals became acute:

Russians might attempt to exploit Turkish weakness increased after the battle of Stalingrad; A. Halûk Ülman, *Türk-Amerikan Diplomatik Münasebetleri 1939-1947: İkinci Cihan Savaşının Başından Truman Doktirinine Kadar* (*Turkish-American Diplomatic Relations 1939-1947: From the Beginning of the Second World War to the Truman Doctrine*) (Ankara: Ankara Üniversitesi Siyasal Bilgiler Fakültesi Yayınları, No. 128-110, 1961), p. 40.

[11] Churchill, *The Hinge of Fate*, p. 710.   [12] *Ibid.*, pp. 710-11.

[13] En route to Adana, Churchill had composed an opening statement which he delivered at the beginning of his talks with Turkish leaders. "It was meant to be," he writes, "a wooing letter containing an offer of platonic marriage both from me and the President"; *ibid.*, pp. 706-709.

[14] Aydemir, *The Second Man*, p. 261.

"They may in the summer try to force their way through the center." Soon Turkey might want to assume the offensive especially if "by pulling one brick out of the wall," the Turks could be the ones to cause the whole structure to collapse. What Turkey needed, the Prime Minister declared, were tanks, arms, and weapons, and especially instruction on how to use them. "I have been particularly distressed at the spectacle of the Turkish army" which has not been able to get into the war on account of its lack of the modern equipment so "decisive" on the battlefield. This has made me fully comprehend the attitude of Turkey, Churchill added. "We [British] have ourselves no false pride on these points. . . ." The Americans, he continued, were showing the British how to operate much modern equipment. Britain could do the same for Turkey now. This would be particularly true of airfield construction. As soon as the "nests are ready" and Turkey prepared for war, Churchill promised, at least 21 British air squadrons would be moved in.[15]

The Turks remained skeptical. İstanbul was a city built of wood, subject to the terrible fate of Belgrade should the Germans wish to exact vengeance, they argued.[16] Germany, though no longer capable of waging a blitzkreig against the Allies, was certainly still strong enough to reduce to rubble twenty years of the republic's efforts. The Nazis could overrun the Straits, dealing a great blow to Allied interests in the Aegean. Turkey's single coal field at Zonguldak was only thirty minutes' flying time from German airbases in Bulgaria and thus easily destroyed.[17] Turkish industrial installations could be counted "on a single hand":[18] three fuel refineries never working to full capacity, an electrical plant

[15] Churchill, *The Hinge of Fate*, pp. 706-709.

[16] Aydemir, *The Second Man*, p. 134.

[17] Turkish policy-makers were concerned that the Germans might bomb the Zonguldak coal installations; Ataöv, *Turkish Foreign Policy*, p. 107; Sir Hughe Knatchbull-Hugessen, *Diplomat in Peace and War* (London: Murray, 1949), pp. 182-92.

[18] Aydemir, *The Second Man*, p. 134.

at Çatalgazi. "With a single stroke"[19] Turkish industrial capacity could be wiped out. Thus time and again Turkish leaders attempted to impress upon Churchill their immediate need for arms.

The conversations of the first day ended when the British Prime Minister retired at 1 A.M. He awakened early and composed a list of propositions which he hoped would be acceptable to the Turks. These he called his *Pensées Matinales* or "Morning Thoughts: Note on Post-War Security."[20] A résumé of these thoughts, given to Ambassador Steinhardt by the British Ambassador in Ankara the day after Churchill presented them to the Turks, includes the following:

1. Britain will ask nothing of Turkey that is not in her interest and will never ask Turkey to enter the war if such action might lead to disaster. Accordingly he sought no present commitments of Turkey.

2. The German need for oil and desire to expand eastwards might cause the Axis in desperation to attack Turkey. By reason of this threat Turkey must be strong and her armament increased during the next few months.

3. Even should Germany not attack Turkey, Turkish interests may dictate that she intervene in the Balkans to prevent anarchy. Such a condition could arise as a result of increasing German weakness, trouble in Bulgaria, a quarrel between Rumania and Hungary over Transylvania, or more extensive Greek or Yugoslav resistance. Thus the possibility of Turkey becoming a belligerent must be considered.

4. Without becoming a belligerent Turkey might at some time consider taking the same position as the United States before it entered the war, by a "departure from strict neutrality." Thus Turkey might grant permission to use Turkish airfields from which to bomb the Rumanian oil fields, the Dodecanese Islands and Crete.

[19] *Ibid.*   [20] Churchill, *The Hinge of Fate*, pp. 711-12.

Germany and Bulgaria would submit to such action "not wishing to excite Turkey to more active belligerency."

5. Russia has renounced all territorial gains beyond her June 1941 frontiers. Should Turkey become a full belligerent she will receive the fullest aid and will have the right to all guarantees for her territory and rights after the war. Great Britain would give these guarantees independently of any other power. Churchill expressed the belief that Russia would give the same guarantees and that "President Roosevelt would gladly associate himself with such treaties and that the whole weight of the United States would be used in the peace settlement to that end. At the same time one must not ignore the difficulties which the United States constitution interposes against prolonged European commitments."

6. It is important that Turkey be "among the winners" to assure her security after the war. Even after Germany is crushed Turkish cooperation will still be necessary.

7. At the end of the war the United States will be the strongest nation and will desire solid international structure which will spare the United States from having to enter future European wars. This structure will call for disarmament of the aggressors and an association of nations stronger than before.[21]

These points and a military understanding were accepted in the late morning of January 31.

Two military decisions were taken at Adana. The Allies would build up Turkish stocks of armaments quickly to a point at which their defense forces would have a full year's reserve; second, in the event Turkey did enter the war, the British promised to provide air protection over specified areas including İstanbul and İzmir. The British also promised to provide certain units of field support. A "self-con-

[21] The Ambassador in Turkey (Steinhardt) to the Secretary of State, Ankara, February 2, 1943, *Foreign Relations*, 1943, IV, 1,060-65 at p. 1,061.

tained" air squadron under British command along with British anti-tank and anti-aircraft units to be placed under Turkish command would begin operations once the Turks began to fight. Lists of equipment to be transferred to Turkey were drawn up. These came to be known as the Adana lists.[22]

THE AMBIGUOUS AFTERMATH OF ADANA

On February 2, Churchill wired Stalin that "there is no doubt" the Turks "have come a long way towards us," although, he added, he had "not asked for any precise political engagement or promise about entering the war on our side." He stated that Turkey would participate in the Allied cause possibly before the end of the year by a "strained interpretation of the neutrality" similar to that once invoked by the Americans. "They may allow us to use their airfields for refueling for British and American bombing attacks," he wrote, and "I am telegraphing you to range them more plainly than before in the anti-Hitler system."[23] President İnönü, however, seems to some degree to have succeeded in his attempts to impress upon Churchill the extent to which he was concerned about Stalin's postwar intentions. Churchill informed the Russian Premier that the Turks were apprehensive over their political position in view of the great strength of the Soviet Republic. "They would, I am sure," he added, "be very responsive to any gesture of friendship on the part of the U.S.S.R."[24] Stalin, however, seems not to have been impressed either with Churchill's close personal relationship with İnönü, which the Prime Minister claimed to have established, nor by the need to reassure the Turks:

The international position of Turkey remains very delicate. . . . It is not clear to me how in the present circum-

22 *Ibid.* 23 Churchill, *The Hinge of Fate*, pp. 713-14.
24 *Ibid.*, p. 714.

stances Turkey thinks to combine her obligations *vis-à-vis* the U.S.S.R. and Great Britain with her obligations *vis-a-vis* Germany. Still, if Turkey wishes to make her relations with the U.S.S.R. more friendly and intimate let her say so. In this case the Soviet Union would be willing to meet Turkey half-way.[25]

Stalin did not hesitate to contradict the Prime Minister's assessment of what the Turks would do to assist the Allied cause. It is evident, however, from what Churchill had wired Stalin that he regarded his mission to Adana as having been at least moderately successful. And success, in this instance, as defined by Churchill, could not have been less than to draw Turkey into the war—at first as a benevolent, rapidly mobilizing neutral, then as a limited participant, permitting its airbases to be used, and then, finally, as the partner of the Western Allies in the Balkans. Stalin's evaluation was more accurate. The Turks left Adana feeling that they had not been committed—not morally, and certainly not politically—to any of these actions.[26]

Turkish policy-makers returned to Ankara believing that Churchill had put before them a number of options which they could select as time went by in the light of their assessment of the prevailing military and political situation. Indeed, Churchill's not requiring them to commit themselves on the spot to a specific course of action created a general sense of relief among Turkish policy-makers and the Turkish public.[27] And Churchill, upon his return to London, attempted to squelch all rumors which alleged that the Turks had entered into a specific arrangement with the British. When the *Times* hinted that a secret Anglo-Turkish agreement had been signed at Adana to liberate the Aegean and Greece,[28] Churchill, speaking to Parliament on February 11,

[25] *Ibid.*, p. 715.
[26] Former President İsmet İnönü in a personal interview with the author.
[27] Ülman, *Turkish-American Diplomatic Relations*, p. 40.
[28] *Times*, London, February 2, 1943.

cautioned against such speculation lest it "get Turkey in trouble."[29] He noted that "Turkey is our ally" but that the Allies must wait "to see how the story unfolds chapter by chapter, and it would be very foolish to try to skip on too fast."[30] Turkish commentary followed a similar line. Turkish newspapers were careful to point out, in the words of the Director of the Press Bureau, that "no demands had been made upon Turkey and Turkey had undertaken no engagements."[31] Asım Us, among others, attempted to discount speculation that the British Prime Minister had come to Adana in order to put before Turkish leaders the campaign Turkey would have to fight in 1943.[32] Us argued that if such had been the case, the meeting at Adana would have taken place prior to the Casablanca Conference since it was at Casablanca that the Allies established their 1943 offensive plans "up to the last detail." Turkish policy-makers, therefore, left Adana believing that they had gained time and possibly matériel without committing themselves. As Nadi suggests, the Adana Conference and subsequent events represented a sort of "interesting chess game" in which İnönü and the rest would concede a little after the Western Allies had conceded a lot.[33] In retrospect, therefore, it appears that the Adana meeting was not a success, neither from the Turkish nor the British point of view. Churchill did not succeed in committing the Turks to a policy of more direct

[29] Great Britain. Parliament. House of Commons. *The Parliamentary Debates (official reports)*, Fifth Series (London: His Majesty's Stationery Office, 1943), Vol. 386, Cols. 1,478-79.

[30] *Ibid.*

[31] Selim Sarper as quoted in *Tasvir-i Efkâr*, February 3, 1943.

[32] Asım Us, "Adana Mülâkatının Akisleri Üzerinde Bir Düşünce" ("A thought on the repercussions of the Adana Conference"), *Vakit*, February 5, 1953 as quoted in Türkiye Cumhuriyeti Başvekâklet. *Ayın Tarihi (News of the Month)*, February 1943, No. 111 (Ankara: Matbuat Umum Müdürlüğü), pp. 130-31; henceforth all volumes referred to as *Ayın Tarihi*; also see Hüseyin Cahit Yalçın's analysis, "Çörçil'in Türkiye'yi Ziyareti" ("Churchill's visit to Turkey"), *Yeni Sabah*, February 3, 1943.

[33] Nadi, *Opening in the Curtain*, p. 174.

involvement. The Turks did not convince the British that the Russians really were bent on aggressive expansion. Both sides probably thought, however, that they had done a little better at convincing the other than later proved to be the case; and this led to much subsequent British-Turkish misunderstanding and animosity.[34]

The feeling in Ankara after Adana, therefore, remained constant in two crucial respects. Turkish policy-makers continued to regard Soviet ambitions as the principal danger facing them and continued to believe that Britain would conceivably do nothing to restrain those ambitions.[35] Churchill's inadroit assertions that the Soviets harbored only good intentions heightened the fear that Britain might seek to strengthen its position in Europe by a "separate agreement with Russia"[36] and that such an agreement could come "at the expense of Turkey."[37]

---

[34] Erkin, *Turkish-Russian Relations*, p. 227, confirms that Adana left a legacy of misunderstanding: the Turks felt they had impressed upon Churchill the reasons why they needed to act prudently, that is, to remain out of the war, whereas the British Prime Minister left feeling that he had convinced the Turks of the necessity of their fighting. During his conversations with Turkish officials at Adana, Churchill seems not to have fully appreciated their reluctance to get involved directly in the war. Menemencioğlu in the *Menemencioğlu Manuscript*, pp. 272-73, recounts that at one point Churchill in passing referred to certain liberties which he seemed to assume the Turks would permit the British in regard to the Straits. Menemencioğlu writes that he interrupted the British Prime Minister to observe that such privileges if granted would constitute an infraction against the Montreux Convention. "My interruption," Menemencioğlu writes, "seemed undoubtedly to displease Mr. Churchill and he gave me a certain kind of look. . . ." Menemencioğlu interpreted this look to mean "Why do you lack a sense of political reality now?" Menemencioğlu makes it quite clear that the political reality he had in mind was to keep Turkey out of war. In the *Menemencioğlu Manuscript*, p. 270, he also indicates that Churchill at Adana committed the British to creating in Turkey "an independent army." For the British Prime Minister, "No equipment envisaged was sufficient enough or modern enough," he writes.

[35] Ahmet Şükrü Esmer in *Turkish Foreign Policy*, p. 156.

[36] *Ibid.*   [37] *Ibid.*, p. 145.

The conference at Adana did have one result in that Churchill seems to have persuaded the Turks to seek a new diplomatic understanding with the Soviets.[38] On February 13, Foreign Minister Menemencioğlu instructed the Soviet Ambassador in Ankara, Vinogradov, to inform his government that the Turkish Government was willing to start negotiations for the improvement of Soviet-Turkish relations. Following the initial Churchill-Stalin exchange regarding the Adana conference, moreover, the Turkish Government instructed Cevat Açıkalın, as yet Turkish Ambassador in Moscow, to suggest to Molotov that their two countries collaborate in devising a new formula for improving Turkish-Soviet relations. Açıkalın specifically proposed that a Russo-Turkish communiqué similar to the Anglo-Turkish one following Adana be issued.[39] Stalin apprised Churchill of the new Turkish diplomatic effort on March 2.[40] What the Turks had feared at Adana, however, gradually materialized during the months following it: as the Soviet Union's fortunes of war changed, as it came to feel more powerful, it became increasingly anti-Turkish and openly threatening.[41] Molotov rejected Turkish overtures on the grounds that they were inadequate to the task of ameliorating Turkish-Soviet relations which would improve

[38] Aydemir, *The Second Man*, p. 263; this was confirmed in a personal interview with former President İsmet İnönü.

[39] Erkin, *Turkish-Russian Relations*, pp. 240-41.

[40] Churchill, *The Hinge of Fate*, p. 716. Menemencioğlu suggests that the Russians were not at all pleased by Churchill's commitment to reinforce Turkey militarily. In the *Menemencioğlu Manuscript*, p. 273, he states: "This honeymoon did not suit the Soviets and shortly thereafter remonstrances began to be addressed by Moscow to London. According to the Russians, the reinforcement of the Turkish army had nothing to do with the war against Germany."

[41] Ülman, *Turkish-American Diplomatic Relations*, p. 23; A. Ş. Esmer, "Türk-Soviyet Münasebetleri" ("Turkish-Soviet Relations"), *Ulus*, October 21, 1957, suggests that during the war, when the Russians felt weak and threatened, they were careful to act friendly toward the Turks, but whenever they felt strong, they acted antagonistically.

only when Turkey entered the war.[42] Thus the Turkish diplomatic attempt to achieve a modus vivendi with the Russians, prompted by Churchill, met with a rebuff.[43] After the battle of Stalingrad and especially after Adana, the Soviet Union began to criticize Turkey's nonbelligerence vehemently.[44]

Russian criticism of Turkish neutrality after Adana and the Soviet rejection of Turkish attempts to improve diplomatic relations may also have been prompted by German reports that the conference had been held to strengthen Turkey specifically against Russia. Intelligence reports reaching the German Embassy suggested "the Adana Conference was aimed against the Soviet Union" and that, furthermore, "Turkey would actively enter the war on the side of the Allies if or when the German troops are forced back behind the Dnieper River."[45] Erkin suggests that the Russians were aware of such reports and became increasingly suspicious.[46]

Erkin also claims that the Soviets believed that the Turks were pushing for a Balkan federation to work against Soviet penetration of the Balkans. German intelligence conveyed similar reports to Berlin after the Adana conference. Such was not the case. In the words of Turgut Menemencioğlu,

[42] Erkin, *Turkish-Russian Relations*, pp. 240-41.

[43] Aydemir, *The Second Man*, p. 263.

[44] Kemal Baltalı, *Boğazlar Meselesi: 1936-1956 Yıllar Arasında (The Issue of the Straits: Between the Years 1936-1956)* (Ankara: Yeni Desen Matbaası, 1959), p. 109; Baltalı, p. 110, accepts the thesis put forward by Professors Ülman and Esmer that the diplomatic posture of the Soviet Union toward Turkey vacillated according to its fortunes in war.

[45] Central Information, Memorandum, Foreign Ministry in Berlin, Berlin, March 1, 1943, *Captured Files*, NA, T-454, Roll 88, EAP 99/402.

[46] Erkin, *Turkish-Russian Relations*, p. 243; Menemencioğlu, *Menemencioğlu Manuscript*, p. 273, notes that von Papen was not slow to attempt to heighten these suspicions of the Russians by spreading rumors about the decisions taken at the Adana Conference. Von Papen in *Memoirs*, p. 498, gives as the reason for German calm during Churchill's visit, "I had a perfect understanding with the Turkish statesmen."

"Balkan cooperation to stop the war at the Balkan frontier was a thought much cherished by Saracoğlu and the Turkish government immediately before the war," but "ideas of a Balkan Federation in 1942 were only utopian."[47] He correctly argues that the Turks would have wanted such a federation by way of preserving the integrity of the Balkan countries and Turkish boundaries by keeping non-Balkan powers out. Turkey would have joined such a federation since "the idea [of one] had been kept alive for ten years." There is a distinction, however, between wanting something in the abstract and concretely seeking to bring it about. After Adana, the prevailing conditions were such that Turkish leaders did not feel that they could aim to create a Balkan federation against Russia—whether or not such Turkish designs were being perceived or assumed in the Kremlin.

Thus the Adana Conference, which Churchill portrayed to Stalin as having brought the Turks closer to the Allies, did little to remove the distrust which had plagued Turko-Soviet and Anglo-Turkish relations. In the face of increasing Soviet resentment, Turkish officials were made to remember the promise of Stalin that if Turkey were ever invaded, "Russia would help."[48] The Russian Premier had uttered this in a friendly tone at a time when the Soviet Union was losing the war against Germany. But now that the Soviet Union was becoming increasingly victorious and Stalin's tone increasingly venomous, his promise to help could mean invasion. Turkish leaders decided that no pretext must be given to the Soviets to invade, and they became more determined than ever to prevent the fighting from being waged on Turkish territory. This made them ever more reluctant to cooperate with the British.

[47] Turgut Menemencioğlu in personal correspondence with the author, September 30, 1969.

[48] Baltalı, *The Issue of the Straits*, p. 109.

SIX

OPERATION FOOTDRAG

THE BRITISH PLAY THEIR HAND WITH RUSSIA AND TURKEY

IN 1943, Great Britain found itself in the unenviable position of having among its allies two nations that perceived their interests to be in opposition: Turkey and Russia. It was a situation to tax even British diplomacy, for all its experience at juggling incompatible demands and interests.

The British Government, through Churchill, Eden, members of both Houses of Parliament, and established non-official voices such as the *Times* of London, repeatedly attempted to reassure the Soviets that His Majesty's Government was ready to defer to Russia's prerogatives in Eastern Europe and to its right to establish and maintain a secure frontier after the war. Such statements, calculated to reassure Stalin, heightened suspicions in Turkey, especially when combined with calls for German dismantlement.

At the same time, however, Churchill was increasing his pressure on the Turks to enter the war. To this end, he had to convince Ankara that its best chance of securing the peace it favored would come in fighting alongside the Allies. The Turks, however, hearing British statements to the Russians, became increasingly resistant to Churchill's advice. As Professor Fahir Armaoğlu has stated, "The more the British spoke of friendship with Russia, the less the Turks became the friends of the British."[1]

Turkish concern about British postwar plans can be traced back at least to December 2, 1942, when Foreign Secretary Eden, speaking to the House of Commons, asserted

[1] Professor Fahir Armaoğlu in a personal interview with the author, Ankara, April 20, 1966.

that the maintenance of peace after the war would depend on the vigilant cooperation of the four Great Powers, Great Britain, the United States, the Soviet Union, and China.[2] Eden was emphatic. The vehicle through which these co-ordinated efforts would take place was to be the United Nations, "based in the first instance on the understanding between ourselves, the United States and Russia." Eden left little doubt as to what he perceived to be the only future source of aggression. "The first need of Europe," he declared, "will be to build up an enduring system of defense against the possibility of renewed German aggression."[3] As for relations with the Soviet Union, "there was no reason why there should be any conflict of interest between the Soviet Government and ourselves." Eden rejected the notion that ideological differences should or need make cooperation impossible.[4]

The plaudits in the House of Commons were not echoed in Turkey. The press lost little time in opening fire on this blueprint for Big Three action. Necmettin Sadak, in *Akşam*, for example, wondered emphatically what would happen if one of the guardian-states began to pursue an aggressive policy. He stated that it was perfectly conceivable that an imperialist government might come to power. Europe would then be at a loss. The European political system outlined by Eden assumed Big Three collaboration, but would this collaboration continue after the enemy had been defeated, Sadak asked.[5] The Turks had been able to sound

[2] Great Britain. Parliament. House of Commons. *The Parliamentary Debates (official reports)*, 1942, Cols. 1,253-56. It should be mentioned that his statement included qualifications presumably designed to re-assure such elites as Turkish foreign-policy makers, e.g., "I have spoken of four Great Powers, ourselves, Russia, the United States of America and China, but I must make it plain that I do not visualize a world in which those four Powers try to clamp down some form of big-Power dictatorship over everybody else." The Turks, however, heard him to be calling for just this.

[3] *Ibid.*   [4] *Ibid.*, Col. 1,527.

[5] Necmettin Sadak, *Akşam*, December 6, 1942.

out the British on this issue. As we have seen, Churchill at Adana took a positive view of future relations with the Soviet Union.

The Turks did not wait long after Churchill departed to be confirmed in their apprehensions about British policy toward Russia. An editorial in the *Times* and a speech by Churchill created consternation in Ankara. On March 10, 1943, the *Times* of London published an editorial which argued: 1) the postwar peace will depend on the primacy of the Big Four Powers and on their willingness to use force to prevent future aggression; 2) only two of these four were in Europe, the Soviet Union and Great Britain; 3) consequently, Russia must be responsible for keeping the peace in Eastern Europe while Great Britain must be given similar charge in Western Europe.[6] After the war, the editorial reasoned, the Soviet Union would be in a position to get what it wanted anyway. What mattered was whether Great Britain would be with her or against her:

> Britain has the same interest as Russia herself in active and effective Russian participation in continental affairs; for there can be no security in Western Europe unless there is also security in Eastern Europe, and security in Eastern Europe is unattainable unless it is buttressed by the military power of Russia. . . .[7]

The editorial concluded unequivocally: "Russia will, at the moment of victory so largely due to her outstanding effort, enjoy the same right as her allies to judge for herself of the conditions which she deems necessary for the security of her frontiers."[8] Again, the reaction in Turkey was one of dismay. The Turkish press was clamorous in its denunciations. Yalman, in *Vatan*, noted wryly that Britain had become Russia's mouthpiece and was demanding a feudal

[6] *Times*, March 10, 1943. The length of leading editorials in the *Times* indicates the significance attributed to it by the editors; this editorial occupied fully one and a half columns.

[7] *Ibid.*   [8] *Ibid.*

empire in its name.[9] Cevat Açıkalın informed the author that he, İnönü, and Menemencioğlu knew of this editorial and were deeply distressed by its contents.[10]

Had the Turks at this time possessed exact information about the substance of the discussions taking place in Washington between Foreign Secretary Eden and President Roosevelt (March 12-March 30), they would have felt even more confirmed in their bleak view of the future. During their talks concerning the shape of postwar Europe, Roosevelt declared that only the Big Three, Great Britain, the Soviet Union, and the United States, should be allowed to possess armaments, with the smaller nations, including the neutrals, allowed to possess "nothing more dangerous than rifles."[11] Eden, for his part, assured the President that the Russians "would demand very little territory of Poland, just possibly up to the 'Curzon Line' " and stated his belief that Stalin wanted a strong Poland "providing the right kind of people were running it."[12] Eden also informed Roosevelt that the Soviet Union would probably insist upon absorbing the Baltic States, a thought which troubled the President more than Eden who accepted it more or less as a tol-

[9] Ahmet Emin Yalman, *Yeni Sabah*, March 15-20, 1943; also, *Cumhuriyet*, December 1943. On March 21, 1943, *The New York Times* strongly dissented from the *Times'* editorial of March 10. "American opinion will not look favorably on any proposal to put the small nations of Europe on the execution block in order to purchase Russian confidence and cooperation," it declared. *The New York Times* later reported that it had been gratified to learn that the *Times* had spoken only on its own behalf. The extent to which this was true remains uncertain.

[10] The Turkish statesmen were careful not to reveal their concern publicly. On March 17, 1943, Prime Minister Şükrü Saracoğlu delivered an address to the Grand National Assembly in which he referred to the "friendly hands that all the English statesmen with Mr. Churchill at the head, have extended . . ."; *T.B.M.M. Zabıt Ceridesi*, Seventh Assembly, Third Session, I, March 17, 1943, 25-26.

[11] Eden, *The Reckoning*, p. 431.

[12] Robert E. Sherwood, *Roosevelt and Hopkins: An Intimate History* (New York: Harper & Bros., 1948), p. 709.

erable *fait accompli*.[13] In general, Eden's views of Soviet postwar intentions appear to have been based on a presumption of Stalin's determination to be reasonable and moderate in his claims to postwar "security" for Russia. This was just as the Turks feared. As for the security of the small powers, Roosevelt gave Eden the impression, somewhat alarming even to the Briton, that in Eden's words, Roosevelt "seemed to see himself disposing of the fate of many lands, allied no less than enemy."[14] At the end of their discussions, Roosevelt noted that many territorial questions remained, but that he "did not intend to go to the Peace Conference and bargain with Poland or the other small states. . . ."[15] This, too, reflected the Turks' worst suspicions of Allied attitudes and intentions.[16]

One event which did lend credence to Turkish apprehensions took place a few weeks after Eden returned from Washington—the Soviet rejection of the Polish Government-in-exile. On April 26, 1943, the Soviets broke off diplomatic relations with the Sikorski regime in London and organized their own pro-Russian, communist-dominated government, the Union of Polish Patriots.[17] The Turks, who immediately perceived this as the first step in Russia's attempt to annex eastern Poland, were deeply distressed.[18]

[13] *Ibid.*

[14] Eden, *The Reckoning*, p. 433. For Eden's House of Commons' statement regarding these discussions, Great Britain. Parliament. House of Commons. *The Parliamentary Debates (official reports)*, Fifth Series, Vol. 388, April 8, 1943, Col. 816-23.

[15] Sherwood, *Roosevelt and Hopkins*, p. 710.

[16] Cevat Açıkalın informed the author that İnönü, Menemencioğlu, and Saracoğlu all feared that the Allies would settle major territorial questions among themselves after the war and not permit the smaller powers to influence their decisions.

[17] Feis, *Churchill, Roosevelt, Stalin*, pp. 192-94.

[18] Professors Esmer and Armaoğlu emphasized the effect Russia's treatment of the Sikorski Government had in Ankara. (In personal interviews with the author.)

Yet the British, as far as the Turks could tell, remained oblivious to the dangers.[19] Thus they watched Churchill's activities in North America during the summer of 1943 with deep forebodings.

At the Churchill-Roosevelt meeting in Washington in May 1943, and at the Quebec Conference three months later, the British Prime Minister indeed pushed for Turkish belligerence.[20] He did this, first, by focusing on Italy. On May 12, 1943, Churchill listed the advantages of a campaign to defeat Italy: it would require the Axis to overextend their logistics, thereby "taking the weight off" Russia; it would force Italian divisions to leave the Balkans, thus reducing Axis strength in the area, and encourage Turkey, "who had always measured herself with Italy in the Mediterranean," to enter the war. Churchill declared, "The moment would come when a . . . request might be made to Turkey for permission to use bases in her territory . . . ," which Churchill argued, "could hardly fail to be successful if Italy were out of the war."[21] Controversy exists and per-

[19] Cevat Açıkalın and Feridun Cemal Erkin claim that the Turkish Foreign Ministry was aware of the tensions between the Polish Government-in-exile and the British Government at this time. (In personal interviews with the author.) Eden, during his visit to Washington, made these tensions known to President Roosevelt; Sherwood, *Roosevelt and Hopkins*, p. 710.

[20] Since this was the third Anglo-American summit meeting, the code name of the conference was TRIDENT. For descriptive analyses, Feis, *Churchill, Roosevelt, Stalin*, pp. 126-31; Churchill, *The Hinge of Fate*, Chap. 20, "My Third Visit to Washington," pp. 782-99; Sherwood, *Roosevelt and Hopkins*, pp. 727-34.

[21] Churchill, *The Hinge of Fate*, p. 791. Five days after Churchill had made these remarks, the *Times* published a policy paper which, like Eden's speech of December 2, 1942 and Churchill's statement, March 21, 1943, tended to make Turks even more reluctant to become involved in the hostilities. On May 17, 1943, the *Times* reported that the so-called Postwar Policy Group comprised of 36 members of both Houses of Parliament but mainly Conservatives had presented a paper to the House of Commons. The paper urged that upon the uncondi-

haps always will as to what Churchill had in mind at this time. The one conclusion which emerges clearly is that Churchill wanted to occupy Italy with a view to bringing pressure upon Turkey.

The Americans were prepared, although as ever with reluctance, to agree with Churchill on an invasion of Italy, but for reasons not wholly congruent with those of the Prime Minister. American strategists considered Italy in terms of the western rather than the southeastern front: as a potential airbase against enemy-occupied Europe which could be useful in connection with the opening of the Second Front. In July 1943, American planners hoped "that the measures finally adopted to eliminate Italy would yield a base area for broadcasting air operations against German-controlled Europe."[22] Thus the Americans, even after the decision to attack the Italian mainland had been agreed upon, continued to confound the British Prime Minister. Rather than assist in the reinforcement of the Turkish defenses, as Churchill had hoped, the Americans now decided to withhold support. They opposed sending U.S. heavy bombers to Turkey on the ground that these could be put to better use in missions based in Italy.[23] Insofar as Churchill hoped that the decision to invade would be a stepping stone to further commitments by the Americans in the Eastern Mediterranean, his plans were not to be realized. With the Eastern Mediterranean consigned to low priority by the Americans, the British were still left to play their hand with

---

tional surrender of Germany: (1) Germany be disarmed and demobilized, its war and airplane industries completely dismantled; (2) East Prussia and the Rhineland be taken away from it on a permanent basis; (3) the Allies occupy Germany and remain until the time when "such occupation may with safety be terminated." The paper declared that Germany was not to maintain a defense establishment after the war. The outcry in Turkey was unanimous and included the pro-Soviet *Tan*, May 19, 1943; also, *Vatan*, May 20, 1943, which describes the proposals as being "another Versailles."

[22] *Strategic Planning*, p. 155.   [23] *Ibid.*

the Turks, but were forced to do so without tangible American strategic support.

While Churchill was thus urging the Americans to join the British in utilizing the time available before the cross-Channel attack to expand their efforts in the Eastern Mediterranean, he was concurrently engaged in persuading and preparing the Turks for an active part in such a campaign. He did not succeed any more with them than with the Americans. Whereas the Americans could and did explicitly say no, the much weaker Turkish position made it prudent for them to be less direct, if no less obdurate. As we have seen, at Adana, Churchill promised to provide substantially increased supplies to Turkey. In doing so, he believed—wrongly—that this equipment would ensure Turkish entry into the war. The Turks and the British thus put a different price tag on these supplies. This disagreement, however, was never to come into the open because of the maneuvering of the Turks, who managed to change the issue from *what purpose this equipment* to *what amount of equipment*—a much lower-keyed though, to the British, no less frustrating issue.

THE TURKS DRAG THEIR FEET

At Adana it had been decided that Anglo-Turkish military talks would take place in Ankara soon. On February 26, 1943, under the joint chairmanship of A. C. Arnold, British Military Attaché and Asım Gündüz, Turkish Deputy Chief of Staff, representatives of the two military staffs met. The British determined that they could import no more than 500 to 1,000 tons of equipment into Turkey a day for military purposes. Thus, the plan to support Turkey had to be phased. This is the reason why HARDIHOOD, the operational plan for supplying Turkey in preparation for its entry into the war, was structured into four stages, each to follow immediately upon the termination of the one preceding:

153

First Phase: The provision of twenty-five Royal Air Force squadrons, mainly fighters, with anti-aircraft artillery to protect the airfields.

Second Phase: The provision of a further twenty-five Royal Air Force squadrons, with the necessary anti-aircraft artillery for the defense of Turkish airfields.

Third Phase: The provision of two heavy anti-aircraft regiments, two light anti-aircraft regiments, and a further two anti-tank regiments.

Fourth Phase: The provision of two armoured divisions.[24]

The first phase was never completed.

To supply this scarce equipment was one problem. To press it into service once it reached Turkey, however, proved even more difficult. "Progress was handicapped," writes General Henry Maitland Wilson, Commander-in-Chief of Allied Forces, Middle East Command, "by Turkish inability or unwillingness to appreciate the limitations of the railway system or to give any reliable estimate of their own civil and military demands in war."[25] Wilson thus complains of "tortuous and interminable negotiations with the Turks."[26] What seemed mere obfuscation to Wilson was, however, high policy to the Turks.

An advance planning staff of the Allied Middle East Command set off for Ankara in mid-March 1943, for example, to discuss how to operationalize plans to build up Tur-

[24] Great Britain. *History of the Second World War*. United Kingdom Military Series, J.R.M. Butler (ed.), Vol. v, John Ehrman, *Grand Strategy* (London: Her Majesty's Stationery Office, 1956), 90.

[25] Henry H. Maitland Wilson (Field Marshal Lord Wilson of Libya), *Operations in the Middle East from 16 February 1943 to 8th January 1944* (Supplement to *London Gazette*, November 12 1946, No. 37,786, p. 5,595, para. 286); henceforth referred to as *Operations in the Middle East*. This account written by General Wilson actually points at two specific impediments to British attempts to bolster Turkey's military preparedness: Turkish reluctance or inability to cooperate, and the inadequacy of Turkish railways.

[26] *Ibid.*

key's military capacity.[27] To underline the importance of constructing airfields and related installations before the outbreak of hostilities, Air Marshal Sholto Douglas also visited Ankara in March. The Turks accepted the proposals outlined by the planning staff and Douglas.[28] In a few days, however, the Turks reneged on their agreement and made new, more difficult demands. Wilson decided to journey to Ankara himself.

In the middle of April 1943, meetings took place between Wilson, Marshal Fevzi Çakmak, Gündüz, and their staff assistants in the Ministry of War. Discussions were not allowed to stray beyond the question of defending Turkey. Wilson suggests that the Turks had been briefed not to discuss offensive operations.[29] The questions the Turks did raise had to do primarily with who would command British units in Turkey. This was hardly the issue Wilson had come to Ankara to discuss. He wanted to formulate specific war plans—how Turkey could best fight against the Axis, how its army could be most expeditiously pressed into service, how the Turks could best utilize the equipment they were receiving from the British. Turkish defenses would have to be ranged along the Çatalca and Bolayır lines, Wilson told Çakmak. The British officer advised the chief of the Turkish military staff "not to swan about . . . ," and gave him concrete suggestions as to how the Turkish army should defend its positions.[30] Çakmak listened but remained, typically, circumspect. Wilson ran into similar difficulties when he spoke subsequently with Menemencioğlu and Saracoğlu,

27 *Ibid.*, p. 5,596, para. 291.

28 Henry H. Maitland Wilson (Field Marshal Lord Wilson of Libya), *Eight Years Overseas 1939-1947* (London: Hutchinson and Co., 1949), p. 155.

29 *Ibid.*, pp. 156-57. As will be suggested later, personal relations between İsmet İnönü and Fevzi Çakmak were such that the President of the Republic would hardly have been inclined to entrust Çakmak with the responsibility for discussing with foreign emissaries an issue like how or when Turkey would enter the war.

30 *Ibid.*

only now the resistance became more subtle. The two insisted upon discussing tactical questions whenever Wilson raised political issues and emphasized political issues when Wilson raised tactical questions. Neither Wilson nor Ambassador Hugessen, who attended the meetings between Wilson and Turkish officials, hesitated to be blunt. Wilson writes that both he and Hugessen "hammered in the point that to be of use we must be called in in time."[31] Wilson urged the Turks to accept British anti-tank and anti-aircraft artillery units immediately. He attempted to induce the Turks to evaluate specific military operations. Menemencioğlu and Saracoğlu were not responsive and continued to shift the discussion before the talks ever went too far.

When the Turks did demonstrate an interest in operational aspects of warfare, they exasperated the British as much as when they had exhibited none at all. For example, a member of Wilson's staff, Wilfred Lindsell, came to Ankara in August 1943, to lead a party of Turkish military officers on maneuvers. His mission was, among other things, to instruct the Turks how to maintain and service the equipment they were receiving. Lindsell informed Wilson, however, that they were unwilling students.[32] Wilson comments that the task was nearly impossible anyway, since Turkey's "shortage of mechanics meant that crew members had to be taught the working of the internal combustion engine from page one of the book."[33] The British were thus confounded in the field as well as in staff discussions.

But the most intractable problem of all involved the transportation of goods and equipment within Turkey. To be properly maintained, the fighting units which were to participate in the first three phases of HARDIHOOD required an estimated 1,200 tons of equipment a day, well

---

[31] *Ibid.*   [32] *Ibid.*, p. 157.

[33] *Ibid.*; Aydemir, *The Second Man*, p. 133, states, "Motor vehicles were few and varied. It was said that there were 28 different kinds of trucks in the army." The implication is that the Turks used anything that ran on wheels.

over the maximum which Turkish ports and railways could handle. The British attempted to remedy the situation, but, again, for every problem the British solved, they confronted several more. In March 1943, they allocated 100 locomotives and 2,500 fifteen-ton cargo wagons for use in Turkey, approximately half of which were to be supplied immediately, the other to be held in reserve. This did not eliminate the transportation problem, however, but merely created another: how to meet the fuel needs of these locomotives. As Herbert L. Matthews wrote on March 14, 1943, the "real snag is coal."[34] This did not mean that Turkey was faced with a shortage. The problem was sea transportation to bring the coal to the southern regions of Turkey. "British authorities," wrote Matthews, "believe that already there are a number of locomotives in the south lying idle for lack of coal," as a result of an insufficient number of ships. The British transferred a number of cargo ships to Turkey to help alleviate this situation. But even if there had been *enough* ships to supply *enough* locomotives with *enough* fuel to permit *enough* British engineers to receive *enough* equipment from *enough* ports to build *enough* airports to house *enough* planes which would protect Turkey in the event of war, Turkish policy-makers did not wish HARDIHOOD to succeed, certainly not at the pace the British had in mind.

The heart of the operation was the delivery of 45 air

[34] The Chargé in the United Kingdom ([Herbert L.] Matthews) to the Secretary of State, London, March 14, 1943, *Foreign Relations*, 1943, IV, 1,098. Matthews' full statement reads: "The [British] Foreign Office believes that the real snag is coal. There is no sea transportation available for bringing coal from Zonguldak to the South of Turkey, and the British believe that already there are a number of locomotives in the south lying idle for lack of coal. If coal were available in this area, the British would be willing to hand over more locomotives to the Turks." Although there were rail lines connecting Zonguldak and the south of Turkey, the equipment available at this time was not adequate to the demand. At least, that is what the Turks wanted the British to believe.

squadron units, including 16 heavy-bomber squadrons. In the spring of 1943, Turkish bases could hardly have accommodated as sophisticated a force as this. Turkish airport facilities could have serviced no more than 25 air squadrons and were equipped for dry weather conditions only. Consequently, British engineers drew up plans to develop Turkey's airfield capabilities.[35] These included installing a major advance base near Afyon Karahisar and two others near Milas and Muğla, all of which were to be designed to meet the demands of all-weather flying. The British also promised to locate a Royal Air Force maintenance unit in Çakmak, a road-rail transhipment point in Ulukışla, and proposed to enlarge the port depots at Mersin and İskenderun in order to handle the delivery of construction materials which would be needed to fulfill these plans. In early June, British authorities submitted these proposals, which required bringing substantial numbers of trained British personnel into Turkey. The Turks began operation footdrag in earnest. Wilson reports that,

> Turkish consent to the construction of the advanced base was not given until August, and then only on conditions which made it quite impossible to complete the project by the end of the year. Work had to be carried out by the Turks, under the supervision of only those British personnel already in Turkey, and it had to be disguised as commercial construction. Permission to start on the port depots was not given until December.[36]

Plans to enlarge the gasoline storage facilities in İskenderun, to provide tankage at airfields, to construct hospitals, and to improve communications by laying telephone trunk lines were, writes Wilson, "in all cases . . . delayed by the Turks."[37] This is not to say that the Turks refused to accept British military assistance. The British, with American

[35] *Operations in the Middle East*, p. 5,596, para. 295.
[36] *Ibid.*, para. 296.   [37] *Ibid.*, para. 298.

backing, supplied the Turks with approximately 80 million dollars worth of military equipment in 1943. On December 5, 1943, at the Second Cairo Conference, General Wilson informed Harry Hopkins and Anthony Eden, in Menemencioğlu's presence, that since the Adana Conference Turkey had received "350 tanks, 48 self-propelled guns, nearly 300 anti-aircraft guns (over 100 of them heavy) 300 field and medium guns, 200 mortars, rather less than 500 anti-tank guns, an enormous quantity (about 99,000) of various guns and automatics, 420 mortars, and about one million anti-tank mines for the defence of Turkey."[38] Thus the Turks did allow themselves the luxury of receiving large amounts of military equipment from the British. But as Zeki Kuneralp has suggested, "the Turks hoped that the British would not supply them so that they would have the excuse they needed to stay out of the war." Operation footdrag, or the attempt on the part of the Turks to prevent the British from bringing Turkish logistical capabilities to the point where the Allies could force them into the war, as Kuneralp expressed it, was, "an elegant way of saying no."[39]

[38] Hopkins-Eden-Menemencioğlu Meeting, December 5, 1943, *Foreign Relations: The Conferences at Cairo and Tehran, 1943*, p. 729.

[39] Zeki Kuneralp in a personal interview in London, September 8, 1969. Kuneralp, who had returned to London as Turkish Ambassador only a few days before our conversation, having left the post of Secretary-General of the Turkish Foreign Ministry, served as a political officer in the Turkish Embassy in Romania during the war. Mrs. Nermin Streater recalls that her uncle, Numan Menemencioğlu, and others at the Foreign Ministry believed that Chief of Staff, Marshal Fevzi Çakmak, refused to allow roads to be built on a large scale because he feared that the Russians would use them to invade Turkey. (In a personal interview with the author, London, September 5, 1969.) Although operation footdrag went into full effect during the summer of 1943 and was designed to prevent the construction of air installations, there were earlier signs of it. On June 29, 1939, Hugessen complained about the delays in military staff talks since the Anglo-Turkish Declaration of May 12, 1939. "I have also pointed out difficulties caused by Turkish reticence in regard to harbour defences," the British Ambassador wrote; Sir Hughe Knatchbull-Hugessen (Ankara) to Viscount Halifax, Ankara,

Turkish delaying tactics were directed particularly toward projects which required large numbers of foreign skilled personnel to enter Turkey, such as the construction of airfields. The files of the German Embassy in Ankara show that in July 1943, İnönü received a position paper from the Ministry of Foreign Affairs advising him that work on British air installations was actually proceeding too fast. The paper warned that as a result of this Turkey might be forced into the war. The paper declared:

> British construction of airfields in Turkey is proceeding more rapidly than expected: the fields which had been expected to take one year are being readied after only 5 months, and the British personnel buildings in

---

June 29, 1939, *Docs.Brit.F.P.*, vi, 188-89. Hugessen concluded this message by stating, "It is clear that there is an element of *amour propre* in Turkish attitude." Trumbull Higgins, *Winston Churchill and the Second Front 1940-1943* (New York: Oxford University Press, 1957), p. 51, on the contrary congratulates them for their refusal to go along blindly with the British in 1941: "The Turks were not, however, so incautious as to play the role shortly to be assumed with so little warning by the more febrile Serbs, namely that of the gambit in the Prime Minister's ambitious schemes. Sensibly, the Ankara Government refused the British offers of a few Royal Air Force squadrons from the already overstrained Middle East Command on the grounds that these units were too small to resist a German assault—but were large enough to provoke such an attack." In February 1942, the British informed the American Embassy in London of some of their difficulties. In response to U.S. Ambassador Winant's request for information regarding the British handling of supplies to Turkey, the British reported, "There are already quantities of supplies for Turkey in the Middle East which cannot be sent on because of lack of facilities at the Turkish ports open to British shipping and because the Turks have so far made only four ships available for this purpose. The Turks have done little so far to assist in opening up supply lines into their country"; the Ambassador in the United Kingdom (Winant) to the Secretary of State, London, February 14, 1943, *Foreign Relations*, 1942, iv, 679-80; also, Robert J. Collins, *Lord Wavell 1883-1941: A Military Biography* (London: Hodder and Stoughton, 1947), pp. 255ff; Reader Bullard, *Britain and the Middle East: From the Earliest Times to 1950* (London: Hutchinson's University Library, 1951), p. 127.

Turkey are steadily mounting. Montgomery's army is being gradually transferred to the Syrian-Turkish border and it is quite possible that Turkey may be forced into the war by British staging a *fait accompli*, either by bombing the Romanian oil fields from Turkish airports or by a quick invasion of the Balkans from Syria through Turkey.[40]

Turkish obfuscation thus placated the Germans, to whom an influx of British personnel and air squadrons would have been more provocative than the supply of British military equipment to the Turkish army. Yet the Turks concurrently insisted that without the airfields and air cover, they were obviously in no position to enter the war due to German air superiority. The position seemed illogical to the British, even maddening, because they presumed that the Turks were planning to enter the war on the Allied side. It was, however, perfectly logical to the Turks, who quietly proceeded from the opposite supposition.

The position paper of the Turkish Foreign Minister referred to a possible link-up between Turkish and British forces. Although the British did not plan to invade the Balkans through Turkey against its will, it is true that British forces were preparing in Syria for a link-up with the Turkish army at this time. Such a link-up hinged upon the completion of the airfields and the arrival of British air squadrons. The Turks would not have dragged their feet as they did, had they been certain that such a link-up would have led to a large-scale Anglo-American thrust into the Balkans. But, as Esmer and Erkin have indicated to the author, the British would make no such commitment and

40 Foreign Ministry in Berlin (Waltheur) to Ambassador in Ankara (von Papen), Berlin, August 13, 1943, *Captured Files*, NA, T-120, Roll 2618, Frame E364709. Confirmation that the British were quietly building up a force on the Syrian-Turkish frontier to join the Turks is given by the British liaison officer for the projected link-up, who happened to be the husband of the niece of the Turkish Foreign Minister. Personal interview with Mr. Jasper Streater, London, August 7, 1969.

did not trust the Turks sufficiently to reveal Allied grand strategy.[41] We know now, that, failing to secure American approval for a Balkan campaign, the British had no grand strategy to reveal.

CHURCHILL PLAYS HIS TRUMP

With the fall of Mussolini on July 25, 1943, despite these other frustrations, Churchill renewed his efforts, both with the Turks about the war and with the Americans about the Eastern Mediterranean. He felt that the "collapse of Italy should fix the moment for putting the strongest pressure on Turkey to act in accordance with the spirit of the Alliance, and in this Britain and the United States . . . should if possible be joined or at least supported by Russia."[42] Churchill, with these considerations in mind, left ten days later, on August 5, 1943, for the Quebec Conference with the U.S. President. Roosevelt and the Joint Chiefs resolved that this time they would meet Churchill with their policy firmly set. At the first plenary session of the conference, August 19, 1943, they elicited from the British Prime Minister an agreement to assign top priority to the cross-Channel attack. Churchill accepted this, agreeing to the target date of May 1, 1944. As Henry L. Stimson, the U.S. Under-Secretary of State, wrote, "from this time onward OVERLORD held the inside track."[43]

[41] Ahmet Şükrü Esmer and Feridun Cemal Erkin in personal interviews with the author.

[42] Winston S. Churchill, *The Second World War*, Vol. v, *Closing the Ring* (Boston: Houghton Mifflin Co., 1951), 58; this statement was included in a memorandum which Churchill distributed to the War Cabinet and forwarded to the President on July 26, 1943.

[43] Henry L. Stimson and McGeorge Bundy, *On Active Service in Peace and War* (New York: Harper & Row, 1948), p. 439. The code name for the August conference in Quebec was QUADRANT; see Feis, *Churchill, Roosevelt, Stalin*, pp. 147-53; Churchill, *Closing the Ring*, Chap. 5, "The Quebec Conference," pp. 80-97; Sherwood, *Roosevelt and Hopkins*, pp. 745-50; also, Higgins, *Soft Underbelly*, pp. 91-107.

The results of the meetings reflected little of Churchill's thinking about the Eastern Mediterranean, however. In their final conference report to the President and the Prime Minister, for example, the Combined Chiefs of Staff stated that "the time was not considered right for Turkey to enter the war."[44] They agreed, however, that the United States and Great Britain should continue to supply Turkey with such equipment "as they could spare and the Turks could absorb."[45] Although they were parties to such agreements, the British never stopped believing it would be to Allied advantage to have Turkey enter the war.[46] There was still reason to hope that the Turks could be brought into battle. Churchill decided to play his trump card. On September 9, 1943, while he was in Washington and apparently without informing the President, Churchill cabled General Wilson, "this is the time to play high. Improvise and dare."[47] He thus signaled his forces in the Eastern Mediterranean to launch an attack on Rhodes.

To Churchill, the combined sea and air base of Rhodes, the air base on Cos, and the sea base at Leros together offered a vantage point from which to attack German concentrations in the Balkans and northern Italy, to bomb the Romanian oil fields and refineries at Ploesti, and to defend Egypt and North Africa. Thus Churchill decided on a new initiative if not in conjunction with the United States, then alone. He would take Rhodes. But there was still another reason for his daring to attack Rhodes. He wanted to bolster British diplomatic approaches to Turkey. British capture of Rhodes and gradual control of the Aegean might possibly persuade the Turks to enter the war. At least, Churchill reasoned, British officials would be able to speak with greater authority in Ankara. British plans failed, however, and by the end of 1943, British influence with Turkish offi-

---

[44] *Strategic Planning*, p. 229.   [45] *Ibid.*
[46] *Ibid.*
[47] Churchill, *Closing the Ring*, p. 205.

cials hit a new low.[48] Although the British made several later attempts in 1943 to occupy some of the islands in the Aegean, the failure to take Rhodes marks the beginning of the end of Churchill's campaign to bring Turkey into the war. Not only did the British fail to take over Italian-garri-

[48] Churchill, *ibid.*, p. 220, writes, "Turkey, witnessing the extraordinary inertia of the Allies near her shores, became much less forthcoming. . . ." His deepest resentment toward American officials during the war resulted from their refusal to support him and British forces during this October attempt to capture Rhodes. "General Eisenhower and his Staff seemed unaware of what lay at our fingertips . . . ," Churchill writes. His submission to American strategy on this occasion caused him, as he says, "one of the sharpest pangs I suffered in the war." He concludes on one of his few bitter notes, "The American Staff had enforced their view; the price had now to be paid by the British"; Churchill, *Closing the Ring*, Chap. 12, "Island Prizes Lost," pp. 203-25. The Americans resisted Churchill's pleas not because they did not accept his arguments concerning the potential value of Rhodes. They ran counter to Churchill's proposal because whenever the British Prime Minister said Rhodes, the Americans heard him to imply the Balkans. "Strategically, if we get the Aegean islands, I ask myself," Roosevelt wrote in a missive to Churchill, "where do we go from there?" The President ruled out the Balkans with a firm and decisive no; *ibid.*, pp. 214-15. Churchill, *ibid.*, pp. 207-208, correctly takes notice of the fact that Hitler realized the importance of the islands in the Aegean as well as the strategic significance of Turkish neutrality. Hitler conducted the war on the Crimean front with Turkey in mind. He feared that losses on that front might encourage the Turks to enter the war. Thus he refused to allow his armies to retreat when greater flexibility could have saved scores of men and equipment; see Felix Gilbert, *Hitler Directs His War: The Secret Records of His Daily Military Conferences* (New York: Oxford University Press, 1950), pp. 90-95; also see Alexander Werth, *Russia at War, 1941-1945* (New York: E. P. Dutton and Co., 1964). Werth cites General I. V. Tynlenov, commander of Soviet forces on the Transcaucasian front, as follows: ". . . if instead of trying to do too many things all at once, the Germans had concentrated their forces in the east, they might have broken through the Grozny and even to Baku." Instead, Tynlenov argues, "they were determined to grab the Black Sea coast as well, partly in order to eliminate the Russian Black Sea Navy, which would have had to scuttle itself, and partly in order to get Turkey into the war on the German side"; see also General I. V. Tynlenov, *Cherez tri voiny (Through Three Wars)*

soned Rhodes, but the Germans, meeting little resistance, took it and then went on to take Cos, Leros, and Samos from the British, who had held them almost from the beginning of the Mediterranean war.

The Turkish Escape and Supply Route

Although the British 1943 campaign was stillborn, and despite the fact that the British were actually having to retreat before the Germans in this sector, the Turks gave substantial aid to the Allied side, while retaining their public posture of neutrality. They supplied beleaguered British forces in the Aegean with food and equipment and helped escaping units from the Royal West Kent, Irish Fusilier, and other regiments reach the Turkish mainland safely.

Supplies destined for British-held islands in the Aegean were transported by railroad through Syria across Turkey to Kuşadası, a small but excellent port south of İzmir. From October 9 to November 17 when Leros fell, 1,400 tons of emergency material were shipped to British forces through Turkish hands. From September 28 to November 16, 3,000 tons of goods actually reached Samos and 480 tons reached Leros.[49] Turkish caiques manned by Turkish crews transported these goods. When the British evacuated their forces in the Aegean, furthermore, Kuşadası and Bodrum, further along the coast, were the first stops in their escape route. When General Wilson, for example, on November 18-19 ordered the evacuation of Samos, Turkish caiques brought

(Moscow, 1960). For further elaboration, Alan Bullock, *Hitler: A Study in Tyranny* (New York: Harper & Row, 1962), p. 715; Admiral Karl Doenitz, *Memoirs: Ten Years and Twenty Days* (London: Weidenfeld and Nicholson, 1958), p. 389; Doenitz states, "Hitler regarded it as essential to hold the Crimea as long as possible, because . . . this would inevitably have political repercussions and put great strain . . . on the neutrality of Turkey; also see F. H. Hinsley's *Hitler's Strategy* (Cambridge: Cambridge University Press, 1951), pp. 231-32.

[49] *Operations in the Middle East*, p. 5,591, paras. 245-46.

such personalities as Brigadier Baird, Colonel Tzigantes, commander of the Greek Sacred Squadron, General Solda- relli, the Italian commander, the Greek Archbishop, and hundreds of British and Italian citizens to the mainland.[50] On the evenings of November 20 and 21, Turkish caiques were able to bring more British out of Samos, plus 1,000 Greek civilians and 400 Italian troops: all this while the Germans were occupying the island.[51]

The fact that Foreign Minister Menemencioğlu was per- sonally in charge of these operations further strengthens the evidence that he was neither particularly a foe of Britain nor a friend to the Germans. But neither does it represent a shift in Turkish assessment of their self-interest. Surrepti- tious aid indicated both governmental sympathy for the British and a determination not to translate such sympathy into active public—let alone military—support for the Al- lies. Moreover, the Turkish Government during this period and right to the end of the war in no way revised its basic estimates. Russia was still the enemy, and growing constant- ly in strength. The British and the Americans were mis- guided friends, inadvertently unleashing the Russians to occupy Eastern Europe. But now that the Turks were actu- ally assisting the British retreat from the Aegean, they real- ized that the British hand had been played. Now it was Russia's turn.

[50] *Ibid.*

[51] A Turkish "military informant" in Berlin is cited by von Papen as putting the Turkish position thus: Turkey would not allow the British to compromise its neutrality, but "when a plane flies to one's left one can always shoot to the right. Or if a troop transport violates Turkish waters, one can always fire short or over it. In any event, one would certainly fire." Foreign Ministry in Berlin (Kroll) to Ambassador in Ankara (von Papen), Berlin, March 12, 1943, *Captured Files*, NA, T-120, Roll 2618, Frame E364587.

SEVEN

PRESSURE ON TURKEY MOUNTS: MEETINGS OF FOREIGN MINISTERS

THE MOSCOW CONFERENCE: THE RUSSIANS TRY TO FORCE TURKEY INTO THE WAR

THE Moscow Conference of American, British, and Soviet Foreign Ministers was marked by the extraordinary vigor with which the Soviets pressed for an Anglo-American commitment to force Turkey into the war, a commitment which the United States in particular was reluctant to give, but one which Molotov finally succeeded in obtaining if not as a part of the main conclusions to the conference then at least as an important codicil.

Soviet determination to push Turkey from neutrality into war became evident even before the October conference in Moscow. An article appeared in *War and the Working Class* early in September, which was sufficiently important to be reprinted in *Izvestia*.[1] "The neutrality of Turkey," it declared, "becomes increasingly more favorable and necessary to Germany as Turkey secures the safety of the Balkan flank for the German armies, and allows the Germans to continue to hold very limited forces there and to concentrate the overwhelming proportion of the German troops on the Soviet-German front. . . ."[2] Professor Esmer suggests that it was Stalin's belief at this time that the Western Allies were tolerating Turkish neutrality in order not to weaken the

[1] Translations of this article are in *Daily Worker*, September 4, 1943; also, George E. Kirk, "The U.S.S.R. and the Middle East 1939-1945: Turkey," *Survey of International Affairs 1939-1946: The Middle East in the War* (London: Oxford University Press for the Royal Institute of International Affairs, 1952), p. 458.

[2] *Ibid.*

167

Germans in the Balkans before Britain and the United States were in a position to take the Balkans. He notes that the Russian press began to complain angrily that "The arms England was sending to Turkey were not going to be used against Germany, but rather were to be used to reinforce Turkey against Russia after the war."[3] Against this background of Soviet propaganda, the Moscow Conference opened.

The Foreign Ministers of the Big Three, Hull, Eden, and Molotov, met in Moscow on October 19, 1943.[4] Molotov, as chairman, immediately submitted three requests to Hull and Eden. As ever, the Soviets sought reassurance that the opening of the Second Front would take place in the spring of 1944 as scheduled. The second proposal constituted a demand that the three powers coerce Turkey immediately into the war. The third concerned the use of Swedish air bases. Molotov adjourned the meeting as soon as he had finished submitting these proposals.[5]

Eden immediately informed his chief about the three Soviet demands. Molotov's interest in Turkish belligerence delighted Churchill. The Soviet call for a cross-Channel attack came as no surprise, but their desire to have Turkey in the war immediately did.[6] Churchill instructed his Foreign Secretary to ascertain whether the Russians would be

[3] Professor Esmer in *Turkish Foreign Policy*, p. 158.

[4] Feis, *Churchill, Roosevelt, Stalin*, pp. 191-234; Eden, *The Reckoning*, pp. 472-87; Hull, *Memoirs*, Chap. 92, "Moscow Conference Begins," pp. 1,274-91 and Chap. 93, "Birth of the United Nations Organization," pp. 1,292-1,307.

[5] Churchill, *Closing the Ring*, pp. 284-85.

[6] *Ibid.*; Eden, *The Reckoning*, p. 477; Hull, *Memoirs*, p. 1,279. Churchill, *Closing the Ring*, p. 286, excited by Molotov's remarks asked Eden to ascertain whether the Russians would "be attracted by the idea of our acting through the Aegean, involving Turkey in the war, and opening the Dardanelles and Bosphorous so that British Naval forces could aid the Russian advance and that we could ultimately give them our right hand along the Danube." Churchill, in phrasing his question this way, seems to have obviously wanted to prejudice the Russian response.

interested in "a right-handed evolution," referring to a full-scale Anglo-American invasion of the Balkans.[7] Thus at the very point when his Eastern Mediterranean strategy seemed dead, the Soviets seemingly were about to give it a new lease on life.

At the second meeting, Molotov again emphasized Soviet concern about Turkey.[8] If the British and the Americans were friends of the Soviet Union, if they wished to lighten the burden being carried by Russian armies, then they would surely seek to bring the Turks into the war, he argued. Eden replied, "There was no disagreement between them as to the desirability of bringing Turkey into the war."[9] The British, in effect, thus accepted the principle that the Turks ought to come into the war immediately. Eden, however, was most circumspect. He outlined the obstacles preventing Turkish entry into the war, but specified only those difficulties which related to Turkey's military preparedness, not those pertaining to its political posture, specifically vis-à-vis the Soviet Union. These other considerations were, as the Prime Minister wrote to Eden on October 20, for Eden's "inner thoughts" alone.[10] The Foreign Secretary, knowing that the Americans perceived British interest in southeastern Europe as a threat to the cross-Channel attack, therefore walked the line between seeming overanxiousness and too great a reluctance. He wanted to go along with the Russians but without the opposition of the Americans. Moreover, he was concerned not to arouse Russian suspicions that Britain wanted Turkey in the war for its own political reasons. Thus, when Eden accepted the principle that Turkey be brought into the war, he devoutly recited that the entire question revolved upon logistical and practical matters which had to be considered with a view to ensuring the

[7] *Ibid.*

[8] Record of the Second Meeting of the Tripartite Conference, Moscow, October 20, 1943, *Foreign Relations*, 1943, I, 583-86.

[9] *Ibid.*

[10] Churchill, *Closing the Ring*, p. 287.

success of the cross-Channel attack.[11] Eden also assured his Russian counterpart that the reason why the British continued to supply the Turks with weapons was solely and precisely to enable them to fight against the Germans. Lest Molotov suspect the British of arming the Turks against Russia, Eden confided that "Britain would welcome Turkey's help to drive the Germans out of the Balkans, but Britain was not interested in Turkish intervention in the Balkans once the Germans had withdrawn."[12] He added that Turkish airfields were not as crucial as they had once seemed, since bases in Italy could now be used. Eden concluded, "If, however, our Soviet friends thought we ought to press Turkey, we should be glad to consider the matter." The British position thus fell in line with that of the Soviets.

Having received this satisfactory response from Eden, Molotov's attention turned to Hull. The Secretary of State had listened silently to Eden's exposition of British policy toward Turkey. Now he responded with what became his standard rejoinder during the conference whenever this question arose: he preferred "not to speak on military matters."[13] Hull, like Eden, had also cabled home for instructions after the first session. Hull's chief, unlike Eden's, was not keenly interested in the question of Turkish belligerence. Instead of replying directly to the Secretary of State's message, Roosevelt turned it over to the Joint Chiefs of Staff. The Joint Chiefs, in turn, gave it to the Joint Stra-

[11] Eden told Molotov that Turkey had been promised 25 air squadrons, but also indicated that "We have not got these 25 squadrons in the Eastern Mediterranean and under present conditions Turkey, whose military preparedness is still very backward, would, as our partner in the offensive, be more of a liability than an asset"; *Foreign Relations,* 1943, I, 584. Eden was careful throughout his discussion to omit any mention of Turkey's fear of the Soviet Union, which had been almost certainly communicated to him by the Prime Minister after his return to London from Adana.

[12] *Ibid.,* p. 585. [13] *Ibid.,* p. 584.

tegic Survey Command (JSSC) for its consideration.[14] Response to Hull's request for instructions was further delayed by the disagreement between army planners and the JSSC which ensued over this issue.[15]

Army planners argued against bringing Turkey into the war, restating many of the old arguments and concluding, correctly, that "Turkey did not want Soviet help and would probably demand British and American guarantees to protect it against the USSR . . ." which would divert the Anglo-American forces from the cross-Channel attack.[16] The JSSC, on the other hand, argued that it would be desirable to have the Turks join in the fighting in order to divert the Germans from the Channel defenses. In the end, the Joint Chiefs of Staff took the equivocal position that pending further study Turkey should be neither encouraged nor dissuaded. The Joint Chiefs wanted to ascertain what the Soviet Union would do to protect Turkey should it enter the war. It also wanted to make certain that Turkish belligerence would not jeopardize the cross-Channel attack. Since no such assurance could be given at the time of Hull's message to the President, the Joint Chiefs recommended caution.[17]

[14] The Joint Strategic Survey Command (JSSC) included representatives from all the services and undertook to analyze a broad variety of questions for the Joint Chiefs. In regard to Turkish entry into the war, the JSSC generally subscribed to the position taken by General Marshall that Turkish belligerence would be more a liability than an asset. At this juncture, however, the JSSC apparently reversed itself and argued that Turkey did indeed have a useful function to perform as a belligerent.

[15] *Strategic Planning*, pp. 296-98. [16] *Ibid.*, p. 297.

[17] On October 26, 1943, Secretary of State Hull received the following instructions from the President: "It would not be deemed advisable to push Turkey at this moment into a declaration of war on the side of the Allies since the necessary compensation to the Turks in war material and war supplies including armed forces and ships would divert too much from the Italian front and the proposed OVERLORD operation. However, inquiries could be started on basis of lease by

Hull conveyed the substance of his instructions to the Soviet Foreign Minister. This was not what Molotov wanted nor, apparently, what he felt he could extract from the Americans. For the duration of the conference, he pleaded with Hull to agree to help bring the Turks into the war. Hull, for example, records that on October 25 Molotov accosted him during a recess and stated that the three Great Powers, "should 'suggest' to Turkey that she come into the war and that by this word 'suggest' he [Molotov] meant to suggest peremptorily which meant in effect a command. . . ."[18] Hull refused to respond. Molotov persisted. He told Hull that he could not understand why the Allies should supply Turkey with arms "without getting some fighting out of her."[19] Three days later, Molotov declared that the Russian position was quite simple. Turkey should be forced into the war now because no matter what complications the Allied faced as a result, the problems Hitler would thereby have to face would be even greater. The use of Turkish air bases was not enough. Turkey's full participation was needed, now. Should Turkey refuse, then shipments of armaments should cease. But Turkey, Molotov asserted, could not readily refuse a three-power request.[20] As soon as the formal meetings of the conference ended, Molotov and Eden sat down, on October 31, to determine the best way to coerce the Turks into the war. As Eden wired Churchill, Molotov in the course of this discussion repeated again and again, "that if the three Great Powers were really of the belief that Turkey should come into the

Turkey as a neutral of airbases and transportation facilities"; President Roosevelt to the Secretary of State, Washington, D.C., October 26, 1943, *Foreign Relations*, 1943, I, 644.

[18] Memorandum of Conversation, the Secretary of State in Moscow, October 25, 1943, *ibid.*, p. 634; also, Hull, *Memoirs*, p. 1,297.

[19] *Ibid.* The cited phrase represents Hull's description of what Molotov had to say rather than a direct quotation from Molotov.

[20] Record of the Tenth Meeting of the Tripartite Conference, Moscow, October 28, 1943, *Foreign Relations*, 1943, I, 659-62.

war, she would have no option. . . ."[21] Churchill, for his
part, encouraged at the offset of the conference, had already
decided to launch a new campaign to facilitate Turkish
entry into the war. Whereas American planners had refused
to recommend that the Turks be made to fight, feeling
themselves unwilling or unable to divert sufficient logistic
support to a Turkish front, Churchill seems to have decided, along with the Russians, that it would be well to have
the Turks fight in any case. He appears to have been much
less pessimistic than the Americans about the chances of
Turkish survival were they to be pushed into war with the
supplies already available.[22] This marks the beginning of
the nadir in Anglo-Turkish relations during the war. Turkish policy-makers, particularly Foreign Minister Menemencioğlu, soon gathered the impression that the British and
Russians wished to force their country into the war, whether
or not Turkish cities could be adequately protected,
whether or not Turkish troops could be properly supplied
and reinforced. Eden now told Molotov that he was prepared to meet the Turkish Foreign Minister in Cairo in
order to request, on behalf of the Big Three, the immediate
use of Turkey's airfields and to demand authority to send
submarines through the Straits.[23] Some disagreement between Molotov and Eden ensued. Eden, informing Molotov

[21] Eden, *The Reckoning*, pp. 483-84.

[22] On October 23, 1943, Churchill cabled Eden, "If we force Turkey
to enter the war, she will insist on air support, etc., which could not
be provided without detriment to our main operations in Italy. If, however, Turkey enters on her own initiative, perhaps moving through a
phase of non-belligerency, we should not have the same obligation,
and yet great advantages might be reaped." Churchill concluded, "Personally I would like to see Turkey come in on her own." *Closing the
Ring*, pp. 288-89.

[23] Memorandum of Conversation, Moscow, October 31, 1943, *Foreign
Relations*, 1943, I, 689-90; Memorandum of Conversation, by the Ambassador in the Soviet Union (Harriman), Moscow, November 1, 1943,
ibid., pp. 693-94. Eden told Hull and Harriman what he intended to
say and, after, what he had said to Molotov.

that the British could no longer plan on holding Leros without Turkish help, declared that he wanted to ask the Turks for air bases to protect Leros. Molotov firmly rejected this on the grounds that Turkey should be made to come into the war on an all-out basis.[24] Molotov hinted that the future of the Anglo-Russian alliance depended upon the outcome. Eden seems to have been influenced by Molotov's arguments. On November 1, 1943, Hull reported to the President that Eden had shown him a cable which the British Foreign Secretary had sent to Churchill. Eden admitted in the wire that he had told Molotov that unless Menemencioğlu, along with the Turkish Government, agreed to immediate Allied use of airfields and their right to pass submarines through the Straits, "I should tell him [Menemencioğlu] that our supply of arms and equipment would stop forthwith." Eden went further. If Turkey did not become directly involved in the war against Germany by the end of 1943, the Allies should consider presenting to the Turkish Government a tripartite ultimatum to do so immediately. Molotov, as a result of these remarks, withdrew his objections to the British desire to make their demands for air bases. As Eden wrote,

> . . . our Government was in complete agreement that before the end of the year Turkey should enter the war, and that I was prepared to sign at once on the dotted line to that effect. Question of tactics was [the] only difference between us. He wanted only one bite on [the] cherry while I wanted two.[25]

Molotov and Eden, therefore, agreed to a momentous compromise: before the end of 1943 Turkey should enter the

[24] *Ibid.*, p. 694. Eden, *The Reckoning*, p. 483, states that he and Churchill shared American doubts concerning Turkey's entry into the war. "On the other hand," he writes, "the Prime Minister and I did not want to give a flat negative to the Soviet proposal."

[25] The Secretary of State to the President, Moscow, November 1, 1943, *Foreign Relations: The Conferences at Cairo and Tehran*, pp. 144-46.

war and should be made to place at the disposal of Allied forces air bases and other facilities as desired by their two governments. On November 1, 1943, they initialed the following secret protocol:

It is agreed between the Foreign Secretaries of the Soviet Union and the United Kingdom as follows:

First. In order that Turkey may take her part with the United Nations in hastening the defeat of Hitlerite Germany . . . the two Foreign Secretaries think it most desirable that Turkey should enter the war on the side of the United Nations before the end of 1943.

Second. It is agreed between the two Foreign Secretaries that on behalf of the United Kingdom and the Soviet Governments it should be suggested to Turkey at the earliest possible date, to be agreed upon between them, that before the end of 1943 Turkey should enter the war.

Third. It is further agreed that a request should immediately be made of Turkey to give to the United Nations all possible aid by placing at the disposal of the Allied Forces Turkish air bases and such other facilities as may be agreed upon as desirable by the two Governments.[26]

The agreement that Molotov had sought since the beginning of the conference was thus accepted by the British.

With the protocol initialed, Molotov resumed his efforts to induce the Americans to sign it. He asked Eden to explore with Hull the possibility of making their agreement a tripartite one. Hull wired the President for instructions. This time Molotov's efforts met with success. On November 4 the President informed Ambassador Harriman, Hull having returned to Washington, that "this Government agrees to join Great Britain and Soviet Union in making immediate demand on Turkey for use of air bases and later press-

[26] The Ambassador in the Soviet Union (Harriman) to President Roosevelt, Moscow, November 2, 1943, *Foreign Relations*, 1943, I, 697-98.

ing Turkey to enter the war before the end of the year."[27] Molotov was immensely satisfied, and so was Harriman.[28] And as for Eden, he left Moscow on November 4 in order to meet the Turkish Foreign Minister whom he did not like and believed to be pro-Axis.

MENEMENCIOĞLU AND EDEN AT CAIRO: THE BRITISH PLAY THE RUSSIAN HAND

Everything about the November 5-8 meeting between the Turkish and British Foreign Ministers appears to have gone badly. British Ambassador Hugessen, in Ankara, had known that Eden wanted to see Menemencioğlu and went to convey his knowledge "privately" on November 1. "With many sentences in the conditional mood," Hugessen inquired whether Menemencioğlu would be willing to go to Cairo "at the shortest possible notice."[29] Menemencioğlu answered affirmatively. The Turkish Foreign Minister telephoned

[27] President Roosevelt to the Ambassador in the Soviet Union, Washington, D.C., November 4, 1943, *ibid.*, p. 698. This represented a departure for Roosevelt on the issue of Turkish entry. Harriman's recommendation that the United States join the Anglo-Soviet agreement and Roosevelt's desire to meet the Russians on good terms later in the year probably influenced him. Selim Sarper, who succeeded Cevat Açıkalın as Turkish Ambassador in Moscow, informed the author that he did not know of the secret protocol until many months after its signing and, Sarper stated, neither did the Turkish Government. Sarper suggested, however, that Eden's firm position with Menemencioğlu in Cairo and the nature of his demands indicated to them that there had been some agreement between the British, the Soviets, and quite possibly the Americans in regard to Turkey. (In a personal interview with the author.)

[28] On November 7, Harriman wrote to Roosevelt to express his pleasure at the President's decision regarding the Anglo-Soviet agreement. On this occasion he offered his own explanation of why Molotov had been so anxious to have Turkey in the war. "His [Molotov's] anxiety . . . is I believe due to the fact that he is personally under some criticism by Soviet military authorities . . ."; the Ambassador in the Soviet Union (Harriman) to President Roosevelt, Moscow, November 7, 1943, *Foreign Relations*, 1943, I, 699.

[29] Hugessen, *Diplomat in Peace and War*, p. 195.

Hugessen at 10:00 A.M. on November 2, however, to inform him that he had to go to bed for reasons of ill health.[30] When the invitation finally did arrive, it gave Menemencioğlu only twenty-four hours' notice. Flying conditions were so bad that Hugessen and Menemencioğlu had to make a twenty-four hour journey by train through the Taurus Mountains which was made even more difficult by a cave-in blocking one of the mountain passes. Açıkalın, who accompanied the Foreign Minister to Cairo, remembers Menemencioğlu grimacing with pain on the trip from Ankara.[31]

Menemencioğlu and Eden were not strangers to each other, but there was no friendship between them. Even as the talks began, Menemencioğlu confided to Açıkalın that he considered the Britisher, "a theatrical man" who was "full of himself."[32] Eden, for his part, already had an impression

[30] This account of how the Eden-Menemencioğlu meeting in Cairo was arranged differs from the one circulated at the time of the conference. This alleges that it was Menemencioğlu who had called for the meeting. The American Embassy in Ankara apparently accepted these reports; see, e.g., *Foreign Relations: The Conferences at Cairo and Tehran*, p. 162, n. 3, where the editors of this volume cite an unpublished telegram sent by the Chargé in Turkey, Robert F. Kelley, to the Department of State, which reported that "the meeting between Numan [Menemencioğlu] and Eden has been arranged as the result of an intimation by Numan [Menemencioğlu] that he would like to see Eden upon the latter's return from Moscow." Kelley again reported this on November 8, 1943; the Chargé in Turkey (Kelley) to the President, the Secretary of State, and the Under-Secretary of State (Stettinius), Ankara, November 8, 1943, *ibid.*, pp. 161-62. The *Times* of London, November 8, 1943, went out of its way to correct the erroneous impression that Eden had asked Menemencioğlu to come to Cairo to tell him of the decisions at Moscow. It was Menemencioğlu "who, taking advantage of the presence of Mr. Eden in the vicinity of Turkey," made the request. James Reston in *The New York Times* of the same date reported the same.

[31] Cevat Açıkalın in a personal interview with the author. Besides Açıkalın, Zeki Siren, Turgut Menemencioğlu, and Sadi Kavur traveled to Cairo with Numan Menemencioğlu; *Ayın Tarihi*, Vol. 123 (November 1943), p. 94.

[32] As told to the author by Cevat Açıkalın.

of his Turkish counterpart as quite simply pro-Axis—a view from which Hugessen, the British Ambassador who admired Menemencioğlu, had failed to dissuade him.[33]

Upon his arrival, the British Foreign Secretary conferred first with Sholto Douglas and General H. Maitland Wilson. They decided that ten squadrons of the Royal Air Force would be dispatched to Turkey within the month. Menemencioğlu and Açıkalın, accompanied by Hugessen, arrived in Cairo around noon, November 5, and talks promptly began.

Eden immediately faced the Turkish Foreign Minister with a request to receive the squadrons on Turkish soil within three weeks.[34] Menemencioğlu, surprised by this, refused to treat it as anything less than a demand to go to war.[35] In his account of these conversations, Menemencioğlu asserts that Eden wanted Turkey to enter the war within one month and that, furthermore, Eden sought the use of

[33] Sir Hughe Knatchbull-Hugessen in a personal interview with the author, Barham, England, March 21, 1966.

[34] The Chief of the Division of Near Eastern Affairs (Alling) to the Under-Secretary of State (Stettinius), the Assistant Secretary of State (Berle), and the Adviser on Political Relations (Murray), Washington, D.C., November 9, 1943, *Foreign Relations: The Conferences at Cairo and Tehran*, pp. 164-67 at p. 164. In an apparent effort to keep the Americans informed, Mr. William Hayter, First Secretary of the British Embassy in Washington, informed Paul H. Alling of the substance of the Eden-Menemencioğlu talks. Ambassador Hugessen performed a similar task in Ankara; the Chargé in Ankara (Kelley) to the President, the Secretary of State, and the Under-Secretary of State (Stettinius), Ankara, November 10, 1943, *ibid.* Turgut Menemencioğlu has written of his uncle's position during this conference with Eden, "It was mostly one of getting information about British intentions." (In a letter to the author.)

[35] Alling's report of what Hayter had told him stated that Menemencioğlu "refused to agree that there would be any difference between these two courses of action, contending that to furnish air bases to the Allies would be tantamount to entering the war." It is likely that Eden pressed a particularly sensitive nerve in Menemencioğlu with this request. As has already been mentioned, Menemencioğlu was keenly opposed to any attempt by a major European Power to establish bases in Turkey.

Turkish air bases with this purpose in mind.[36] If Menemencioğlu is correct, it would suggest that Eden had indeed set out to convey Molotov's idea of exerting pressure on Turkey to fight. The record of the discussions between Eden and Menemencioğlu given to the Americans by the British, however, reveals that Eden spoke primarily of air bases.[37] In the British version of these discussions, Eden assured Menemencioğlu that "there was no intention to press the Turks to go into the war on an all-out basis."[38] Whether Eden demanded the use of air bases or actually requested Turkey's immediate entry into the war, Menemencioğlu astutely insisted that the use of Turkish air bases by Allied air squadrons must be treated as indistinguishable from a declaration of war on Germany. The Axis would regard it as such.[39] Menemencioğlu also argued that neither Turkish public opinion[40] nor Allied logistics were as yet ready for immediate Turkish entry.[41] He took the position that noth-

[36] Menemencioğlu in the *Menemencioğlu Manuscript*, pp. 274-75, writes the following: "A surprise awaited me at Cairo. At our first meeting M. Eden gave it to me to know that M. Churchill wished to see Turkey declare war on Germany with a maximum delay of one month." Menemencioğlu records his shock at this; he suggested that they had better discuss the issue in a fuller way first. He writes, "I urged him [Eden] to let us continue our conversation on the whole range of problems of interest to Turkey and to Turco-British relations. When we will have exhausted this subject of capital importance, we could then begin to examine M. Churchill's proposition."

[37] *Foreign Relations: The Conferences at Cairo and Tehran*, pp. 164-67, 174-75.

[38] *Ibid.*, p. 165; Menemencioğlu inquired "What good it would do the Allies if at the end of the war Turkey was militarily exhausted."

[39] Professor Ahmet Şükrü Esmer emphasizes this aspect of the Turkish position in his account in *Turkish Foreign Policy*, p. 160. Esmer writes: "The Turkish delegation plainly indicated that as far as Turkey is concerned there was no difference between giving the Allies air bases on [Turkish] territory and entering the war, and that at that time [Turkey] was not ready to go to war." Aydemir, *The Second Man*, p. 265, esp. n. 1, takes the same position.

[40] Esmer, *Turkish Foreign Policy*, p. 174.

[41] Cevat Açıkalın in a personal interview with the author.

ing short of an Anglo-American commitment to invade the Balkans would make it militarily feasible for Turkey to enter the war[42]—British air squadrons were just enough to enrage the Germans but not enough to guarantee Turkey against invasion. Menemencioğlu thus categorically ruled out any halfway house: Turkey would never be content to play a passive role by furnishing air bases; nor would it "remain on the side line and make faces at the Germans."[43] But Turkey could not actively enter the war unless the British and the Americans could provide adequate protection by their presence in the Balkans. It was an all or nothing proposition.

Although Eden had taken pains to persuade Molotov of the value of a "two bites on the cherry" approach to Turkish entry into the war, believing this to be a kindness to the Turks, it was not so perceived by Menemencioğlu. Professor Esmer has explained that when the British demanded the use of Turkish airfields, as a first step, Menemencioğlu saw this as an attempt to have the second step, Turkish entry into war, come as the result of an attack from the Axis. In this way the British would not seem to have pushed the Turks and would be less responsible for their protec-

[42] In personal interviews with the author, former President İnönü, as well as Cevat Açıkalın and Feridun Cemal Erkin, have confirmed the thesis that an Allied landing in the Balkans had become by this time the *sine qua non* of direct Turkish military participation in war. The evidence is clear that the Americans did not want such a campaign; see *Strategic Planning*, pp. 132-33. It is unclear as to whether Churchill did or not. But there is reason to believe that the Turks urgently wanted the Western Allies to open their Second Front in the Balkans and that, had they done so, the entire Turkish calculation of self-interest would probably have changed from a balance in favor of neutrality to one in favor of fighting.

[43] The Chargé in Ankara (Kelley) to the President, the Secretary of State, and the Under-Secretary of State (Stettinius), Ankara, November 10, 1948, in *Foreign Relations: The Conferences at Cairo and Tehran*, pp. 174-75.

tion. Esmer, for his part, still describes this phase of British policy, as being "senseless and cruel."[44]

What the Turks appear to have feared even more than the unavailability of Anglo-American aid, in the event of their belligerency, was a surfeit of "assistance" from the Soviet Union. It especially annoyed Eden that he had to listen to lengthy discourses on Turkish perception of Russia's Balkan ambitions which seemed to him little more than echoes of Axis propaganda.[45] Menemencioğlu's arguments against the policy of unconditional surrender also appeared this way.[46] Eden had gone to give Menemencioğlu advice, not to receive it; but the Turkish Foreign Minister seemed not to be hearing the Foreign Secretary. Eden telegraphed Churchill during the meetings:

> We had a long, tough day. My persuasions were the less effective as both the Foreign Minister and Açıkalın seemed to be particularly deaf. . . . No one can be so deaf as a Turk who does not wish to be persuaded.[47]

[44] Ahmet Şükrü Esmer in a personal interview with the author. Aydemir, *The Second Man*, p. 264, n. 2, comments critically on what might have happened had the Turks granted the Allies Turkish air bases and access through the Straits: "No document has been published about whether the Soviets had intention of using the Turkish Straits and naval and air bases as an ally if Turkey had entered the war as a full-fledged warrior. But had Turkey entered the war and the Soviets created such a *fait accompli*, I think that the Allies would not have been able to prevent it, because they were not in full control of the Mediterranean and the Aegean. In case of such an event, Turkish-Soviet relations would present complications which are inestimable even now." This parallels Menemencioğlu's own thinking at the time. As Mrs. Nermin Streater informed the author, and as Menemencioğlu's own memoirs bear out, the Turkish Foreign Minister was afraid to grant the British bases, believing that the Russians would undoubtedly demand similar prerogatives.

[45] *Foreign Relations: The Conferences at Cairo and Tehran*, pp. 166, 175.

[46] *Ibid.*, p. 166.   [47] Eden, *The Reckoning*, p. 485.

Eden states that the basic weakness of the Turkish position was that they suspected that the British had made "some deal" with the Russians.[48] He was quite correct, as subsequent research has shown. The Turks did, in fact, perceive Eden to be repeating "exactly" the Russian demands at the Moscow Conference.[49] In their discussions Menemencioğlu very quickly concluded that Eden was doing the bidding of the Soviet Union. "I was not slow," he writes, "in becoming convinced that it was at the instigation of the Russians that M. Eden . . . insisted in Cairo on the precipitous entry of Turkey into the war."[50] On one occasion, Menemencioğlu openly accused Eden of acting as a spokesman not only for Britain but for Russia as well.[51] Eden replied that Menemencioğlu would do well to "face facts . . . Britain was an ally of Turkey but she was also an ally of Russia."[52] This was scarcely a winning argument and made the Turks all the more unwilling to accept British requests.

Menemencioğlu was quite candid in regard to his apprehensions about Russian ambitions, particularly in regard to the Balkan nations and Eastern Europe. He let these concerns become known to the British Foreign Secretary by continually asking him questions concerning Russian intentions. Menemencioğlu admits, without apology, that these

[48] *Ibid.*, pp. 485-86. Eden writes: "The strength of the Turkish position lay in their doubts about Soviet intentions after the war. They feared the growth of Soviet power and that we and the United States would then be far away and unwilling to help them." Despite the secret Anglo-Soviet-American protocol that he himself had signed, Eden goes on to say "the weakness of their [the Turks'] position was an unfounded suspicion that there had been some deal between us and the Russians. . . ."

[49] Esmer in *Turkish Foreign Policy*, p. 160.

[50] *Menemencioğlu Manuscript*, pp. 278-79.

[51] *Foreign Relations: The Conferences at Cairo and Tehran*, p. 181.

[52] Esmer, *Turkish Foreign Policy*, p. 161, suggests that Eden's "irritation" with Menemencioğlu at this point helped to create the unproductive tone of the meeting. In his account, Esmer, as does the author of the present study, makes use of the unpublished memoirs of Michel Sokolnicki.

questions "were in truth very indiscreet."[53] Menemen-cioğlu's eagerness to learn about decisions at Moscow particularly centered on the fate of Poland to which he reverted repeatedly. At one point the Turkish Foreign Minister asked Eden point-blank: "What do you intend to do with Poland?" Eden "became furious," and retorted, "What business is it of yours?" Menemencioğlu replied heatedly, "For us, Poland is the *pierre de touche*."[54]

Eden, in his efforts to compel a change in Turkish policy, even embarked on the counterproductive strategy of threatening the Turks with the Russians, pointing out "the unenviable position in which Turkey would find itself vis-a-vis the Russians in the event it declined to meet British wishes."[55] Eden thus actually did what Churchill had thought about doing at Adana. The Prime Minister, at that time, had told Harry Hopkins he "intended to take the line" that if the Turks were "recalcitrant" he "could not undertake to control the Russians regarding the Dardanelles."[56] As we saw, Churchill was much softer. At the conclusion of their last conference, Eden, in an apparent attempt to end his talks with Menemencioğlu on a cordial note, inquired as to what the Turkish Foreign Minister would advise him to report to Prime Minister Churchill. Menemencioğlu responded, "Pray tell M. Churchill for us to think back to Adana and to reread the document which he gave to us one morning. I am certain that he will understand."[57] Menemencioğlu did promise to submit the Allied requests to his government for its consideration.

His failure to win over Menemencioğlu would not have

[53] *Menemencioğlu Manuscript*, p. 275.

[54] Perhaps the phrase in English which most nearly corresponds to the intent of *pierre de touche* is "proof of the pudding." This exchange is reported in the unpublished memoirs of Michel Sokolnicki and was told to the wartime Polish Ambassador in Ankara by the Turkish Foreign Minister himself.

[55] *Foreign Relations: The Conferences at Cairo and Tehran*, p. 166

[56] Sherwood, *Roosevelt and Hopkins*, p. 683.

[57] *Menemencioğlu Manuscript*, p. 276.

been particularly surprising to Eden had he better understood the basis of Turkish policy, which was to safeguard
now and in the postwar era, first, the independence of Turkey and, second, the independence of the Balkans, if at all
possible. The Turks were not interested in fighting the
Germans. They had no desire to weaken themselves unnec-
essarily, believing it essential to build up and conserve their
strength for a possible future confrontation with a victorious Soviet Union. As already suggested, they suspected the
Russians of wanting the Turks to waste their resources in a
battle with Germany so as to make them, later, more vulnerable to Soviet pressures and designs. They had no territorial ambitions in the Balkans and no national animosity
toward Germany, which had at least respected the essentials
of their neutrality and territorial integrity during the
period of Axis ascendance. If they were to fight, it would
be to protect their present and future position against their
only perceived enemy: the Russians. They were prepared to
go to war to help the British and Americans take the
Balkans ahead of the Russians. But, as Menemencioğlu put
it bluntly to Eden at Cairo, they were not interested in help-
ing to aid "the establishment of Russia in Rumania and
Bulgaria"[58] nor in becoming a route by which Soviet troops
could enter the Eastern Mediterranean. Given these fixed
policy commitments, it did not help the Allied cause to
threaten Turkey with the possibility of Soviet expansionism: it was already the basic assumption in all Turkish
calculations. Nor was it productive to hold out the possibility that, if they were to cooperate with Moscow now,
Russia would be more restrained in their future demands
toward the Turks. This was to stretch Turkish credulity
beyond the breaking point. Eden thus had neither carrot
nor stick with which to confront Menemencioğlu.

Not surprisingly, on November 15, Menemencioğlu called
on Ambassador Hugessen "to inform him that Turkey had

[58] *Turkish Foreign Policy*, p. 161.

rejected England's proposals."[59] Reluctantly, Hugessen pointed out to the Turkish Foreign Minister that it would be difficult, if not impossible, for Britain under the circumstances to justify the continuation of arms shipments to Turkey.[60]

THE NEW TURKISH STRATEGY: A TACTICAL SHIFT

At Cairo, the record reveals, much of the Turkish effort to avoid being forced into the war was centered on an effort to persuade Eden that premature Turkish entry would serve only the interests of the Russians and that these interests would prove to be inimical not only to Turkey, but to the Western Allies, as well. This effort, at least insofar as convincing Eden was concerned, failed dismally. Thereafter, Turkish strategy appears to have undergone a change. No longer did the Turks attempt to warn the Western Allies of future Russian designs on Eastern Europe. They now concentrated on purely logistical and military-tactical arguments to resist Allied demands while leaving their perceptions of the Soviet threat quietly in the background. They

[59] *Ibid.*, p. 160. Although Turkey said no to the Allies at this time, there is evidence that İnönü was already thinking ahead to a time when he might no longer be able to resist Allied pressures. Aydemir in his biography cites—neither confirming nor denying it—an account of a meeting in mid-November between İnönü and a delegation from the Congress of the Turkish Historical Society at which İnönü is reported to have told them: "The day is very close. The Turkish nation is about to enter the war for the interests of the nation. Our national interests dictate this. You are teachers. You will spread to the four corners of the country. You will help the country get accustomed to this hardship from now on. Turkey will enter this war"; Aydemir, *The Second Man*, p. 135.

[60] Memorandum by Mr. [Foy D.] Kohler of the Division of Near Eastern Affairs, *Foreign Relations: The Conferences at Cairo and Tehran*, pp. 180-82; "Plainly, if the Turks did not use the weapons which were being provided to them against the Germans," Hugessen had said at Cairo, "the Soviets could only believe they were intended for use against the Russians."

seem to have agreed that the British and Americans were not prepared to accept their counsel or their reasoning in this respect.

On the evening of November 13, three days after his return to Ankara, Menemencioğlu launched into the new strategy in a conversation with Ambassador Steinhardt.[61] Reporting to him on his Cairo talks, he listed his disagreements with Eden in eight points which, the Foreign Minister argued, militated in favor of continued Turkish neutrality. All eight are military in nature. Together, they form a kind of plea against the British effort to push Turkey into war. Not a word is said about the Soviet menace or about postwar settlements in the Balkans. As Menemencioğlu gave them to Steinhardt, the eight points were:

(1) The Turkish Government prefers to discuss Turkey's entry into the war rather than the mere granting of air bases as in its opinion the granting of air bases would inevitably involve Turkey's entrance into the war.

(2) Eden, although proposing action by Turkey tantamount to entry into the war, failed to indicate what if any assistance the Turks might expect from the Allies.

(3) The Turkish Army is not equipped for offensive action and . . . must anticipate the devastation of İstanbul and İzmir . . . its railroad system paralyzed . . . with the resultant demoralization of the transportation system leading to starvation. . . .

(4) The readiness of the Turks to sanction Turkey's entry into the war has been adversely affected by the failure of the British to send adequate forces to take over and hold the islands in the Aegean.

(5) In the absence of strong Allied forces in or immediately available to Turkey, particularly aviation, the Turkish Government must consider the probability of a vio-

[61] The Ambassador in Turkey (Steinhardt) to the President, the Secretary of State, and the Under-Secretary of State (Stettinius), Ankara, November 14, 1943, *ibid.*, pp. 190-92.

lent Axis reaction to the granting of air bases. . . . Should the Germans desire an easy victory to restore their prestige the foregoing probability would become a certainty.

(6) The request of Eden that Turkey grant air bases or enter the war prior to December 3 affords insufficient time to make the necessary military preparations and to prepare public opinion.

(7) It was unreasonable for Eden to ask for air bases or for Turkey's entrance into the war without at least a partial disclosure of Allied military plans in respect of the Near East and the Balkans.

(8) There would not be the slightest hesitation on the part of the Turkish Government to enter the war were Anglo-American forces to land in the Balkans as this would imply the availability of adequate Allied forces to support Turkey.[62]

This shift in Turkish strategy—from an emphasis on the political dangers of premature entry to one on purely military concerns—was apparently accepted at face value by Ambassador Steinhardt. On November 15, Soviet Ambassador Vinogradov, in Ankara, confided in Steinhardt that he had not attempted to see Menemencioğlu since the latter's return to Ankara because he thought it preferable to let the British Ambassador try to find out alone whether political or military considerations were primarily responsible for holding the Turks back from the fighting.[63] Steinhardt

[62] *Ibid.*, pp. 190-91.

[63] *Ibid.*, p. 200. Hugessen had apparently reported to Vinogradov that Turkish obduracy was based primarily on political considerations, namely, fear of Soviet motives and aspirations, particularly in the Balkans which, Hugessen told Vinogradov, the "Turks look upon in somewhat the same light as the British look upon the low countries." *Ibid.*, pp. 193-94. Although this report of the British Ambassador's statement comes at third hand, from Steinhardt via Vinogradov, it appears substantially accurate. Ambassador Hugessen confirmed to the author that, throughout this period, he had "the closest possible working relationship with 'Vino,'" meeting with him for dinner at least

gathered the impression that Vinogradov had been explicitly ordered to stay out of the Anglo-Turkish talks unless the Turks approached him first. It fell to Steinhardt, drawing on his recent conversation with Menemencioğlu, to convey to Vinogradov that the Turks had already received what they needed by way of assurances as a result of the Moscow Conference but were hesitating to comply with Allied demands for military reasons.[64]

This is significant because Steinhardt had, by this time, already received a full account of the Cairo discussions from Hugessen which clearly revealed the predominance of political over military concerns in Turkish thinking. Yet Steinhardt appears to have been ready not only to accept the new Turkish line put to him, but anxious to convey it to the Soviet Ambassador. The probable reason for this is not difficult to deduce. The position of the United States throughout the war—as most recently evidenced at Moscow—had been one of reluctant agreement to put pressure on Turkey to force it into the war.[65] Cevat Açıkalın states that Stein-

once a week. It seems plausible that Hugessen would have given Vinogradov a full and accurate account of the Cairo meeting. (Sir Hughe Knatchbull-Hugessen in a personal interview with the author.)

[64] The Ambassador in Turkey (Steinhardt) to the President, the Secretary of State, and the Under-Secretary (Stettinius), Ankara, November 16, 1943, *Foreign Relations: The Conferences at Cairo and Tehran*, pp. 119-20.

[65] Averell Harriman, as U.S. Ambassador to Moscow, had been one of the relatively few advocates of a truly hard U.S. line toward Turkey—perhaps because his posting led him to put much weight on Russian feelings in the matter. The United States, he urged, should "immediately intensify in the most realistic manner" its pressure on the Turks; Memorandum by the Assistant Secretary of War (McCloy), based on a conversation with Harriman, Cairo, November 21st? [sic], 1943, *ibid.*, p. 266; "We should," Harriman said, "apply at least as much pressure as Eden had recently done with some success"; *ibid.* General George C. Marshall, on the other hand, noted that "the U.S.S.R. evidently wants Turkey into the war as a cold-blooded proposition. The Soviets definitely want something, and we should find out what it is"; Joint Chiefs of Staff Minutes, Meeting of the President with the Joint

hardt placed no pressure on the Turks during this period to enter the war.[66] At the same time, the United States was anxious that Turkish recalcitrance be interpreted to Russia as inoffensively as possible. The new Turkish line, in its emphasis on fear of German military power and the weakness of the Allies in the Eastern Mediterranean, was far more accommodating of the American position than had been the hard anti-Soviet political line pursued at Cairo. Cevat Açıkalın confirms that Turkey, at this point, deliberately selected the purely military argument as the one more likely to bolster its neutrality.[67] Once Turkish policy-makers

---

Chiefs of Staff, November 28, 1943, *ibid.*, p. 481. Neither view, however, prevailed with the President who simply concluded that he "did not have the conscience to urge the Turks to go into the war," although he was not prepared to disrupt Allied unity nor cause offense to the Russians either; *ibid.*, p. 480. The result was a U.S. policy at this time of somewhat nominal adhesion to the tripartite position adopted at Moscow.

[66] Cevat Açıkalın in a personal interview with the author.

[67] Açıkalın, in an interview, indicated that this was a purely tactical shift. In fact, the political concern over Russian intentions was still more important in Turkish thinking than the still real but lesser fears of German military capacity. Açıkalın revealed that in the third week of November 1943, approximately ten days after Menemencioğlu had returned from Cairo, he had called upon Vinogradov at his Foreign Minister's behest. "Look," Açıkalın said to the Russian Ambassador, "the Germans have 17 fresh divisions in Bulgaria." Vinogradov interrupted: "Fifteen." "Alright," Açıkalın continued. "You want us to come into the war." Vinogradov nodded. "Well in that case, we are ready and willing to fight, *but* only in Bulgaria and only if you or the British or the Americans fight alongside of us." Açıkalın reports that Vinogradov became ecstatic repeating several times, "Good, good." Not a week had gone by, Açıkalın claims, before the Russian Ambassador returned, this time with a dour expression. "Russia can handle Bulgaria alone," he told Açıkalın. "Turkey must fight, but only in Greece; that is where she can be of greatest use, particularly to Turkey's ally, Great Britain." "What if our capital were to be occupied by the Germans as reprisal?" Açıkalın now asked. "Well," Vinogradov said reassuringly, "do not worry, we shall come and help you." Açıkalın reports that at this point he rose from his chair and said, "That, Sir, is exactly what we do not want." Cevat Açıkalın in a personal interview with the

had decided that the Americans had joined the British in placing close relations with Russia above skepticism over Russian intentions, they thereafter spoke only of military preparedness and the inadequacy of Turkish defenses, no longer of the dangers of Soviet expansionism.

The Americans accepted this as at least a convenient, if not entirely convincing argument. It served to give weight to American reluctance to become embroiled in a British campaign in the Eastern Mediterranean, and it was the one argument for leaving Turkey alone which least offended the Russians. On November 20, as the President was en route to the Tehran Conference, Secretary Hull informed him that the Turks had decided in principle to enter the war but that military considerations, primarily those concerning defense against a German attack, were preventing them from taking actual steps.[68] He also told Roosevelt that Anglo-Turkish military talks had revealed a wide divergence on estimated Axis strength. Hull suggested that this divergence reflected the self-interest of both parties and indicated that Steinhardt believed a compromise could be reached on the amount of further military assistance required to enable Turkey to withstand the Axis.

On the afternoon of November 16, Menemencioğlu appeared before the parliamenatry group of the CHP. He presented a formal report of his discussions in Cairo, requested on behalf of the government the right to declare war against the Axis if necessary, but above all, reaffirmed his, the President's, and Prime Minister's intention to keep Turkey out of the war if possible. The caucus began at 5:30 P.M. and did not end until 3:00 A.M., nine and one-half hours later.

---

author. The incident was used by the Turks to confirm two suspicions: that the Russians wanted Bulgaria for themselves and that they would use Turkish entry into the war as an excuse to insist that Soviet troops be given passage through Turkey.

[68] The Secretary of State to the President, Washington, D.C., November 20, 1943, *Foreign Relations: The Conferences at Cairo and Tehran*, p. 261.

To this day, what was said on this occasion has been kept secret, although we know a heated and sometimes acrimonious debate ensued.[69] Menemencioğlu claims that, during this session, he assumed an important role in obtaining approval of the government's motion to accept British demands.[70] He also indicates that the motion included the condition that Turkey enter the war *only* after the Turkish army had received "a minimum of materiel necessary to permit them to resist the enemy sufficiently."[71] Menemencioğlu immediately transmitted this decision to the British Ambassador, stating that the decision in principle to enter the war had been taken and that it only remained to determine the timing of Turkey's intervention. Menemencioğlu told him that if Britain were to furnish sufficient supplies, it would be Britain that would fix the time. If on the other hand, British deliveries were slow or insufficient, then it would be Turkey, and Turkey alone, that would make the choice of when to enter the war.[72] Menemencioğlu also told Hugessen that the Turkish Government had set still another condition on its entry. Turkey would not enter the war until specific plans had been drawn up for the cooperation of Turkish and Western Allied forces in the Balkans.[73] İnönü would emphasize this at his Cairo meeting with Churchill and Roosevelt.

[69] Kâzım Özalp in a personal interview with the author. Özalp indicated that factions did form during this momentous debate and one was openly pro-Axis.

[70] *Menemencioğlu Manuscript*, p. 283.

[71] *Ibid.*

[72] *Ibid.*, pp. 283-84; also, Hugessen, *Diplomat in Peace and War*, p. 196.

[73] Erkin, *Turkish-Russian Relations*, pp. 247-48, suggests that this second condition, posing the principle of Turko-Anglo-American military cooperation in the Balkans, was of great importance. Although the Turks had sought this all along, after November 16, 1943, it became a matter of official Turkish policy that Turkey's belligerence could only take place as part of a coordinated and cooperative effort in the Balkans by the Western Allies.

EIGHT

PRESSURES ON TURKEY AT
THE SUMMIT: MEETINGS OF
HEADS OF GOVERNMENT

THE FIRST CAIRO CONFERENCE: A BRIEF HANDSHAKE

BY November 1943, the time had come for the Americans
and the British to ask their Soviet allies just what they intended for Europe in the postwar era. Thus Churchill and
Roosevelt traveled to Cairo and Tehran, attended by their
staffs that altogether numbered over 500 persons.

The President and the Prime Minister had desperately
wanted to touch base with Stalin and had offered to travel
to meet him.[1] The Soviet Premier's insistence upon Tehran
caused Roosevelt particular difficulties, however. Tehran
was so far from Washington that Roosevelt feared he might
not be able to continue to fulfill the domestic obligations
of the presidency. In the course of a lengthy correspondence,
Roosevelt suggested a number of alternatives including
Ankara, but to no avail. Stalin insisted on remaining near
the battlefront.[2]

[1] See, e.g., President Roosevelt and Prime Minister Churchill to Marshal Stalin, Quebec, August 18, 1943, *Foreign Relations: The Conferences at Cairo and Tehran*, pp. 20-21.

[2] Roosevelt expressed his concerns regarding Tehran in several messages to Stalin: "Personally, my only hesitation is the place but only
because it is a bit further away from Washington than I had counted
on. My Congress will be in session at that time and, under our constitution, I must act on legislation within ten days. In other words, I
must receive documents and return them to the Congress within ten
days and Teheran makes this a rather grave risk if the flying weather
is bad"; President Roosevelt to Marshal Stalin, Washington, D.C., September 9, 1943, *ibid.*, p. 24; also, President Roosevelt to Marshal Stalin,
Washington, D.C., October 14, 1943, *ibid.*, pp. 31-32. For Stalin's insist-

Churchill did not mind traveling to Tehran but had first wanted to meet the President alone in Cairo. Churchill conceived of the preliminary meeting with the President, now referred to as the First Cairo Conference, as a final opportunity to coordinate Anglo-American strategies, that is, to bring strategy closer to his thinking, particularly as regards the Eastern Mediterranean. But the President apparently had had enough of the Prime Minister's pleading and decided to put Chiang Kai-shek and if possible V. M. Molotov between them. Without telling Churchill, he invited both to Cairo. Plainly, Roosevelt was anxious not to give offense to Stalin by seeming to gang up on the Soviet leader.[3] Churchill did not accept these tidings happily.[4]

What Churchill had feared, eventually occurred. Roosevelt used their precious four days in Cairo, November 22-26, 1943, to confer not with Churchill or the British Imperial Staff but with Chiang. Roosevelt "took an exaggerated view of the Indian-Chinese sphere," Churchill writes, with the result that the "Chinese business occupied first instead of last place in Cairo."[5] The fact is that the President may well have kept himself deliberately too busy to confer with Churchill. In any event, Churchill "amazed" Eden with the patience he displayed in courting Roosevelt. "W. [Winston] had to play the role of courtier and seize opportunities as and when they arose."[6] But when the President promised

---

ence upon remaining near the front, Marshal Stalin to President Roosevelt and Prime Minister Churchill, Moscow, August 24, 1943, *ibid.*, p. 22; also, Marshal Stalin to President Roosevelt, Moscow, October 19, 1943, *ibid.*, pp. 33-34.

[3] Churchill, *Closing the Ring*, p. 319.

[4] For the Prime Minister's grave "misgivings," Prime Minister Churchill to President Roosevelt, London, November 12, 1943, *Foreign Relations: The Conferences at Cairo and Tehran*, pp. 81-82. "I thought . . . the British and American Staffs would have 'Many meetings' before being joined by the Russians or Chinese," Churchill wrote. "I still regard this as absolutely essential. . . ."; also, Churchill, *Closing the Ring*, pp. 317-18.

[5] *Ibid.*, p. 328.   [6] Eden, *The Reckoning*, p. 491.

Chiang to undertake an amphibious operation in the Bay of Bengal with what would have to have been the very landing craft that Churchill had wanted for operations in the Aegean, Churchill could no longer remain acquiescent. "This would have cramped projects," he wrote.[7] On November 29, he registered his dissent in a statement addressed to the Combined Chiefs of Staff. Churchill eventually prevailed upon Roosevelt to withdraw his commitment to Chiang.[8] But these were not happy days for Churchill. Therefore, as a result of accident or design, the First Cairo Conference failed to be a conference in anything but name. It was a stopping point, a handshake more than anything else.

THE TEHRAN CONFERENCE: THE SOVIET REVERSAL

Tehran had been taken from pro-Nazi elements only a few months before the conference convened and was still full of sympathizers. Thus first thoughts upon arrival naturally turned to matters of personal safety.[9] This permitted Stalin an opportunity for an important maneuver. Within minutes after Roosevelt had arrived, Stalin sent messages to the President urging him to leave the American Embassy and move into the Russian one. The British and the Russian embassies were situated near each other, but the American Embassy was a good mile away and would necessitate the President's driving through the narrow streets of Tehran several times a day. Roosevelt accepted Stalin's invitation.

There was another advantage besides security in having the Americans and the Russians occupy the same compound. Not only did it protect the President from possible assassination, it also isolated him from Winston S. Churchill. The President went to Tehran hoping to gain Stalin's confidence and believed that he could accomplish this by

[7] Churchill, *Closing the Ring*, p. 328.
[8] *Ibid.* "Even so," Churchill wrote, "many complications arose."
[9] *Ibid.*, pp. 342-43.

convincing the Russian Premier that he desired the opening of the Second Front as much as Stalin himself. Roosevelt almost certainly feared that this would be made more difficult by the importunities of Churchill who undoubtedly would insist upon a hearing for his Balkan and Turkish plans. The outcome of all this was that Roosevelt and Stalin did have several private meetings[10] and, in pursuing the logic of their own ends, came to the decision that it would not be to their advantage to have the Turks fight.

At Tehran, Roosevelt became even more determined to keep the Turks from making a thrust at the Dodecanese lest they thereby involve American might in a Greek campaign and thus threaten preparations for the cross-Channel attack. The President's intention to oppose Churchill's "Turkish plans" became evident the first day of the Tehran Conference, November 28, in a meeting with the Joint Chiefs on the morning of the day the first plenary meeting was scheduled. Roosevelt pelted his Chiefs of Staff with questions dealing with British policy toward Turkey.[11] "Suppose we can get the Turks in, what then," he asked. General Marshall responded by warning that much equipment and possibly much manpower would have to be diverted to the Aegean. Marshall also discounted the British claim that the Turks could alone hold the Straits against the Germans.[12] Admiral King declared that the United States would almost inevitably get involved in the Dodecanese if Turkey entered the war. The President, apparently con-

[10] Churchill was upset by this and sought out the Russian Premier alone as well. "The fact that the President was in private contact with Marshal Stalin and dwelling at the Soviet Embassy, and that he had avoided ever seeing me alone since we left Cairo . . . led me to seek a direct personal interview with Stalin. I felt that the Russian leader was not deriving a true impression of the British attitude"; *ibid.*, p. 375.

[11] Meeting of the President with the Joint Chiefs of Staff, November 28, 1943, Joint Chiefs of Staff Minutes, *Foreign Relations: The Conferences at Cairo and Tehran*, pp. 476-82 at p. 478.

[12] *Ibid.*, pp. 478-79.

vinced, eventually renounced all intentions of forcing the Turks to fight.[13]

The President carried through on this during the first plenary meeting and seems to have personally condoned operation footdrag. After promising to urge the President of Turkey to bring his country into the war, Roosevelt declared that "if he were in the Turkish President's place, he would demand such a price in planes, tanks and equipment that to grant the request would indefinitely postpone OVERLORD."[14] When Churchill suggested that it might be possible to divert some forces and supplies from the Pacific theater to the Eastern Mediterranean,[15] Roosevelt declared that "it was absolutely impossible to withdraw any landing craft from that area."[16] So important did Harry Hopkins consider this that he wrote out a statement for the record in longhand. No landing craft were available for an attack on Rhodes, he wrote, and even if any were to become available, no decision had been taken as to where they might best be used. Moreover, no promise of an amphibious landing, "implied or otherwise" was to be made to the Turks.[17]

These tensions between the British and the Americans were not new. Ever since Casablanca, the Americans had disagreed with the British on the question of the feasibility of Turkey's entrance into the war. What was striking at Tehran was that Stalin now reversed the position his Foreign Minister had so strongly taken at the Moscow Conference and, instead of supporting the British on the question

[13] *Ibid.*, p. 480. The minutes read: "The President said that he did not have the conscience to urge the Turks to go into the war."

[14] First Plenary Meeting, November 28, 1943, Bohlen Minutes, *ibid.*, pp. 487-97 at p. 496.

[15] Tripartite Luncheon Meeting, December 1, 1943, Bohlen Minutes, *ibid.*, p. 587.

[16] *Ibid.*

[17] *Ibid.*; also, Sherwood, *Roosevelt and Hopkins*, p. 793, and pp. 794-95 for a facsimile of Hopkins' note.

of Turkey, now sided with the Americans.[18] In the intervening months the Soviets had made more progress in the field and perhaps had by now concluded that Turkish help was likely to be more trouble than it was worth. This conclusion is borne out by Stalin's concern as to where the Turks would fight and who would fight alongside them: in particular, whether Anglo-American forces would go into Bulgaria with the Turks. Indeed, Stalin asked this directly of Churchill and the President. Churchill responded in the affirmative.[19] Using Roosevelt's line of argument with Churchill, Marshal Stalin admonished Churchill that it was not wise to scatter British and the American forces.[20] He suggested that it would be better to concentrate all efforts upon OVERLORD and to consider the other campaigns as diversionary. Stalin added that he had lost hope of Turkey entering the war and was now certain that it would not, "in spite of all the pressure that might be exerted."[21]

In Moscow, Molotov had sought Turkish entry into the war with tenacious insistence. He did not at that time wish to entertain any doubts concerning Turkish compliance. Turkey could not readily refuse a three-power request, he had argued. That was on October 28. Now on November 28, he and Stalin were suggesting that the Turks could not be brought into the war no matter what the Allies threat-

[18] First Plenary Meeting, November 28, 1943, Combined Chiefs of Staff Minutes, *Foreign Relations: The Conferences at Cairo and Tehran*, pp. 497-508 at p. 507. William Hardy McNeill, *America, Britain, and Russia: Their Co-operation and Conflict 1941-1946*, Vol. III, *Survey of International Affairs 1939-1946*, Arnold J. Toynbee (ed.) (London: Oxford University Press for the Royal Institute of International Affairs, 1953), p. 353, states, "Churchill's hope of finding Stalin sympathetic to his Turkish and Aegean projects was rudely blasted"; Churchill, moreover, lost whatever support he may have received from Roosevelt regarding Turkish entry once the President realized that Stalin was now tending to oppose it.

[19] *Foreign Relations: The Conferences at Cairo and Tehran*, p. 505.
[20] *Ibid.*   [21] *Ibid.*

ened and that, in any event, Turkish entry would act as a strategic liability to the Allied cause.[22]

Despite this new Soviet-American combination, Churchill continued to pursue his Mediterranean and Balkan policies, but to no avail. Turkey's entry into the war would divert nine Bulgarian divisions and leave the Germans alone to

[22] Several reasons have been offered to explain why the Soviets reversed themselves on the question of Turkish entry into the war. McNeill, *America, Britain, and Russia*, p. 352., n. 2, for example, writes, "What may have led Stalin to give up Turkey and the Mediterranean in favour of Overlord cannot be said with any certainty. He may have been thinking in terms of post-war spheres of influence; but if so, one must wonder why the same calculation had not dominated his behaviour in October and November when he had seemed willing and anxious to bring Anglo-American troops into the Balkans in support of Turkey's belligerency. Stalin's changed attitude may reflect some internal debate within the Russian Government, but Deane . . . says that he was convinced that the change in the Russian 'line' was simply a deliberate manoeuvre to 'throw the opposition off balance.'" McNeill concludes by suggesting that "This may well be the correct explanation," although it hardly helps to explain Molotov's own driving interest in the question at the Moscow Conference. Erkin, *Turkish-Russian Relations*, pp. 242-43, suggests that the Soviets wanted the Turks to enter the war when it seemed likely that they would be defeated or at least devastated by the Germans. "A victorious Turkey," however, Erkin writes, "would be a great restraint on the Russians in the realization of their plans in the Balkans." Aydemir, *The Second Man*, pp. 267-68, concurs in this: at Moscow the Soviets wanted Turkey to enter the war under orders, "to join the war by virtue of an order and not to become a voice at the peace conference." Aydemir argues that "the Soviets were intimidated by İnönü's demand first that he be given an 'equal voice' at the Cairo meeting and secondly that Turkey be treated as a powerful nation after the war." Aydemir suggests that it was this latter condition that influenced Stalin's position. Russian sources published thus far do not shed new light on this; see, e.g., Vladimir P. Potemkin, *Politika Umirotvoreniia Agressorov I Borba Sovetkogo Soiuza Za Mir* (Moscow: Gozpolitizdat, 1946); S. Belinkov and I. Vasilev, *O Turetskom 'Neitralitete Vo Vremia Vtoroi Mirovoi Voiny* (Moscow: Gozpolitizdat, 1952); Nikolaevich Ivanov Lev, *Ocherki Mezhdunarodnykh Otnoshenii v Period Vtoroi Mirovoi Voiny, 1939-1945* (Moscow: Adka. Nauk SSSR, 1958). Perhaps Riker's size principle entered into Stalin's calculations; see below, Chap. xv, pp. 323-25.

fight in Yugoslavia and Greece. Britain, he assured Stalin, "had no ambitious interests in the Balkans but merely wanted to pin down the German Divisions there."[23] In his difficult position, Churchill even hit upon the surprising tactic of playing on Soviet ambitions. If the Allies could agree on an ultimatum to Turkey, he would personally point out to the Turks that their refusal to accept "would have very serious political and territorial consequences for Turkey particularly in regard to the future status of the straits."[24] It was actually Churchill, not Stalin, who threatened at Tehran to alter the status of the Straits after the war as reprisal against the Turks. Later he noted that such a large land mass as Russia "deserved" access to a warm-water port and suggested that this could be settled agreeably "as between friends."[25] Since Churchill had raised the

[23] Second Plenary Meeting, November 29, 1943, Bohlen Minutes, *Foreign Relations: The Conferences at Cairo and Tehran*, pp. 533-40 at p. 536. Churchill, *Closing the Ring*, p. 355, reports that Stalin responded to his question on whether or not the Turks should be made to enter the war by saying, "'I am all in favour of trying again. We ought to take them by the scruff of the neck if necessary.'" The Combined Chiefs of Staff Minutes of the first plenary meeting, however, register the opposite and cite Stalin as having indicated that Turkey could not be brought in by force; *Foreign Relations: The Conferences at Cairo and Tehran*, p. 505, esp. n. 5; Churchill's version so completely contradicts the rest of Stalin's utterances at Tehran as to suggest a misunderstanding on the Prime Minister's part. It may also represent his hopeful wishing. Interestingly, Professor Esmer in his recent study cites Churchill's version as the authentic one while agreeing that Stalin opposed an Anglo-American expedition. Esmer in *Turkish Foreign Policy*, p. 162, suggests that at this time, "Russia could not dwell on the subject of Turkey's neutrality. What it could do was to lessen the aid being sent to Turkey, to prevent Turkey and the Westerners [Britain and the United States] from embarking upon the Balkans with large forces." Esmer offers no explanation of why Stalin had reversed himself. Molotov, after all, did dwell on the subject of Turkish neutrality at Moscow.

[24] *Foreign Relations: The Conferences at Cairo and Tehran*, p. 536.

[25] Roosevelt-Churchill-Stalin Luncheon Meeting, November 30, 1943, Bohlen Minutes, *ibid.*, pp. 565-68 at p. 566.

question, Stalin obligingly inquired about the regime of the Dardanelles. "Since England no longer objected," Stalin said, "it would be well to relax that regime." Churchill agreed but warned against trying to alter the status of the regime while still attempting to bring the Turks into the war. "No need to hurry . . . ," Stalin replied, indicating that he was "merely" interested in discussing the question in general terms.[26] Churchill also said they all hoped to see Russian ships on every sea. "Lord Curzon," Stalin reminded the Prime Minister, "had had other ideas."[27]

The Churchillian tactics in this respect were, and remain, puzzling. Even Eden, at lunch with Molotov on November 30, confessed that he simply did not know what the Prime Minister meant.[28] It seems plausible, however, that the British leader was deliberately whetting Soviet appetites in order to be able to threaten the Turks with being abandoned to these Russian aspirations in the event they failed to enter the war. It was not a strong hand Churchill was playing at Tehran, and his tactics reflect it.

In a limited way, however, the tactic succeeded. At the December 1 luncheon meeting of the three leaders, Churchill again urged that they address one last, joint summons, stressing, on the one hand, the advantage to the Turks of sitting at the peace table alongside them and on the other, the penalties of failure.[29] In the event such a final demand was made and again rebuffed, Churchill said that he personally would "favor a change in the regime of the Straits," and the British "would wash their hands of Turkey, both now and at the peace table."[30] True, Churchill did not succeed in getting an ultimatum issued, but the three leaders

[26] *Ibid.* [27] *Ibid.*, p. 567.

[28] Hopkins-Eden-Molotov Luncheon Meeting, November 30, 1943, Ware Minutes, *ibid.*, pp. 568-75. Asked by Molotov to enlarge on what Churchill had meant by his remarks concerning the future of the Straits, Eden replied, "Frankly, I do not know."

[29] Tripartite Luncheon Meeting, December 1, 1943, Bohlen Minutes, *ibid.*, pp. 585-93 esp. pp. 587-89.

[30] *Ibid.*, p. 588.

did agree, at least, to a joint message inviting İnönü to an immediate meeting in Cairo. For lack of any other agreement in regard to the Turks, the three agreed to endorse the idea of conferring directly with the President of Turkey. Whatever pleasure Churchill may have derived from having the door to Turkish entry thus kept ajar, he was too perspicacious to entertain high hopes. The Turks would perform in their "usual behavior," he prophesied. "If you suggested a small move they [would say] they preferred the big. And if you suggested the big, they [would say] they were not ready."[31] Coming from such a master at political maneuvers, this was high if begrudging recognition.

THE SECOND CAIRO CONFERENCE:
İNÖNÜ CONFRONTS ROOSEVELT AND CHURCHILL

Turkish leaders, observing the Tehran Conference from Ankara, were filled with concern. They feared that Stalin would try to maneuver the Western Allies into forcing Turkey into the war ill-prepared. This would expose the Turks to German retaliation from which the Russians would then be in a position to "save" them.

Whether or not this is a correct interpretation of Stalin's tactics at Tehran, it is certainly true that, to the Turks, this fear of Russia was their central reality.[32] They believed, on the one hand, that it was essentially the Russians who, through the British, were trying to push them into the war and that it was also the Russians who, again through pressure on the British, were responsible for the delays in supplying them with adequate amounts of war equipment. The conclusion reached by Turkish leaders was that Russia, for

[31] *Ibid.*, p. 589.

[32] For a discussion of the Turkish state of mind at this time, see Esmer in *Turkish Foreign Policy*, p. 161. He suggests that the Turks believed that Russia wanted to see Turkey weakened: he also says that at this time "the anxiety was born in Turkey that Britain had aligned its policies with those of Russia. . . ." As we have seen, however, this anxiety hit the Turks much earlier.

its own reasons, wanted the Turks to fight, to fight at the end of a very short leash held by the Russians.[33] This view is not entirely borne out by the evidence, which suggests that the British had reasons of their own for wanting the Turks to fight, and that the British and the Americans had problems and priorities of their own which affected the rate of supplies delivered to Turkey. But the Turks, from their uncomfortable and exposed position, saw the Russians as the moving evil genius behind all their difficulties and the British, increasingly, and the Americans to a lesser extent, as the unwitting tools of Soviet imperial designs.

When İnönü received his invitation to meet Roosevelt and Churchill in Cairo, a heated discussion took place in the Council of Ministers as to how to respond.[34] Eventually, it was decided that it was in Turkey's self-interest to reply in the affirmative, providing that "a free exchange of views would take place" and that their meeting would not be merely "a matter of communicating a decision already taken at Tehran between the British, Americans and Russians. . . ."[35] These were the conditions that İnönü set on his acceptance which Roosevelt, at least, happily granted. "Please tell the President that I am especially happy to have the occasion to talk with him," Roosevelt instructed Steinhardt after he had received İnönü's qualified acceptance. "Assure him that he is being invited to a 'free discussion as between equals.' "[36] İnönü had thus successfully asserted his right to negotiate freely and on equal terms.

In agreeing to go to Cairo, İnönü was aware that he still had some room to maneuver. He suspected that, whatever

[33] Erkin, *Turkish-Russian Relations*, pp. 256-57.

[34] *Menemencioğlu Manuscript*, p. 276.

[35] *Ibid.*; also, Papers on Arrangements for the Conference with Turkish Officials, Attachment 2, the British Ambassador in Turkey (Knatchbull-Hugessen) to the British Embassy in Egypt, Ankara, December 2, 1943, *Foreign Relations: The Conferences at Cairo and Tehran*, p. 663.

[36] The President to the Ambassador in Turkey (Steinhardt), Cairo, December 2, 1943, *ibid.*, p. 664.

the Western Allies were saying in public to appease the Russians, President Roosevelt and his advisers were becoming, if possible, even less interested in the whole Aegean theater. İnönü also told the author that he suspected that Roosevelt was becoming increasingly preoccupied with the Far East.[37] Moreover, he believed that the Americans would hesitate to commit Turkey to war if it seemed that this would subject Turkish populations to devastation. Thus İnönü prepared to depart.

Five planes came to Adana to transport the party of Turkish officials to Cairo. Two returned carrying only luggage. İnönü decided to leave his entire military staff home. Not one Turkish soldier, with the exception of the President's aide-de-camp, Celal Üner, came to Cairo. This enabled İnönü to say, as he was often to do, that he was not in a position to discuss military technicalities,[38] a useful delaying tactic in the negotiations.[39]

President İnönü and his party left Ankara secretly in mid-afternoon of Friday, December 3. Some eighteen hours later they arrived in Adana, where to İnönü's surprise, not only Roosevelt's plane commanded by Major John Boettiger, the

[37] Former President İnönü informed the author that his talks with the U.S. President confirmed these suspicions. İnönü claims that by this time, Roosevelt had developed "an obsession" concerning China and the war against the Japanese. (In a personal interview.)

[38] Unlike the Adana Conference where a substantial number of Turkish officials were on hand to negotiate with Churchill and his party, only a few Turks attended the Cairo Conference. Besides İnönü there were Menemencioğlu, Açıkalın, Celal Üner, Selim Sarper, Turgut Menemencioğlu, and Sadi Kavur, the Foreign Minister's *chef de Cabinet*. They comprised the entire Turkish delegation. With them, traveling in the same party, flew British Ambassador Hugessen and the Soviet Ambassador in Ankara, Vinogradov. The latter went to Cairo at İnönü's personal invitation but without instructions from his government. It had been expected that, in addition to Vinogradov, the Soviets would be represented by Vyshinsky.

[39] This despite the fact that İnönü was himself a distinguished general who told the author that he always applied military and strategic reasoning to the problems of foreign policy.

President's son-in-law, but also Churchill's plane commanded by his son, Captain Randolph Churchill, awaited
him. This at once created a small crisis of protocol which
Foreign Minister Menemencioğlu resolved by ruling that
İnönü would travel in Roosevelt's plane, while he would
travel in Churchill's. It did not escape Turkish attention
that the incident was symbolic of a certain lack of coordination in the policies of the British and the Americans toward
them.

It was not only a wild divergence between the British
and the Americans that İnönü and Menemencioğlu detected. There was, upon arrival in Cairo, clear evidence of
a much wider gulf between the British and the Americans
on the one hand and the Soviets. As Menemencioğlu noted
in sizing up the situation, "from the first day, we saw that
M. Vyshinsky shone by his absence." The absence of the
Soviet Deputy Commissar for Foreign Affairs, Menemencioğlu felt certain, "could not be fortuitous."[40] It tended to
confirm the Turks in their suspicion that the Russians
wanted Turkey to fight, but as dependents of the Russians,
not with strong support from the Western Allies and especially not alongside a strong Anglo-American expeditionary

[40] *Menemencioğlu Manuscript*, p. 278; United States Ambassador
Steinhardt put an entirely different gloss on Vyshinsky's absence. He
wrote that Vyshinsky telephoned him to say that his delay in arriving
at the conference "had been in no sense intentional but had resulted
from his instructions arriving in Algiers a few hours after he had left
there for Naples. . . ." Vyshinsky told Steinhardt that he left for Cairo
immediately after he received his orders to attend the meeting with
Turkish officials. He did not arrive, however, until after the Turkish
delegation had left; the Ambassador in Turkey (Steinhardt) to the
Chief, Division of Near Eastern Affairs (Alling), Ankara, December 24,
1943, *Foreign Relations: The Conferences at Cairo and Tehran*, pp.
858-59. Steinhardt seems to have believed the Deputy Commissar for
Foreign Affairs. He reports that Vyshinsky was "quite satisfied" with
what had transpired at the conference. "What impressed me more than
anything else," Steinhardt wrote, was that Vyshinsky did not expect
the Turks to enter the war by December 31 or even by February 15.
Vyshinsky indicated that the Russians were not averse to this.

force in the Balkans.[41] It seemed, therefore, quite comprehensible to the Turks that the Russians were not interested in this meeting, the purpose of which, as the Turks saw it, was an Anglo-American attempt to prepare them for a deliberate entry into the war, possibly alongside the Western Allies.

The Turkish tactics at Cairo, as they emerge from the records, interviews, and memoirs, were to conserve strength by remaining neutral for as long as possible, to obtain the maximum of armaments, and thus to prepare themselves for any eventuality posed by the Russians. They were prepared to go to war if the Allies insisted, but only if they supplied the necessary arms and, above all, sent a British or Anglo-American force into the Balkans.

The obvious way to advance these tactics, which had not changed much since Adana, would have been to argue that the Soviets must now be seen as the principal future threat to Europe, and that Turkish military power would be built up and conserved for the day, rapidly approaching, when Turkey, the United Kingdom, and the United States must send a strong force into the tottering Balkans to head off the communist menace. The confrontation between Eden and Menemencioğlu at Cairo had, however, convinced Turkish leaders that this candid approach had lost all utility. The author asked President İnönü whether he tried to caution Roosevelt against Stalin. İnönü indicated he had not, declaring,

> I did fear that the British and the Americans would enter into an agreement with the Russians which would sacrifice the interests of Turkey but I could not say this. The Americans and the British were Allies of Russia and they were still fighting. I had to watch events closely and then find the correct diplomatic methods to deal with them.[42]

[41] Cevat Açıkalın in a personal interview with the author.
[42] Former President İsmet İnönü in a personal interview with the author.

The records of these talks thus show that the Turks at Cairo no longer made any effort to communicate their premonitions regarding Soviet postwar intentions to the Western Powers.[43] It had become clear to the Turks that talk of Russian imperialist Bolshevism was not the politic line to pursue with Roosevelt and Churchill. Even when the British opened up this topic, they refused to be drawn in. Instead, the Turks embarked on a less candid policy, but one which they had reason to believe could be more likely to succeed, if not with the British then at least with the Americans. They emphasized the inadequacy of the military aid received so far and their general vulnerability to German attack. They made steep demands for more equipment which they claimed was essential to protect them against their German menace, but which could only have been provided by the Anglo-Americans at the cost of undercutting preparations for the cross-Channel attack. And they played for "a little more time."[44] They no longer tried to argue

[43] Eden was not unaware of the change that had come over the Turks; "fear of Russia was not mentioned again," he writes; "instead the Turks based their reluctance on their country's military unpreparedness . . ."; Eden, *The Reckoning*, p. 497. Foreign Minister Menemencioğlu tells of only one exception—and that was off the record, during an informal meeting he and İnönü had with Roosevelt. The U.S. President was, he reports, telling the two Turkish leaders of the favorable impressions gained of Stalin at Tehran: "his spirit of moderation and his sincere desire to continue to cooperate with the Americans and the British after the victory." Roosevelt went on to tell them that Soviet truculence had been the result of an inferiority complex, brought on by Western intrigues against the Russian revolution, but that Soviet success in the war had wiped out this inferiority complex, making the Russian leaders "once again men like we are." Menemencioğlu wrote that he told Roosevelt: "Mr. President, I know very well what you believe, but I implore you to beware of the superiority complex which may follow." *Menemencioğlu Manuscript*, p. 282.

[44] Numan Menemencioğlu, *ibid.*, p. 299, reports that during one of the meetings, when İnönü seemed to be succeeding in his efforts to convince Roosevelt that the Turks needed "a little more time," Eden leaned forward and whispered in a voice loud enough to be heard by the Turkish translator: "But Mr. President, you forget we have a com-

their case for a policy which would have geared Turkey's role primarily to the need for containing Soviet expansionism. Instead, İnönü and Menemencioğlu now focused entirely on the other argument open to them: they should not be pushed away from neutrality until their military build-up would give them reasonable assurance against German retaliation.[45]

The Turks stated this case with great care and eloquence. İnönü argued that only 4 per cent of the supplies on the Adana lists had actually been delivered.[46] "Practical considerations" would have to be met before the Turks could afford to antagonize the Germans, who might be losing but still had the angry power of a wounded animal.[47] First,

---

mitment vis-à-vis the Russians." This remark further convinced the Turkish Foreign Minister that the British, to curry favor with the Russians, had agreed to try to force the Turks into the war. The Russian leaders, Menemencioğlu comments, "wanted to see us in the war in order to have one day the possibility of delivering us from the invader."

[45] Turgut Menemencioğlu suggests that the Turks were ready to go to war on three conditions: "first, a common strategic theater of cooperation . . . the Allies should abandon their stale military front in Italy and land in the Balkans, for example, in the Adriatic, so that Turkish and Allied armies could cooperate; second, a minimum amount of defense equipment, especially anti-aircraft for the defense of big cities . . . should be promised to Turkey; third, a month or two should be allowed for the Turkish government to prepare its public opinion and to come to agreements with interested governments that were not represented in the Cairo Conference—meaning the Soviet Union whose agreement Turkey wanted to have explicitly." (In personal correspondence with the author.) There is little doubt that had these conditions been fulfilled the Turks would have entered the war, but, equally, no doubts exist that the Turks in making them knew that they would not be met.

[46] Erkin, *Turkish-Russian Relations*, p. 253.

[47] In this the Turks were reinforced by Ambassador von Papen, who, kept informed of British-Turkish air base negotiations by the spy Moyzich (Cicero), warned that "the day on which Ankara would decide to put Turkish bases at the disposition of the Allies, these would immediately be destroyed and Germany would take offensive action

Turkey's "minimum essential requirements" must be met and the three nations must draw up a joint "plan of preparation."[48] İnönü vowed that his country "had mobilized everything she had, even matériel dating from the middle ages."[49] But many Turkish requests had been deferred, promised deliveries had not been made, some supplies were obsolete, and the available equipment was woefully inadequate. Moreover, there had been no joint planning to draw up what İnönü called "the plan of collaboration"—a joint strategy for a Balkan campaign which would ensure, as İnönü described it, effective coordination between Allied and Turkish units. "What would suit Turkey best would be that she should fight side by side with British and American contingents in her own part of the world," İnönü declared.[50]

It was "naturally essential" that such matters be studied by experts and the Turkish President expressed the hope that this would be studied "on a big basis." Such joint planning would, however, take time. Of course, given their global perspective, President Roosevelt and Mr. Churchill could simply assign Turkey a specific role in a campaign developed by their Chiefs of Staff. But there did not appear to be a plan, or if there was, it had not been disclosed to the Turks. Turkey, İnönü declared, could not accept "a demand to come into the war blindly, with a statement that when Turkey had entered the war she would be told what her part was to be."[51] This approach worked admirably in maintaining the split between Roosevelt and Churchill.[52]

---

against Turkey even before the first British airplane touched the soil of İzmir"; reported by Erkin, *ibid.*, p. 258.

[48] First Tripartite Meeting of Heads of Government, December 4, 1943, United States-United Kingdom Agreed Minutes, *Foreign Relations: The Conferences at Cairo and Tehran*, pp. 690-98 esp. pp. 695-96.

[49] *Ibid.*   [50] *Ibid.*   [51] *Ibid.*, p. 696.

[52] Cevat Açıkalın has suggested that the Turks understood the nature of the differences separating the President and Prime Minister. (In a personal interview with the author.)

Roosevelt was plainly sympathetic and was generally impressed by Turkish arguments and entreaties. The Turks were careful to encourage him in this by their deft handling of British attempts to disqualify their position, which sometimes involved their juggling the issues at hand. Menemencioğlu argued at one point, for example, that trucks at the rate of 300 a month had been promised at Adana, while actual deliveries had been little more than half of that number. The Adana lists had become a "dead letter" while "deliveries did in fact represent a very small proportion of promises."[53] Eden countered by stating that he could not accept these figures, and General Henry Maitland Wilson went on to list the substantial amounts of equipment that had in fact been delivered to Turkey. Hopkins was surprised by the amounts mentioned by Wilson and said so.[54] On such occasions, the Turks would leap ahead by shifting to various other arguments including the fact that there had been no "general plan."[55] This was typical: if Churchill, for example, offered to increase the number of British technicans working on Turkish air bases, İnönü or Menemencioğlu stated that it was essential that in the period of preparation the Germans should not be provoked by the presence of British personnel.[56] The result was that Roosevelt sided with the Turks and not Churchill. "If he were a Turk," the President told Churchill on December 4, 1943, he would require more aid than Britain had thus far supplied before he would bring Turkey into the war.[57]

At the end of the discussions, İnönü also argued that Tur-

---

[53] Hopkins-Eden-Menemencioğlu Meeting, December 5, 1943, United States-United Kingdom Agreed Minutes, *Foreign Relations: The Conferences at Cairo and Tehran*, pp. 726-33 at p. 729.

[54] *Ibid.*   [55] *Ibid.*, p. 730.

[56] Third Tripartite Meeting of Heads of Government, December 6, 1943, United States-United Kingdom Agreed Minutes, *ibid.*, pp. 740-47.

[57] Quadripartite Dinner Meeting, December 4, 1943, *ibid.*, p. 698; Roosevelt did attempt at the end of the conference to convince İnönü that it would be in Turkish interests to enter the war, but halfheartedly; *ibid.*, e.g., pp. 741, 745.

key could not go to war because ". . . the period of mud in Thrace had not yet begun."[58] Another reason was that one class of military recruits had been discharged while a new class was still being trained. Such matters were of a technical nature, İnönü explained, and he "could not go further into detail" since his military experts "were not with him."[59] He also stated that entry into the war was a serious political decision. If he made it he would be going, he stated, against the decision of the Grand National Assembly, although he knew, of course, that he had already received authorization in principle from his parliamentary caucus. Perhaps, sensing that such arguments were subterfuge and that the German threat was not the one uppermost in Turkish minds, Churchill at various earlier times tried to interest Turkish leaders in speculation about Russia. He also urged the Turks to throw in their lot with the Allies now, so that

> Turkey would sit on the Bench with Russia. . . . Turkey's great friend and Ally felt it would be a pity if she now missed her chance. In a few months, perhaps six, German resistance might be broken, and Turkey, if she did not accept the invitation now, might then find herself alone, not on the Bench, but wandering about in Court. It would be dangerous if Turkey now missed the chance. . . . There were risks either way. But if Turkey associated herself with the United Nations she would also be associated with Russia, one of the strongest military Powers in the world, if not the strongest, at any rate in Europe and Asia.[60]

Such remarks reflect Churchill's awareness of the Turkish fear of Russia, but, needless to add, his policies on how to

[58] Churchill-İnönü Meeting, December 7, 1943, United Kingdom Minutes, *ibid.*, pp. 751-56 at p. 753.

[59] *Ibid.*

[60] On December 4, 1943, and in plenary session, Churchill declared that he had "always realized that Turkey's preoccupation was Russia"; *ibid.*, p. 694. For the quotation, *ibid.*, p. 691.

deal with these fears were vastly different from those of İnönü and Menemencioğlu. In any event, as already mentioned, the Turks were no longer prepared to discuss the matter.

İnönü and his subordinates had their fixed views of Soviet postwar intentions. They did not believe that those intentions would be altered in the least, but would be only bolstered by Turkey's entry into the war.[61] This was their view and it determined their policy. But, as we have now seen, at Cairo it never appeared on the surface of their arguments. Instead they stuck doggedly to the position that they were, in principle, committed to entering the war on the Allied side, but were as yet too vulnerable to German counterattack to be anything but an Allied liability. As matters now stood, the Turkish Foreign Minister insisted, "the vital centers of Turkey such as İstanbul, İzmit, İzmir, Ankara, and the coal basin of Zonguldak would immediately be annihilated by the Germans. . . ."[62] The Turkish population, he said, "would not understand being precipitated into the war solely in order to receive blows without having the possibility itself of rendering some [blows] in return."[63] Churchill was not impressed with this argument, for he felt the Turks simply were dragging their feet;[64] but

[61] *Menemencioğlu Manuscript*, p. 279; Erkin, *Turkish-Russian Relations*, p. 258.

[62] *Menemencioğlu Manuscript*, p. 284.

[63] *Ibid.*

[64] At the conclusion of the Second Tripartite Meeting of the Heads of Government, December 5, 1943, *Foreign Relations: The Conferences at Cairo and Tehran*, p. 718, Churchill declared that "the discussion seemed to have got into a difficult circle. We [the Allies] were satisfied that no preparation could be effective without the introduction of personnel while the Turks refused the introduction of personnel because of the danger of provoking Germany." Earlier, Churchill had forcefully tried to place the blame for Turkey's unpreparedness on operation footdrag, that is, on Turkish shoulders: "The Turks had not taken full advantage of the school and tuition opportunities offered to them and this had affected their ability to absorb the available material." Air Marshal Sholto Douglas supported Churchill by pointing out that

Roosevelt understood: the Turks simply did not "want to be caught with their pants down."[65]

Despite Roosevelt's manifest understanding of the Turkish position, there were moments of high-pressured persuasion during the conference. The conversations between Eden and Menemencioğlu, with Harry Hopkins trying to act as mediator, were particularly rancorous.[66] At one point Hopkins felt constrained to remind Menemencioğlu that the Allies really had Turkish interests at heart. They wanted Turkey to fight "willingly and whole-heartedly," even ". . . if she could not have all she wanted." He reminded the Turkish Foreign Minister that the Allies, too, did not have all they wanted when they entered the war. The "main point," Hopkins declared, "was that the war had reached a critical stage." Thousands of Allied nationals might be saved if Turkey entered the war this year, but he added, "Turkish participation might not be useful very long after that date [January 1]." Hopkins declared that Allied military and political opinion was unanimous in believing that Turkish belligerence could shorten the war. He conceded, however, that, "In the last analysis a country went to war in its own interests." He assured Menemencioğlu that everything possible would be done to minimize the dangers to Turkey, but noted that "if . . . discussions were prolonged about the adequacy of material, etc., Turkey's entry would be futile."[67]

Such attempts to persuade the Turks were, however, far milder than Eden had wanted and the Turks had feared. The ultimate result was to postpone decision and to give the Turks further time. No ultimatum was issued. Instead, a military mission was to go to Ankara for further discussion—including the thorny question of infiltrating British personnel—on preparing the air bases. The Turks did agree

---

70 aircraft including 54 Hurricanes and 18 Beauforts "had been waiting ready for the Turks to collect for the last three months."

65 *Ibid.*, p. 713.   66 *Ibid.*, pp. 726-33.   67 *Ibid.*, p. 732.

"in principle" to enter the war, but this was a hollow concession. They reserved the right to decide for themselves, by February 15, 1944, whether they would consent to Allied use of the air bases. They made no commitment to permit British technicians and officers to man the bases. It was agreed that formulation of the joint military plan of collaboration was to begin, but this could be only tentative at best, while the Turks were still considering the "general political repercussions" of entry. If, after due consideration, the response was negative, the Allies agreed that there would be no recriminations and that the Allies would not issue blame on the Turks.[68] However, the equipment intended for Turkey would have to be sent elsewhere.[69]

At the final meeting of the three heads of government, Hopkins urged Roosevelt, in a note, to meet İnönü for a few minutes privately in a last attempt to urge him to be ready to go to war by February 15, 1944.[70] Roosevelt waited until the appropriate moment and adjourned the meeting. He requested İnönü to remain in order to say good-bye.[71] Roosevelt "expressed the hope that Turkey would join the United Nations actively to defeat the Axis by February 15th." İnönü responded, "I was willing to soften my requirements to enter the war but not to relinquish them." Roosevelt "agreed that everything had to be done to protect

[68] This summary is from Esmer in *Turkish Foreign Policy*, p. 164.

[69] These generous sentiments seem not to have been shared by the British and not by Eden in particular. At the parting between the British and the Turks, Eden reminded İnönü and Menemencioğlu that "if the time for Turkey's entry into the war came and went, it was inevitable that the spirit of the Alliance would be affected"; *Foreign Relations: The Conferences at Cairo and Tehran*, p. 754.

[70] For a facsimile of this note, the President's Special Assistant (Hopkins) to the President, Cairo, December 6 (?) [sic], 1943, *ibid.*, p. 817.

[71] An editor's footnote, *ibid.*, p. 747, n. 13, in regard to Hopkins' suggestion that the President ask İnönü to be ready for war by February 15, states "No record has been found showing whether Roosevelt did so." İnönü and Turgut Menemencioğlu, who translated for İnönü and Roosevelt on this occasion, assure the author that Roosevelt did ask to see the President alone.

Turkey." Roosevelt also told İnönü that "he [Roosevelt] completely understood my [İnönü's] reluctance to bring Turkey into the war."[72] Erkin reports that President İnönü took the occasion of this private meeting to thank Roosevelt "warmly for having occupied with so much grace and skill the role of intermediary and moderator between the opposing theses that separated the British and the Turks."[73] Well he might have been thankful, for Roosevelt had, by his lukewarm support of Eden and Churchill and his receptivity to the Turkish argument, given the Turks yet another reprieve. Menemencioğlu wrote that in the American President's company "the state of my soul had been touched by grace."[74] To Churchill and Eden it was a grace that passed all understanding.

Nevertheless, it appears that the Turkish leaders were not wholly unresponsive to Churchill's arguments. No doubt, İnönü and his Foreign Minister both realized that there was something to the Britishers' claim that the best way to deal with the Russians was to come into the war as a full-fledged member of the Alliance. Germany, they saw, had lost the war and Turkish security now lay in the hands of the Allies. If Turkey did nothing to help in the war, how could its leaders expect the British and the Americans to do anything for their security vis-à-vis Russia after it was over? There is evidence that at Cairo İnönü took this advice from the Western Allies seriously, if not to the degree of rushing into war, then at least to the extent of contemplating the establishment of a dialogue with the Soviet Union, whether prefatory to an actual entry into the war or not.

For all its inconclusiveness, the Second Cairo Conference

[72] The substance of this conversation was related to the author by former President İsmet İnönü in a personal interview; Turgut Menemencioğlu has written of this meeting: "Roosevelt made friendly gestures and used a very reassuring tone." (In a letter to the author, September 30, 1969.)

[73] Erkin, *Turkish-Russian Relations*, pp. 254-55.

[74] *Menemencioğlu Manuscript*, p. 281.

is important in another respect. It marks the beginning of the end of the first phase, and the beginning of the second phase of Turkish wartime diplomacy. The first phase was designed, essentially, to meet a military threat, from the Soviets as well as the Nazis; the second was an attempt to curb the political influence of Russia in Eastern Europe. The Second Cairo Conference marks the turning point in Turkish foreign policy from a wartime strategy designed to ward off military dangers to a policy directed toward the potential political conflicts during the final stages of the war and in the postwar world.

PART III
TURKEY'S EFFORTS TO
CONTAIN ALLIED VICTORY

NINE

A TIME OF ESTRANGEMENT

THE DETERIORATION OF ANGLO-TURKISH RELATIONS

A CROWD of thousands including Prime Minister Şükrü Saracoğlu, the Council of Ministers, most of the members of the Grand National Assembly, and a proportionate number of the Turkish bureaucracy jubilantly greeted İsmet İnönü upon his return to Ankara. One foreign diplomat remarked that it was as if "the Turks had returned from a peace conference as the victorious party."[1]

At a news conference called immediately upon his arrival, which carefully excluded Axis or pro-Axis newsmen, Menemencioğlu declared that they had indeed returned to Ankara extremely pleased.[2] He emphasized the significance of Turkish collaboration with the Allies which, he confided, was not always effective but "as we were able to see at Cairo, is nevertheless precious."[3] The Foreign Minister nodded in agreement when one journalist suggested that Turkey had entered the Allied camp without becoming a belligerent.[4] Another correspondent questioned the Foreign Minister on Turkey's relations with Russia. Menemencioğlu responded that the subject of Russia had been at the heart of the discussions in Cairo and that Turkish-Soviet relations emerged

[1] Personal interview with a member of the British diplomatic mission in Ankara during the latter part of the war who remains in government service and wishes to remain anonymous.

[2] *Hariciye Vekili Numan Menemencioğlu, Kahire mülâkatı münasebetile, Müttefik ve Türk gazetecilerine beyanatta bulundu (The Foreign Minister makes a declaration to the Turkish and Allied press about the Cairo Conference)* in *Ayın Tarihi*, Vol. 121 (January 1943), pp. 42-43.

[3] *Ibid.*, also *News Chronicle*, London, December 10, 1943.

[4] *Ibid.*

strengthened. Turkey's relations with the Soviet Union were thus almost as good as those with Great Britain.[5] This was true to the extent that İnönü and his Foreign Minister may have returned from Cairo willing, once more, to explore the possibility of a diplomatic understanding with the Russians. But the Turks were still extremely skeptical. Yet in a way Menemencioğlu's reply was valid. If Turkey's bonds with Russia were, at this point, almost as strong as those with Britain, Anglo-Turkish relations in the early months of 1944 were becoming increasingly strained.

As a result of the Cairo talks, the British sent a military mission to Ankara in early January headed by Air Marshal Linnell. The British came to negotiate arrangements for the preparation of Allied air bases, while the Turks' objective was to obtain more military supplies. The Linnell mission quickly became mired in the same difficulties as befell every British negotiating team sent to Turkey since Adana.

British efforts to talk about getting the air bases operational ran into a by now broadly familiar sequence of objections. The Turks complained that they were not privy to overall Anglo-American war strategy for the Eastern Mediterranean.[6] They estimated German strength at ten times the British intelligence figures and demanded no less than 500 Sherman tanks and 300 fighter planes and 180,000 tons of matériel immediately.[7] The Turks also claimed that the British were exaggerating the number of their personnel needed to prepare the bases while refusing to train Turks for the job.[8] Erkin's summation is:

> The imperceptible misunderstandings which had sprung up in the course of the conversations at Adana now became more precise and serious. The parties present

[5] *Ibid.*, also, *Manchester Guardian*, December 14, 1943.

[6] Feridun Cemal Erkin in a personal interview with the author.

[7] The Ambassador in Turkey (Steinhardt) to the Secretary of State, Ankara, January 18, 1944, *Foreign Relations*, 1944, v, 816-17; also, *The New York Times*, March 5, 1944.

[8] *Menemencioğlu Manuscript*, pp. 286-87.

did not even always speak the same language. The two
points of view were separated by a deep chasm.[9]

The long-standing apprehensions of the Turks were exacer-
bated by the tenor and direction of these negotiations. As
usual, cardinal among these was the fear that Britain and
Russia had secretly agreed that Eastern Europe would go to
the Russians in return for Soviet recognition of paramount
British interests in the western part of the Continent. Menemencioğlu, during the Linnell negotiations, hinted as much
in his complaint to Ambassador Steinhardt that "there must
be a political reason . . . for the British desire that Turkey
remain on the defensive after entering the war."[10] The
Turkish Foreign Minister was more explicit in his private
memoirs. He noted that the British had selected only southern locations for their bases, except for a small installation
at İzmit. Who or what was to protect the northeast and the
littoral of the Black Sea, he wondered. The answer, Menemencioğlu decided, was: the Russians. Once British bases
were established to strike at central Europe, would the Russians not want equal rights to attack the retreating Germans
in the Balkans? Menemencioğlu wrote that he had wondered whether the British were not deliberately confining
themselves to bases in the south of Turkey to leave room for
the Russians to use the north; he had wondered whether
they would not later "force his hand" vis-à-vis the Russians.
He records having felt that he might some day be in the
position of having to exclude Soviet aircraft from Turkish
soil, by force if necessary:

> The British, it is true, were going to establish them-
> selves solidly in the south. But why was the area in the
> north being left empty? Empty in preparation for what?
> I was tormented by these reflections. . . .[11]

9 Erkin, *Turkish-Russian Relations*, p. 255.
10 *Foreign Relations*, 1944, v, 816-17.
11 *Menemencioğlu Manuscript*, p. 287.

Again, these were not thoughts to be revealed openly, and so the negotiations bogged down in logistical detail, problems of personnel, and the other familiar issues.

The British suspected that Turkish obduracy was in part the result of their belief, partially confirmed in Cairo, that the Americans did not support the British position in these negotiations. The British military mission had not been in Ankara a week when the Department of State received an *aide-mémoire* from the British Embassy in Washington requesting that the United States "back up any representations that the British Ambassador in Ankara may make. . . ."[12] On January 8, 1944, Secretary of State Hull informed the President that the British intended to take the line that this was Turkey's last chance to join the war effort and that if they refused, the British Government would have to "reconsider its whole Turkish policy."[13] Hull recommended a different emphasis: that they authorize Steinhardt to "make it clear" to the Turks that the United States would welcome their active support in the war. But he advised against instructing Steinhardt to back up more stringent representations the British might make. Roosevelt consented to this and Steinhardt was so notified on January 11. Steinhardt proceeded as instructed and on January 14 made it "unmistakably clear" to Menemencioğlu that the United States desired the Turks in the war.[14] This effort was too general and halfhearted to make any difference to the stalled Linnell negotiations, and Linnell and his subordinates abruptly left Ankara on February 3. No reason for the hasty departure of the military mission was given to the

[12] Memorandum by the Secretary of State to President Roosevelt, Washington, D.C., January 8, 1944, *Foreign Relations*, 1944, v, 814.

[13] *Ibid.*

[14] The Ambassador in Turkey (Steinhardt) to the Secretary of State, Ankara, January 14, 1944, *ibid.*, pp. 815-16; also, the Secretary of State to the Ambassador in Turkey, Washington, D.C., January 11, 1944, *ibid.*, pp. 814-15.

Turkish Government in order to force it "to draw its own conclusions."[15]

In the discussions, the Turks had been most disturbed at never being able to induce the British to commit themselves concerning where and how and with what Allied troop support Turkish forces were to fight in the Balkans.[16] Indeed, they were never able to get the Allies to commit themselves to any kind of Balkan campaign. At Cairo, the Turkish Foreign Minister had again offered to bring the Turks into the war following any substantial Anglo-American invasion of the Balkans.[17] The demise of the Linnell mission brought the offer to the fore again. In his unpublished memoirs, Menemencioğlu recalls an encounter at a dinner in Ankara, early in January 1944, at which he offered to put in writing Turkey's commitment to enter the war thirty days after an invasion of the Balkans, or, he added, "even in the West."[18]

[15] The Ambassador in Turkey (Steinhardt) to the Secretary of State, Ankara, February 4, 1944, *ibid.*, pp. 817-18.

[16] Esmer in *Turkish Foreign Policy*, p. 167, writes: "As a result of the 'crisis of confidence' there was a thick curtain of mystery over the joint military plans and cooperation. This curtain was not lifted until after the end of the war. In fact, England and the United States were reluctant to give information about their plans to Turkey. Turkey showed that even a war in the Balkans, which was the only area in which Turkey would show any activity, was an issue upon which the three major nations could not come to definite agreement."

[17] Erkin, *Turkish-Russian Relations*, pp. 261-62.

[18] Erkin, *ibid.*, recounts being told of this by Menemencioğlu himself, but in his book omits the phrase "even in the West" which appears in the *Menemencioğlu Manuscript*, p. 292. Which version is the correct one is important historically because the question is, did Menemencioğlu commit Turkey to war on the condition that the Western Allies open the Second Front, regardless of where the attack came, either in the Balkans or Western Europe. Turgut Menemencioğlu, who acted as the official translator for the Turkish delegation at both Cairo meetings with Allied officials, in response, first affirms that Turkish policy at the end of 1943 was that only a landing of British or British and American forces in the Balkans would suffice to bring the Turks into the war. He suggests, however, that this was subject to evolution and that his uncle

Menemencioğlu noted, however, that Hugessen did not even bother to come by the next day as they had arranged to collect the written offer.[19] Soon thereafter the Linnell mission left Ankara and "little by little the British began to abstain from all cordiality and they no longer appeared even to see us, in order not to have to greet us."[20] Apparently the British had given up on the Turks, particularly, on Numan Menemencioğlu.

The departure of the British military mission marks the nadir in Anglo-Turkish relations during the war. Even Hugessen, who speaks little but praise of the Turks, notes that after the Linnell mission departed "a period of some difficulty followed, during which we made no attempt to conceal our disappointment."[21] The British also solicited

---

may well have used the phrase "even in the West" as a ruse to test Anglo-American intentions. He writes: "As the conversation with the British Ambassador took place over a month after the Cairo Conference and as by that time the possibility of a Second Front in spring became more realistic, an evolution of the original idea of military cooperation [between Turk and Anglo-American troops] in the same strategic theater may have been possible. I doubt this, but mention it as a possibility. It is also possible that the phrase was used as a kind of recrimination: 'You bring pressure on us but you are not ready to cooperate or assist us. We are not even sure that you will open a Second Front in time or alleviate the counter-thrust which will fall on us if we enter the war as of now. At least if that took place we might know your intentions and capabilities better. . . .'" Ambassador Menemencioğlu concludes, "These are hypothetical words to express some doubts which I know existed in my uncle's mind at the time." (In a letter to the author, Ankara, September 30, 1969.)

[19] *Menemencioğlu Manuscript*, p. 289.

[20] *Ibid.*, p. 290.

[21] Hugessen, *Diplomat in Peace and War*, p. 200; Irena Sokolnickia reports that the British Ambassador led a campaign to exclude Menemencioğlu from social events to which members of the British Embassy had been invited. Mrs. Sokolnickia reports that on several occasions, Hugessen approached her to request that she not invite the Turkish Foreign Minister to attend a dinner or a party which Hugessen was planning to attend. She claims that she habitually rejected such requests. Hugessen, however, denies that he ever made such requests or

American support in rebuking the Turks, especially Mene-mencioğlu, socially as well as diplomatically. On February 4, one day after the departure of the British military mission, Hull received a request from the British Government that Ambassador Steinhardt be instructed to keep his social relations with the Turks at minimum. Roosevelt agreed and Hull wired Steinhardt "to 'cool off' in your relations with the Turks. . . ."[22]

British and American arm shipments to Turkey ceased immediately. The British were so determined to sever ties with Turkey that they ordered a Turkish ship leaving Port Said, loaded with arms, to "discharge her cargo before sailing."[23] Lend-lease war deliveries also stopped, although the British carefully avoided suspending all commercial transactions lest the Turks retaliate by suspending chromite deliveries.

Years later, Cevat Açıkalın was to write of this period, "In the excited and passionate atmosphere of those times, there were many who raised critical voices about Turkey's attitude."[24] No voice was sharper than that of the *Times* of London. In two articles, both published in February 1944, the *Times* announced that Anglo-Turkish relations were "deadlocked" and "stagnated."[25] In an article entitled "Turkey and the Powers: Misgivings since the Cairo meeting," the *Times* declared that the British military mission had found Turkish demands "to be exaggerated and disproportionate with Turkish power of absorption. . . ." This in itself might not seem so bad, the *Times* reported, were it not for the factors that were creating "a *crise de confiance*."[26]

---

that there was ever a personal vendetta pursued by the British against Menemencioğlu. (In personal interviews with the author.)

[22] The Secretary of State to the Ambassador in Turkey (Steinhardt), Washington, D.C., February 7, 1944, *Foreign Relations*, 1944, V, 818.

[23] A. C. Edwards, "Impact of the War on Turkey."

[24] Cevat Açıkalın, "Turkey's International Relations."

[25] *Times*, London, February 9, 1944.

[26] *Ibid.*; Esmer, in *Turkish Foreign Policy*, pp. 165-67, also speaks of

In this connection the *Times* came as close as any printed source to admitting that the *crise de confiance* was due to the personal antagonism between Menemencioğlu and Eden as well as to the British comprehension of operation foot-drag. In regard to the antagonism, the Special Correspondent of the *Times* in Ankara stated that "the present trial . . . is due to misunderstandings and possibly to fits of ill temper. . . ." As for Turkish procrastination, the *Times* declared that although Turkey paid lip service to the Alliance, its leaders had no intention of fulfilling their obligations. Turkish arguments and demands were "mere subterfuges put forward to evade that issue." In a follow-up article, February 26, entitled "Hesitation in Ankara," the *Times* linked Turkish reluctance to come to the assistance of the Allies with its fear of the Soviet Union.[27] "Turkish suspicion and fear of Soviet Russia are as tenacious as are all suspicions and fears derived from inherited habit which cannot be rationally justified. . . ." The *Times* warned Turkey that if its leaders wished to play a significant role in Balkan affairs after the war, they had better placate the Russians and begin to cooperate with the Allies.

As might be expected, this deeply troubled the Turks. Sadak, in *Akşam,* published a series of editorials objecting to the *Times*' position on the grounds that it transformed the "sensitive issues" of foreign policy into "street politics."[28]

---

the period of March-June 1944 as one which involved a crisis of confidence between Turkey and Britain and places the blame squarely on the British.

[27] *Times,* London, February 26, 1944.

[28] An example of Sadak's comments after the first article in the *Times* is conveniently found in *Ayın Tarihi,* Vol. 123 (February 1944), pp. 27-29, i.e., "İngiltere ile Türkiye arasında görüş ayrılığı varımıdır?" ("Are there differences of views between England and Turkey"), Necmettin Sadak, *Akşam,* February 11, 1944; for an example of his writing after the second *Times* article appeared, "Şimdiye Kadar Kaç Defa Harbe Girecektik" ("How many times would we have entered the war up until now"), *Akşam,* February 29, 1944, as in *Ayın Tarihi,* Vol. 123 (Feb-

Admitting that the reports in the *Times* conveyed the impression of inside information, Sadak declared that they were "completely biased" and did not seem even "to believe in their own logic." To counter them, he voiced the usual line of Turkish arguments—insufficiency of arm deliveries from the West, the need to coordinate war strategy—and put the blame on Britain for the crisis of confidence. The Turks had remained steadfast in upholding the Alliance. The British had wavered in meeting their commitments. It was natural that people did not want to go to war, especially for nothing but cheap honors. Falih Rıfkı Atay took a similar approach.[29] The Turks knew what they were signing when they had entered into the agreement with Britain, but they did not wish to fight blindly. Atay conceded that there were strains in the Alliance. "An active alliance," he wrote, "will not sleep in the files in the basement where documents are kept." Thus Turkish public reaction to the articles in the *Times* was to downgrade the issue from a crisis of confidence into a squabble among partners, to staunchly uphold the role Turkey had played in the war, to place whatever blame there was squarely back on Britain's shoulders. But pressures on the Turkish Government were mounting.[30]

ruary 1944), pp. 41-43. There were no differences between what Sadak wrote after the first and second *Times* articles except that he became increasingly more bitter about the British wanting to force Turkey into the war; Esmer, in *Turkish Foreign Policy*, p. 166, refers to Sadak's February 29 editorial and quotes it as follows: ". . . the statements of the *Times* concerning the undefined benefits we are to gain at the end of the war if we enter it, and the cheap honors we will be deprived of if we do not enter it, have created neither enthusiasm nor fear in the Turkish public."

[29] Falih Rıfkı Atay, "Müttefikimiz İngiltere'de" ("Our ally is in England"), *Ulus*, February 18, 1944, as in *Ayın Tarihi*, Vol. 123 (February 1944), pp. 37-38.

[30] On February 8, 1944, one day before the first article in the *Times* appeared, Menemencioğlu told von Papen that "Turkey could not allow her relations with her British and American allies to get any worse"; von Papen, *Memoirs*, p. 521.

The *Times* had advised the Turks to show interest in working with the Russians. Menemencioğlu decided to do this.

MENEMENCIOĞLU APPROACHES THE RUSSIANS

While relations between Turkey and the British thus deteriorated, the Turks made another effort to sound out Soviet intentions and to explore the possibility of better relations with Russia as Roosevelt and Churchill had urged at the Cairo meeting. The Turkish Foreign Minister did this with grave doubts. The Russians, he felt, were simply lying low. He wrote,

> the Russians had manifested a total disinterest. They had even denied being the promoters of the British proposals. They did not want to disquiet Turkey, the insistence of their British allies appearing sufficient to achieve their goal. If [the Russians] were not wishing to disquiet the Turks, it must have been because they intended something very disquieting.[31]

Nevertheless, after Cairo, and at British urging to "establish an area of agreement in order to avoid becoming the object of Soviet hostilities during and after the war," Menemencioğlu decided to approach the Russian Government in the person of Soviet Ambassador Vinogradov and to suggest that their two governments negotiate a treaty guaranteeing the independence and neutrality of the Balkan States after the war. Menemencioğlu says that "such a treaty would have opened the door to an extensive collaboration between the two countries."[32] The Turkish Foreign Minister thus set out to discover Russia's intentions. "Turkey," Menemencioğlu told Vinogradov, "does not have to be the wall separating Britain from Russia but a path of union uniting these two

[31] *Menemencioğlu Manuscript*, pp. 290, 3g-4g; note the *Menemencioğlu Manuscript* includes an insert between pp. 290-91 which Menemencioğlu paginated with the symbols, 1g-5g.

[32] *Ibid.*, pp. 290, 2g.

countries which were already allied."[33] The Russian reply, according to Menemencioğlu, was that the Soviet Union considered itself in basic agreement with this, but that there remained "the grave obstacle" of Soviet involvement in a war in which Turkey continued to be a nonparticipant. If Turkey would agree "to erase this difference" by entering the war without delay, the Soviet Union would be prepared to conclude with her not only a limited treaty of consultation, but a general act of mutual assistance.[34]

With that, the exchanges ended. Menemencioğlu wrote that the twin specters of a still-powerful Germany at Turkish frontiers and of Soviet assistance that would undoubtedly take the form of defense forces which would never leave Turkish soil made him understand why the Russians had been so aloof at the Cairo talks. Obviously, the Soviets were not interested in Turkey's entering the war adequately armed and militarily supported by the Anglo-Americans. The Russians wanted the Turks in the war, but "mutually assisted" by Russia. Thus Menemencioğlu perceived his doubts to have been validated.

In any event, the approach to Russia had led only to a rebuff. It was criticized by one of the Foreign Minister's principal assistants as "technically counterproductive and unwise."[35] With Turkish-British relations "virtually at zero,"[36] Turkish-Soviet relations filled with foreboding, and Germany on the verge of collapse, Turkey entered the middle of 1944 uncomfortably isolated.[37] Diplomatic skill had spared it the ravages of war, but there was a feeling that the same diplomacy had ill-prepared Turkey for security in the approaching postwar era.

[33] *Ibid.* [34] *Ibid.*, pp. 290, 3g.
[35] Erkin, *Turkish-Russian Relations*, p. 281.
[36] *Ibid.*, p. 263. [37] *Ibid.*, p. 264.

TEN

THE SHIFT IN INTERNAL POLICY

INCREASING Allied victories, the diplomatic "freeze" imposed on Turkey by the United States and Britain, the discontinuance of military supplies from the West, the failure of negotiations with Russia, all these factors began to exert their irresistible pressures on the course of Turkish policies in the spring and summer of 1944. In Erkin's words:

> If Turkey were to decide to remain outside the war, British-Turkish harmony would be broken; Great Britain would perhaps no longer concern itself with Turkish affairs and Russia would be left completely free to take up its problems with Turkey in its own way.[1]

Ambassador Hugessen had put it to Saracoğlu that "very soon Turkey would have to choose between the alternatives of entering the war or finding itself all alone after the war."[2] Even the United States seemed to have joined the British in abjuring all responsibility for what happened to Turkey. During this period, therefore, the Turks began to modify their policies both internally and externally in order to placate the Allies. In order to appease the British and Americans, they repealed the *Varlık Vergisi* or tax on wealth which had deeply offended the sensibilities of the Western democracies; to win the favor of the Russians, they suppressed the Pan-Turanian movement which, among other things, had worked toward the liberation of Turkic ethnic groups within the Soviet Union.

[1] Erkin, *Turkish-Russian Relations*, p. 263.
[2] Esmer in *Turkish Foreign Policy*, p. 157.

230

THE VARLIK VERGISI

On November 11, 1942, the Turkish Grand National Assembly levied the *Varlık Vergisi*. Ostensibly, this tax was designed to force those individuals who were amassing large fortunes on account of the war to pay taxes commensurate with their returns.[3] It was also presumably designed to withdraw large amounts of money from circulation as a deflationary device. In proposing this legislation, Prime Minister Saracoğlu told the members of the Grand National Assembly that it was a tax designed to bear down on "people who had earned a lot of money during the war,"[4] such as merchants and property owners. He further explained that assessments would be made by local committees from which there could be no appeal except through the Assembly and that this would help to meet swollen government expenditures.[5]

From its inception, however, the law occasioned strong protests. During the actual debate in the Assembly, when it was passed, objections to the *Varlık Vergisi* were raised on the grounds that it was contrary to principles of law."[6]

[3] *Varlık Vergisi Hakkında Kanun* (Law on Tax on Wealth), Law No. 4305, effective November 11, 1942, is most conveniently found in *Düstur*, Üçüncü Tertip (Third Format), Vol. XXIV at p. 9; also, Türkiye Cumhuriyeti Başbakanlık. Neşriyat ve Müdevvenat Genel Müdürlüğü) (Office of the Prime Minister of the Turkish Republic. General Directorate of Press and Publications), *Resmî Gazete (Official Record)*, No. 5255, November 11, 1942 (Ankara: Devlet Matbaası, 1942); henceforth *Resmî Gazete*; T.B.M.M. Üyeleri için Bastırılmıştır (Publications for the Members of the Grand National Assembly), *Sicil-i Kavanin (Register of Laws)*, Vol. XXIII at p. 901; henceforth *Sicil-i Kavanin*.

[4] *T.B.M.M. Zabıt Ceridesi*, Sixth Assembly, Third Session, November 11, 1942, Vol. 28, p. 21; for debate on the *Varlık Vergisi*, pp. 14-29; for the text of the law, pp. 29-32.

[5] *Ibid.*, p. 22. Minister of Finance Fuat Ağralı, of course, delivered an address supporting the government's position; *ibid.*, pp. 24-25.

[6] *Ibid.*, p. 23; although Ali Râna Tarhan gave the government his support, he did express certain reservations which suggest that he had his doubts concerning the legality of the law.

The publicized purpose of the tax was to further social justice by taxing the rich. But, as Nadir Nadi has written, "according to a more specific explanation, which was whispered from ear to ear, or even at times declared out loud, a second objective of the tax was to free the market from the control of the minorities and open it to Turks."[7] Thus, he notes, "our Jewish, Greek Orthodox and Catholic citizens who were proud of being Turkish citizens had to sell out their property and wealth for nothing. . . ."[8] This view conveys a more accurate picture of the *Varlık Vergisi*.

The enforcement of the law was both discriminatory and repressive. On January 18, 1943, Ambassador Steinhardt, a member of the Jewish faith, reported that he could no longer doubt that the tax discriminated against minority groups, since the evidence was "irrefutable."[9] The local tax boards were applying the tax in an uniformly discriminatory way, so that it seemed evident that they had received their directives from the central government.

Stringent measures were taken against defaulters. Persons convicted of not paying the tax were subject to ninety days' imprisonment and confiscation of property. In February and March of 1943, the daily newspapers in İstanbul and Ankara announced that attempts to escape seizure or to spread "false propaganda" about the injustice of a personal assessment would subject guilty parties to deportation or hard labor. Citizens condemned to hard labor were first interned

[7] Nadi, *Opening in the Curtain*, p. 178. Despite the accuracy of Nadi's description of excesses of the tax, it should be noted his discussion seems essentially designed to embarrass İsmet İnönü.

[8] *Ibid.*

[9] The Ambassador in Turkey (Steinhardt) to the Secretary of State, Ankara, January 18, 1943, *Foreign Relations*, 1943, IV, 1,079-81. Local tax boards throughout Turkey divided profit-making enterprises into two categories, the "M" category for those of the Müslim faith and the "G" category, for *gayrimüslim*, or non-Muslim. Members of minority communities fell into the latter and were taxed at harsh, often prohibitive, rates; Geoffrey Lewis, *Turkey* (New York: Frederick A. Praeger, 1960), p. 117.

at Kadıköy, Haydar Paşa, Kartal, Pendik, or Maltepe and later sent to the labor camp at Aşkale, near Erzurum.[10] The interned received two and a half liras per day, half of which was immediately returned to the government against their debts, the remaining half being used for personal expenses, food, clothing, etc. Provisions were made to employ the families of men sent away. Approximately 4,000 were arrested in all.[11]

No procedure for appeal was established except that of direct petition to the Grand National Assembly. By January 15, 1943, 3,000 petitions had been filed.[12] The committee on petitions of the Assembly and the Ministry of Finance then announced that appeals would be considered only after full payment of the tax and that overcharges would be repaid.

By March 15, 1943, 300 people had been sent to the camp at Aşkale only 3 of whom bore Turkish names, the rest being Jewish, Greek, or Armenian. This pattern continued for the duration of the tax. Steinhardt informed the State Department that even Turkish officials, including the Prime Minister, recognized that injustices were occurring.[13] Nadi and Faik Ökte, who was in charge of collecting the revenues of the *Varlık Vergisi* in İstanbul, confirm this.[14] Both individuals assert that although the tax hit the minorities, the government "did not touch the landowners, who owned textile factories, commission collectors, who did business

---

[10] These events received wide attention in Britain. On January 28, 1944, the *Times* reported, "The authorities are proceeding with the punishment of defaulters. . . . A number of people, mostly Jews and non-Moslems . . . have been arrested and are being kept in hotels at Moda before being sent to Aşkale, near Erzurum, where they will do compulsory labours for public works."

[11] Ahmet Emin Yalman in a personal interview with the author.

[12] *Foreign Relations*, 1943, IV, 1,079-81.

[13] *Ibid.*

[14] Faik Ökte, *Varlık Vergisi Faciası* (*The Tragedy of the Capital Levy*) (İstanbul: Nebioğlu Yayınevı, 1951).

with the government, and the contractors."[15] Members of minority groups who were not Turkish citizens were equally taxed at exorbitant rates. This produced constant difficulties with foreign governments, Axis and Allied alike.

During this episode most embassies, including the German, the Bulgarian, and the Greek, submitted formal protests to the Turkish Government. The American Embassy thought "strong and direct language to the Turks was thoroughly justified. . . ."[16] Eventually, there was in Ankara a sustained clamor against the tax from foreign diplomats.

As for the Turkish press, it carried full reports of the *Varlık Vergisi*, its regulations and its penalties, as well as the names of those who had been sent to Aşkale, but failed to comment editorially. Ahmet Emin Yalman, however, broke this silence by publishing an article in *Vatan*, October, 1, 1943, under the headline: "The *Varlık Vergisi* must be wound up: it has become a chronic disease."[17] Yalman, himself of Jewish origins, stated that the tax was a result of

---

[15] Nadi, *Opening in the Curtain*, pp. 178-79.

[16] Memorandum by the Adviser on Political Relations (Murray), Washington, D.C., February 19, 1943, *Foreign Relations*, 1943, IV, 1,084-85. In regard to the practice of taxing foreign citizens, Geoffrey Lewis comments, "It being a principle of international law that a state may not tax foreign subjects more heavily than its own nationals, orders were given that foreign residents in Turkey were to be treated like the Ms, except for Jewish subjects of the Axis Powers. In practice, not only these but many other foreigners were assessed as Gs; citizens of Greece, in particular tended to be lumped together . . ."; *Turkey*, p. 119. The American Embassy became involved in three cases: the first was an American citizen working in Turkey named Nicholas Balladur who was taxed at a higher rate than Turkish employees earning the same salary; the second instance arose when the Socony-Vacuum Company was "taxed doubly"; the third involved the firm of Sadullah, Mandel and Levy which was taxed at a rate double the value of its capital investment, most of which was owned by American citizens. As a result of Steinhardt's personal protest to the Turkish Prime Minister, Sadullah, Mandel and Levy ended up paying a fraction of the original amount assessed, while the taxes imposed on Balladur and Socony-Vacuum were completely canceled; *Foreign Relations*, 1943, IV, 1,079-81.

[17] *Vatan*, October 1, 1943.

a "contagious disease," anti-Semitism, which was raging in
Europe and had "produced a wound which needed heal-
ing." On October 1, 1944, one year after he began criticizing
the tax, *Vatan* was suspended and Yalman himself was sent
to Aşkale. Lest it be thought otherwise, Yalman described
the labor camp to the author as "a healthful place. The people who were forced to be there had a good time, although
most resented their exile deeply."[18] *Vatan* resumed publication on March 23, 1945.

Aydemir, however, defends the tax as an "unavoidable
need, not an act of capriciousness." He indicates that after
the death in August 1942 of Prime Minister Refik Saydam,
"price control and adjustment measures disintegrated"; the
government urgently needed more funds for itself and
thought it advisable to withdraw excess currency from an
inflationary market.[19] Aydemir admits that "even today the
tax remains as an accusation against İnönü's career" and
that İnönü at the time paid particular attention to the implementation of the tax because he knew that he would
ultimately be accountable for it.[20]

When the tax was passed,[21] it was estimated that it would
yield 465 million lira. By March 17, 1943, Saracoğlu reported to the Assembly that the tax had yielded 225 million
lira which had "dispelled the clouds" on the country's fiscal
horizon. "Much money which was being spent in an un-
thinking and harmful way had now been removed from
circulation," he declared.[22] By February 1944, almost 315

18 Ahmet Emin Yalman in a personal interview with the author.
19 Aydemir, *The Second Man*, pp. 228-30.
20 *Ibid.*, p. 233. When the author asked former President İnönü to
comment on the *Varlık Vergisi*, he said, "It was a tax on all the Turks."
21 *T.B.M.M. Zabıt Ceridesi*, Sixth Assembly, Third Session, November 11, 1942, Vol. 28, pp. 14-29.
22 *Ayın Tarihi*, Vol. 111 (March 1943), p. 17. The repeal of the tax
on wealth came in a series of steps: it was brought before the committee
on finance of the Assembly on March 13, discussed on the floor of the
Assembly on March 15, and technically repealed on March 17, 1944.
For text of the repeal, *Varlık Vergisi Bakayasının Terkine Dair Kanun*

million lira had been collected.[23] Of this amount almost 280 million lira had come from the "wealthy minorities."[24] The *Varlık Vergisi* was canceled on March 15, 1944, and the repeal took effect two days later. All penalties yet to be enforced or in progress were written off as were the taxes, amounting to 108 million lira, which had not been collected.

In explaining the repeal, Finance Minister Fuat Ağralı indicated that "part of the uncollected revenues cannot be collected and that the other part cannot be collected without subjecting the taxpayers to extreme hardships or complete poverty." The repeal was pictured as an actuarial readjustment, since "there is no operational use in keeping this balance on our records from year to year. . . ."[25] It was, however, also a positive response to pressure, particularly from the United States, and a gesture toward better relations between the Turks and the Western Allies. Franz von Papen detected this, and he attributed the repeal of the tax to the desire on the part of Turkish statesmen to appeal to the United States.[26] The *Varlık Vergisi* had placed the Turks even further outside the camp of the Western Allies. By March 1944, the revenues collected were a luxury they could no longer afford. The repeal of the *Varlık Vergisi* marks the point when the Turkish Government began to face up to the realities of the postwar world in earnest.

(*Cancellation of Remaining Uncollected Tax on Wealth*) (*Düstur*, Third Format, Vol. xxv), p. 173; *Sicil-i Kavanin*, xxv, 97; *Resmî Gazete*, No. 5657, March 17, 1944.

[23] For the debate, *T.B.M.M. Zabıt Ceridesi*, Seventh Assembly, Twenty-Ninth Session, March 15, 1944, I, 34, pp. 44-46; for the text of the repeal act, pp. 46-47; Aydemir, *The Second Man*, p. 233, gives the same figures as presented here.

[24] *Ibid.*, p. 233.

[25] *T.B.M.M. Zabıt Ceridesi*, Seventh Assembly, Twenty-Ninth Session, March 15, 1944, I, 45.

[26] Ambassador in Ankara (von Papen) to Foreign Ministry in Berlin, Ankara, June 16, 1943, *Captured Files*, NA, T-120, Roll 2618, Frame E364618.

THE PAN-TURANIAN QUESTION

Another clear indication that the Turkish Government was attempting to bend with the course of world events came in May 1944, when it openly suppressed those working to propagate Pan-Turkic and Pan-Turanian ideas.[27] In a single sweep, the government arrested the small but significant group of extremists who had, since the beginning of the war, called for the unity of all Turkish peoples. The wide publicity which the government gave these arrests and the timing of its action indicate that its goal was not simply to punish a group of dissident elements but to gain favor with the Soviet Union and possibly induce its leaders to act moderately.[28]

During the war, the Pan-Turanian movement in Turkey was divided into a number of groups. The one thing they did share in common, however, was resentment, bordering on hatred, toward the Union of Soviet Socialist Republics.

[27] Charles Warren Hostler, *Turkism and the Soviets: The Turks of the World and Their Political Objectives* (London: George Allen and Unwin, Ltd., 1957), pp. 199-206, defines the differences between Pan-Turkism and Pan-Turanism: "Pan-Turkism was born under the reciprocal influence of the Eastern Turks threatened by 'Russianization,' and Western Turks exposed to Russian expansion. Pan-Turanism (seeking unity among Turkish, Mongol and Finnish-Ugrian peoples), in contrast to Pan-Turkism (seeking unity of Turkish peoples), followed in the wake of Russian expansion in the Balkans, and is correlated to Turkish and Hungarian experiments in anti-Slav collaboration." The movement in Turkey during the war had elements of both Pan-Turkism and Pan-Turanism but will be referred to here simply as the Pan-Turanian movement.

[28] Charles Warren Hostler, "Trends in Pan-Turanism," *Middle Eastern Affairs*, Vol. III, No. 1 (January 1952), 3-13 at p. 10; Hostler writes: "The great publicity given the arrests in the press was doubtless designed to placate the Soviet Union against which the movement must ultimately have been directed, and to help improve Russo-Turkish relations." Analysts on the staff of the *Review* agreed: Turkish leaders "refrained from acting until they judged that the denunciation of the movement would gain good marks for them in Moscow"; *Review*, November 15, 1944, Series N, No. 37, p. 181.

They, therefore, were inevitably perceived by the Russians as a threat to them. It was this that made the government finally take action against them.

This does not suggest, however, that the Turkish Government favored or actually supported their activities prior to this time. On the contrary, to do so would have violated one of the basic tenets underlying all Turkish foreign policy, the preservation of Turkey's boundaries.[29] Some authors have suggested that Turkish policy-makers may have sympathized with the Pan-Turanists as a result of their mutual feelings toward the Soviet Union.[30] Admittedly, the suppression of the movement could have come much earlier.[31]

[29] On October 10, 1941, while Karl Clodius was in Ankara, he and Numan Menemencioğlu discussed the Pan-Turanian issue. Although Menemencioğlu admitted that "Turkey could not remain disinterested in the fate of 40 million people of Turkish origin in Russia," the then Secretary-General of the Foreign Ministry, in the words of Clodius, "repeatedly stressed that Turkey had no aspirations outside her present borders"; the Deputy Director of the Economic Policy Department to the Foreign Ministry, Ankara, October 10, 1941, *Docs.Ger.F.P.*, III, 632-33. Clodius added that he believed that Menemencioğlu was the "spiritual leader of Turkish foreign policy" rather than Saracoğlu. On July 5, 1943, Menemencioğlu addressed himself to the Pan-Turanian question on the floor of the Assembly and declared: "We wish only prosperity and happiness to Turks outside of Turkey's borders. Aside from this, all our policies, all our Turkism [exclusively] concerns the Turks who have entered the borders of this nation"; *T.B.M.M. Zabıt Ceridesi*, Seventh Assembly, Forty-Fourth Session, July 5, 1943, I, 13-14.

[30] See, e.g., George Lenczowski, *The Middle East in World Affairs* (Ithaca, N.Y.: Cornell University Press, 1952), p. 142; Hostler, *Turkism and the Soviets*, p. 180, also hypothesizes that "Possibly these irresponsible, extreme groups were tolerated by the Turkish government as an ideological preparation for the Turkish youth in the event of war with Soviet Russia. . . ."

[31] Nadir Nadi, *Opening in the Curtain*, p. 184, is quite explicit on this point: "At a time when it became plain that the Allies were going to win the war, May, 1944, drastic measures were taken against the racists. Their leaders were captured and imprisoned. If, however, the same people had been prosecuted seriously earlier, at the time when they were ridiculing Atatürk after his death and when they were propa-

There is no documentary evidence, however, which establishes a working arrangement between the Turkish Government and the Pan-Turanians. Yet, since the movement played and continues to play a role in Turkey's relationship with the Soviet Union, it behooves us to identify, if only briefly, the Pan-Turanian leaders, their ideologies, their partisans in government, and to discuss the influence, if any, these elements wielded over decision-making in Ankara and upon the unfolding of international events.

PAN-TURANIAN ELEMENTS

A central figure in the Pan-Turanian movement during the World War was A. Zeki Velidî Toǧan.[32] Born in the district of Başkırıa, a province in the southern Urals in Russian Turkestan, he demonstrated his militant political activism early by becoming the prime mover in a Muslim organization that was working during the Russian Revolution to create an autonomous state of Başkırıa. For the rest of his life, Toǧan devoted his efforts to arousing Turkey's interest in the Turkic peoples within the Soviet Union. He did always with a view to convincing the Turkish Government that an independent Turkestan was a concrete and realizable goal. His prolific writings, therefore, possess a distinct anti-Soviet flavor. In a major study published during the war, for example, Toǧan presented a long diatribe against what he described as the "new Russianism," an organized attempt by the Soviets to destroy Turkish culture in Turkestan.[33] "The present new Russianism," he wrote in 1942, "takes the following shape":

---

gandizing themselves freely in schools and periodicals, the racist movement could have been prevented at the outset or at least restrained."

[32] For a fuller outline of Toǧan's life, Hostler, *Turkism and the Soviets*, pp. 218-19.

[33] A. Zeki Velidî Toǧan, *Bugünkü Türkili (Türkistan) ve Yakın Tarihi (Today's Turkestan and Its Recent History)*, I, *Batı ve*

1). to combine communism with Russian imperialism as two basic complementary concepts and to follow a double-faced political line against subservient satellite countries and the world;

2). to express the Russian nation's purpose of world domination as a "sacred ideal" and to become a devoted and warring nation deeply ready to die in order to realize its national objectives in this way;

3). to increase Russian population. . . .

4). to make certain that the Russians are mobile and agile enough to be transplanted to the parts of Asia that have to be invaded;

5). to perfect the system of dictatorship and maximum administrative centralization to provide for effective expansion and conquest.[34]

Toğan suggested that the way to counteract the effects of the new Russianism was for the Turkish Government to try to bolster Turkish culture among the people living in the Ukraine, Caucasus, Mongolia, and Turkestan.[35] Language, he argued, would serve as a barrier to their complete Russification.[36]

Reha Oğuz Türkkan, a student of Zeki Velidî Toğan while Toğan held a professorship in Turkish history at the University of İstanbul, organized a secret racist society in 1938 and was very active until arrested by the government

---

Kuzey Türkistan (West and North Turkestan) (İstanbul: Arkadaş İbrahim Horoz ve Güven Basımevleri, 1942), p. 590.

[34] *Ibid.*

[35] *Ibid.*, p. 592; Toğan goes on to say, "Russians are not bad people. What makes them bad is four centuries of imperialism. . . ."

[36] Toğan in *ibid.*, pp. 598-99, likens Russian rule in Turkestan to that of British colonization of India and argues that the only way open to both subordinate peoples to maintain their identity is to preserve their language. Toğan also remarks, *ibid.*, p. 598, that "The English do not want an independent Turkic-Islamic state but would abide by a *fait accompli* and seek mercantile advantages."

in May 1944.[37] More fanatical than his mentor, at least in outward appearance, Türkkan and the publication he edited, *Bozkurt* (*Gray Wolf*), propagated a brand of racial superiority that was little different from that of Nazism.[38] In its official declaration on the arrests of the Pan-Turanian leaders, the government cited Türkkan as a confirmed racist who was working to subvert the central government.[39]

Another prominent racist, perhaps the most rabid of all, but for that no friend of Türkkan, was Nihat Atsız, who combined racism with an obsessive hatred of communism and the Soviet Union.[40] He, through a number of publica-

[37] Hostler, *Turkism and the Soviets*, pp. 181-82; Hostler, "Trends in Pan-Turanism," p. 7; Karpat, *Turkey's Politics*, pp. 265-66; also, Reha Oğuz Türkkan, "The Turkish Press," *Middle Eastern Affairs*, Vol. I, No. 2 (May 1950), 142-49.

[38] Türkkan (*ibid.*, p. 143) claims that periodical publications, magazines, and the like were less under government control in Turkey during the war than newspapers. He writes also that ". . . any group could put out a periodical, and if it was suspended for any reason, it was not too difficult to start over again with a new weekly or monthly." This may help to explain the comparatively large number of periodical journals that were published by the Pan-Turanian movement during the war. In July 1943, Menemencioğlu was called upon to answer allegations in a publication entitled *En Büyük Tehlike* (*The Greatest Danger*) which claimed that Pan-Turanian propaganda was running rampant in Turkey. Menemencioğlu stated that he was aware of the claims being made in *En Büyük Tehlike* but denied their validity by saying that ". . . there is no nationalism or racism in Turkey in the way that this book suggests and we are aware of no manifestations along this line"; *T.B.M.M. Zabıt Ceridesi*, Seventh Assembly, Forty-Fourth Session, July 5, 1943, I, 14. Menemencioğlu also spoke of the freedom of the press and publications, its advantages and disadvantages.

[39] See "Irkçılık ve Turancılık Tahrikatı Yapanlar Hakkında Hükümetin Tebliği" ("Government's declaration concerning [those] involved in racist and Turanist provocations") in *Ayın Tarihi*, Vol. 126 (May 1944), pp. 21-23; also Erer, *Prohibitionists*, pp. 115-16.

[40] In regard to Nihat Atsız, see Hostler, *Turkism and the Soviets*, p. 183; Hostler, "Trends in Pan-Turanism," p. 9; Karpat, *Turkey's Politics*, p. 266, n. 43; Fethi Tevetoğlu, *Türkiye'de Sosyalist ve Komünist Faaliyetler 1910-1960* (*Socialist and Communist Activities in Turkey*

tions, *Tanrıdağ*, *Atsız*, and *Orhun*, argued that only pure
Turks should be allowed to hold high government positions, that excessive tolerance of minorities was a dangerous
thing for Turkey, that war was edifying, and that only
racism could serve as the basis of nationalism.[41] In an article
published in *Orhun*, February 20, 1934, Atsız wrote, "The
eternal enemy of the Turkish nation is the entire world.
This history gives us eternal advice: there are three internal
enemies, communists, Jews, and flatterers."[42] It was Atsız
who precipitated the government's action against the Pan-
Turanists in May 1944.

Early in 1944, on February 20 and March 21, Atsız published two "open" letters to Prime Minister Saracoğlu in
which he attacked the Prime Minister, the party, and what
he described as subversive Leftist student elements. "The
purpose of these lines," Atsız wrote in his first open letter to
Saracoğlu, "is to ask you why Turkism is only [applied] in
words and never passes into action."[43] This was a double-
pronged insult to the Prime Minister since it suggested that
Saracoğlu paid lip service to Pan-Turanist ideals without
ever transforming them into action.[44] In his letter, Atsız

1910-1960) (Ankara: Ayyıldız Matbaası, 1967), *passim.* Kemal Karpat,
Turkey's Politics, p. 265, no. 40, describes the Atsız-Türkkan feud as
follows: "The polemic between Reha Oğuz Türkkan and Nihat Atsız,
two racialist leaders, in 1941-1943, centered around mutual accusations
of lack of 'blood purity' and each one of the contestants dug into the
other's genealogy to prove that neither was a one hundred per cent
ethnic Turk."

[41] Hostler, "Trends in Pan-Turanism"; Alexander Henderson, "The
Pan-Turanian Myth in Turkey Today," *Asiatic Review*, N.S. 41, No.
145 (January 1945), pp. 79-90 at p. 83.

[42] Tevetoğlu, *Socialist and Communist Activities in Turkey*, p. 483,
n. 303.

[43] For the two open letters of Atsız to Saracoğlu, *ibid.*, pp. 607-609;
for the quotation see p. 608.

[44] Tevetoğlu, *ibid.*, p. 607, makes the same case; he cites Saracoğlu
as having "insincerely" said, " 'We are Turks, Turkists and will always
remain Turkists. To us Turkism is a blood issue as well as a matter

also complained that Leftist students had broken up Pan-Turanian meetings being held at the community center in İstanbul. "The worst of all these demonstrators are university students," Atsız wrote,

> most of them studying with state money. That means the state is unknowingly feeding snakes, red-eyed sneaky and poisonous snakes. When these snakes become doctors tomorrow and go to the various parts of the country on duty, the first thing they will do will be to sabotage activities. They will stab the country in the back and they will be agents of foreign armies who will bring the red dawn that they have been waiting for to Turkey.[45]

The second open letter directly attacked the CHP by decrying what Atsız described as being hatred of race and family, its opposition to religion and war, and its subversion of nationalism in the disguise of fighting fascism.[46]

As a result of these letters, a slander suit was brought against Atsız by Sabahaddin Âli, whom Atsız had described as being a traitor to Turkey.[47] Hasan Âli Yücel, Minister of Education, and Falih Rıfkı Atay, editor of *Ulus*, supported Âli's case against Atsız. The court hearing of the case, April 26, 1944, was disrupted by violent demonstrations conducted by pro-Turanist students. They personally assaulted Sabahaddin Âli.[48] Atsız, apparently emboldened, immediately published a statement denouncing all "Leftist" intellectuals. The government decided to act. On May 9, 1944, the Pan-Turanian leaders were arrested.[49]

---

of conscience and culture. . . .' " Tevetoğlu then attacks Saracoğlu for having brought a case against Atsız.

[45] *Ibid.*, p. 610.   [46] *Ibid.*, pp. 612-17.   [47] *Ibid.*, p. 606.

[48] Erer, *Prohibitionists*, pp. 121-22; also, Karpat, *Turkey's Politics*, p. 267, n. 44.

[49] Lenczowski, *The Middle East in World Affairs*, p. 146; Hostler, *Turkism and the Soviets*, p. 185; Hostler, "Trends in Pan-Turanism," p. 10. Gotthard Jäschke, *Die Turkei in den Jahren 1942-1951: Ge-*

On May 18, 1944, the Council of Ministers approved the "taking of necessary actions and measures" by the Ministry of the Interior against "those involved in racist and Turanist provocations."[50] An official declaration was released stating that investigations had established that the arrested persons were "indoctrinating citizens with principles other than true nationalism" and were thus plotting against the constitution. For such purposes, the declaration charged, "they have set up secret organizations, action programs, and organs of propaganda."[51] On May 19, 1944, President İnönü, introduced by Minister of Education Hasan Âli Yücel, delivered a lengthy and widely publicized speech in

---

schichtekalender mit Namen und Sachregister (*Turkey in the Years 1942-1951: Chronology with Names and Events*) (Wiesbaden: Otto Harrassowitz, 1955), pp. 25-26. The government published a collection of racist and Turanist articles in 1944 as a way of condemning the movement's ideology; *Irkçılık-Turancılık* (Ankara: Türk İnkılâp Enstitüsü Yayını, No. 4, 1944).

[50] "Irkçılık ve Turancılık Tahrikatı yapanlar hakkında Hükümetin Tebliği" ("Government's declaration concerning [those] involved in racist and Turanist provocations") in *Ayın Tarihi*, Vol. 126 (May 1944), pp. 21-23. The names of those originally arrested by the government are: İzzettin Şadan, Nihat Atsız, Tahir Akın Karaoğuz, Mustafa Hakkı Akansel, Hakkı Yılanlıoğlu, Tesbihcioğlu, Kadircan Kaflı, Azerî M. Altınbay, Abdulkadir İnan, San'an Azer, Samet Caferoğlu, Ahmet Caferoğlu, Ali Dursun Tevetoğlu, M. Şakir Ülkütaşır, Yusuf Kadıgıl, Mükrimin Halil Yınanç, Sepicioğlu, Nurullah Barıman, Hamza Sadi Özbek, Orhan Şaik Gökyay, Hüseyin Avni Göktürk, Cafer Seyit Ahmet Kırımer, Muharrem Feyzi Togay, Ali Genceli, A. Zeki Velidî Toğan, Akdes Nimet Kurat, Nebil Buharalı, Reha Oğuz Türkkan, Hüseyin Namık Orkun, Remzi Oğuz Arık, Mehmet Halit Bayrı, Bedriye Atsız, Ziyaettin Fahri Fındıkoğlu, Hüsnü Emir Erkilet, Müftüoğlu Mustafa Tatlısu, Zeik Sofuoğlu, Gülcan Tevetoğlu, Uluğ Turanlıoğlu, Ali Haydar Yeşilyurt, Nejdet Sancar, Cemal Oğuz Öcal, Nihat Sami Barnalı, Peyami Safa, Fethi Tevetoğlu, Elmas Yıldırım, Osman Turan, İsmet Tümtürk.

[51] *Ibid.*; Aydemir, *The Second Man*, p. 250, refers to the Pan-Turanian movement as "amateurish plots" and suggests that the memory of these arrests will engender criticism of İnönü in the future.

the Sports Stadium of Ankara.[52] İnönü's speech, among the most significant of his career, made three points: the Pan-Turanists were a danger to the Turkish Republic; Turks wanted no part in an adventurist policy and desired no more territory; the Soviet Union was the historical friend of Turkey. In regard to the Pan-Turanists, "there are such things that can be initiated only after the constitution and governmental law have been violated," İnönü declared. "Therefore, under a mask of brilliant ideas, we are confronted with an attempt against the very existence of the republic and the Grand National Assembly." İnönü warned his countrymen that "the plotters are trying to deceive all of us, gradually and progressively, our children of ten and ourselves." İnönü also affirmed Turkey's traditional renunciation of adventurism.

> In everybody's mind there was the idea that if we ever got any power we would be involved in adventurist and aggressive politics. The republic, however, has seen the fundamental value of civilized living, in the existence of an atmosphere of security among the family of nations.[53]

İnönü sought to make it clear that this was a matter of preference and choice: ". . . our national policy is far from looking for adventures outside the country . . . this is not a

[52] "Millî Şef İnönü'nün 19 Mayıs Gençlik Bayramı münasebetile gençliğe hitaben söylediği nutuk" ("National Leader İnönü's speech to the youth on the occasion of the May 19 youth holiday"), Ayın Tarihi, Vol. 126 (May 1944), pp. 23-29; for the specific quotations see pp. 27-28; Hasan Âli Yücel, in introducing İnönü declared, "the first condition of success in national issues is to believe in Atatürk first and İnönü second and to act according to what they say"; ibid., pp. 22-23. Falih Rıfkı Atay and Necmettin Sadak, not surprisingly, immediately published editorial defenses of the speech; see, e.g., "Millî Şefin Milletine büyük dersi" ("The National Leader's big lesson to his nation"), Akşam, May 21, 1944, as in ibid., pp. 157-59; Falih Rıfkı Atay, "Cumhurreisimizin nutku" ("The speech of our President"), Ulus, May 21, 1944 as in ibid., pp. 159-60.

[53] Ibid., pp. 27-28.

policy of obligation or of necessity but a policy of faith and understanding." His speech, finally, emphasized good Turkish-Soviet relations. After referring to Pan-Turanism in Turkey as a "harmful and sick manifestation of recent times," İnönü stated:

> In view of this, it is necessary to understand the Republic very well. When the national liberation movement ended, we were friends with only the Soviet Union [unlike] the other neighbors [that] still keep vividly in their minds all the memories of the old hostilities.[54]

İnönü's Youth Day speech of May 1944 leaves little doubt that it was aimed at Soviet ears as well as at the youth of Turkey.

PAN-TURANIST PARTISANS IN GOVERNMENT AND THEIR INFLUENCE ON DECISION-MAKING

The question next arises, did these elements, the individuals involved or their ideas, play a role in formulating Turkish foreign policy, that is, did they influence Turkish policymakers to take certain courses of action which fostered their goals or favored their values? In the author's view the answer is quite clearly negative. As Leo D. Hochstetter has remarked, "American intelligence during the war never found any evidence that connected İnönü or Menemencioğlu with the Pan-Turanists."[55] Neither has the present author.[56] Hostler, a knowledgeable observer, however, states

[54] *Ibid.*

[55] In a personal interview with the author, September 8, 1969.

[56] A wide variety of individuals interviewed in the course of this study have gone on record to deny that either İnönü or Menemencioğlu were attracted to Pan-Turanist possibilities. The list includes such men as Professor Ahmet Şükrü Esmer, Professor A. Suat Bilge, Professor Enver Ziya Karal, Professor Fahir Armaoğlu, as well as Cevat Açıkalın and Zeki Kuneralp. Former President İnönü personally denied ever having been in any way "a friend" to the Pan-Turanists. Mrs. Nermin Streater and Turgut Menemencioğlu categorically discount

"One may conclude that highly placed persons in the Turkish state had plans ready to exploit all the possibilities the German-Soviet war and a collapse of the USSR could furnish for the realization of Pan-Turkish ideals."[57] Lothar Krecker also alleges that the government, in the person of Nuri Paşa [Killigil], played a double game of officially condemning Pan-Turanism but privately sounding out the German Foreign Office on the possibility of setting up an autonomous state between Turkey and the Soviet Union.[58] Neither of these authors, however, furnish much new documentary evidence beyond that published in 1947 by the Soviet Union in the *Secret Documents*.

The documents in *Secret Documents* describe the activities of General Hüseyin Hüsnü Emir Erkilet, General Ali Fuad Erden, Hüsrev Gerede, Turkish Ambassador in Berlin until 1943, and Nuri Paşa, brother of the famous Enver Paşa. The Turkish Chief of Staff, Fevzi Çakmak, and the editor of the *Türkische Post*, General Âli İhsan Sâbis, are also implicated. On August 5, 1941, moreover, von Papen informed the German Foreign Ministry that "government circles in Turkey were showing an interest in the Turkic peoples in Azerbaijan." Along with Nuri Paşa and Zeki Velidî, neither of whom were in the government, von Papen mentioned Şükrü Enis Bahça, a deputy in the Assembly from

any suggestion that Numan Menemencioğlu may have considered the establishment of a Turkic state between Turkey and the Soviet Union to have been a real possibility or that he may have worked in favor of such a goal. Perhaps one of the central theses of this study deserves reiteration at this point: Turkish foreign policy during the war up until June 1944 was the result of decisions taken by İnönü and Menemencioğlu alone although assisted by several others. Menemencioğlu was the central and dominant figure in the Foreign Ministry. There can be no talk of Pan-Turanist ideals influencing Turkish foreign policy unless one can establish that İnönü and Menemencioğlu were guided by them. No writer has yet succeeded in doing this, and much evidence to the contrary seems to exist.

[57] Hostler, *Turkism and the Soviets*, p. 177.

[58] Krecker, *Germany and Turkey in the Second World War*, pp. 211-15.

İstanbul, Memduh Şevket, the Turkish Ambassador in Afghanistan, and Ahmet Said Cafer, who von Papen wrote, was "not to be trusted in any way" since he was a Turkish Government spy. It is these men who emerge as Pan-Turanist partisans in the *Secret Documents* collection.[59] The most important thing that can be said of them, however, is that they operated around the periphery of power and decision-making in Ankara during the war.[60] This includes Fevzi Çakmak.

Fevzi Çakmak was, to be sure, an important individual in Ankara during wartime. He was a companion of Atatürk, a sound engineer, and by 1939 his name had become almost synonymous with the title of his office, Turkish Chief of Staff. He ruled the armed forces with an iron hand until he reached the retirement age of sixty-eight. On November 24, 1941, an intermediary named Garoun informed the German Foreign Ministry that Çakmak, although "not at liberty of expressing this officially," was, as Garoun put it, "closely interested in Turanism."[61] On May 13, 1942, von Papen informed the German Foreign Ministry that General Mürsel Baku had told him that Çakmak was prepared to help the Pan-Turanian movement by allowing civilians devoted to the cause to leave for Germany, if they so desired.[62] Çakmak, however, refused, "for the time being," to grant permission for military officers to do the same.[63] On June 1,

[59] Von Papen to the German Foreign Ministry, Therapia, August 5, 1941, *Secret Documents*, pp. 36-37; also, Hostler, *Turkism and the Soviets*, pp. 172-75.

[60] This study of Fevzi Çakmak and the other generals implicated in the Pan-Turanist movement might well have been placed in Chapter 1 of this study. It was felt, however, that their relationship to the Pan-Turanian movement was of such significance as to warrant placing this discussion, particularly of their overall relationship to İnönü and Menemencioğlu, in the present context.

[61] Hentig to Erdmansdorf and Wehrmann, Berlin, November 24, 1941, *Secret Documents*, p. 48.

[62] Von Papen to the German Foreign Ministry, Ankara, May 13, 1942, *ibid.*, pp. 74-75; Hostler, *Turkism and the Soviets*, p. 175.

[63] *Ibid.*

1942, Garoun had another conversation in the Foreign Ministry in Berlin during which he indicated that Çakmak believed that it was almost inevitable that Turkey would have to fight in the Baku region. This represents the substance of the proof marshaled in *Secret Documents* to prove that Çakmak was a Pan-Turanian sympathizer.

Hostler, furthermore, writes, "they [the documents cited in *Secret Documents*] do reflect the sympathies of certain of his [İnönü's] key advisers."[64] Hostler then refers to George Lenczowski who identifies Marshal Çakmak as the one "key adviser."[65] A closer look at the relationship between İsmet İnönü and Fevzi Çakmak, however, reveals that even if Çakmak were attracted to Pan-Turanian ideals, and the evidence is hardly conclusive, his influence with İnönü was minimal. On the contrary, there were great tensions between the two men and it was İnönü who forced Çakmak to retire in January 1944. Çakmak's biographer, Süleyman Külçe, writes, "President İnönü was known by the entire world as an overly cautious person. Of course Fevzi Paşa knew of this characteristic. But whenever the situation permitted, the Marshal would call him a coward rather than overly cautious."[66] During the war, İnönü undermined Çakmak's role by personally relying upon the Assistant Chief of Staff, Asım Gündüz, in matters related to high government policy.[67] İnönü could have extended Çakmak's appointment by pushing back, in his case, the compulsory age

[64] *Ibid.*, p. 176; also Lenczowski, *The Middle East in World Affairs*, p. 142.

[65] *Ibid.*

[66] Süleyman Külçe, *Mareşal Fevzi Çakmak: Askerî, Hususî Hayatı* (*Marshal Fevzi Çakmak: His Military and Personal Life*) (2nd ed.; İstanbul: Cumhuriyet Matbaası, 1953), I, 65. On the question of whether Çakmak was a Pan-Turanist, Zeki Kuneralp has said: "Fevzi Çakmak may have been favorably disposed to the Germans but was never an outright Pan-Turanist." The author tends to agree with this view; Kuneralp also succinctly describes Çakmak's relationship with İnönü as follows: "No love was ever lost between Çakmak and İnönü." (In a personal interview with the author.)

[67] Külçe, *Mareshal Fevzi Çakmak*, I, 65.

of retirement. "But this," Külçe suggests, "was [for İnönü] an opportunity not to be missed."[68] In any event, Çakmak's influence in regard to foreign-policy issues was highly circumscribed at this time by İnönü. This held true almost without question, to policies concerning the Pan-Turanian problem.

If it is not possible to count Çakmak among İnönü's key advisers, it is even less accurate to do so in the case of Ali Fuad Erden, Hüseyin Hüsnü Emir Erkilet, Âli İhsan Sâbis, or even Hüsrev Gerede, let alone Nuri Paşa. Erden and Erkilet, for example, were typical of that class of Turkish generals who had studied under German military instructors around the time of the First World War and who deeply admired Germany throughout their lives.[69] Erden, head

[68] *Ibid.* For a copy of the telegram İnönü sent to Çakmak when the general retired, see *ibid.*, pp. 294-95; also *Ayın Tarihi*, Vol. 122 (January 1944), p. 31. The analysis of the İnönü-Çakmak relationship and particularly the circumstances of Çakmak's retirement rendered by Külçe is confirmed by Nizamettin Nazif Tepedelenlioğlu and Fethi Tevetoğlu. Nizamettin Nazif Tepedelenlioğlu, *Ordu ve Politika (Army and Politics)* (İstanbul: Bedir Yayınevi, 1967), pp. 361-62, writes, ". . . it was thought that Marshal Fevzi Çakmak would remain at the head of the army . . . until the day he died. . . . As a matter of fact, some were excessively optimistic in saying, 'Who would dare [to fire him]?' The Marshal will never leave the position of the head of the army. İsmet İnönü easily proved the opposite." Tepedelenlioğlu also outlines the security precautions İnönü apparently took the day the news of Çakmak's retirement was to be announced. Several cavalry units were posted in the streets of Ankara to prevent demonstrations; see Tevetoğlu, *Soviet and Communist Activities in Turkey*, p. 314. Tepedelenlioğlu and Tevetoğlu are associated with İnönü's rivaling political interests. Admiral Andrew Brown Cunningham (of Hyndhope), seems to have detected the split between Çakmak and Turkish officials; see *A Sailor's Odyssey* (New York: E. P. Dutton and Co., 1951), p. 214, where Cunningham writes, "As I saw it, they [Turkish officials] were divided among themselves, and the Marshal [Çakmak] had been difficult to control since Kemal's death." Cunningham was a fleet admiral in the British navy and visited Turkey immediately after the signing of the Anglo-French-Turkish agreement of October 1939.

[69] Kâzım Özalp has said, "Many army officers liked the Germans because they had been trained by them, had fought alongside them in

of the Turkish Military Academy, and Erkilet, a two-star retired general, moreover, visited Hitler at the Fuehrer's general headquarters in East Prussia on October 28, 1941. Both returned from this trip, which took them to the front where German troops were still defeating the Russians, in a state of near euphoria.[70] In an audience with İnönü, Çakmak, and Saracoğlu, they informed the Turkish President that "all that was left of Russia was its snow."[71] But again their relationship with İnönü was, at best, tenuous. During the war, Erkilet wrote for *Cumhuriyet* and was clearly identified with the more extremist elements in the Pan-Turanian movement.[72] Although a well-known figure, his views even on military developments were not considered reliable by İnönü and were certainly not given any weight in policymaking.[73] Erden, somewhat less openly identified with the Pan-Turanian camp although universally recognized as being pro-German, was closer to İnönü but hardly a key adviser, particularly on this issue.[74] In October 1945, when the Court of Cassation revoked the sentences that had been imposed on the Pan-Turanists arrested in May 1944, Erden was one of the presiding judges. "İnönü was angry with me

the First Great War, and continued to admire their discipline. This included Fevzi Çakmak who deeply admired them." (In personal interview with the author.)

[70] Professor Ahmet Şükrü Esmer in a personal interview with the author.

[71] Esmer in a personal interview. For Erden's account of his and Erkilet's visit, Erden, *İnönü*, pp. 210-13.

[72] *Secret Documents* contains an entire chapter, pp. 169-86, devoted to the work of Erkilet.

[73] Cevat Açıkalın in a personal interview with the author.

[74] This is not to suggest that Erden did not share Pan-Turanist ideals; see the Ambassador in Turkey (von Papen) to the Foreign Ministry in Berlin, Ankara, July 14, 1941, *Docs.Ger.F.P.*, p. 176, in which von Papen reports that Erden had told him, in von Papen's words, "Turkey would be pleased if in the Caucasus a federation of the local tribes, which are in greater or less degree related to the Turks, could be established while east of the Caspian Sea formation of an independent Turanian state would be regarded as the best solution."

in 1945," he writes. "My guess is that the time he was angry with me was when the racists were being tried at the Military Court."[75]

The case for Âli İhsan Sâbis' not having acted as a key adviser is even more patent. Closely associated with the Ebuzziya family and German operations in Turkey during the war, Sâbis, in 1943, published his memoirs in which he accused Kâzım Özalp and Halil Paşa [Kut], among others, of profiteering and of irresponsible action during the First World War.[76] On October 16, 1943, Özalp—who, as suggested above, *was* close to İnönü and Halil Paşa—and Osman Okyar sued Sâbis for defamation of character. Another indication of the distance between Sâbis and the decision-making circles of the Turkish Government came in March 1944, when Saracoğlu recommended to the members of the Assembly that they not revoke Hüseyin Cahit Yalçın's parliamentary immunity in order to allow Sâbis to sue him.[77] Yalçın, in a series of articles, had virulently reacted to Sâbis' book, especially its pro-German tendencies,[78] and Sâbis attempted to bring him to court. Saracoğlu, by virtue of his recommendation to the Assembly prevented this.

[75] Erden, *İnönü*, p. 230.

[76] Âli İhsan Sâbis, *Harb Hatıralarım* (*My War Memoirs*), Vol. I (İstanbul: Inkılâb Kitabevi, 1943). A second volume was published in Ankara in 1951 by the Güneş Matbaası.

[77] On the subject of revoking Yalçın's immunity, *T.B.M.M. Zabıt Ceridesi*, Seventh Assembly, March 8, 1944, I, 27 and Enclosure No. 37.

[78] For a sampling of the articles written by Yalçın in regard to Sâbis and his book, "Bir Fena Kitap" ("A bad book"), *Tanin*, September 20, 1943 and "Fena Kitabın Lekeli Muharriri" ("The shady writer of the bad book"), *Tanin*, September 26, 1943. In his memoirs, pp. 50-51, Sâbis suggested that the Second World War was a continuation of the first. During the First World War, he wrote, "The French and English Ambassadors said 'Russia is our ally; whatever they do not want, we do not want; whatever is against their interests is against our interests. The Germans are our enemy. Since everything the Germans attempt presents a threat to us, it is our duty to oppose Turkey's attitude toward Russia.'" Sâbis concluded, "The political situation described by these words in 1914 is not different from the political situation of the

In regard to Nuri Paşa, Lothar Krecker alleges that this individual went to Berlin in 1941 to discuss the Pan-Turanian issue at the behest of the Turkish Government.[79] Krecker, however, produces no evidence that connects Nuri Paşa's visit to the government. The author, therefore, tends to agree with Zeki Kuneralp that "Nuri Paşa did not represent the government. He was a businessman who harbored certain dreams, but his influence over policy-makers in Ankara was nil."[80]

Krecker also suggests that Nuri Paşa was in official contact with the Turkish Embassy in Berlin. This says a good deal about the Ambassador in Berlin, Hüsrev Gerede, but very little about Gerede's superiors in Ankara. Gerede did indeed entertain dreams of an autonomous Turkish state on the east of the Caspian Sea. On August 5, 1941, for example, he approached Weizsäcker in the German Foreign Ministry to discuss the possibility of uniting the Turkic people in the Caucasus into a single puppet buffer state.[81] This and other conversations conducted by Gerede, however, in the author's view reflect Gerede's personal sentiments rather than his official instructions from Ankara. Krecker does concede, "astounding as it may seem," that Gerede was acting alone.[82] Interestingly, Gerede, in a conversation with Rib-

---

Second World War. . . ." Sâbis later revealed his resentment toward İnönü for the treatment he received in May 1944.

[79] Krecker, *Germany and Turkey in the Second World War*, pp. 211-15; in this connection, Krecker, p. 213, refers to a message from von Papen to the German Foreign Ministry dated April 6, 1942, which reports that Prime Minister Saracoğlu had told von Papen that although Turkey could not officially support Germany in finding a solution to the Pan-Turanian question, the Turkish Prime Minister had nevertheless "given permission to certain persons in an unofficial capacity to communicate [with German representatives] about this." The reader is left to draw his own conclusions.

[80] Zeki Kuneralp in a personal interview with the author.

[81] Memorandum by the State Secretary (Weizacker), Berlin, August 5, 1941, *Docs.Ger.F.P.*, XIII, 284.

[82] Krecker, *Germany and Turkey in the Second World War*, p. 210.

bentrop on August 25, 1941, informed the German Foreign Minister "that his country had absolutely no ambitions outside its present borders."[83] Thus it would seem that Gerede out of personal motivations sought to generate enthusiasm in Berlin for an autonomous Turkic state in the Caucasus. Krecker alleges that the Turkish Government unofficially approved of his doing so. His proof is highly circumstantial, however, and succeeds in demonstrating only that İnönü, Menemencioğlu, and Saracoğlu knew of the work being done by Gerede and the other Pan-Turanists and that they were temporarily allowing it to continue. This may have indeed changed had Germany, in fact, defeated Russia. Pan-Turanian ideas and movements, as Hochstetter has said, "were like weeds ready to spring up."[84] Turkish foreign policy would undoubtedly have had to adjust to the new circumstances created by German dominance. But how they would have handled such a situation is speculative, and there is nothing in the records revealed to date that is capable of demonstrating that İnönü, Menemencioğlu, or Saracoğlu sought to help Germany out of Pan-Turanist ambitions.

The documentary evidence, therefore, thus far uncovered does not allow us to establish any links between the Pan-Turanian movement and the men in Ankara that wielded power. As von Papen advised Ribbentrop in May 1941, it was "erroneous to assume that . . . promises of areas . . . could influence the course which the Turkish Government is determined to pursue in the interest of its clean reputation."[85] Eventually, so it seems, Ribbentrop decided to heed the advice of his ambassador in Ankara and instructed von Papen to abstain from discussing the Pan-Turanian issue with Turkish officials. He wrote:

[83] The Foreign Minister (Ribbentrop) to the Ambassador in Turkey (von Papen), Berlin, August 25, 1941, *Docs.Ger.F.P.*, XIII, 373-75.

[84] In a personal interview with the author.

[85] The Ambassador in Turkey (von Papen) to the Foreign Minister (Ribbentrop), Ankara, May 29, 1941, *Docs.Ger.F.P.*, XII, 913-15.

When we take into account the fact that these issues do not provide Turkey with a sufficient enticement to shift its general policy towards the belligerent nations in our favor, there is no reason for us to give them any guarantees or to participate in Turkey's wishes and demands.[86]

Thus, as Hostler correctly points out, the waning of the movement's prospect of success came even before the Russians began to defeat Germany.[87]

İnönü's attempt to placate the Soviets by seizing the opportunity presented by the publication of the open letters of Nihat Atsız failed, however. Insofar as he hoped to influence Soviet behavior toward Turkey, which was, to repeat, very much at the heart of his decision to suppress the Pan-Turanists, İnönü met with disappointment. The Russians

[86] The Foreign Minister (Ribbentrop) to the Ambassador in Turkey (von Papen), Berlin, September 12, 1942, *Secret Documents*, pp. 105-106. Another early indication of the fact that the Germans were not intending to unify the Turkic elements within the Soviet Union into an autonomous state was the fact that they treated Turkic prisoners of war, both those who were captured while fighting in the Russian army and those who were captured while imprisoned in Russian labor camps for anti-Soviet activity, equally severely. One would have thought that had the Germans intended to create a viable resistance movement that would have led to a separate state, they would have begun by winning the loyalties and channeling the energies of the group that was already disaffected. For a description of the conditions in German prisoner of war camps in Turkestan and the Caucasus, Tahir Çağatay, *Türkistan: Kurtuluş Hareketile İlgili Olaylardan Sahneler (Scenes from Events Concerning The Liberation Movements)* (İstanbul: "Yas Türkistan" Yayını, 1959), p. 24.

[87] Hostler, *Turkism and the Soviets*, p. 184; Hostler, however, goes on to suggest that this and Turkish neutrality in general were "provoked by the Nazi's arrogance and intention not to permit anyone to share in their booty in the USSR." This thesis is parallel to the Russian view which alleges that Turkey intended to invade the Soviet Union during the Second World War. For a resounding denial that the Turkish Government ever planned to attack the Soviet Union in order to pursue Pan-Turanist possibilities, see Ömer Rıza Doğrul, "Turkish Foreign Policy Since the Revolution," *Pakistan Horizon* (June 1951), pp. 61-67, esp. p. 64.

continued to attack Turkish neutrality as favoring the Germans and treated the trials of the Pan-Turanists as mere whitewash. A shift in internal policy alone in mid-1944 would not do. Turkey had to realign its foreign policy as well.

ELEVEN

REALIGNMENT OF TURKISH
FOREIGN POLICY

ALONG with their shift in internal policy, Turkish officials, particularly İnönü, took four important steps in the early part of 1944 to bring Turkey's foreign policy into closer correspondence with emerging realities. In response to British and American demands, Turkey ceased transporting chromite to Germany, virtually closed the Straits to Axis ships, dismissed Foreign Minister Menemencioğlu, and severed diplomatic and economic relations with Germany.

THE CESSATION OF CHROMITE DELIVERIES TO GERMANY

During January and February, the Turks had actually increased deliveries of chromite to Germany. The American Ambassador had not only joined his British colleague in protesting this imprudent action, which was attributed to the anti-Soviet preoccupation of the Foreign Minister, but had recommended that "appropriate action" be taken to destroy the Maritza Bridge linking Bulgaria with Turkey in order to eliminate the railway used to transport the chromite.[1]

[1] The Ambassador in Turkey (Steinhardt) to the Secretary of State, Ankara, February 18, 1944, *Foreign Relations*, 1944, V, 819. In April 1944, the Turkish Foreign Minister attempted to justify these increased deliveries. He argued on the floor of the Grand National Assembly that, first, the British in 1940 had been offered an option for twenty years on the whole of Turkish chromite production but had refused; secondly, in 1943, with British agreement, shipments to Germany had begun in return for shipments of German armaments. "Our principle for trading with Europe," Menemencioğlu stated, "is goods for goods. We have used this principle . . . so strictly that we have taken care not to ship

In March, the British and the Americans considered the utility of further economic sanctions. The Western Allies could have ceased preemptive buying or could have blockaded Turkish ports. Steinhardt and Hugessen opposed the first on the grounds that while it would have no immediate effect on the Turkish economy it would allow the Germans to gain control of the Turkish financial market. The Turkish economy, moreover, seemed immune to pressures from a blockade.[2] The State Department concluded: "It is doubted that Turkey's standard of living is such that it is economically vulnerable to blockade action."[3] Moreover, a blockade would have had the effect of making the Turks even more dependent on the Axis. Thus the State Department reasoned the arsenal of weapons to use against the Turks was "pitifully bare."[4] This was not wholly true, for the Turks themselves were conscious of their growing dependence on British and American good will in the face of Soviet advances. The Western objective, however, was to speed the Turks toward a realignment of their policies with pressures strong enough to achieve these changes quickly, yet not so strong as to weaken the Turks to the point of making them more dependent on the Germans.

On April 19, 1944, the British and the American ambassadors presented Menemencioğlu with notes of protest against the chromite shipments.[5] For Hugessen it was his

---

the corresponding goods before the [imported] goods have arrived. . . ." If chromite shipments to Germany had been rising, it was because of increased German supplies to the Turks, the Foreign Minister concluded; consult *T.B.M.M. Zabıt Ceridesi*, Seventh Assembly, First Session, April 20, 1944, IX, 96.

[2] The Ambassador in Turkey (Steinhardt) to the Secretary of State, Ankara, April 5, 1944, *Foreign Relations*, 1944, V, 822-25.

[3] The Secretary of State to the Ambassador in Turkey (Steinhardt), Washington, D.C., March 30, 1944, *ibid.*, pp. 820-22.

[4] *Ibid.*, p. 821.

[5] The Ambassador in Turkey (Steinhardt) to the Secretary of State, Ankara, April 15, 1944, *ibid.*, pp. 825-26.

first meeting with the Turkish Foreign Minister in weeks, and it was a "chilly ten minutes."[6] Although the contents of the notes were identical, Menemencioğlu's meeting with Steinhardt took place in a friendlier atmosphere. "Numan [Menemencioğlu] accepted the note," Steinhardt wired the State Department, "in a friendly spirit indicating a cooperative state of mind" and declared that he "had no particular desire to trade with Germany." Menemencioğlu also indicated that he was unable to understand why the Allies "had not long since taken action to relieve him from his 'dilemma' by destroying means of transportation between Turkey and Germany. . . ."[7] As they parted, Menemencioğlu told Steinhardt that he would give the note "careful consideration." The following day, he informed the American Ambassador that shipments of Turkish chromite would be reduced to 4,000 tons per month as against the 6,752 tons delivered in February.[8] Five days later, on April 20, he announced the cessation of all chromite shipments to Germany. Menemencioğlu explained to the Grand National Assembly that a neutral state was under an obligation to sell indiscriminately if at all to both sides of a war. Because of its alliance with Britain, "the nucleus and basis of our foreign policy," Turkey was not neutral. Thus, he announced that shipments of chromite to the Axis would cease.[9]

A related issue was trade in strategic goods between Turkey and the pro-Axis Balkan States of Hungary and Romania. As late as May 3, 1944, the Allies were dismayed that Turkey had signed a new trade agreement with Hungary. On May 10, Steinhardt and Hugessen again took their

[6] The phrase is Hugessen's; also, the Ambassador in Turkey (Steinhardt) to the Secretary of State, Ankara, April 15, 1944, ibid., p. 827.

[7] Ibid., pp. 825-26.

[8] The Ambassador in Turkey (Steinhardt) to the Secretary of State, Ankara, April 15, 1944, ibid., pp. 826-27.

[9] T.B.M.M. Zabıt Ceridesi, Seventh Assembly, First Session, April 20, 1944, IX, 98.

protests to Menemencioğlu. The Turkish Foreign Minister replied that his country could not afford the "luxury of severing trade with the Axis."[10] He indicated instead, that the United States and Britain "would always have the opportunity to prevent the export of strategic materials" by compensating Turkey for the goods it would otherwise receive from the Axis. For example, not a ton of Turkish exports would go to Romania if Britain or the United States would furnish equivalent amounts of oil now being supplied by the Axis.[11] Nevertheless, the Western Allies maintained their diplomatic pressure, much to the annoyance of the Foreign Minister who complained that the Allies were encroaching upon Turkish sovereignty.[12] On May 26 the Turkish Government gave way, submitting to the British and Americans a draft agreement affirming its intention not to export chromite to the Axis and also promising to keep its export of other strategic commodities to below half of export levels in the previous year.[13] Steinhardt and Hugessen both recommended, with minor modifications, acceptance of this draft. Steinhardt, however, was quickly forced to take issue with the British who wanted to maintain "constant pressure" on the Turks before signing the agreement. Nonacceptance would only serve to publicize strained Anglo-Turkish relations, Steinhardt argued, while acceptance would indicate to the Turkish Foreign Minister that he "is on notice that further demands will shortly be made."[14] Steinhardt's arguments prevailed. The agreement

[10] The Ambassador in Turkey (Steinhardt) to the Secretary of State, Ankara, May 12, 1944, *Foreign Relations*, 1944, v, 841-42.

[11] *Ibid.*

[12] The Ambassador in Turkey (Steinhardt) to the Secretary of State, Ankara, May 23, 1944, *ibid.*, p. 848.

[13] The Ambassador in Turkey (Steinhardt) to the Secretary of State, Ankara, May 26, 1944, *ibid.*, pp. 851-52.

[14] The Ambassador in Turkey (Steinhardt) to the Secretary of State, Ankara, June 2, 1944, *ibid.*, pp. 857-59. Steinhardt was reacting to a message from the Department of State, May 31, 1944 (*ibid.*, p. 856), in which he was asked to comment on British suggestions that " 'con-

was signed and the Allies did indeed begin to make new demands on the Turkish Government. These involved passage of Axis ships through the Straits.

MENEMENCIOĞLU'S RESIGNATION AND THE CLOSURE OF THE STRAITS TO AXIS SHIPS

Article 4 of the Montreux Convention provides that in time of war when Turkey is not a belligerent, ships of commerce, no matter what the flag or cargo, shall have liberty of passage through the Straits.[15] This right is subject to a provision set out in Article 3, that Turkey may establish a sanitary inspection post at either entrance to the Straits where ships may be stopped and inspected.[16] This check is to be

---

stant pressure between now and launching of Second Front' should be maintained on the Turks as a means of maintaining a threat to the Germans." Steinhardt replied: "I am at a loss to follow the argument that when Numan [Menemencioğlu] objects to continued pressure by contending that what is asked is tantamount to a rupture of relations with Germany the British 'will let him argue like this until the attack opens and then tell him frankly that this [is] what is wanted.' I don't see what the British will gain after the attack has opened by telling Numan [Menemencioğlu] 'frankly' that a rupture of relations with Germany is what is wanted as they have been telling him this since December."

15 The first sentence of Article 3 of the Montreux Convention reads: "All ships entering the Straits of the Aegean Sea or by the Black Sea shall stop at a sanitary station near the entrance to the Straits for the purposes of the sanitary control prescribed by Turkish law within the framework of international sanitary regulations"; League of Nations, *Treaty Series*, Vol. CLXXIII, No. 4015, "Convention regarding the Regime of the Straits, with Annexes and Protocol, signed at Montreux," July 20, 1936, pp. 213-41 at p. 219. For an account of Turkey and the Straits, James T. Shotwell and Francis Deák, *Turkey at the Straits: A Short History* (New York: The Macmillan Co., 1941); Harry N. Howard's works on the subject are definitive.

16 Article 4 in part reads: "In time of war, Turkey not being belligerent, merchant vessels under any flag or with any kind of cargo, shall enjoy freedom of transit and navigation in the Straits. . . ."

effected as rapidly as possible. For no other reason may vessels be halted in transit.

Feridun Cemal Erkin points out that the right of sanitary inspection in Article 3 was won by Turkey at Montreux over the opposition of many delegations and was accepted only after Turkey promised to hold these inspections to the minimum time required to carry out the formalities.[17] Otherwise, Turkish authority to interfere with free passage was formally reduced to near zero. Nevertheless, Erkin states, Turkish insistence on the right of sanitary inspection was in reality a device to give itself, "under cover of sanitary control," the means to examine the cargo of ships destined for countries "whose attitude at a given moment might appear suspect," and to ascertain whether ships claiming to be vessels of commerce really were.[18]

During wars in which Turkey is neutral, the Convention prohibits most vessels of war of a belligerent power from passing through the Straits except in specified circumstances.[19] Article 8 and Annex II of the Convention define the prohibited belligerent vessels in terms of tonnage, equipment, speed, and function.[20] The definition does not include vessels of less than 100 tons displacement and is ambiguous in its application to small vessels which are auxiliary to conventional warships or which by their nature are not clearly intended or capable of performing only as vessels of

[17] Erkin, *Turkish-Russian Relations*, p. 272.

[18] *Ibid.*, pp. 272-73.

[19] Article 19 of the Montreux Convention permits the wartime passage of nonbelligerent vessels of war, but prohibits the passage of warships of belligerents other than those engaged in a collective military action arising from an obligation under the Covenant of the League of Nations or from assistance being "rendered to a State victim of aggression in virtue of a treaty of mutual assistance binding Turkey, concluded within the framework of the Covenant of the League of Nations. . . ."

[20] Article 8 specifies Annex II as the section that defines categories of ships.

commerce or as vessels of combat.[21] The problem of definition in wartime is further complicated by the fact that merchant vessels of belligerents are ordinarily armed against attack.

During January and February 1944, the British Ambassador complained to Turkish authorities about German vessels, which he alleged were auxiliary vessels of war, being allowed to pass through the Straits. On each occasion, the Turks claimed to have satisfied themselves that the vessels were in the range of 20 to 40 tons and had carried commercial cargoes.[22] The British had insisted that these ships were of the type used for combat in the Aegean or had hidden armaments including gun-carriages. The Turks had maintained that gun-carriages were normal equipment for merchant vessels of combatants, and that these did not change the commercial character of the vessels in question.[23]

At the end of May, the British Embassy notified the Turks that five German E.M.S. class vessels were about to pass through the Straits, and that they were armed with cannons, Bofors, and depth charges. These were stopped by the Turks on May 26. On May 29, the German Embassy complained that eleven more vessels had been stopped at one end of the Straits and six more at the other. The Germans, insisting that these vessels were purely commercial and carried cargoes of lumber, fodder, and charcoal, demanded that they be allowed to pass. According to the Turks, inquiry revealed nothing unusual about the vessels and they were allowed through.[24]

Then, at the beginning of June, the British Ambassador reported that three German "war-transports" and three

[21] Annex II, Sec. C (6) of the Montreux Convention defines auxiliary vessels as "naval surface vessels the standard displacement of which exceeds 100 tons (102 metric tons), which are normally employed on fleet duties or as troop transports, or in some other way than as fighting ships, and which are not specifically built as fighting ships. . . ."

[22] Erkin, *Turkish-Russian Relations*, pp. 274-75.

[23] *Ibid.*, p. 275.   [24] *Ibid.*, p. 276.

E.M.S. type vessels were heading for the Straits and again asked that they be stopped. One, the *Kassel*, refused to be inspected and was not permitted to pass from the Black Sea.[25] The Turks were thus in a dilemma. Erkin notes that he advised Menemencioğlu to make use of Article 24 of the Convention, which could be read to entrust Turkey with the task of using its discretion in the application of the Convention, but that the Foreign Minister rejected his proposal, "preferring to adhere strictly to the letter of the Convention."[26] The Foreign Minister asked for and received von Papen's personal assurances that the vessels were not ships of war. He thereupon gave permission for them to pass.[27] The British reaction was one of unrelenting if not wholly unwarranted moral outrage.[28] Speaking in Parliament, Foreign Secretary Eden referred to "this unsatisfactory attitude" and said that "His Majesty's Government are profoundly disturbed by the fact that the Turkish Government should have lent themselves to this palpable manoeuver. . . ."[29] He particularly objected to "the inadequate and hurried inspection" to which the German ships were being subjected by Turkish authorities.

These protests merely indicated to Menemencioğlu that the British Government was demanding the closure of the Straits to all German vessels, not merely those prohibited by

[25] *Ibid.*   [26] *Ibid,* p. 279.

[27] Esmer in *Turkish Foreign Policy,* p. 167.

[28] The British case had been theoretically weakened by the fact that they themselves had long violated Turkish neutrality with the tacit approval of the Turkish Government. Captain Stephen W. Roskill of the Royal Navy observes in his official history, "our protests [regarding the Axis warship] were . . . weakened by the fact that we could not deny that our own light naval forces had not shown too scrupulous a regard for Turkish neutrality when conducting operations against the enemy's Aegean garrisons and shipping." *The War At Sea 1939-1945,* Vol. III, Stephen W. Roskill, *The Offensive* (London: Her Majesty's Stationery Office, 1960), p. 317.

[29] Great Britain. Parliament. House of Commons. *The Parliamentary Debates (official reports),* Fifth Series, Vol. 400, Col. 1,987.

the Convention; it was a matter of the definitions adopted at Montreux, no longer suiting one of the principal signatories.[30] The Turkish Foreign Minister proposed to the British Government that the meaning and application of the terms of Annex II in regard to small auxiliary vessels be submitted to an impartial foreign jurist, perhaps a Swiss, and that meanwhile, until the jurist had completed his considerations, the passage of suspected vessels be halted. Both the Germans and the British rejected this procedure as being too slow. In the end, the Turks insisted on a full inspection of the *Kassel*, which the Germans had refused, and found that it possessed 9-millimeter armor plate, cranes of 31-ton capacity for transporting tanks, 5 machine guns, 2 cannons, submarine detection equipment, depth charges, and 65 chests of ammunition![31] "In brief," Erkin concludes, "the inspection confirmed the information of the British Ambassador."[32] The Turks protested to Germany on the violation of the Convention and thereafter prohibited the passage of all E.M.S. and Mannheim class vessels. They also ordered the intensive inspection of all German vessels applying to pass through the Straits. These decisions were announced by Prime Minister Saracoğlu, who had taken over the Foreign Ministry the day of the announcement. Menemencioğlu resigned "so that Turkish-English relations would not deteriorate."[33]

The Allies were especially gratified by the resignation of Foreign Minister Menemencioğlu, who was generally believed to be pro-Axis.[34] His departure was less a factor than

[30] Erkin, *Turkish-Russian Relations*, p. 276; this rendition of Menemencioğlu's thinking is confirmed in the *Menemencioğlu Manuscript*, p. 293.

[31] *Ayın Tarihi*, Vol. 127 (June 1944) in the *Hâdiselerin Takvimi (Calendar of Events)*, pp. 6-7.

[32] Erkin, *Turkish-Russian Relations*, p. 277.

[33] Baltalı, *The Issue of the Straits*, p. 121.

[34] *Keesing's Contemporary Archives, 1943-1946*, Vol. V (London: Keesing's Publications, Ltd.), June 24-July 1, 1944, p. 6,526, for exam-

a symbol of Turkish realignment. Menemencioğlu's foreign policy accorded with that of İnönü and virtually all Turks in having sought throughout the period of German ascendancy to preserve Turkey by neutrality.[35] In the period of Allied ascendancy he had cooperated with the British within the limits of a more benign neutrality and had sought to warn the West of the need to work with Turkey to prevent the Soviets from capturing the Balkans. This policy had now come to the end of its utility. The Germans were beaten, the Soviets were clearly going to "liberate" Eastern Europe and the Anglo-Americans were not prepared to launch a major offensive in the Eastern Mediterranean. To have failed to shift from this consistent and hitherto near-unanimous Turkish policy would only have alienated the British and, to a lesser extent, the Americans; it would have left Turkey isolated in the face of events in Eastern Europe

---

ple, reported, "It was pointed out in London that N. Menemencioğlu had generally been regarded as the Minister largely responsible for the Turkish refusal to enter the war on the side of the Allies. . . ."

[35] Turgut Menemencioğlu emphasizes that although his uncle's opinions usually prevailed in matters concerning foreign policy, there was in any event more often than not unanimity among Turkish foreign policy-makers. Thus it is impossible to specifically sort Menemencioğlu's policies from those of İnönü. Turgut Menemencioğlu writes: "I would not say that Numan could set policy with autonomy, but he had the Ministry under his absolute control and he directly influenced policy by his clear position and unwavering attitude in his contacts with the Turkish government, the President and members of Parliament. He took part in Cabinet meetings and his analysis or explanation prevailed. Fortunately, most of the time, the President, Prime Minister and the army shared his opinions. Sometimes, especially when new events occurred, differences would appear. Rarely, toward the end, some clashes also took place. In general, Turkish policy was conducted in a very harmonious manner." (In a personal letter to the author.) Zeki Kuneralp confirms this analysis: "Numan was made a scapegoat by İnönü in order to help Turkey wash its hands clean once the Allies began to win the war. Menemencioğlu, however, never took a major decision without consulting İnönü, so his policies and those of İnönü were actually one and the same." (In a personal interview with the author.)

which the Turks could no longer hope to alter. Thus the realignment had become necessary, and, to make it dramatic and visible, İnönü asked the Turkish Foreign Minister to resign.[36]

That Menemencioğlu became the symbol of this realignment was made inevitable by his unwillingness to conciliate the British in the matter of Axis shipping through the Straits. The fact of his unwillingness does not, however, necessarily confirm the view that the Foreign Minister was essentially pro-Axis. His own reflections on the events leading to his resignation indicate that in this as in most other major crises, Menemencioğlu's thoughts were of the Soviet Union. "Those whom we may favor merely because they are our allies," he wrote, "may one day use it against Turkey if we give in to them and allow the treaty law of the Montreux Convention to become an instrument of our national politics." What then, he asked, "of our enemies who are only waiting for a single default" to confirm their thesis that Turkey is neither strong enough nor responsible enough to enforce the Convention scrupulously. "What means of defense would we then have against the Russians if it were to be violated even just this once for the British; the Russians, too, could and undoubtedly would demand that the Convention be sacrificed to a moment's political exigency."[37] Thus it can be faithfully reported that Menemencioğlu assumed an adamant position over passage of the German ships because he feared the effects that a single transgression would have on the Soviet Union. Menemen-

[36] Feridun Cemal Erkin in a personal interview with the author has described the events during the day Menemencioğlu resigned. It was an angry day for İnönü and Menemencioğlu both.

[37] *Menemencioğlu Manuscript*, p. 294; Cevat Açıkalın and Nihat Erim have claimed that in legal terms, at least, Menemencioğlu interpreted the provisions of Article 19 correctly in allowing these small, partially dismantled, auxiliary vessels to pass through the Straits. Erim, later to become Secretary-General of the CHP, was then a young legal aide in the Foreign Ministry and headed a commission to study the case. (In a personal interview with the author.)

cioğlu reasoned if Turkey could be seen to have violated the letter of the Convention, the Russians would either require a revision of the Straits or, more to the point, would demand the right to patrol the Straits. Menemencioğlu was simply not prepared to put other considerations ahead of the Soviet danger.

The British Ambassador, however, at the height of the crisis, had gone over Menemencioğlu's head with a personal appeal from Churchill to İnönü. Hugessen recalls the vehemence with which he presented the Allied case. "I spoke for nearly an hour without interruption, and at the end İnönü finally nodded. I knew I had won."[38] Indeed he had. "İnönü sacrificed Menemencioğlu to placate the British," Professor A. Suat Bilge has said.[39] The Foreign Minister was now clearly out of step with the rest of his government's policies. "Numan forgot the politics of the situation," as Açıkalın has rightly stated.[40]

SEVERANCE OF RELATIONS WITH GERMANY

Menemencioğlu was now out of the way, chromite shipments from Turkey to the Axis had stopped, and Turkish exports to Axis countries were reduced by half from the previous year. On June 23, Eden contacted Hull and proposed joint action to force the Turks to discontinue relations with the Axis. Hull agreed to support the British in their representations to the Turkish Government and notified Steinhardt of this on June 28.[41]

[38] Sir Hughe Knatchbull-Hugessen in a personal interview with the author.

[39] In a personal interview with the author.

[40] In a personal interview with the author.

[41] In this as in other matters relating to Turkey's realignment, Foreign Secretary Eden seems to have advocated a tough line. In an *aide-mémoire* to the Department of State, the British Embassy indicated that Eden was of the opinion that the Western Allies should follow Menemencioğlu's dismissal "with some concrete suggestion of their own. . . ." Eden advised that they "not lag behind" the Soviet Union

The same day, Ambassador Harriman elicited Molotov's opinion on this approach. Molotov was not impressed with what he saw to be a halfway measure. He told Harriman: "If we had expected Turkey to enter the war in 1943 it would not be logical to reduce our demands after our military successes which should be convincing to the Turks."[42] Despite these Russian objections, on June 13, one week after the Allied Normany landings, Hugessen submitted to Prime Minister and acting Foreign Minister Şükrü Saracoğlu a British request that Turkey break off diplomatic relations with Germany. Saracoğlu protested that the British Government was requiring Turkey to take action that was "dishonorable" and which the Grand National Assembly would not approve. Hugessen is reported to have replied that he hoped the Turkish Government would not hold to this position "since it would have a most unfortunate effect in London."[43] During the interview, Saracoğlu again broached the possibility of an Anglo-Turkish entry into Bulgaria as a preferred alternative. The British Ambassador replied that he knew of no Allied plans to invade the Balkan Peninsula and in any case was not in a position to discuss the issue.[44]

The British position in this phase of relations with Turkey was that a break in relations with Germany would be very useful, having a strong psychological effect on Germany and being capable of immediate execution. Such a request for the cessation of economic and diplomatic "relations could be acted upon without delay, involved . . . no

in telling the Turks to break diplomatic relations with Germany or enter the war; *aide-mémoire*, the British Embassy to the Department of State, Washington, D.C., June 23, 1944, *Foreign Relations*, 1944, V, 860-63.

42 The Ambassador in the Soviet Union (Harriman) to the Secretary of State, Moscow, June 28, 1944, *ibid.*, pp. 863-65.

43 The Ambassador in Turkey (Steinhardt) to the Secretary of State, Ankara, June 30, 1944, *ibid.*, pp. 866-67.

44 *Ibid.*

military commitments, and would have nearly the same moral effect on Germany and in the Balkans as would a declaration of war."[45] The British, therefore, took the position that a break with Germany was an excellent way for the Turks to "clarify" their policy which "had become obscure and confused by recent events." The British, promising to come to Turkey's assistance should the Germans attack,[46] also promised to try to compensate the Turks for whatever disruption the break might cause the Turkish economy.

The United States broadly supported this British line of approach, indicating that it must be made clear to the Turks and particularly to the Russians that a breach of diplomatic relations "was regarded as only a first step towards active belligerence."[47] It, too, believed that such a first step would bring benefits: the expulsion of German personnel and Axis agents from Turkey, the right to fly over Turkish territory, and the possible use of Turkish air bases.[48] General Marshall, however, again warned that the United States should make it clear to Turkey and its allies it was not "thereby committed to military, naval, or air support of any campaign in the Balkans."[49] Marshall reiterated his opposition to any diversion of resources from operations already underway in the Mediterranean.

[45] A close paraphrase of Hull; see Hull, *Memoirs*, p. 1,374.

[46] *Aide-mémoire*, the British Embassy to the Department of State, Washington, D.C., July 12, 1944, *Foreign Relations*, 1944, v, 879-81.

[47] Hull, *Memoirs*, p. 1,374.

[48] *Strategic Planning*, p. 505. The strategy section of the Joint Chiefs continued to advise Marshall not to allow Turkey to come into the war. The United States would have to supply the bulk of equipment and technicians to bring a Turkish attack to successful fruition. Planners in the Pentagon also seemed apprised of the political dangers which might result from a Turkish attack on Bulgaria. "If the Turks attacked Bulgaria," the strategy section reasoned, "Soviet forces would be brought into the southern Balkans, and neither the Turks nor the British wanted that to happen."

[49] Hull, *Memoirs*, p. 1,375.

The Soviet Government, however, remained disinterested in these maneuvers. Their position remained one of demanding that Turkey either enter the war or that it be left isolated.[50] Churchill tried to move Stalin from this and to enlist his interest in a tripartite demand for a diplomatic break. "The Turkish alliance," he reminded the Soviet leader, "was very dear" to Germany. A break in relations with Turkey "would be a knell to the German soul."[51] Stalin's reply arrived in London on July 15:

> As you know on the initiative of the Turkish Government we resumed negotiations with it last May and June, and twice made the same proposal that the three Allied Governments made at the end of last year. Nothing came of that either. As regards any half-hearted step by Turkey I do not at the moment see how it can benefit the Allies. In view of the evasive and vague attitude which the Turkish Government has assumed in relation to Germany, it is better to leave Turkey to herself and to refrain from any further pressure on her. This implies, of course, that the claims of Turkey, who has evaded fighting Germany, to special rights in postwar affairs will be disregarded.[52]

Ambassador Harriman reported that the Soviets were being careful not to allow Turkey's severance of relations with Germany to take on the aura of a concession to the Soviet Union. On June 13, after a conversation with Vyshinsky, Harriman further reported that the Soviets refused to regard Turkey's severance of relations as a valid preliminary step to active belligerence. Turkish action was too little and

---

50 *Ibid.*, p. 1,373.

51 Union of Soviet Socialist Republics. Ministry of Foreign Affairs, *Correspondence Between the Chairman of the Council of Ministers of the U.S.S.R. and the Presidents of the U.S.A. and the Prime Ministers of Great Britain During the Great Patriotic War of 1941-1945.* (Moscow: Foreign Languages Publishing House, 1957), the Premier to the Prime Minister, Moscow, July 15, 1944, p. 236.

52 *Ibid.*

came too late, Vyshinsky had claimed. "There was no time for a second step." The reason why the Russians were remaining "aloof," Harriman correctly surmised, was that they hoped to derive whatever benefits that came from Turkish action without recognizing any consequent obligation to Turkey.[53]

The Soviets, with their troops massed along the Romanian border, now perceived no gain to themselves in a gesture that might have the effect of giving the Turks a claim to preferment. When, on August 2, 1944, the Turks announced the break, it was coldly received by *Pravda* as "calculated opportunism."[54] From the United States, on the other hand, came a small hint of a new rapprochement. On August 4, the Joint Chiefs of Staff were reported to have agreed that if a campaign were to develop in the Balkans, "the United States would be willing to . . . see if portions of Turkish requests for aid could be made available."[55]

Speaking on August 2 in the Grand National Assembly, Prime Minister and Acting Foreign Minister Saracoğlu said that the break in diplomatic relations merely reflected the established lines of Turkish policy.[56] Turkey had never been neutral but rather had been on the side of Great Britain throughout the war. Now that the British and the United States governments had requested this specific step on Turkey's part, Turkey would comply. Saracoğlu noted that it was a "just" request and took cognizance of the fact that the British had agreed to compensate the Turks for economic losses sustained as a result of the break in relations. The

[53] The Ambassador in the Soviet Union (Harriman) to the Secretary of State, Moscow, July 30, 1944, *Foreign Relations*, 1944, v, 894-95; closely paraphrased.

[54] See the *Times*, London, September 12, 1943, for a rendering in English.

[55] *Strategic Planning*, p. 505; also Chairman, Joint Chiefs of Staff (Marshall) to Under-Secretary of State (Stettinius), August 4, 1944, *Foreign Relations*, 1944, v, 897.

[56] *T.B.M.M. Zabıt Ceridesi*, Seventh Assembly, August 2, 1944, I, 5.

Prime Minister informed the Assembly that the British were "very pleased" with Turkey's decision. He also assured the deputies that "this decision . . . is not a decision for war." Of the Assembly's 492 members, 411 voted for the resolution which was moved by leading members of the Parliamentary Group of the CHP.[57] The motion was supported by Ali Râna Tarhan of the Independent Group of the CHP who said that his party "shares the opinion that this action is a requirement of our alliance. . . ."[58] The Turks had thus brought their foreign policy into line with Allied demands. They now waited to see if the Allies would respond in kind.

[57] They were: Hasan Saka (Trabzon), Kâzım Özalp (Balıkeşir), M. Ş. Esendal (Bilecik). The vote to sever relations with Germany was (technically) unanimous since there were none against, with the rest abstaining or absent.

[58] *T.B.M.M. Zabıt Ceridesi*, Seventh Assembly, August 2, 1944, I, 6.

TWELVE

TURKEY BETWEEN EMERGING SPHERES

ALLIED VICTORIES DURING THE SUMMER
AND FALL OF 1944

THE MONTHS following Menemencioğlu's resignation saw the Allies sweep into areas that had been controlled by the Axis since the beginning of the war. In June the cross-Channel attack had finally taken place and by September, British and American penetration into northwestern Europe seemed secure beyond question. By November 1, moreover, the British had established themselves in Greece and were beginning to assist the partisans under Tito to rout out German troops. Soviet advances were equally impressive. By late September both Finland and Romania had capitulated. In early October, the Soviet army attacked Hungary and the Hungarian Government quickly called for an armistice. The battle for Poland took longer. For three months, September, October, November, Soviet forces tarried along the Vistula while Poles engaged Germans in bloody conflict. When Soviet occupation forces finally entered Warsaw in December, there was hardly any resistance left in Poland.

As ever, the Turks watched these developments with mixed feelings: gladdened by the liberation of Axis-occupied nations but also fearful that the liberation would turn out merely to substitute one occupation force for another. In his various moves to realign Turkey with the Allies, İnönü, as we have seen, hoped once again to have benevolent relations with the West, particularly the British, and to forge a modus vivendi with the Russians. When the attempt by Foreign Minister Menemencioğlu to engage the Soviets in meaningful negotiations failed, it became all the more urgent for Turkey to draw closer to the British and the Americans. Thus İnönü took the steps he did. At the same time, it was necessary, as a matter of prudence in relation to the Russians and because İnönü did not wish to antagonize or embarrass the Americans and the British, to guard the tone of the Turkish reaction to developments and, in general, to disguise Turkish fears as hopefulness.[1]

Indeed, for a time, there seemed to be reason for hope. The Soviet Union had committed several actions which seemed to reveal an intent to pursue a moderate policy. The Tripartite Allied Declaration on Iran, signed in mid-December 1943, for example, guaranteed Iranian independence after the war and relieved Turkish fears that the Russians would insist upon remaining there after the war. The Czechoslovak-Soviet treaty, signed on December 12, 1943, was equally reassuring. Eduard Beneš, who had traveled to

[1] Selim Sarper provided certain insights which contributed to this analysis in a personal interview with the author, Ankara, July 21, 1968; Selim Sarper served as Turkish Ambassador to the Soviet Union from March 1943 until after the war. Fahir Armaoğlu, in a personal interview, has also said, "Upon seeing that the collapse of Germany was imminent and with it that of the European balance, the Turkish Government felt the necessity of playing up to the Soviet Union." This was true in relation to the United States and Britain as well. On September 12, 1944, for example, Saracoğlu called Ambassador Steinhardt into his office. Steinhardt found the Prime Minister in a "rather troubled state of mind." The Turkish Prime Minister expressed his inability to comprehend the unfavorable attitude in Britain and the United States toward Turkey and stated that despite its compliance with the British request to sever relations with Germany, "London continued to evidence irritation and dissatisfaction with the Turk Government." Steinhardt suggested that perhaps bad feelings resulted from the fact that Turkey had not yet entered the war. Saracoğlu retorted that the Turks had been waiting over the past few months for a specific request from the British or the Americans but that it had not been made. It was "hardly advisable," he said, for the Turkish Government to take the initiative. Saracoğlu made it clear that they were ready to comply with British and American wishes; the Ambassador in Turkey (Steinhardt) to the Secretary of State, Ankara, September 12, 1944, *Foreign Relations*, 1944, V, 899-900.

Moscow for the purpose of negotiating the treaty, found Stalin and Molotov accommodating: Russian occupation forces would not interfere in Czechoslovakia's internal affairs and would transfer the civil administration to Czech authorities as soon as possible. The Turkish press applauded these events and suggested that they demonstrated Moscow's good intentions and the fact that the Soviets were working closely with the British and the Americans.[2]

This held true in regard to Soviet treatment of Romania. As Russian armies began to cross the Pruth River on April 2, Molotov issued a conciliatory statement which promised that the Soviet Union would seek to preserve Romania's social structure as well as its territorial integrity. When Russian armies finally did bring about the downfall of the Antonescu Government in Romania, the Soviets seemed to be acting in accordance with Molotov's pledge. On August 23, King Michael accepted Soviet armistice terms and on August 25 declared war on the Axis. He also appointed a coalition government, under General Constantine Sanatescu, which was comprised of moderate political elements. The same day, Molotov seemed to give his consent to these developments by officially repeating the generous conditions he had enunciated in April. These mild Soviet actions and pronouncements were considered by some of the Turkish press as a hopeful sign of change in Moscow's policies.[3]

[2] See, e.g., *Ulus*, December 15, 1944; *Tanin*, December 16, 1944; *Cumhuriyet*, December 18, 1944.

[3] See, e.g., *Tanin*, April 5, 6, and June 30, 1944; *Akşam*, April 4 and August 27, 1944; on September 15, 1944, Sadak, in *Akşam*, published an editorial entitled "Romanya mütarekesi ve Sovyetler Birliğinin harp sonu sulh ve emniyet tertipleri" ("The Romanian Armistice and the end of war, peace and security measures of the Soviet Union") in which he stated that the armistice with Romania, which had been signed by the Soviet Union alone, reflected the intentions of all three of the Allies. All things considered, he wrote, the conditions imposed upon Romania "cannot be considered ruthless or excessive for a defeated enemy"; *Ayın Tarihi*, Vol. 130 (September 1944), pp. 254-55. It should also be mentioned that during this period, the Turkish press carried news of the Soviet Union's mild treatment of Finland.

Nevertheless, while the Turks were going out of their way to give no offense to the Russians and were even willing to applaud Soviet policy, they, in the words of one observer, continued to "show more fear of Russia than they ever have [shown] of Germany."[4] What brought Turkish apprehensions concerning the ambitions of the Soviet Union to a near fever pitch in September 1944, notwithstanding the moderate Soviet position toward Iran, Czechoslovakia, Finland, and Romania, was the Russian invasion of Bulgaria.

Soviet Occupation of Bulgaria and the Reaction in Turkey

As the Turks watched the Russians march through Romania, they feared that Bulgaria would be the next to fall; consequently, they urged the Bulgarians to take action that might prevent a Soviet invasion. During July and early August, Turkish publicists, Hüseyin Cahit Yalçın, Asım Us, and Ahmet Emin Yalman recommended that the Bulgarians institute their own speedy adjustments in policy by overthrowing their pro-Axis regime and by declaring war on the Axis.[5] Bulgaria, they suggested, could now take pride in the fact that it had never declared war on the Soviet Union.

Although the Bulgarians waited until the Soviets declared war on August 29, it seemed, for an instant, as if they were planning to heed Turkish advice. In early September, the pro-Axis Bulgarian Government did fall and a new cabinet headed by Constantine Muraviev, a member of the right-wing Agrarian Party, immediately attempted to shore up its position with the Allies, especially the Russians. In early morning, September 5, Muraviev issued a statement in which he renounced all further collaboration with the Nazis, promised to begin negotiations immediately with the

---

[4] Richard Mowrer, *Chicago Daily Mail*, September 14, 1944; Mowrer had just visited Ankara.

[5] See, e.g., *Tanin*, July 7, 31, and August 5, 1944; *Vakit*, July 5, and August 5, 11, 1944; *Vatan*, August 18, 1944.

British and the Americans on the terms of an armistice, and pledged that his government would pursue friendly relations with Russia. *Tass*, however, immediately disavowed this as fraudulent and insufficient. On September 8, the Muraviev Government attempted to appease the Russians further by breaking diplomatic relations with Germany and by calling for an armistice with the Soviet Union. Soviet troops under Marshal Tolbukhin, however, had already begun to invade Bulgaria. On September 9, Kimon Georgiev, the pro-Soviet leader of the Fatherland Front, emerged as the head of the Bulgarian Government, having forced the young King Simeon II to consent to the new regime. The Turks thus found themselves suddenly bordering a nation which had long been irredentist toward Thrace and Macedonia, had long openly coveted a port on the Aegean, and which had now become the instrument not only of Bulgarian nationalism but of Soviet expansionist aspirations as well.

What particularly alarmed the Turks was the possibility of a synthesis between Bulgarian irredentism and Soviet-supported communist aggression. There had long been pro-Russian feelings in Bulgaria; the Bulgarians had not declared war on the Soviet Union and the Germans had even been afraid to allow Bulgarian troops to fight against the Russians for fear that they would defect.[6] Now a pro-Soviet government had been established in Sofia and at a time when Russia was coming to occupy all of the Balkans. The Turks wondered whether the Russians might thus try to help the Bulgarians gain control over Salonicka.

[6] For a brief description of Turkish suspicion toward Bulgaria and an analysis of its causes, Aptulahat Askın, *Atatürk'ün Dış Politika İlkeleri ve Diplomasisi (Principles of Atatürk's Foreign Policy and Diplomacy)* (İstanbul: İnkılâp ve Aka Kitabevleri, 1966), p. 126. From the Turkish point of view, their rift with Bulgaria has been caused to some extent by Bulgaria's historically pro-Russian attitude and by its inveterate irredentism. As C. L. Sulzberger observed: "Scratch a Bulgarian and you are likely to find an irredentist"; *The New York Times*, November 1, 1968. Turks apparently tend to agree.

The public reaction to developments in Bulgaria was pro-
nounced: black-out regulations, a rush for gold, hoarding
on a wide scale.[7] Rumors alleging that Turkey was about
to be invaded by the Soviet Union became widespread.[8]
Ankara, however, attempted to remain calm. Certain members of the Turkish press, close to the government, tried to
put a favorable light on the Russian invasion of Bulgaria.
Necmettin Sadak, for example, indicated that the Soviet
Union was acting in consonance with the British and the
Americans and that the invasion only suggested that the
Soviets intended to treat all defeated Axis countries alike.[9]
He later declared that the Bulgarians had committed a
number of foolish mistakes and were now in the process of
being slapped by "big brother," the Soviet Union.[10] Bulgaria had tried to fool the world, but the Soviets were dem-
onstrating that the world had not been deluded by them.

Not every voice in Turkey, however, was willing to be
subdued to appease the Russians. Hüseyin Cahit Yalçın
found the Soviet declaration of war on Bulgaria difficult to
understand since the reasons proffered by way of justification were neither "convincing nor soothing."[11] Admitting
he was no friend of the Bulgarian Government or its policies, Yalçın declared that he was unable to detect serious
enough fault on the part of the Bulgarians to warrant Soviet
declaration of war. He also refused to accept the notion that
in declaring war on Bulgaria, the Soviets were acting for the
United States or Britain. On the contrary, the declaration
of war was an attempt by Russia to show the Americans and

---

7 For a fuller description, Geoffrey Lewis, *Turkey*, pp. 120-21.

8 *Ibid.*

9 Necmettin Sadak, "Sovyet Rusya'nın Bulgaristan'a harb notası"
("Soviet Russia's declaration of war on Bulgaria"), *Akşam*, September
7, 1944, as in *Ayın Tarihi*, Vol. 130 (September 1944), pp. 269-70.

10 Necmettin Sadak, "Sovyet Rusya ordularının Bulgaristanı işgal
etmeleri hadisesi" ("Soviet Russian army's invasion of Bulgaria"),
Akşam, September 10, 1944, as in *ibid.*, pp. 271-73.

11 "Rus-Bulgar harbi oldu-bitti" ("The *fait accompli* of the Russian-
Bulgarian war"), *Tanin*, September 7, 1944, as in *ibid.*, pp. 270-71.

the British that "there will be only one influence in the Balkans and that influence will be exclusively the Russian influence." Yalçın added, "This is what the Soviets want to get across to the Anglo-Saxons: the Balkans are a special game preserve of the Soviet Union."[12] On this occasion, Yalçın tried to arouse the British to the seriousness of the danger by asserting that the Russians were also bent on controlling the Straits, the Aegean and, possibly, Greece, a position which he later modified. If the Soviets advance toward the Straits, the new strategic capabilities brought on by the war will make it necessary for them to gain a hold on the surrounding regions, Yalçın argued. "Churchill will not swallow this very easily," Yalçın concluded, "but he will not be able to open his mouth." Thus Yalçın, the only Turkish publicist who had urged Turkey in mid-1943 to honor its commitment to the British by entering the war regardless of whether they invaded the Balkans, now tried to warn Churchill about the danger inherent in not stopping the Russians before they tried to gain control of the Straits and the Aegean.

The necessity of not provoking the Russians did not escape Yalçın. On September 15, after the Russian invasion of Bulgaria had been accomplished, Yalçın took care to note that the relations between the Turkish and Soviet governments were "extremely normal and even friendly," despite occasional attacks against Turkish policy emanating from Russian newspapers and radio broadcasts.[13] Yalçın discounted the significance of these attacks for as long as official relations between the two countries remained good. The Russian invasion of Bulgaria would not have caused concern, Yalçın suggested, had not the Soviets seemed to have "stormed into the Balkans by elbowing the Americans and

[12] *Ibid.*

[13] "Türkiyede endişe ve Türkiyede Sülkûn ve itimat" ("Anxiety or tranquillity and confidence in Turkey"), *Tanin*, September 15, 1944, as in *ibid.*, pp. 78-79.

the British aside" while Bulgarian representatives were in Cairo ready to fulfill Allied requests. Thus even Yalçın, who had expressed repeated doubts concerning Soviet ambitions, tried to place the Bulgarian invasion in a plausible if not happy light. The initial refusal of the Bulgarian Government to withdraw its forces from Greek and Yugoslavian territory, however, made this effort seem thankless.

It had become evident that the Soviet Union was in a position to dominate Bulgarian affairs. Reports from Britain, statements by both Churchill and Eden, moreover, had indicated that the Western Allies agreed that Bulgarian divisions should be made to depart from foreign soil at once. Yet for several weeks during September and October, Bulgarian forces remained stationary. The Turks correctly guessed that the British and Soviets were in disagreement over the terms of the Bulgarian armistice,[14] and it was for this reason that the order for Bulgarian troops to leave was not being given.[15] Asım Us publicly declared that the armistice agreement between Bulgaria, England, and America was being delayed on account of the fact that while the British were demanding that Bulgarian forces leave Thrace and Macedonia at once, the Bulgarians were "taking advantage of the leniency of the Soviet army in Bulgaria and were

[14] Selim Sarper in a personal interview with the author.

[15] Selim Açıkalın in a personal interview with the author. On October 15, 1944, Necmettin Sadak, in an editorial in *Akşam* entitled "Bulgaristan'dan gelen acayip haberler karşısında" ("The strange news from Bulgaria"), stated that it was impossible to comprehend the reasons why Bulgarian forces were not being withdrawn, given the fact that Prime Minister Churchill and Foreign Secretary Eden had declared that they were to be so. "Just as we do not understand it," he wrote, "there is no one in England who understands it either." Sadak then raised the crucial question: "Since Bulgaria knows of this decision of the Allies, what does it rely on in finding so many excuses and trying not to let go of the land it is holding?" Sadak responded by stating that the Bulgarians were relying upon their good relations with the Soviets "to bargain for its century-old aims"; *Ayın Tarihi*, Vol. 132 (October 1944), pp. 348-50.

attempting [to hatch] some complicated plots."[16] Indeed, it took no less than a personal agreement between Churchill and Stalin to resolve the issue.

At the end of October, Bulgarian forces were finally withdrawn from occupied Salonicka and eastern Yugoslavia. The command to depart was issued by the Soviets as a result of an agreement between them and the British that was arranged during Churchill's visit to Moscow, October 9-18. Churchill and Stalin agreed that the Bulgarian Government would evacuate its troops and that the Russians would be given the dominant voice in Bulgarian affairs. This second aspect of the agreement was not made publicly known, and the Turks greeted the news of the Bulgarian armistice agreement with pleasure tempered by the hope that the Bulgarians would now forever renounce dreams of a greater Bulgaria. Yalçın, observing that the conditions imposed upon Bulgaria had been mild, stated that it should "consider itself fortunate."[17] Yalçın hoped that in signing the treaty the Bulgarians would realize the futility of such dreams as coming down to the Aegean Sea or setting up an independent Macedonia. Sadak, commenting on pro-Soviet demonstrations in Sofia, stated that he hoped the revolution in Bulgaria would become "a big gain" for the Balkans by producing "a new mentality freed of desires for expansion and imperialistic opportunity."[18] Turkish hopes in this regard were quickly shattered, however, by the irredentist speeches of Georgiev and his Foreign Minister Stainov and later by the Pan-Slavic statements of Tito.

Anxieties in Turkey ever since Georgiev had come to power revolved around the fear that Bulgaria's intransigent

[16] Asım Us, "Bulgaristan mütarekesi" ("The Bulgarian Armistice"), *Vakit*, October 6, 1944, as in *ibid.*, Vol. 131 (October 1944), pp. 350-51.

[17] Hüseyin Cahit Yalçın, "Bulgaristan mütarekesi" ("The Bulgarian Armistice"), *Tanin*, November 4, 1944, as in *ibid.*, Vol. 132 (November 1944), pp. 267-68.

[18] Necmettin Sadak, "Bulgar mütarekesi ve Balkan milletlerinin emniyeti" ("The Bulgarian Armistice and the security of the Balkan nations"), *Akşam*, November 8, 1944, as in *ibid.*, pp. 269-71.

attitude was due to Russian plans for a confederation among the Slavic states, a plan that could involve Soviet occupation of the territory stretching between the Black Sea and the Adriatic, including Salonicka.[19] The armistice agreement and the Bulgarian withdrawal from Salonicka and Yugoslavia had relieved some of these apprehensions. But in January 1945, a victorious Tito along with Georgiev broached the subject of Pan-Slavism once again. The reaction in Turkey was sharp and immediate. Yalçın, for example, accused Tito of committing a "blunder" by speaking of the brotherhood of the Slavic nations.[20] He reminded the Yugoslav leader that his country had been liberated from Bulgarian as well as German occupation. Yalçın wrote that Tito had declared that Yugoslavia was friendly with Bulgaria not only because they were geographical neighbors, but because they were both Slavic nations. "The purpose is plain: to create a Slavic bloc in the Balkans in which Bulgaria will also be a member." Yalçın, commenting on the prevalence of Pan-Slavism in Yugoslavia and Bulgaria, asserted that opportunism was the reason for it. "In order to save themselves from punishment and to emerge from the war with even greater profits than before, the Bulgarians have taken to speculating on the concept of Slavism. . . ."[21] Yalçın later become more specific as to what kinds of profits the Bulgarians and Yugoslavs were seeking:

[19] Cavit Oral in a personal interview with the author. On January 19, 1945, *Haber* published an editorial by Hüseyin Cahit Yalçın entitled "Kahire yolu Moskova'dan geçermiş" ("The road to Cairo passes through Moscow"), which alleged that the Bulgarian Foreign Minister Stainov realized that the work of British and American representatives in Cairo, attempting to design the Bulgarian Armistice, would eventually be subsumed by the Russians. What was happening in Cairo was less important than what was decided in Moscow; see, *ibid.*, Vol. 134 (January 1944), p. 434.

[20] "Balkanlarda kendisini gösteren tehlike" ("The danger that is arising out of the Balkans"), *Tanin*, January 13, 1945, as in *ibid.*, pp. 174-76.

[21] *Ibid.*

Already it cannot be denied that the most prevalent current in Tito's Yugoslavia is general Slavic sentiment. The initial step for this is the Bulgarian-Yugoslav brotherhood. The issue of an independent Macedonia is being used as a lever by the Slavic element in their attempt to descend to the Aegean Sea as a bloc, to destroy Turkish-Greek unity, and to grasp the domination of the Balkans.[22]

Thus by January 1945, the Turks, despite their guarded hopefulness, felt encircled by Soviet imperialist designs and Bulgarian and Yugoslav Pan-Slavism. This made British efforts to liberate and establish a stable government in Greece seem even more important in their eyes.

THE BRITISH OCCUPATION OF GREECE: A TIME OF TRIBULATION

In the face of Soviet advances on the Continent, the British did indeed try to salvage a corner of the Balkans, but their attempt to take Albania was foiled at least in part as a result of the work of Kim Philby. On September 15, however, the British realized the first step in their long-awaited dream of liberating Greece. On this date, British land forces occupied the island of Kythera, off the Peloponnesus. On October 5, just as the Red army was entering Yugoslavia by agreement with Marshal Tito, the British entered Petras on the mainland. By October 14, Athens and Piraeus were liberated. The Turks greeted the news of the British invasion of Greece with intense relief. Atay declared that the British landing was tantamount to the opening of a second front in the Balkans; Yalçın asserted that the British had not forgotten their vital interest in preserving the freedom and independence of the Balkan and Mediterranean nations.[23] In an obvious attempt to counter the Bulgarian-Yugoslav axis, the

[22] "Davayı kaybeden bir kıral" ("The king that lost the cause"), *Tanin*, January 25, 1945, as in *ibid.*, pp. 184-85.

[23] See, e.g., *Ulus*, September 28, 1944; *Tanin*, September 28, 1944.

Turkish press at this time began to speak of Graeco-Turkish identity of interests. The picture suddenly clouded, however, when Communist demonstrations broke out in Athens on November 4, 1944.

Throughout the war, the Greek resistance movement had been divided into a number of competing groups, the most prominent of which were EDES, led by Colonel Napoleon Zervas, and the communist-inspired ELAM-ELAS. The British, in order to hasten the defeat of the Germans, had supplied all Greek resistance groups with arms and found, to their dismay, that besides using them against the enemy they were fighting each other. Churchill, for months prior to the liberation of Athens, had feared the outbreak of civil war in Greece. On November 4, his fears were realized and civil war did break out. As a result, British occupation forces under General Scobie became heavily engaged in large-scale military operations against well-armed communist forces that the British had equipped themselves. Churchill ruefully admitted that he had underestimated the danger of the communist underground. "I must admit that I judged them on their form against the Germans," he declared. "They were simply taking our arms, lying low and awaiting the moment when they could seize power."[24]

The Turkish press welcomed strong British action against the communist rebels. Yalçın, in particular, was glad that the British were not hesitating for fear of being described as fascists. "The word 'fascist' has become a curse word espe-

[24] Great Britain. Parliament. House of Commons. *The Parliamentary Debates* (*official reports*), Fifth Series, Vol. 407, January 18, 1945, Col. 402; also, see Hüseyin Cahit Yalçın's comments on Churchill's statement, "Mr. Churchill'in Yunanistan hakkındaki beyanatı" ("Mr. Churchill's declaration on Greece"), *Tanin*, January 25, 1945, as in *Ayın Tarihi*, Vol. 134 (January 1945), pp. 180-82; in this statement, Yalçın described Greek communist forces as more Trotskyite than those in Moscow. For an outline of Graeco-Turkish joint defense preparations before the war, Alexander Papagos, *The Battle of Greece 1940-1941* (Athens, Greece: The J. M. Scazikis "Alpha" Editions, 1949), pp. 43-70, 127-34.

cially for the communists. To them anybody who is not on their side is a fascist."[25] Yalçın also spoke out in this instance against the principle of noninterference which was being used by the communists as "a trap set up against the democracies."[26] For his part, Falih Rıfkı Atay indicated that although Turkey wanted to remain neutral, it could not remain disinterested since the interests of Turkey and the Balkans were at stake in the conflict raging in Greece.[27]

Although the Turks were disturbed by events in Greece, their concern was mitigated to some degree by the fact that the communist rebels seemed to be acting independently of Stalin. Turkish observers correctly perceived that the Soviets were not attempting to further complicate the British position by openly taking sides or by supplying the rebels with arms. Yalçın gratefully reported that the Soviet Union had dissolved the Comintern and thus had given the world notice that it would take no responsibility for the provocations all over the world. "There is no need," Yalçın wrote, "therefore, to worry about Moscow sponsoring foreign communist rebellions. . . ." Moscow, he added, had distinguished itself from Trotskyism in that it now sought to consolidate communism within the borders of the Soviet Union rather than to impose it in foreign countries.[28] Toward the end of the year, the situation in Greece did indeed seem to ease. Churchill and Eden confronted ELAM-ELAS leaders on December 25, and on January 14 a truce was declared between them and the British-backed government

[25] "Komünistler ve mülteciler" ("Communists and Refugees"), *Tanin*, December 5, 1944, as in *Ayın Tarihi*, Vol. 133 (December 1944), pp. 284-85.

[26] "Demokrasi harbinin ilk kazanılan muharebesi" ("The first battle won in the war of democracy"), *Tanin*, December 10, 1944, as in *ibid.*, pp. 288-89.

[27] "Bir komşumuzun acıklı durumu" ("The sad situation of one of our neighbors"), *Ulus*, December 8, 1944, as in *ibid.*, pp. 286-87; also, Asım Us, "Yunanistandaki dahilî harb hali" ("The state of internal war in Greece"), *Vakit*, December 8, 1944, as in *ibid.*, pp. 285-86.

[28] "Komünistler ve mülteciler," *ibid.*, pp. 284-85.

of the regent, Archbishop Damaskinos. For its part, the Turkish Government played a small but important role in fostering the settlement by publicly disclaiming all rights to the Dodecanese islands. One must look further, however, for an understanding of Yalçın's position at this time. Quite clearly he hoped to display satisfaction that Stalin had hesitated to become an active party in the Greek conflict. Yalçın had spoken earlier, moreover, of Soviet intentions not to impose communist ideology upon the nations being invaded by them. He declared, for example, on October 6,

. . . it is necessary to think of the Stalin era within the Soviet Union as communism's departure from the objective of establishing a proletarian dictatorship all over the world [to be replaced by the attempt] to reinforce the structure of socialism only within the Russian borders.[29]

In this Yalçın was addressing himself to the guarantee offered by Molotov that the Soviets would seek to preserve the social institutions of countries invaded. "It is plain from this guarantee," Yalçın wrote, "that Soviet armies will not enter the various countries as a communist army." Yalçın suggested that this alone should serve to relieve some of their anxieties.

Yalçın's purpose at the end of 1944, however, was not to urge acceptance of abstract promises. It was not enough to claim that Soviet armies were not invading the countries of Eastern Europe and the Balkans in order to impose communism upon them. It was equally important that Soviet armies not become an instrument of Russian imperialism.

. . . we cannot forget that these invasions also have a tomorrow. Radio Moscow, who gives open guarantees against anxieties that communism will be forced on other nations, has never touched upon this aspect of the problem. This is the point, however, that is occupying the

29 "Sovyetlerin prensipleri" ("Soviet principles"), *Tanin*, October 6, 1944, as in *ibid.*, Vol. 131 (October 1944), pp. 330-31.

minds of people particularly in the Middle East [Turkey]. Although we learn once again that the Soviet program recognizes, as a basic principle, compliance with all the nations' independence, we also see and know very well how these principles are applied in the field of "realistic" politics.[30]

The recognition of a country's independence did not prevent a large nation from trying to grab a large chunk of it, Yalçın advised. Insofar as the Soviets are concerned, "They come up with the excuse of strategic borders and try to take with their left hand what they have left with their right." In writing this, Yalçın had a specific fear in mind: the division of Europe into spheres of influence. The Soviet armies would invade Eastern Europe in the name of the Allied war against Nazi Germany and might remain with the consent of the British. Although evidently willing to obtain whatever could be gained by emphasizing the fact that Stalin seemed bent on reinforcing socialism in one country, he could not help but fear that communism would eventually be imposed upon an entire region, the region surrounding Turkey. This colored his and other observers' perceptions of the meeting between Churchill and Stalin in Moscow and suggests how the Turks viewed Stalin's refusal to assist communist elements in Greece: there was an agreement between the British and the Russians that had parceled out regions to each, leaving the Russians dominant in the East and the British dominant in the West.

THE CHURCHILL-STALIN MEETING OF OCTOBER 1944 AND THE DECISION TO ESTABLISH SPHERES OF INFLUENCE

Turkish observers, caught between Greece, Eastern Europe, and the Balkans, judged events largely on the basis of what specific developments signified about the political intentions of the Great Powers. The fear that Britain and Russia

[30] *Ibid.*

would divide Europe into spheres of influence had been prevalent in Turkey, as we have seen, from the very first days the Allies began to defeat Axis armies. During the fall and winter of 1944, these fears became stronger. It was becoming increasingly evident that the Russians were the dominant force in the East, whereas the British seemed to be functioning alone in the West. Although there were geographical as well as historical reasons why this should be, apprehensions in Turkey were aroused in early 1944, by rumors that Stalin had accepted a British plan to partition Europe into spheres of influence, giving Russia supremacy over the Balkans, including Romania, eastern Yugoslavia, and Bulgaria. As Anne O'Hare McCormick reported on March 4, 1944, "Reasonably or unreasonably the Turks fear Russia. They are . . . a border state and the suspicion that Moscow seeks to erect her 'cordon sanitaire' by drawing all the nations along the frontier in her own orbit makes them exceedingly wary."[31] The Turks feared that a world divided into spheres of influence would diminish the viable independence of the smaller nations. They could not be certain, moreover, where Turkey would fall in such an international system. They doubted whether the British would fight to keep them out of the Russian orbit and deeply feared that they would be left to face a dominant Soviet Union alone. This also made the Pan-Slavic issue all the more vexing at the end of 1944.[32] In any event, these fears help to explain why Turkish officials continued to try to win the good graces of Britain, despite their concerns over British policy, and why they were subdued in discussing Soviet intentions.

Some substance for believing that the Russians and the British had indeed divided Europe into spheres of influence

[31] Anne O'Hare McCormick, heir to the *Chicago Tribune* combine, was highly critical of Churchill's policies in regard to the Soviet Union on the grounds that they were allowing the Soviets to expand into the Mediterranean and Balkan regions. The quotation is from the editorial page of *The New York Times*, March 4, 1944.

[32] Selim Sarper in a personal interview; also, Erkin, *Turkish-Russian Relations*, pp. 259-60.

was provided by Lincoln MacVeagh, the United States envoy to the émigré Greek and Yugoslav governments in Cairo. On June 19, 1944, MacVeagh leaked a story to C. L. Sulzberger of *The New York Times*, alleging that "Initial steps towards outlining zones of 'initiatives' in the Balkan peninsula have been agreed upon by the British and Soviet governments. . . ."[33] MacVeagh's report asserted that Greece would fall under British protection while Romania was to fall under that of the Soviet Union. Sulzberger suggests that MacVeagh informed him of this because he was furious over the "private deal between London and Moscow" and wanted it made known to the world.[34] Cevat Açıkalın has indicated that the Turkish Government did become aware of such reports and that İnönü suspected they were true.[35] Indeed, they were: as early as May 1944, Churchill had broached the subject with Roosevelt and Stalin of assigning spheres of "responsibility" to the Great Powers.

Churchill had represented this as a temporary scheme. The Allied armies were advancing along different fronts and on-the-spot administrative decisions had to be taken. "We do not of course wish to carve up the Balkans into spheres of influence," Churchill had informed the President, "and in agreeing to the arrangement we should make it clear that it applied only to war conditions. . . ."[36] Roosevelt and especially Hull were deeply skeptical about Churchill's plan. But the President, after reversing himself twice, notified the British and Soviet governments that the United States had accepted the "spheres" arrangement, but only for a three-month trial period.[37] With this agreement in his

[33] C. L. Sulzberger, in the *International Herald Tribune*, September 3, 1969.

[34] *Ibid.*

[35] In a personal interview with the author.

[36] Winston S. Churchill, *The Second World War*, Vol. VI, *Triumph and Tragedy* (Boston: Houghton Mifflin Co., 1953), pp. 73-74.

[37] The President consulted Secretary of State Hull who became concerned that such an agreement, despite Churchill's intentions, would lead to a political division of Europe. At first Roosevelt agreed with

pocket, Churchill went to see Stalin. The Moscow meeting between Churchill and Stalin has been immortalized by Churchill's own description of it:

> The moment was apt for business, so I said, "Let us settle about our affairs in the Balkans. Your armies are in Roumania and Bulgaria. We have interest, missions, and agents there. Don't let us get at cross-purposes in small ways. So far as Britain and Russia are concerned, how would it do for you to have ninety per cent predominance in Roumania, for us to have ninety per cent of the say in Greece, and go fifty-fifty about Yugoslavia?" While this was being translated I wrote out on a half-sheet of paper:

Roumania	
Russia	90%
The others	10%
Greece	
Great Britain	90%
(in accord with U.S.A.)	
Russia	10%
Yugoslavia	50-50%
Hungary	50-50%
Bulgaria	
Russia	75%
The others	25%

Hull and informed Churchill of this. In mid-June 1944, however, while Hull was away from Washington, Roosevelt notified Churchill that he had decided to consent to the British initiative. The State Department, uninformed of the President's reversal, proceeded on the assumption that Roosevelt still objected to any proposal which implied a division of Europe and submitted an *aide-mémoire* to the British Embassy to this effect. To make matters even more confusing, Roosevelt had a change of heart when his Secretary of State returned to Washington and wired Churchill that he could no longer accept Churchill's scheme. But the British Government had already informed the Soviets that they had received the President's approval and were now ready to accept this temporary division of Europe. On July 15 the State Department finally agreed; Feis, *Churchill, Roosevelt, Stalin*, pp. 341-42.

I pushed this across to Stalin, who had by then heard the translation. There was a slight pause. Then he took his blue pencil and made a large tick upon it, and passed it back to us. It was all settled in no more time than it takes to set down.

Of course we had long and anxiously considered our point, and were only dealing with immediate war-time arrangements. All larger questions were reserved on both sides for what we then hoped would be a peace table when the war was won.

After this there was a long silence. The pencilled paper lay in the centre of the table. At length I said, "Might it not be thought rather cynical if it seemed we had disposed of these issues, so fateful to millions of people, in such an offhand manner? Let us burn the paper." "No, you keep it," said Stalin.[38]

The agreement between Churchill and Stalin left Hungary and Yugoslavia partially open to British and American supervision. The administration of the occupying forces in Bulgaria, Romania, Hungary, etc. was to be under the aegis of a tripartite Allied commission of the United States, Britain, and Russia. This agreement, however, represents an important step in the postwar division of the world into separate conflicting blocs. At Moscow, Stalin also served notice on Churchill that he would seek a revision of the Montreux Convention, a suggestion to which Churchill gave general agreement pending a discussion of specifics at the next tripartite summit meeting.

The news of the agreement between Churchill and Stalin, of course, was not released, but the Turks reacted to the conference as they did to on-going events in Eastern Europe and the Balkans, with mixed feelings. Necmettin Sadak chose to compliment the Soviet Union on its "honest politics";[39] Asım Us suggested that Britain and Russia were

[38] Churchill, *Triumph and Tragedy*, pp. 227-28.
[39] "Moskova konuşmaları, Balkan meselesi ve Türkiye" ("Moscow

working together in a cordial atmosphere and that they were both pleased with Turkish neutrality.[40] *Ulus*, in a series of articles, however, defined the Turkish position more precisely: the smaller nations would never be satisfied with a system of spheres of influence which permitted the Great Powers to manipulate their destinies.[41] The small powers were insisting upon the creation of an international system that would guarantee their freedom from intervention or Great Power domination. The well-known political commentator for *Ulus*, Burhan Belge, writing in the *Aylık Siyasî İlimler Mecmuası* (*Monthly Political Sciences Magazine*) added that the "three big nations are jointly and victoriously assuming the position of the world's political and administrative authority. . . ."[42] Belge feared that this would tend to make the Great Powers seek to "eliminate opposition" to their suzerainty over their respective domains. He noted that not only Germany and Japan, but also France and Italy had been eliminated as serious contenders for a major voice in world affairs. On December 31, 1944, Yalçın offered a similar analysis, commenting on a chance remark by the British Prime Minister in which Churchill had indicated that unless the communist guerrilla forces gave up their struggle, a tripartite "trust" comprised of the major powers would be set up to rule Greece.[43] Yalçın warned the

negotiations, the Balkan issue and Turkey"), *Akşam*, October 16, 1944, as in *Ayın Tarihi*, Vol. 131 (October 1944), pp. 40-42.

[40] "Moskova müzakereleri ve Türkiye" ("Moscow negotiations and Turkey"), *Vakit*, October 18, 1944, as in *ibid.*, pp. 42-44.

[41] *Ulus*, September 14, 17, 18 and October 14, 24, 1944; on October 31, 1944, however, Falih Rıfkı Atay, in an article in *Ulus* entitled "Bulgarlarla mütareke" ("Armistice with the Bulgarians") praised the agreements reached between Churchill and Stalin. "Everything was solved in the Moscow meeting," he wrote in an apparent attempt to mitigate whatever ill-effects Turkish skepticism may have had in Moscow, London, and Washington; *ibid.*, pp. 219-20.

[42] Burhan Belge, "Moskova Buluşması" ("Moscow meeting"), *Aylık, Siyasî İlimler Mecmuası*, Vol. XIX, No. 163 (October 1944), 408-13.

[43] "3 ler tröstü" ("The three power trust"), *Tanin*, December 31, 1944, as in *Ayın Tarihi*, Vol. 133 (December 1944), pp. 295-97.

Greek partisans as well as his countrymen against this "brief and simple" threat: "A major power's interference and take-over of the administration in any part of Europe will certainly cause counterreactions immediately in other parts." Yalçın added, "This is the route that may take us directly to spheres of influence, protectorates, and annexations."[44] But the route had already been chosen by the Great Powers. This too quickly became apparent to the Turks. In a prescient analysis, Necmettin Sadak stated that the lines dividing Europe had already become permanent and that the only question remaining was how Germany would be ruled.[45] "It is possible to predict tomorrow's events from today's examples," Sadak began. "One might regard [the issue of] postwar governments and administrative styles in all of these countries to be already decided or settled, because people and liberation governments have already been established." Sadak indicated that the Mediterranean area, the Adriatic Sea, Greece, and Italy constituted Britain's security sphere, while Romania, Hungary, Czechoslovakia, and Poland fell well within the Russian. Writing one day after the Yalta Conference had begun, Sadak stated that the only outstanding issue was whether the free German committee in Moscow or another government to be selected by the Allies would eventually assume power in Germany. "Whatever the decision," Sadak concluded prophetically, ". . . the entire eastern region of Germany . . . will remain under Soviet occupation for a long time and, from the point of view [of preserving] Soviet security, all the nations lying between the Soviet Union and Germany will remain under Soviet occupation as well." These thoughts made the search in Turkey for postwar security a pressing need.

[44] *Ibid.*

[45] "Harbin bitişi sulhun gelişi" ("The ending of war, the coming of peace"), *Akşam*, February 5, 1945, as in *ibid.*, pp. 138-39.

THIRTEEN

THE SEARCH FOR POSTWAR SECURITY

THE DUMBARTON OAKS CONFERENCE

AT Cairo and Tehran, Allied leaders agreed to allow their representatives to consider in the coming months the matter of an international security organization. The United States, in particular, was determined to lead the way toward the establishment of a system of collective security that would regulate the settlement of disputes. The Dumbarton Oaks Conference, which included delegations from China, the Soviet Union, the United States, and Britain, was held between August 21, 1944 and October 9, 1944, in order to work out the precise details of such an organization. Indeed, the broad outlines of what eventually became the United Nations took shape at this time.

The one major disagreement which arose during the conference concerned voting procedures; that is, "to what extent would the Great Powers share with others the right to shape and decide policy and action."[1] In more specific terms, the issue revolved around the question of the veto in the Security Council. The Soviet Union insisted upon the unanimity rule, the right of each permanent member to veto all major decisions coming before the Security Council. The United States attempted to convince the Russian delegation to agree that members of the Security Council who were party to a dispute should not be allowed to vote on matters dealing with that dispute. After lengthy debate, a compromise was worked out: the Security Council could try to bring about a peaceful settlement of a dispute without having to have the unanimous consent of its members: the

---

[1] Feis, *Churchill, Roosevelt, Stalin*, p. 431.

permanent members would be allowed to exercise the right of veto, however, in cases requiring the use of force to settle disputes.

As might be expected, the reaction in Turkey to this was mixed. Hüseyin Cahit Yalçın complained that the draft organization conceived at Dumbarton Oaks, if adopted, would provide little real security for the smaller states.[2] "The new organization only provides for action to be taken against the small countries," he wrote. Nothing could be done to prevent the big nations from taking action against the weaker ones. If one of the big powers said no, measures under consideration could not be taken by the Security Council, Yalçın observed. Not all comment in Turkey was as skeptical. Nuri Eren, for example, defended the Dumbarton Oaks proposals on the grounds that the Security Council would play a forceful role and that it opened up the possibility of "founding an international military staff with a force ready for immediate action."[3] Such then was the dialogue in Turkey concerning the Dumbarton Oaks Project.

While being concerned that the future world peace-keeping organization not become merely a vehicle for Great Power domination, Turkish policy continued, meanwhile, to seek the friendship and protection of the United States and Great Britain through gestures designed to strengthen good relations with them. On January 3, 1945, the Turkish Government announced that it had decided to break off diplomatic relations with Japan. Although Admiral Leahy called this "one of the best evidences of the certainty of complete Allied victory,"[4] the Turks saw it as it was: a some-

[2] Hüseyin Cahit Yalçın, "Dünyanın sulhünü koruyacak yeni Teşkilât" ("The new organization to protect world peace"), *Tanin*, October 10, 1944, as in *Ayın Tarihi*, Vol. 131 (October 1944), pp. 229-30.

[3] Nuri Eren, "Dumbarton Oaks Konferansı," *Aylık Siyasî İlimler Mecmuası* (*Monthly Political Sciences Magazine*), Vol. XIX, No. 164 (November 1944), 423-44 at p. 432. Nuri Eren at the time of writing is the Deputy Chief of Mission of the Turkish delegation to the United Nations.

[4] Leahy, *I Was There*, p. 286.

what irrelevant, symbolic act. On December 28, 1944, Steinhardt had told Hasan Saka, the new Turkish Foreign Minister, that the Allies wanted Turkey to sever its ties with Japan. Saka replied that there was no advantage to the Turks in doing this, "but that if 'Turkey's allies' believed such action profitable . . . ," Turkey would certainly oblige.[5] Two days later, the Turkish Government officially informed Steinhardt of its compliance. One other gesture was that the Turkish Government, also in January, began to permit the passage of Allied ships carrying war matériel to the Soviet Union.[6] The opening of the Straits was a happy event in Turkey, but some interpretations in Britain and the United States were troubling to the Turks. Yalçın, for example, expressed his concern over the fact that certain publications in England and the United States were conveying the impression that the Straits had been closed as a result of a decision of the Turkish Government. Yalçın made it clear that the Straits had remained open throughout the war and that goods from the Western Allies did not flow to Russia through the Straits solely because the Germans had hitherto controlled the Aegean.[7] The meeting of the Big Three Powers at Yalta soon relegated these concerns to the back pages.

[5] The Ambassador in Turkey (Steinhardt) to Secretary of State, Ankara, December 28, 1944, *Foreign Relations*, 1944, v, 900; for the entire record of Turkey's break with Japan at the request of the United States and Britain, see pp. 900-904.

[6] Erkin, *Turkish-Russian Relations*, p. 284.

[7] Hüseyin Cahit Yalçın, "Boğazların açılması" ("The opening of the Straits"), *Tanin*, January 17, 1945, as in *Ayın Tarihi*, Vol. 134 (January 1945), pp. 58-59; Yalçın wrote: ". . . we recall certain publications in the West, particularly in America. These articles reflected a deep ignorance of the true conditions of the Straits just like the articles that were written prior to World War I. For instance, mention was made [in these articles] of the Russian need for the open seas and the Straits were regarded as a pressure-valve in our hands to be opened or closed whenever we wanted." Yalçın denied that this was true and again claimed that the Straits had been kept open during the war, but that German control of the approaches to the Dardanelles had closed them to Allied shipping.

THE CRIMEA CONFERENCE: THE ENDING OF WAR

The Yalta Conference, convened on February 4 and lasting until February 11, created grave foreboding in Ankara. The Turkish Government was at this time primarily concerned that Western leaders, and Churchill in particular, intended to side with Stalin in seeking a revision of the Montreux Convention.[8] Professor Esmer, for example, notes that "the possibility of Churchill's giving concessions to the Russians . . . worried the Turkish Government since Churchill was angry at Turkey and expressed at every opportunity his intention of having nothing further to do with the Straits."[9] Although this does not correctly perceive Churchill's state of mind at Yalta, where he championed Turkish interests, it does correctly reflect the anxious state of isolation still felt by the Turks.

The Turkish question was not paramount at Yalta, but many of the other decisions did, directly or indirectly, affect Turkish interests and concerns. The veto power, slightly encumbered, was accepted by the Big Three as the basis for the wielding of real power in the proposed new peace-keeping organization. Russia agreed to the American proposal that a permanent member should abstain from voting when it was itself a party to a dispute, but only in matters of "peaceful settlement." In relation to "enforcement" resolutions, the Great Powers would still be in a position to cast an unfettered veto.

As regards Poland, Stalin persuaded Churchill and Roosevelt to accept his basic position, in regard to territorial and political arrangements, in return for a promise to hold free and general elections one month after final Polish liberation. The final agreement, reluctantly signed by both Roosevelt and Churchill reads, "The Provisional Government which is now functioning in Poland should therefore be re-

---

[8] Selim Sarper in a personal interview with the author.

[9] Esmer in *Turkish Foreign Policy*, p. 169.

organized on a broader democratic basis. . . ."[10] This agreement thus granted the communist regime in Warsaw official Allied sanction. Henceforth Stalin was able to claim *validly* that the Big Three had recognized the provisional government as the legitimate new Polish government.[11]

The Yalta Conference also encompassed the future of the Balkan nations. In response to State Department directives warning that the Allied Control Commissions in Central Europe and the Balkans were not functioning properly because the Soviet Union seemed determined to bring them under its sole control, Roosevelt submitted a document to the conference entitled "The Declaration on Liberated Europe." Eventually signed by Churchill, Roosevelt, and Stalin, this pledged that the Big Three would help the liberated nations meet their pressing political and economic problems through democratic means.

On top of this formally impressive but politically vacuous agreement came Roosevelt's surprising announcement to the conferees that American forces would not remain in Europe more than two years after the end of the war. Stalin had reason to feel pleased.[12]

Although not a central issue in the minds of the three heads of state at the Yalta Conference, Turkey did receive attention in two of the eight plenary sessions, each time in a different connection. In the fifth plenary meeting, Stalin used Turkey as a symbol in raising the issue of which states should be admitted into the United Nations and which should be excluded. The President responded that only those nations that had declared war on Germany should be granted the status of an Associated Nation and suggested March 1945 as the deadline for the as yet uncommitted to

10 Feis, *Churchill, Roosevelt, Stalin*, p. 528.

11 *Ibid.*

12 Yalta Papers, First Plenary Meeting, February 4, 1945, Bohlen Minutes, Crimea Conference, *Foreign Relations: The Conferences at Malta and Yalta*, pp. 573-80 at p. 577.

declare war on Germany. Referring to Turkey, Stalin declared that certain nations had "wavered and speculated on being on the winning side."[13] Churchill, however, defended the Turks. He asserted that if a large group of hitherto uncommitted nations were to declare war at this time it would have an effect on Germany's morale. Turkey's candidacy "would not be greeted with universal approbation," Churchill said, but he also asserted that Turkey had entered into an alliance with them "at a very difficult time" and had proved both "friendly and helpful."[14] Stalin agreed to allow Turkey to become an Associated Nation if it declared war on Germany by the end of February. Churchill greeted this with expressions of "gratification."

Despite Stalin's amiability, he served notice on February 10, 1945, that he expected the regime of the Straits to be revised at the end of the war. Stalin declared that ". . . it was impossible to accept a situation in which Turkey had a hand on Russia's throat," adding that he did not intend to "harm the legitimate interests of Turkey."[15] The President, apparently not fully up to the challenge of the discussion, responded irrelevantly by saying that the United States and Canada shared a frontier of over 3,000 miles without a fort and with no armed forces and expressed the hope that other frontiers would eventually exist "without forts or armed forces on any part of their national boundaries." The Prime Minister agreed that a revision of the Montreux Convention seemed to be in order, saying that ". . . the present position of Russia with their great interests in the Black Sea should not be dependent on the narrow exit."[16] Churchill proposed that the matter be taken up at the next meeting of Foreign Ministers. He also suggested that the

[13] Yalta Papers, Fifth Plenary Meeting, February 8, 1945, Bohlen Minutes, *ibid.*, pp. 771-82 at p. 773.
[14] *Ibid.*
[15] Yalta Papers, Seventh Plenary Meeting, February 10, 1945, Bohlen Minutes, *ibid.*, pp. 897-906 at p. 903.
[16] *Ibid.*

Turks be informed that this was being considered and that they be given an assurance that their independence and integrity would be respected. Stalin accepted these suggestions. With regard to the proposal that they immediately inform the Turks of what was afoot, Stalin remarked, ". . . it was impossible to keep anything secret from the Turks. . . ."[17]

With the decision to convene a conference on April 25 at San Francisco to prepare the charter for the postwar United Nations Organization, the Yalta Conference ended. On February 14, on their way home, Churchill and Eden again visited Athens, the precarious Western toe-hold on the Balkans.

Just how precarious was this Western toe-hold, and how vacuous were the promises made to small states in the Yalta "Declaration on Liberated Europe," came to be demonstrated within a few weeks of the ending of the Yalta meeting. On February 28, the Romanian Government resigned under pressure from internal communist and Soviet military forces. Mr. Viyshinsky's personal insistence compelled King Michael to authorize Mr. Pietro Groza to form a new communist-controlled regime on March 6.[18] The British and American governments continued to protest to the Soviet Union that their representatives on the Allied Control Commissions were being ignored by the Soviet authorities in Romania, Bulgaria, and Hungary. The U.S. and Britain refused to recognize the Groza regime. They also demanded the withdrawal of Yugoslav communist forces from Italian territory, only to be met by the Tito Government's insistence that it had a right to all territory its forces had "liberated." On April 6, representatives of the American- and British-supported Polish Government-in-exile who had been negotiating with Soviet officials in Moscow were reported missing by Polish authorities in London. The communist-

17 Ibid.
18 Feis, Churchill, Roosevelt, Stalin, p. 566.

dominated Lublin regime, furthermore, was being firmly established by the Russians in Warsaw. In the period between the end of the Yalta Conference and the opening of the San Francisco Conference on April 25, therefore, whatever hopes might still have been entertained regarding Soviet intentions in Eastern Europe were severely diminished. On the contrary, the last months of the war in Europe clearly confirmed the predictions of the future that had been made since early 1943, since an Allied victory had become probable, by such Turkish leaders as İnönü and Menemencioğlu and by editors such as Yalçın. This was, however, small comfort to the Turks who were now "extremely worried" by developments.[19]

THE TURKISH DECLARATION OF WAR

Turkey at last entered the war against Germany and Japan on February 23, 1945.[20] Speaking in the Grand National Assembly, Prime Minister Saracoğlu said: "From the first moments of danger the Turkish Republic committed its words, arms, and heart to the democratic nations and up until today progressed along the same course in the decisions of its parliament and government."[21] In the Assembly debate, it was emphasized that the declaration of war was "the natural consequence of [Turkey's] alliance with Britain within the framework of our friendship with the Soviets."[22] Although Turkey was now formally entering the war, since the day it had made its alliance with the Allies it had its

[19] Zeki Kuneralp in a personal interview with the author.

[20] The motion in the Grand National Assembly to declare war on Germany and Japan was made by Ali Râna Tarhan, Faık Öztrak, Kâzım Özalp, and Memduh Şevket Esendal; it was passed by a unanimous vote of 401 votes.

[21] *T.B.M.M. Zabıt Ceridesi,* Seventh Assembly February 23, 1945, First Session, I, 131; also, Esmer in *Turkish Foreign Policy,* pp. 169-70.

[22] Şemsettin Günaltay (Sivas), *T.B.M.M. Zabıt Ceridesi,* Seventh Assembly, February 23, 1945, First Session, I, 127.

army mobilized.[23] The entry into war was thus presented as only the last act in the unbroken record of Turkish compliance with the terms of the alliance with Britain, according to the chairman of the Parliamentary Group of the CHP, Faık Öztrak.[24] It was also stated that one of the basic, consistent strands of Turkish policy had always been friendship with the Soviet Union:

During these [past] five years, Republican Turkey has remained loyal to this principle at times when our great neighbor, the Soviet Union, was living in its darkest days. . . . National leader İnönü has advised us to be faithful to this great and valuable friend in every event and in every movement.[25]

The declaration of war was in no sense the result of pressure exerted on Turkey.[26]

Such were the reasons which the Turks wished to place on public record to impress the Allies, the Turkish public, and history. The real reason for the decision was, however, to enable the Turks to participate in the United Nations Conference on International Organization at San Francisco and to placate the Allies. Turkey was simply no longer in a position to refuse. Moreover, there was no danger, now, of being attacked or of having to fight. Foreign Minister Hasan Saka told the Assembly the new British Ambassador to Turkey, Sir Maurice Peterson, had conveyed to him the message from Yalta: only those nations which had declared war on Germany before March 1, 1945, would be invited to San Francisco. "This recent proposal that the English Government has made . . . now gives our nation the possibility and the opportunity to contribute strongly to the Allied cause," he declared.[27]

23 Risah Kaplan (Antalya), *ibid.*, p. 129.
24 Faık Öztrak (Tekirdağ), *ibid.*, pp. 130-31.
25 M. Ökmen (Aydın), *ibid.*, p. 128.
26 E. Erişirgil (Zonguldak), *ibid.*, p. 130.
27 Hasan Saka (Trabzon), *ibid.*, pp. 126-27. Editorials in the Turkish

THE SOVIET NOTE OF MARCH 19, 1945

Turkish entry into the war coincided with the final denoue-
ment of Soviet power in the Balkans: the link-up with Tito,
the consolidation of communist power by the Georgiev and
Groza regimes, and the armistice with Hungary. The British
had failed to take Albania and were hard put to support a
noncommunist regime in Greece. Among non-Axis leaders,
İnönü and his "kitchen" of foreign policy decision-makers
and advisers had been the most vigorous in expressing a
view of Soviet intentions which had been intensely unpopular with British as well as American officials at the time, but
which was now already coming to be shared by Churchill and, after April 12, by President Truman. To have
been right in pointing to the Soviet threat was not, however,
a virtue calculated to make Turkey secure in its relations
with the victorious Soviet Union. Nor could its unpopular-

---

press emphasized points similar to those expressed in the Assembly: the
declaration of war was due to Allied pressure; it would not require
Turkey to fight; it would allow Turkey to participate in the proceed-
ings of San Francisco; see e.g., Falih Rıfkı Atay, "Dünkü tarihî karar"
("Yesterday's historcial decision"), *Ulus*, February 25, 1945, as in *Ayın
Tarihi*, Vol. 135 (February 1945), pp. 50-51; Asım Us, "Harb ilânı
kararımızın mânasi" ("The meaning of our declaration of war"), *Vakit*,
February 24, 1945, as in *ibid.*; Necmettin Sadak, "Türkiye Birleşmiş
Milletler arasında" ("Turkey among the United Nations"), *Akşam*, February 24, 1945, as in *ibid.*, pp. 51-52; Hüseyin Cahit Yalçın, "Türkiye'nin
son kararı" ("Turkey's final decision"), *Tanin*, February 24, 1945, as in
ibid., pp. 52-54; Nadir Nadi, "Tarihî karar" ("The historical decision"),
Cumhuriyet, February 24, 1945, as in *ibid.*, pp. 58-59; Cavit Oral, "Realist siyaset" ("A realist policy"), *Bugün*, February 25, 1945, as in *ibid.*,
pp. 59-60. Cavit Oral wrote: "Politics is an occupation that should have
no basis in sentimentality. The basic thing in politics is to be realistic
and to seek one's own interests." Etem İzzet Benice, "Hayırlı oldu ve
hayırlı olacak" ("It was and will be intrinsically good"), *Son Telgraf*,
February 24, 1945, as in *ibid.*, pp. 54-55, agreed by emphasizing that
the reason Turkey declared war was that it wished to comply with the
decisions of the Crimea Conference so that it would be allowed to participate in the San Francisco Conference.

ity, its "sense of isolation,"[28] be remedied by a last-minute declaration of war against the Axis. The Soviet Union had a genuine grievance against Turkey for its attempt to sow suspicions among the Allies regarding Russian postwar intentions and for Turkey's failure to enter the war. The Soviet Union, which had not chosen to fight Hitler, believed that it had a strong case against Turkey, which had also chosen to stay out of war. In victory, Russia now proceeded to press that case.

On March 19, 1945, the Soviet Union began its long-expected campaign against Turkey by denouncing the Turko-Soviet Treaty of Neutrality and Nonaggression, originally signed in Paris on December 17, 1925. This treaty, initially made for a period of three years, had been granted continued life by three protocols. The last had extended the treaty to November 7, 1945. One of the stipulations in the last protocol was that should one of the contracting parties wish to revise the treaty, it must give six months' notice before the expiration date. As a result, on March 19, Molotov handed Selim Sarper, the Turkish Ambassador in Moscow, a note which stated, "This Treaty no longer corresponds to actual conditions nor for the changes brought about by the war and thus requires fundamental alterations."[29] On March 21, *Izvestia* published the following comment:

> It is no secret that during the present war Soviet-Turkish relations at specific moments might have been better than they were. It is not in the interest of the two countries automatically to extend the terms of an agreement concluded in a totally different situation.[30]

Four days later, *Pravda* wrote:

> During the present war, relations of the Soviet Union with other powers connected by friendly treaties devel-

[28] The phrase is that of Zeki Kuneralp, personal interview.
[29] Erkin, *Turkish-Russian Relations*, p. 287.
[30] *Review*, Series N, No. 47, p. 51.

oped more and more successfully, while relations with Turkey were regulated by a treaty which long since has been outdated.[31]

Selim Sarper was immediately called home for consultations.[32]

On April 4, 1945, the Turkish Government submitted a conciliatory reply to the Soviet Union attesting to its willingness "to examine with attention and good-will any proposal that the Soviet Government would suggest for the conclusion of a treaty better adapted to the present interests of the two countries."[33] The Turks were inclined to the view that Russia's timing of the denunciation suggested a desire to "counteract any benefits Turkey might receive as a consequence of her adhesion to the United Nations and to deprive her of whatever systemic international stability she might thereby otherwise have acquired."[34] Nevertheless, the Turkish Government did endeavor to explore the terms of a new treaty and of Soviet friendship in general. The Soviets refused to be hurried into discussion of a new treaty, proposing instead that the Turks make recommendations. This the Turkish Government was loath to do, since it wished to see what kinds of proposals the Soviets actually intended to make. The ball, so to speak, was in the Russian court. As for improving the climate of relations between the two nations, the most concrete suggestion was that of Ambassador Vinogradov: "put an end to the Turkish press campaign against the Soviet Union and, above all, reduce M. Yalçın to silence."[35] The Turks did attempt to heed this advice.

Despite the concern of İnönü and his subordinates, the Turkish press, once allowed to discuss the Soviet note of

[31] Ibid.

[32] Selim Sarper in a personal interview with the author.

[33] See the Chargé in Turkey (Packer) to the Secretary of State, Ankara, April 7, 1945, Foreign Relations, VIII, 1,231.

[34] Erkin, Turkish-Russian Relations, p. 287.

[35] Ibid., p. 231.

March 19, 1945, openly, attempted to place it in the most favorable light possible. The editorial in *Ulus*, April 8, 1945, written by Mümtaz Faık Fenik, which reaffirmed the existence of close and friendly relations between Turkey and the Soviet Union, serves as a model.[36] Fenik argued that the note was "unquestionably inspired" by Russo-Turkish friendship. Circumstances had changed since the treaty of 1925 had been signed and, as Fenik inquired, "what could be more natural than to desire a new agreement which will be substituted for the old [but which will] have the same characteristics of complementing the mutual interests of Turkey and the Soviet Union." Fenik, indicating that the Turkish Government had gladly accepted the Soviet note, represented the Soviet move as an attempt on the part of the Soviet Union to consolidate relations between Turkey and the Soviet Union. "As long as good intentions prevail in the new negotiations," Fenik concluded, "we can be certain that results will be easily obtained." Other editorials were structured along similar lines: the Soviet Union wished to revise the treaty with Turkey and Turkey had accepted; the Turkish Government regarded this as a happy and favorable development since it would undoubtedly place Soviet-Turkish relations on a sounder footing; finally, all during the war, elaborate and close discussions between the Soviet Union and Turkey had taken place and the two countries were in fundamental agreement. As *Yeni Sabah* put it, "Whenever Russia and Turkey have had a *tete à tete*, they have always come to an agreement."[37] Asım Us, published in *Vakit* an equally optimistic statement, as did Nadir Nadi.[38] "It is futile to look for a bad intention toward

[36] Mümtaz Faık Fenik, "Türkiye ve Sovyetler" ("Turkey and the Soviets"), *Ulus*, April 8, 1945, as in *Ayın Tarihi*, Vol. 137 (April 1945), pp. 68-69.

[37] *Yeni Sabah*, "Rusya ile Türkiye, başbaşa konuştukları vakit daima anlaşabilmişlerdir" ("Whenever Russia and Turkey have had a *tete à tete*, they have always come to an agreement"), April 8, 1945, as in *ibid.*, pp. 64-65.

[38] Asım Us, "Türkiye'nin Sovyetler Birliğine cevabı" ("Turkey's re-

our government within the main lines of the policy being carried out by our northern neighbor," Nadi asserted.

Hüseyin Cahit Yalçın, while toeing the line with the assertion that the Soviet Union intended to pursue friendly relations with Turkey, subtly introduced a number of reservations.[39] Yalçın specifically referred to the fact that the Soviets had not informed the British and American governments in advance and that the timing of the note had been particularly unfortunate since Turkey had only recently declared war on the Axis Powers. But the overall tone and tenor of Yalçın's remarks were designed to reduce anxieties concerning the Soviet move. He took satisfaction in the fact, for example, that the Soviet Union had notified the Turkish Government of its intention to cancel the treaty of 1925 in advance, whereas it could have acted summarily. Yalçın also called attention to the traditional reluctance of the Soviets to reveal their "personal affairs even to their closest friends." Perhaps it was for this reason, Yalçın suggested, that the Soviets had not informed their Western Allies in advance of the March 19 note. Yalçın emphasized that the tranquillity in Turkey as a result of the note was not feigned but genuine, since, he declared, "The Russians do not want land or bases from us." Yet, we now know, the Turkish Government, İnönü in particular, was deeply concerned by the Soviet note of March 19. Selim Sarper has indicated that the optimism expressed in the newspapers at this time was at government behest; it was as yet the policy of the Turkish Government to put a happy sheen on Soviet moves toward Turkey.[40] In early April 1945, this was becoming increasingly more difficult to do, however, since the

---

ply to the Soviet Union"), *Vakit*, April 8, 1945, as in *ibid.*, pp. 65-67; Nadir Nadi, "Türk-Sovyet dostluğunun yarını" ("The future of the Turkish-Soviet friendship"), *Cumhuriyet*, April 9, 1945, as in *ibid.*, pp. 69-70.

[39] Hüseyin Cahit Yalçın, "Türk-Rus münasebetleri" ("Turkish-Soviet relations"), *Tanin*, April 14, 1945, as in *ibid.*, pp. 70-72.

[40] Selim Sarper in a personal interview with the author.

Soviets were opening up a public barrage against Turkey. On April 3, for example, Moscow radio lambasted the Turkish press and accused it of being pro-Nazi.[41] On April 18, *Izvestia* continued the attack by describing the trial of the Pan-Turanists as a whitewash.[42] Attention in Turkey, therefore, turned with genuine eagerness on April 25, 1945, to San Francisco and the opening of the Conference of the United Nations.

THE SAN FRANCISCO CONFERENCE: THE TURKISH PERSPECTIVE

The Turkish delegation at San Francisco was headed by Foreign Minister Hasan Saka, and included the Ambassador to the United States, Hüseyin Ragıp Baydur as well as Feridun Cemal Erkin. On his arrival at San Francisco, Saka called on Molotov but received no further enlightenment as to Russian terms for a new treaty.[43] The Turkish delegation thus turned its attention to the business of the conference.

Ever since the Yalta conference, Turkish observers had been critical of the plans being put forward by the victorious powers for a postwar international system. Sadak, writing in *Akşam*, had pointed out that the original conception of an international peace-keeping organization appeared to be undermined by the proposed voting procedures. A Great Power, he argued, could only be controlled in a dispute if it

---

[41] *Review*, Series N, No. 49, p. 75.

[42] *Ibid.*; Baltalı, *The Issue of the Straits*, pp. 110-11, lists the specific criticisms leveled against Turkey by the Soviets at this time: 1) the Turkish pact or alliance with Germany before German invasion of Russia; 2) Turkey brought their armed forces to the eastern Anatolian front when the German army moved to the Volga; 3) Turkish declaration of war against Axis Powers came only after definite Allied victory; 4) Turkey did not permit ships that were bringing aid to Russia to pass through the Straits; 5) Turkey traded with Germany during the war and delivered large amounts of strategic goods. This represents the brief against Turkey which Soviet authors still hold to today.

[43] Eren, *Prohibitionists*, p. 293.

were willing to vote against itself—a highly unlikely eventuality. "It is hard to believe this system will work unless one also believes that the Big Five are like angels who would never attack the weak."[44] Ever since states were formed, Sadak continued, it had always been the Great Powers that had generated aggression and war. For his part, Asım Us in *Vakit* praised the "beautiful" idea of a United Nations peacekeeping force, but expressed the fear that it could only be used against small states on account of the veto power to be given the Big Five in the Security Council. "Therefore, the new United Nations to be founded on this formula will be nothing but a building without a foundation."[45] The Big Five, in agreement with two other members of the Security Council, would have the voting power to "erase any small country right off the world map." On the other hand, a single veto could prevent all the rest of the members from saving a small nation attacked by one or more of the Great Powers.[46]

The Turks were not alone in voicing these concerns which were widely shared by the small powers at San Francisco. They, in particular, however, had more than hypothetical reasons for concern, as they specifically feared attack by a Great Power.[47] Thus they regretted the proposed struc-

[44] Necmettin Sadak, "Anlaşılmıyan, fakat ehemmiyetli bir nokta" ("A hard to understand but very important point"), *Akşam*, February 20, 1945, as in *Ayın Tarihi*, Vol. 135 (February 1945), pp. 280-82.

[45] Asım Us, "Kırım formülünün sakatlığı" ("The shortcomings of the Crimea formula"), *Vakit*, March 28, 1945, as in *ibid.*, Vol. 136 (March 1945), pp. 228-30.

[46] *Ibid.* For similar views, Necmettin Sadak, "Büyük, Küçük, Ortanca" ("Big, Small, Medium"), *Akşam*, April 11, 1945, as in *ibid.*, Vol. 137 (April 1945), pp. 292-94; Sadak wrote: "In order to eliminate the class differentiation which creates discrimination among countries as between their rights, there should be no differentiation between large and small nations . . ."; also *Ulus*, April 12, 1945, which declared its opposition to dividing nations into categories with different rights. It stated, "only one category of states exists; even the smallest possesses the rights of statehood."

[47] Selim Sarper in a personal interview with the author.

tural defect that would have prevented the organization, as they understood it, from coming to their help in the event of a Soviet invasion. The veto, Turkish observers believed, would give Russia an advantage within the organization, preventing the noncommunist states from being able to utilize their numerical preponderance. There was concern, too, over what the veto in the United Nations might do to the power relationships in the postwar world community, that it would tend to perpetuate a world of Great Power hegemony in which each smaller nation would seek to align itself with a power willing to use the veto on its behalf. To remain neutral, to remain outside the conflicts of the Great Powers, would become increasingly difficult if not impossible.

The San Francisco Conference did not, essentially, modify those provisions of the draft scheme for a United Nations Organization to which the Turks took exception. In the words of the Turkish political scientist Mehmet Gönlübol:

> The conflicts between the large nations and the small at San Francisco almost always resulted in victory for the large nations. This was because the negotiations took place within a political framework arising out of the role of the host countries during the war. . . .[48]

It was this wartime reality which underlay the veto. Similarly, it was for this reason that the small countries were not in a position to "mellow" the Dumbarton Oaks' proposals of the Great Powers.[49] Moreover, Turkey, in particular, was not in a position to exercise much influence over the work of the San Francisco Conference. It had only gained the right to participate "at the last moment"[50] as a result of the sufferance of the victorious powers. Esmer reports that the Turkish delegation felt isolated from the Great Powers dur-

48 Gönlübol, *Atatürk and the Foreign Policy of Turkey*, p. 160.
49 *Ibid.*
50 Esmer in *Turkish Foreign Policy*, p. 172.

ing the conference.[51] "Since the prospective organization was basically to be composed of the winning countries," he wrote, "and since the world after the war was to be run according to the wishes and best interests of these countries, Turkey, which had carefully avoided entering the conflict during the war, was seriously concerned about the negative effects of its nonbelligerence."[52] For this reason, the Turks decided to ratify the Charter of the United Nations.

Returning home, the Turkish delegation urged that the imperfect bargain struck at San Francisco was the best Turkey could have received. "The articles of the United Nations agreement that granted privileges to the big nations," Mümtaz Soysal reports, "worried some of the Members [of the Assembly] and these did not refrain from expressing their concern. . . ."[53] Defending the charter before the Assembly, Foreign Minister Hasan Saka stated:

> Not just we, not just the other small nations, but the preparers of the Dumbarton Oaks Project themselves grant that this work [project] is not a perfect [project]. . . . But if we bear in mind the political realities of today, the efforts spent [in preparing the project] have not been futile. . . . Positive results in international relations can only be obtained through mutual sacrifice. If everybody were to persist in his own viewpoint, there would be no chance for coming to an agreement.[54]

Imperfect as the charter may have been, Saka explained, it was better than its only realistic alternative: anarchy.[55]

This was scarcely fullsome praise, and the subsequent debate, although going through the ritual of approval, was remarkably restrained in its enthusiasm. The deputy from Ankara, M. Ökmen, noted that the veto power "marred"

---

[51] *Ibid.* [52] *Ibid.*

[53] M. Soysal, *Foreign Policy and the Parliament*, p. 117.

[54] *T.B.M.M. Zabıt Ceridesi*, Seventh Assembly, August 15, 1945, First Session, I, 156.

[55] *Ibid.*, p. 157.

the treaty, but comforted himself with the hope that the Great Powers would abide by their professed intention to use it sparingly. After all, he reasoned, if one could not rely on such promises, then one could not rely upon treaties, either.[56] Whether the organization's purpose would be defeated by the veto depended upon its use in practice, which, in turn, depended on the "good or bad intentions" of each of the Big Five. "In fact," Yavuz Abadan remarked, "no legal formula can prevent, restrict, or eliminate the effects of bad intentions."[57]

Although favoring the charter's ratification, Deputy Recep Peker was critical of the Turkish delegation's failure to press harder for limitation of the veto. "We are not among the big nations in terms of our population and technical capabilities. Therefore, we had the right to demand that the mechanism of the Security Council function effectively against any nation that would attempt an armed aggression against us," he argued.[58]

Many Turks, therefore, from the very beginning, perceived the Charter of the United Nations to be a flawed instrument, based on the unity and good will of the Great Powers. In the absence of such a spirit of unity and good will, they saw it as severely limited in its ability to keep the peace and protect the sovereignty of smaller states. They correctly perceived that Turkey, like the other small and medium-sized nations, would soon become embroiled in Great Power politics, if not conflict, and that the United Nations would not be of great help in these circumstances. Hüseyin Yalçın summed up the mood of the day when he asked, "Why . . . was the world so dejected, in spite of victory?" To this he responded:

> The reason was not far to seek: none of the ends for which the war had been fought had been achieved. It was true that Nazism and Fascism had been defeated; but had

56 *Ibid.*, pp. 159-60.   57 Yavuz Abadan, *ibid.*, p. 162.
58 *Ibid.*, p. 172.

the fear of aggression been dissipated? Had freedom and independence been assured to the small nations? Whenever they raised their voices they were reprimanded and silenced. They were told: "You are too weak to protect yourselves. It is the responsibility of the Great Powers to see that the nations live at peace." The war had been fought in vain. The sword of Damocles still hung over the heads of the small nations. Power continued to dominate the world.[59]

This was the mood in Ankara as the war finally came to an end.

[59] *Tanin*, June 6, 1945.

FOURTEEN

A HISTORICAL NOTE:
THE PREDICTED SOVIET
DEMANDS ON TURKEY

ON June 7 and 18, Selim Sarper, representing his government in Moscow, had conversations with Soviet Minister
Molotov which confirmed the most dire expectations regarding Soviet postwar ambitions entertained in Ankara
since the beginning of hostilities.[1] The Russians demanded
the cession of Kars and Ardahan, Turkey's easternmost
provinces, the Soviet militarization of the approaches to the
Dardanelles and the Bosphorus, and a revision of the Montreux Convention with a view to giving the Soviet Union
greater legal control over the regime of the Straits.[2] Thus
began the Turko-Soviet confrontation of 1945, which helped
to usher in the period now known as the Cold War.

It seemed diabolical to the Turks that the Russians chose
the time of universal rejoicing and relief to begin their campaign against them.[3] Soviet timing, however, was well
chosen. From San Francisco emanated the hopeful euphoria
of universal peace.[4] Soviet and American troops were em-

[1] The Ambassador in Turkey (Wilson) to the Acting Secretary of
State, Ankara, July 7, 1945, United States, Department of State, *Foreign
Relations of the United States: Diplomatic Papers*, 1945, *The Conference of Berlin (The Potsdam Conference)*, I (Washington, D.C.: United
States Government Printing Office, 1960), 1,031; henceforth referred to
as *Foreign Relations: The Potsdam Conference*. See also Erkin, *Turkish-Russian Relations*, p. 295.

[2] The Ambassador in Turkey (Wilson) to the Acting Secretary of
State, Ankara, June 18, 1945, *Foreign Relations: The Potsdam Conference*, pp. 1,020-21.

[3] Selim Sarper in a personal interview with the author.

[4] For a description of the Turkish mood at this time of celebration

bracing on the Elbe. Turkey's obstinacy in relation to Russia—a nation that had done so much in cooperation with America and Great Britain to defeat the Axis—would seem a discordant, ungracious note.

The Turks were not abandoned, however. Suprisingly, almost instantly, the wartime grievances of the British toward the Turks vanished. On June 18, the day of the second Sarper-Molotov conversation, the British Government urged the United States to make "firm representations" to the Soviet Government, arguing that the Russians were renouncing "explicit assurances" given by Stalin at Yalta to respect the sovereign integrity of Turkey.[5] At least one Turkish fear, the fear that Great Britain would sacrifice them in order to divide Europe with the Russians into spheres of influence, did not materialize. The British, aware of Soviet intentions, became increasingly supportive of Turkish interests. This, Selim Sarper claims, was deeply appreciated in Ankara.[6]

The Americans, however, temporarily hesitated to join the British. Although the U.S. Ambassador in Turkey, Edwin C. Wilson, along with others such as Averell Harriman, were informing Washington of the seriousness of the Soviet threat to Turkey and the West,[7] the State Depart-

---

for the Allies and great danger to Turkey, Erkin, *Turkish-Russian Relations*, pp. 296-97. Erkin describes the ceremony of the signing of the United Nations Charter in the San Francisco Opera House: "There was but one delegation among those gathered at San Francisco, ours, which, absorbed wholly in the prospects of the morrow's reverses and adversity, was not able to join in the general gaiety."

[5] The Acting Secretary of State to the Ambassador in Turkey (Wilson), Washington, D.C., June 23, 1945, *Foreign Relations: The Potsdam Conference*, pp. 1,028-29.

[6] In a personal interview.

[7] On April 26, 1970, Henry Raymont in the Sunday edition of *The New York Times*, p. 30, reported that documents in the Franklin D. Roosevelt Library at Hyde Park, New York, recently made available to the public reveal that U.S. Ambassador William C. Bullitt warned the President on this account throughout the war. In a memorandum

ment preferred to see things in a more favorable light. In response to the British request that they both formally object to the Soviet treatment of Turkey, the State Department declared that the Sarper-Molotov talks had been conducted in a "friendly atmosphere."[8] It also warned that an Anglo-American protest might create an "unfortunate background" to the Potsdam meeting.

These hesitations were spelled out in more precise terms on June 29, 1945, in a State Department briefing paper.[9]

---

dated August 10, 1943, Bullitt counseled against "a new policy of appeasement" being advocated by certain circles inside the British Government, this time, toward Russia. As early as December 5, 1941, Bullitt advised Roosevelt, "Don't let Churchill get you into any more specific engagements than those in the Atlantic Charter. Try to keep him from engaging himself vis-a-vis Russia." The findings of the present study indicate that the Turkish Government was also deeply concerned about the possibility that after the war the British would seek to appease the Russians.

[8] *Foreign Relations: The Potsdam Conference*, pp. 1,028-29. A debate concerning the significance of Russian demands also occurred in Turkey. In a number of articles published during the latter part of June 1945, for example, Hüseyin Cahit Yalçın and Zekeriya Sertel entered into a bitter dispute. Sertel accused Yalçın of trying "to create an atmosphere of public anxiety" by spreading false rumors about the Soviet Union. The Soviets, Sertel argued, were committed to the independence of all nations and "it was inconceivable that the Soviet Union would commit such a monumental error [of violating this principle] before the very ink of its signature [on the U.N. Charter] was dry." Yalçın vehemently disagreed. "Promises and signatures are meaningless for the Red Fascists," he wrote. "For them there is only opportunity and the taking of advantage. . . . If there is no resistance, they will conquer Iran, then India, China, and finally the sun and the moon." Also see, Zekeriya Sertel, "Türk efkârının aydınlığa ihtiyacı vardır" ("Turkish opinion needs enlightenment"), *Tan*, June 28, 1945, as in *Ayın Tarihi*, Vol. 139 (June 1945), pp. 139-42; Hüseyin Cahit Yalçın, "Zincirini Koparan ihtiraslar" ("Ambitions that exceed their limits"), *Tanin*, June 30, 1945, as in *ibid.*, Vol. 139 (June 1945), pp. 144-45.

[9] Briefing Book Paper: United States Policy Toward Turkey, Washington, D.C., June 29, 1945, *Foreign Relations: The Potsdam Conference*, pp. 1,015-17.

Britain and Russia had eyed Turkey "jealously" for centuries, the paper argued, and British desires to bolster the Turks were really designed to induce the Turks to resist Russian overtures seeking to bring Turkey into the Soviet orbit. The United States should, the paper declared, maintain "a detached but watchful attitude" while "the interplay of British and Soviet policies on the Turkish stage" took its course. The United States could exert pressure on any of the parties at any time in the future. For the time being, the paper concluded, it was "preferable" from the point of view of U.S. interests "for Turkey either to have special alliances in both directions or no alliance at all."[10]

This subdued stance was quickly altered. At Potsdam the conflicts between Soviet and American interests and policies became more sharply drawn. By the time the Truman Doctrine was enunciated, Greece and Turkey had become the focal point of East-West confrontation. The United States was thus forced to take the lead in defending Western interests against Soviet expansionist aims which became nowhere clearer than in respect to Turkey. The "hand with the Turks," which Churchill had requested and received at Casablanca, was now for the Americans alone to play.

[10] *Ibid.*

FIFTEEN

CONCLUSION: SUMMARY ANALYSIS

TURKISH foreign policy and the coming of the Cold War is
the story of a coalition that was never forged and of diplomatic communication that never produced meaningful
negotiations. The reasons for this have already been suggested; it remains only to summarize and, where possible,
to provide some generalization.

The stubborn refusal of the Turkish Government to actively join in the Allied war effort represents a consistent
set of interpretations of the content and meaning of its
operational code that proscribed adventurism but clearly
defined the Soviet Union as archenemy. Turkish neutrality
was, in effect, a balance struck between the conflicting tugs
of interventionism and noninterventionism with the latter
constantly winning over the former. Turkish reluctance to
assume a more activist diplomatic posture did not reflect
satisfaction with British and American policies toward the
Soviet Union. On the contrary, it testifies the extent to
which the Turks believed the Western Allies to be misguided in their handling of the Russians.

For one thing, İnönü and his subordinates quietly hoped
for the development of an international political system
that would keep rein on Soviet expansionism through the
mechanisms of a viable balance of power. The Turks perceived their security as well as that of other small nations
in the postwar world to be inextricably tied to the creation
of a process of systemic equilibrium among the Great Powers. Consequently, they considered Allied policy of unconditional surrender, initially enunciated by Roosevelt, to be
an egregious error. True to their operational code, they perceived such a policy as an open invitation to Stalin to ex-

tend the Soviet domain. That Stalin would try to do so had been, in their view, highly probable; British and American subscription to the doctrine of unconditional surrender made it, as far as they were concerned, inevitable. Thus with the "turning of the tide," Turkish concern became double-pronged: given their assumptions concerning Russian postwar ambitions, they feared either that the British and Americans would be forced to negotiate a spheres of influence agreement placing Turkey well within the Soviet orbit, or that an all-out conflict between Russia and Britain assisted by the United States would break out soon after the defeat of Germany, enveloping Turkey, possibly transforming it into a battlefield or, at the very least, finally giving Soviet Russia the pretext it needed to attempt to fortify the Straits. To Turkish officials, then, British and American policies toward Russia seemed to portend alternative futures that would leave them with no more an appealing choice than that of the frying pan or the fire.

The Turkish Government, however, never fully apprized British and American representatives of their anticipations of Soviet behavior for a variety of reasons: İnönü's innate sense of caution, the nonadventurist principle of its operational code, the foreign policies of Britain and the United States that seemed to encourage Soviet expansionism. Under these circumstances, a Turkish policy initiative that involved a commission of anti-Soviet behavior, even if only in the form of warnings to the West, seemed out of the question.

İnönü was occasionally tempted to reveal his deep-seated reservations to Churchill and to Roosevelt as well. But his meetings with these men convinced him that they were too deeply committed to their own policies toward Stalin to appreciate any interference from him. Perhaps this was inevitable. It may be that İnönü faced an impossible task in trying to alter the behavior of the British and Americans in relation to Russia, particularly when the Allied coalition was based not only on ideological or cultural perceptions of "goodness" but on the highly instrumental grounds of a common enemy in a fight for survival. İnönü, after all, could only speak to the Western Allies of traditional Turkish fears of revisionist Russia. But to have done so would undoubtedly have struck the entire decision-influencing establishment in Ankara as adventurist in the extreme. Most individuals in this group tended to fear that at the very least such initiatives would force them to become totally dependent upon the British and Americans for their security by antagonizing the Russians. Appearing to be anti-Soviet even *with* Western guarantees seemed to the Turks to be almost as adventurist as without. They wished in no way to become the protected creature of any of the Great Powers, including Britain and the United States. A more interventionist posture, they believed, would place them in this position, even if it did not lead to outright invasion by the Soviets. The Turks, therefore, wanted to inveigle Britain and the United States into protecting them but without offending the Russians in the process—a matter, perhaps, of eating their cake and having it too. They thus sought to obtain the benefits of systemic security without becoming openly aligned or opposed to the goals or purposes of any one of the Great Powers. They wanted the security of Great Power protection but without cost to their national sovereignty, and a policy of noninvolved neutrality seemed the only answer.

Fundamentally their quest for Great Power protection without adventurism does not set them apart from other small nations. Small powers, almost by definition, must seek security through a mobilization of resources outside their borders. As Rothstein has observed, *"A small Power is a state which recognizes that it can not obtain security primarily by use of its own capabilities, and that it must rely fundamentally on the aid of other states, institutions, processes, or developments to do so."*[1] But when Turkish policy-

[1] Robert L. Rothstein, *Alliances and Small Powers* (New York: Columbia University Press, 1968), p. 29; italics in the original. Turkish policy-

makers sought the security that only the British and Americans could provide, they hoped to do so without losing their standing as a sovereign nation. Offending the Soviets and having to rely on the British and the Americans might, in their view, have done just this. To cite Rothstein again,

> The perspective from which Small Powers view the problems of security may make them reluctant to ally *solely* on the basis of power and interest. The point holds true, at least to some extent, even in the limiting case: in the situation where a Small Power perceives the threat that it faces in an immediate military sense. In the circumstance, it appears bound to seek the aid of the strongest available Great Power. However, reluctance to accept the obvious criteria as decisive, a reluctance which probably perforce will be overcome in light of the nature of the threat, rests on theoretical perception of ancient lineage. Alliance with superior power is inherently dangerous for a Small Power. The outcome may differ very little from the effect of merely procrastinating. The Small Power may not move from insecurity to security, but from insecurity to the status of a satellite.[2]

The central goal of Turkish foreign policy during the period under review, then, was an Anglo-American commitment guaranteeing Turkish security against the Soviet Union, but one which would not appear to be anti-Soviet in design. Only such an agreement, preferably carried out in the form of a coordinated Turkish-Anglo-American campaign in the Balkans and the Crimea, designed as much to

---

makers entertained what Raymond Aron has described as "defensive ambitions," that is, "safeguarding its autonomy, maintaining its own manner of life, not accepting subordination of its internal laws or of its external action to the decrees of others"; for Aron's discussion of defensive power, see his *Peace and War: A Theory of International Relations*, Richard Howard and Annette Baker Fox (trans.) (Garden City, N.Y.: Doubleday & Co., 1966), pp. 82-88.

[2] *Ibid.*, p. 61; italics in the original.

establish a *cordon sanitaire* between Russia and Turkey as to defeat the Axis, could have produced an alliance that would have brought Turkey into war.

Communication between Turkey and the Western Allies, however, never reached a stage of candor where it could deal with such a delicate issue. British and American officials, especially the distrusted Eden, failed to create an atmosphere in which the Turks felt free even to state this proposal as a condition for their entry into the war. Although Turkish belligerence was the main goal of the British, certainly a matter of the highest priority for the Russians during the Moscow Conference of October 1943, and at times partially supported by the American Government, the Allies never induced Turkish diplomats to discuss openly their conditions. On the contrary, the more insistent Churchill became, the less willing the Turks became to reveal their real position.

The insufficiency of British policy as perceived by Turkish policy-makers is perhaps best illustrated with reference to Riker's size principle. The size principle holds that:

In n-person, zero-sum games, where side-payments are permitted, where players are rational, and where they have perfect information, only minimum winning coalitions occur.

And that:

In social situations similar to n-person, zero-sum games with side-payments, participants create coalitions just as large as they believe will ensure winning and no larger.[3]

In other words, parties tend to form the smallest alliance sufficient to win or to alter the power ratio between them and the enemy but no larger than necessary so as to distribute the rewards of victory to the fewest possible mem-

---

[3] William H. Riker, *The Theory of Political Coalitions* (New Haven: Yale University Press, 1962), pp. 32-33; italics in the original.

bers. The size principle assumes that a utilitarian rationality guides the players who inevitably perceive even their coalition-partners as competitors. This assumption ignores the role of what William A. Gamson calls "nonutilitarian strategy preferences," ideological influences or policy preferences other than those of strict maximization of reward. Steven Rosen has also pointed out that "Even for redistribution alliances, benefits of winning may be divisible noncompetitively."[4] Or, partners to a coalition may be seeking different elements of the enemy's resources so that after victory there may be noncompetitive sharing.

For their part, Turkish policy-makers tended to perceive the relations between the British and the Americans as being noncompetitive, grounded not only in utilitarian necessity but in traditional commonality that transcended immediate interest. Britain and the United States, as Churchill and Roosevelt often proclaimed during the war, had ties that amounted to "a special relationship." İnönü regarded the partnership between the Soviet Union and the Western Allies, however, to be one of strict pragmatism that would devolve into an intense competition once the war ended.[5]

[4] Steven Rosen, "A Model of War and Alliance," in Julian R. Friedman, Christopher Bladen, and Steven Rosen (eds.), *Alliance in International Politics* (Boston: Allyn and Bacon, Inc., 1970), pp. 215-37 at p. 235; for Rosen's criticism of Riker's theory, see pp. 234-37; also see Bruce M. Russett's discussion in the same collection, "Components of an Operational Theory of International Alliance Formation," pp. 238-58; Russett's article originally appeared in the *Journal of Conflict Resolution*, XII, 3, 285-301.

[5] This analysis does not mean to suggest that İnönü or the other members of the Turkish Government had read or were aware of the size principle as such. Starting from the assumption that Soviet policy would inevitably turn competitive against the British and Americans, however, İnönü tended to set policy in accordance with the precepts of the size principle. When, for example, Riker writes the following, he is also shedding light on some of the crucial elements in İnönü's reasoning once the Allies began to win the war (*Theory of Political Coalitions*, pp. 67-68):
"Total war has further this interesting feature: If one side actually

CONCLUSION

Thus, again, for Turkish policy-makers the crucial question was why did the British want Turkey to enlarge the belligerent Allied coalition.

Given İnönü's belief in the inexorability of an expansionist Soviet foreign policy, British designs to expand the Allied coalition by bringing Turkey into the war made sense only in intracoalition competitive terms. Both British and Turkish interests might be served if Turkey, by coming into the war, could lend support to an Anglo-American attempt to contain Soviet Russia. Churchill's most cogent argument on behalf of Turkish belligerence, from İnönü's and Menemencioğlu's point of view, was that Turkey could thus play an active role in the establishment of a postwar settlement. Such a role had meaning to the Turks only in the context of British and American policy toward Russia and the systemic conditions that would prevail once Germany had been defeated. But British representatives never spoke in these terms. All pressures on Turkey to join the Allied coalition were seen in this light. As already suggested, had the Turks ever been convinced that they would be able to head off the Soviets by cooperating with an Anglo-American campaign in the Balkans that would place a ring around Russian expansionism without seeming to be purposefully anti-Soviet, they probably would have done so. The British and American governments never recognized these perceptions, however, and the diplomacy that resulted reflected the consequent breach in which the Turks stubbornly held on to

wins, that is, if one side is exhausted before the other, then victory, by removing the losers, transforms a (probably minimal) winning coalition into a grand coalition. And, if we accept characteristic function theory, grand coalitions are worthless. Assuming, as I shall, that winners in total war retain for some time after victory the zero-sum habits of thought engendered by their very participation in it, then they will reject a coalition of the whole and begin to squabble among themselves. Presumably they will seek to substitute for it something that approaches a minimal winning coalition. If, in fact, they actually do so, their action constitutes further verification of the size principle."

325

their neutrality as their best protection, despite warnings and threats, promises and predictions.[6]

The fact that British and Turkish policies remained so far apart throughout the war reflects diplomatic as well as coalition behavior. It demonstrates the extent to which communication between the Turks, the British, and the Americans never reached the degree of candor that might have permitted meaningful exchanges on Anglo-American policy toward the Russians. Turkish failure to comprehend, let alone influence, British policy reflects a reluctance on İnönü's and Menemencioğlu's part to use diplomatic channels during the war for purposes of negotiating a contract. In this sense, negotiations between the Turks and the Allies can be said never to have reached a meaningfully functional stage.

What one means by "negotiations" assumes analytical significance here. Different conceptions of the negotiating process set different standards for assessing what is sufficient or necessary for negotiations to occur. Many definitions of negotiations differ primarily on the extent to which the search for contract is regarded as being necessary to any process of interaction before it can be termed "negotiation." Fred Charles Iklé seems to demand the most in his definition of negotiations by way of contractual bargaining when

[6] I. William Zartman, *The Politics of Trade Negotiations between Africa and the European Economic Community: The Weak Confront the Strong* (Princeton, N.J.: Princeton University Press, 1971), pp. 206-11, suggests that divergent positions in negotiations are combined by limiting alternatives through four pairs of means: promise and prediction, threat and warning, commitment and obligation, and *fait accompli* and simple incapacity. Each pair has a volitional and nonvolitional component so that "promise refers to a volitional adjunct to agreement whereas prediction provides gratification through the agreement itself," and "threat is volitional whereas warning refers to future consequences beyond the warner's control." Churchill and Eden, in heading Allied diplomacy in Turkey, used warnings, threats, promises, and predictions by way of trying to influence Turkish behavior but never succeeded in narrowing the political gap between the two countries.

he writes, "As used here, negotiation is a process in which explicit proposals are put forward ostensibly for the purpose of reaching agreement on an exchange or on the realization of a common interest where conflicting interests are present."[7] Arthur Lall seems to require the least by defining international negotiations as "the process of consideration of an international dispute or situation by peaceful means, other than judicial or arbital processes, with a view to promoting or reaching among the parties concerned or interested some understanding, amelioration, adjustment, or settlement of the dispute or situation."[8] I. William Zartman describes negotiation as "the process of combining divergent viewpoints to produce a common agreement."[9] Each of these definitions provides the opportunity for a different analysis of the negotiating process. To understand Turkish diplomacy during the war, however, perhaps the most useful is one suggested by Jack Sawyer and Harold Guetzkow: "Negotiation is a process through which two or more parties—be they individuals, groups, or larger social units—interact in developing potential agreements to provide guidance and regulation of their future behavior."[10] This formulation is particularly relevant to the present analysis because it points to contract or future predictability as the main goal of negotiations.

For our purposes, negotiations occur whenever presumably independent parties interact on the basis of a mutually shared intention or expectation of establishing some form of contractual relationship. Contract is defined here simply as an agreement involving the mutual predictability of future behavior. To the degree that conflicting parties in-

[7] Fred Charles Iklé, *How Nations Negotiate* (New York: Harper & Row, 1964), pp. 3-4.

[8] Arthur Lall, *Modern International Negotiation: Principles and Practice* (New York: Columbia University Press, 1966), p. 5.

[9] Zartman, *The Politics of Trade Negotiations*, p. 202.

[10] Jack Sawyer and Harold Guetzkow, "Bargaining and Negotiation in International Relations," in Kelman, *International Behavior*, pp. 466-520 at p. 466.

teract but avoid whatever kinds of communication are necessary or appropriate to achieve predictability on future
conduct, i.e., contract, they are avoiding or preventing negotiations from taking place. Not that success is the sole measure of process. Some negotiations do end in failure; the
parties have attempted to agree on a contract but find that
it is impossible. But it is this search for behavioral predictability on the part of two or more autonomous agencies that,
for the purposes of the present analysis, constitutes the minimum or necessary standard for negotiations. The search for
contract, moreover, is essentially a processual criterion that
leaves open the question of substantive issue. Parties seeking an agreement on future predictability may do so in regard to trivial matters or in relation to highest concerns,
but negotiations can be said to exist as long as predictability
of future behavior is involved. Occasionally, however, parties to a conflict may substitute trivial, procedural, or specious issues in order to appear, for whatever reason, to be
"negotiating" without either intending or expecting to
reach agreement on future behavior. When this is done in
such a way as to 1) avoid or prevent an earnest search for
contractual agreement and 2) through devices that are largely designed to deceive the antagonist into thinking that
negotiations are actually taking place, the interrelationship
between the parties involved becomes not one of negotiation but, rather, almost by definition, one of manipulation.[11]

During the period under review, there was one and only
one proper subject for negotiations as far as the Turks were
concerned: the future behavior of the British and the Americans concerning the Russians. Not that the Turks ever explicitly stated this. Instead, they tried to tempt the British

[11] Frederick W. Frey defines "manipulation" as a specific form of
"power relationship that is intended and recognized by the influencer
and anti-intended and unrecognized by the influencee"; see his "Concepts of Developmental Administration and Strategy Implications for
Behavioral Change," Massachusetts Institute of Technology, unpublished monograph, p. 26.

and Americans into contractual negotiations with nothing more ardent than a number of veiled warnings. One example is the admonitions Churchill received from İnönü and Saracoğlu during the Adana meeting. Another is Açıkalın's ploy with Vinogradov in 1943. Perhaps the most candid statement of Turkish policy-concern uttered to bring about real negotiation was Menemencioğlu's during his fateful meeting with Eden in Cairo in November 1943. Here the Turkish Foreign Minister openly revealed his government's desire to establish a contractual arrangement with Britain concerning Russia. Eden's perceived reaction and demand that Turkey enter the war within a month seemed to eliminate this as a possibility, and the Turks were, as a result, totally unwilling to reveal themselves at the summit meeting in Cairo one month later.

A less candid and decidely more manipulative method to obtain predictability from the British Government was to lure them into the Balkans by offering to enter the war as part of an Anglo-Turkish-American expeditionary force. The Turkish Government informed the British time and again that they were prepared to join the Allied war effort, but only if the Allies would field a force in the Balkans or in any adjacent area and supply the Turkish military command with battle plans in advance. The Turks attempted to manipulate the British and the Americans by emphasizing the German menace whenever they outlined these proposals, even though their real goal was the establishment of a defensive perimeter against Soviet Russia. Although their concern lest İstanbul, İzmir, and Zonguldak be bombed was real enough, their omission of the Soviet threat in conversation with British and American representatives bespeaks of manipulation, not negotiation. Yet, although manipulative, these Turkish offers to join the war effort do in part represent negotiation-bids designed to help pave the way toward a contractual relationship. They went as far as the Turks ever did go toward an actual commitment in regard to their belligerence. The degree to which negotiations between the Turks and the British failed, however, can be measured by the fact that the two governments totally failed to work toward a contractual relationship on the basis of these offers. An Anglo-Turkish expeditionary landing in the Balkans was the very alternative both were presumably considering as a device to lure the United States into the Balkans. Yet they never "negotiated" over the question. For both, ambiguity remained the better part of valor.

Given their perceptions that they could not get the kind of guarantees that they assumed they needed from the British or the Americans, Turkish policy-makers deployed a diplomatic strategy designed to impede Great Power policies that might be later used as a pretext to force Turkey into the war or, worse, to invade it. Since their aims at systemic influence seemed impossible to achieve or at least too risky, they settled for the lesser goal of preserving their neutrality whatever the ultimate consequences. Diplomacy and strategy devolved into a series of avoidance stratagems.

Diplomacy, as defined by Zartman, is "the pursuit of national policy goals through international communication."[12] "Strategy" here is "the art of devising or employing plans or stratagems towards a goal."[13] The term "stratagem" refers to "an artifice or trick in war for deceiving and outwitting the enemy" or more simply "a cleverly contrived trick or scheme for gaining an end."[14] With the exception of the brief episodes in which the Turks tried to elicit contractual agreements from the British and Americans, their foreign policy in terms of practice and performance can be described analytically as a series of stratagems designed to deceive the Great Powers into letting them alone. The diplomatic strategy of Turkish foreign policy thus consisted of the following two stratagems:

12 Zartman, *The Politics of Trade Negotiations*, p. 200.
13 As in *Webster's Third New International Dictionary*.
14 *Ibid.*

Stratagem Number 1

Enter explicit but vague agreements in principle with the members of both Great Power coalitions, if necessary, but when in disagreement, reserve opposition to operational or implementational issues or areas; when pressured to accept operational solutions by the Great Powers, impede progress in the field through the creation of obfuscating conditions and prohibitive demands, that is, agree in the upper range of issue-formulation but manifest opposition in the lower ranges. If called upon to defend such practice, do not admit to it and try to assume the offensive by arguing that the Great Power has failed to live up to its part of the original bargain.

Stratagem Number 2

To prevent a Great Power from imposing an implementation strategy, stress the power and destructive intentionality of the other coalition and the likelihood of attack in the event of such implementation.[15]

Turkish diplomats, during their meetings with representatives of the Great Powers, often employed these two stratagems in order to appear to be negotiating while in effect merely stalling for time. The Turks realized that they could not afford to appear unwilling to negotiate with the Allies. On the other hand, they were not prepared to enter the war on the terms offered by the British. By using these stratagems, they seemed to be in earnest agreement with the Allied position but actually were able to delay the execution of those Allied policies they believed might threaten their neutrality. They entered into the informal agreement with the British at Adana, for example, only to exploit the high degree of latitude provided by its terms, in order to delay actual execution.

15 For another treatment, see Annette Baker Fox, *The Power of Small States*, esp. Chap. VII, "The Influence of Small Powers," pp. 180-88.

331

This is illustrated by the process we have named operation footdrag. The Turks sacrificed gains in military capability in order to prevent an influx of British troops called for in the agreement and accepted by İnönü at Adana. In the Turkish view, this was precisely the kind of assistance that could become a kiss of death, either by leading to a German attack or a Russian invasion on the grounds that what one ally could do another ally might do. The result was repeated measures at the low or mid-echelons on the Turkish part that successfully prevented the British from implementing the Adana agreements. When confronted with this fact during the Cairo Conference in December 1943, both İnönü and Menemencioğlu retorted by referring to the Adana lists of military supplies that they claimed the British had failed to deliver. Much Allied matériel had in fact been supplied them, more than they could possibly use. Even had the Allies been able to meet the letter of the Adana lists, they would not have gone to war in the absence of an Anglo-American expeditionary landing in territory adjacent to Turkey. This, however, they never openly admitted. This is typical of Stratagem Number 1. Turkish representatives would agree in principle with an Allied or, for that matter, Axis position, and delay action through the creation of operational difficulties. When put to task in subsequent conferences, they pointed to Great Power failure to fulfill the acts of performance agreed to in the original decision. We see the manifestations of this stratagem most clearly in the December 1943 conference in Cairo, but it remained a part of Turkish foreign policy until the *pro forma* declaration of war against Germany on February 23, 1945.

To supplement Stratagem Number 1, Turkish diplomats often employed Stratagem Number 2 by emphasizing the destructive intentionality of the other side. In response to Allied demands to enter the war, for example, they would speak of the inevitability of German attack. Whenever the Germans, on the other hand, requested certain forms of assistance, like being allowed to transport Axis forces through Turkish territory, the Turkish reaction would be to underscore the likelihood of Russian attack. These fears were, of course, not entirely divorced from real possibilities. But at least in relation to the Allies, expressions of these concerns were combined with Stratagem Number 1 and used to permit the Turks to assume the bargaining offensive. By employing Stratagem Number 2, the Turks were able to make demands on the Allies, for delivery of vast amounts of goods or the opening of an Anglo-American front in the Balkans, demands which they felt could probably not be met.

In the use of these two stratagems, the Turks put their faith in policies that were essentially incrementalist in nature. As suggested by C. E. Lindblom and David Braybrooke, such policies are "better described as moving *away* from known social ills rather than as moving *toward* a known and relatively stable goal."[16] Eventually this strategy caused a very real rupture with the Allies, so much so that İnönü began to fear that perhaps the British would leave them to the mercy of the Soviets. Turkish diplomacy thus began to shift by sending a series of new signals more closely identifying Turkey with the Allied cause. These shifts at first took the form of changes in domestic policy, like the repeal of the *Varlık Vergisi*, the elimination of Menemencioğlu, and only later included foreign-policy initiatives like the severance of diplomatic relations with Germany.

Thus to the very end, Turkish foreign policy remained incremental, seeking day by day to adjust to changes in the political conditions affecting Turkey, but without ever accepting the risks entailed in trying to play systemically oriented politics. In this, Turkish leaders were acting not

[16] For a complete presentation of Lindblom and Braybrooke's interesting discussion of incrementalism, see their *A Strategy of Decision-Making: Policy Evaluation as a Social Process* (New York: The Free Press, 1963), esp. pp. 61-79.

only in conformity to the norms of their country's founding ideology, but with a view to their position as representatives of a small state surrounded in a universe of war but not yet a party to its violence. For them it was enough merely to survive the war with their sovereignty intact. Perhaps they may be faulted for this. Perhaps they might have early and more actively joined in the Allied effort while attempting to make the British and Americans more aware of their perceptions of postwar Soviet policies. The consequences to Turkey and the world would surely have been significant. But to condemn Turkish policy-makers, notably İnönü, in this way is to judge them for playing small state diplomacy rather than Great Power politics. And is this not precisely the failure of such fallen giants as Sukarno and Nkrumah. İnönü may have tried to do more; but he could have achieved much less.

BIBLIOGRAPHY

BOOKS

Aksın, Aptulahat. *Atatürk'ün Dış Politika İlkeleri ve Diplomasisi (Principles of Atatürk's Foreign Policy and Diplomacy)*. İstanbul: İnkılâp ve Aka Kitabevleri, 1966.

Almond, Gabriel A. *The American People and Foreign Policy*. New York: Frederick A. Praeger, 1960.

Archer, Laird. *Balkan Journal: An Unofficial Observer in Greece*. New York: W. W. Norton & Co., 1944.

Aron, Raymond. *Peace and War: A Theory of International Relations*, Richard Howard and Annette Baker Fox (trans.). Garden City, N.Y.: Doubleday & Co., 1966.

Arzık, Nimet. *Bitmeyen Kavga: İsmet İnönü (Unending Quarrel: İsmet İnönü)*. Ankara: Kurtuluş Matbaası, 1965.

Atak, Sadık M. *Harp Sonrası Dünya 1945-1966 (Postwar World, 1945-1966)*. Ankara: Ankara Basını ve Ciltevi, 1966.

Ataöv, Türkkaya. *Turkish Foreign Policy: 1939-1945*. Ankara: Ankara Üniversitesi Siyasal Bilgiler Fakültesi Yayınları, No. 197-179, 1965.

Atatürk, Mustafa Kemal. *A Speech Delivered by Ghazi Mustafa Kemal, President of the Turkish Republic, October 1927*. Leipzig: K. F. Koehler, 1929.

Aydemir, Şevket Süreyya. *İkinci Adam: İsmet İnönü 1938-1950 (The Second Man: İsmet İnönü 1938-1950)*. Vol. II. İstanbul: Remzi Kitabevi, 1967.

Badoglio, Pietro. *Italy in the Second World War: Memoirs and Documents*. New York: Oxford University Press, 1948.

Baldwin, Hanson W. *Great Mistakes of the War*. New York: Harper & Bros., 1949.

Balta, Tahsin Bekir. *Türkiyede Yasama-Yürütme Münasebeti* (*Legislative-Executive Relations in Turkey*). Ankara: Ankara Üniversitesi Siyasal Bilgiler Fakültesi Yayınları, No. 100-32, İdarî İlimler Enstitüsü Yayınları, No. 9, 1960.

Baltalı, Kemal. *Boğazlar Meselesi: 1936-1956 Yıllar Arasında* (*The Issue of the Straits: Between the Years 1936-1956*). Ankara: Yeni Desen Matbaası, 1959.

Bayur, Yusuf Hikmet. *Türkiye Devletinin Dış Siyasası* (*Foreign Policy of the Turkish Government*). İstanbul: İstanbul Üniversitesi Yayınları, No. 59, 1942.

Belinkov, S. and I. Vasilev. *O Turetskom 'Neitralitete Vo Vremia Vtoroi Mirovoi Voiny*. Moscow: Gozpolitizdat, 1952.

Beloff, Max. *The Foreign Policy of Soviet Russia 1929-1941*. Vol. II. London: Oxford University Press, 1949.

de Belot, Raymond. *The Struggle for the Mediterranean 1939-1945*. James A. Field, Jr. (trans.). Princeton, N.J.: Princeton University Press, 1951.

Berkes, Niyazi. *The Development of Secularism in Turkey*. Montreal: McGill University Press, 1964.

Bilsel, Cemal. *Türk Boğazları* (*Turkish Straits*). İstanbul: Akgün Matbaası, 1948.

Bradley, Omar N. *A Soldier's Story*. New York: Henry Holt & Co., 1951.

Bryant, Arthur. *The Turn of the Tide: A History of the War Years Based on the Diaries of Field-Marshal Lord Alanbrooke, Chief of the Imperial General Staff*. Garden City, N.Y.: Doubleday & Co., 1957.

Bullard, Reader. *Britain and the Middle East: From the Earliest Times to 1950*. London: Hutchinson's University Library, 1951.

Bullock, Alan. *Hitler: A Study in Tyranny*. New York: Harper & Row, 1962.

Burçak, Rıfkı Salim. *Türk-Rus-İngiliz Münasebetleri: 1791-1941* (*Turkish-Russian-English Relations: 1791-1941*). İstanbul: Aydınlık Matbaası, 1946.

Butcher, Harry C. *My Three Years with Eisenhower*. New York: Simon and Schuster, 1946.

Byrnes, James F. *Speaking Frankly*. New York: Harper & Bros., 1947.

Çağatay, Tahir. *Türkistan: Kurtuluş Hareketile İlgili Olaylardan Sahneler (Scenes from Events Concerning the Liberation Movements)*. İstanbul: "Yaş Türkistan" Yayını, 1959.

Carr, Edward Hallett. *German-Soviet Relations between the Two World Wars, 1919-1939*. Baltimore: The Johns Hopkins Press, 1951.

Catroux, General Georges. *Dans La Bataille de Mediterranée (In the Battle for the Mediterranean)*. Paris: Rene Julliard, 1949.

Cebesoy, Ali Fuat. *Gl. Ali Fuat Cebesoy'un Siyasî Hatıraları (General Ali Fuat Cebesoy's Political Memoirs)*. İstanbul: Vatan Neşriyatı, 1957.

Churchill, Winston S. *The Second World War*. Vol. IV. *The Hinge of Fate*. Boston: Houghton Mifflin Co., 1950. Vol. V. *Closing the Ring*. Boston: Houghton Mifflin Co., 1951. Vol. VI. *Triumph and Tragedy*. Boston: Houghton Mifflin Co., 1953.

Ciano, Count Galeazzo. *The Ciano Diaries 1939-1943*. Hugh Gibson (ed.). Garden City, N.Y.: Doubleday & Co., 1946.

———. *Ciano's Diplomatic Papers*. Malcolm Muggeridge (ed.). Stuart Hood (trans.). London: Odhams Press, Ltd., 1948.

Clark, Alan. *Barbarossa: The Russian-German Conflict, 1941-1945*. New York: William Morrow & Co., 1965.

Collins, Robert J. *Lord Wavell 1883-1941: A Military Biography*. London: Hodder and Stoughton, 1947.

Dallin, David. *Soviet Russia's Foreign Policy, 1939-1942*. New Haven: Yale University Press, 1943.

Deane, John R. *The Strange Alliance*. New York: The Viking Press, 1950.

Devereux, Robert. *The First Ottoman Constitutional Period: A Study of the Midhat Constitution and Parliament*, Baltimore: The Johns Hopkins Press, 1963.
Doenitz, Admiral Karl. *Memoirs: Ten Years and Twenty Days*. London: Weidenfeld and Nicholson, 1958.
Duru, Kâzım Nami. *Cumhuriyet Devri Hatıralarım (My Memoirs of the Republican Era)*. İstanbul: Sucuoğlu Matbaası, 1958.
Duverger, Maurice. *Political Parties*. London: Methuen & Co., Ltd., 1954.
Eden, Anthony. *Facing The Dictators*. London: Cassell, 1962.
————. *The Reckoning: The Memoirs of Anthony Eden*. Boston: Houghton Mifflin Co., 1965.
Eisenhower, Dwight D. *Crusade in Europe*. Garden City Books edition, 1952. Garden City, N.Y.: Doubleday & Co., 1948.
Emeny, Brooks. *The Strategy of Raw Material: A Study of America in Peace and War*. New York: The Macmillan Co., 1944.
Erden, Ali Fuad. *İsmet İnönü*. İstanbul: Burhanettin Erenler Matbaası, 1952.
Erer, Tekin. *Basında Kavgalar (Press Quarrels)*. İstanbul: Rek-Tur Kitap Servisi Yayınları, 1965.
————. *Yasakçılar (Prohibitionists)*. İstanbul: Toker Matbaası, 1965.
Erkin, Feridun Cemal. *Les Relations Turco-Soviétiques et La Question Des Détroits (Turkish-Russian Relations and the Question of the Straits)*. Ankara: Başnur Matbaası, 1963.
Esmer, Ahmet Şükrü. *Yeni Türkiye (The New Turkey)*. İstanbul: Nebioğlu Yayınevi, 1959.
Esmer, Ahmet Şükrü, Oral Sander, and the members of the Political Science Faculty of the University of Ankara. *Olaylarla Türk Dış Politikası: 1919-1965 (Turkish Foreign Policy with Events)*. Ankara: Dışişleri Bakanlığı Matbaası, 1968.

Feis, Herbert. *Churchill, Roosevelt, Stalin: The War They Waged and the Peace They Sought.* Princeton, N.J.: Princeton University Press, 1957.

Fox, Annette Baker. *The Power of Small States: Diplomacy in World War II.* Chicago: The University of Chicago Press, 1959.

Fox, William T. R. *The Super-Powers.* New York: Harcourt, Brace & Co., 1944.

Frey, Frederick W. *The Turkish Political Elite.* Cambridge: The Massachusetts Institute of Technology Press, 1965.

Friedman, Julian R., Christopher Bladen, and Steven Rosen (eds.). *Alliance in International Politics.* Boston: Allyn and Bacon, Inc., 1970.

Gafencu, Grigore. *Prelude to the Russian Campaign.* E. Fletcher-Allen (trans.). London: Frederick Muller, Ltd., 1945.

Gallagher, Matthew P. *The Soviet History of World War II: Myths, Memories and Realities.* New York: Frederick A. Praeger, 1963.

de Gaulle, Charles. *The War Memoirs.* Vol. i. *The Call to Honor, 1940-1942.* New York: Simon and Schuster, 1955. Vol. ii. *Unity.* New York: Simon and Schuster, 1959.

Geshkoff, Theodore I. *Balkan Union, A Road to Peace in Southeastern Europe.* New York: Columbia University Press, 1940.

Gilbert, Felix. *Hitler Directs His War: The Secret Records of His Daily Military Conferences.* New York: Oxford University Press, 1950.

Gökalp, Ziya. *Türkçülügün Esasları (The Foundations of Turkism).* Ankara: Matbuat ve İstihbarat Matbaası, 1923.

Gönlübol, Mehmet and Cem Sar. *Atatürk ve Türkiye'nin Dış Politikası: 1919-1938 (Atatürk and the Foreign Policy of Turkey).* İstanbul: Millî Eğitim Basımevi, 1963.

Gordon, David L. and Royden Dangerfield. *The Hidden Weapon: The Story of Economic Warfare.* New York: Harper & Bros., 1947.

Gövsa, Alaettin İbrahim. *Türk Meşhurları Ansiklopedisi (Encyclopedia of Famous Turks).* İstanbul: Yedigün Neşriyatı, 1946.

Gözübüyük, A. Şeref and Suna Kili (eds.). *Türk Anayasa Metinleri (Turkish Constitutional Texts)* (Ankara Üniversitesi Siyasal Bilgiler Fakültesi İdarî İlimler Enstitüsü Yayın, No. 2). Ankara: Ajans-Türk Matbaası, 1957.

de Guingand, Francis. *Operation Victory.* New York: Charles Scribner's Sons, 1947.

Hart, Basil Henry Liddell. *The German Generals Talk.* New York: William Morrow & Co., 1948.

von Hassell, Ulrich. *The von Hassell Diaries 1938-1944.* Garden City, N.Y.: Doubleday & Co., 1947.

Heyd, Uriel. *Foundations of Turkish Nationalism: The Life and Teachings of Ziya Gökalp,* London: Luzac & Co., 1950.

Higgins, Trumbull. *Soft Underbelly: The Anglo-American Controversy over the Italian Campaign 1939-1940.* New York: The Macmillan Co., 1968.

―――. *Winston Churchill and the Second Front 1940-1942.* New York: Oxford University Press, 1957.

Hinsley, F. H. *Hitler's Strategy.* Cambridge: Cambridge University Press, 1951.

―――. *Sovereignty.* New York: Basic Books, 1966.

Hizarcı, Suat (ed.). *Hüseyin Cahit Yalçın.* İstanbul: Varlık Yayınları, No. 550, 1957.

Hostler, Charles Warren. *Turkism and the Soviets: The Turks of the World and Their Political Objectives.* London: George Allen and Unwin, Ltd., 1957.

Hugessen, Knatchbull Sir Hughe. *Diplomat in Peace and War.* London: Murray, 1949.

Hull, Cordell. *The Memoirs of Cordell Hull,* Vol. II. New York: The Macmillan Co., 1948.

Hurewitz, Jacob C. *Diplomacy in the Near and Middle East: A Documentary Record*, 2 vols. Princeton, N.J.: D. Van Nostrand & Co., 1956.

Iklé, Fred Charles. *How Nations Negotiate*. New York: Harper & Row, 1964.

Jäschke, Gotthard. *Die Turkei in den Jahren 1942-1951: Geschichtekalender mit Namen und Sachregister (Turkey in the Years 1942-1951: Chronology with Names and Events)*. Wiesbaden: Otto Harrassowitz, 1955.

Kallay, Nicholas. *Hungarian Premier*. New York: Columbia University Press, 1954.

Karacan, Ali Naci. *Lozan Konferansı ve İsmet Paşa (The Lausanne Conference and İsmet Paşa)*. İstanbul: Maarif Matbaası, 1943.

Karagöz, Âdem Ruhi. *Bulgaristan Türk Basını: 1879-1945 (Turkish Press in Bulgaria: 1879-1945)*. İstanbul: Üniversite Matbaası, 1945.

Karal, Enver Ziya. *Türkiye Cumhuriyeti Tarihi: 1918-1944 (History of the Turkish Republic: 1918-1940)*. İstanbul: Millî Eğitim Basımevi, 1945.

Karpat, Kemal H. *Political and Social Thought in the Contemporary Middle East*. London: Pall Mall Press, 1968.

————. *Turkey's Politics: The Transition to a Multi-Party System*. Princeton, N.J.: Princeton University Press, 1959.

Kelman, Herbert C. (ed.). *International Behavior: A Social-Psychological Analysis*. New York: Holt, Rinehart and Winston, 1965.

Kesselring, Albert. *Kesselring: A Soldier's Record*. New York: William Morrow and Co., 1954.

Khadduri, Majid. *Independent Iraq: A Study in Iraq Politics since 1932*. London and New York: Oxford University Press, 2nd ed., 1958.

————. *Modern Libya: A Study in Political Development*. Baltimore: The Johns Hopkins Press, 1963.

————. *War and Peace in the Law of Islam*. Baltimore: The Johns Hopkins Press, 1955.

Kili, Suna. *Kemalism.* İstanbul: Robert College Publications, 1970.

Kılıç, Altemir. *Turkey and the World.* Washington, D.C.: Public Affairs Press, 1959.

Kinross, Lord Patrick. *Atatürk: The Rebirth of a Nation.* London: Weidenfeld and Nicholson, 1964.

Lord Kinross (J.P.D. Balfour). *Atatürk: A Biography of Mustafa Kemal, Father of Modern Turkey.* New York: William Morrow and Co., 1965.

Kirk, George E. *Survey of International Affairs 1939-1946: The Middle East in the War.* London: Oxford University Press for the Royal Institute of International Affairs, 1952.

Kop, Kadri Kemal (ed.). *Millî Şef İnönü'nün: Hitabe, Beyanat ve Mesajları (National Leader İsmet İnönü: Addresses, Declarations and Messages).* Ankara: Recep Ulusoğlu Basımevi, 1941.

Krecker, Lothar. *Deutschland und die Turkei im Zweiten Weltkrieg (Germany and Turkey in the Second World War).* Frankfurt am Main: Frankfurter Wissenschaftliche Beitrage Vittorio Klostermann, 1964.

Külçe, Süleyman. *Mareşal Fevzi Çakmak: Askerî, Hususî Hayatı (Marshal Fevzi Cakmak: His Military and Personal Life).* Vol. 1. İstanbul: Cumhuriyet Matbaası, 2nd ed., 1953.

Kurat, Yuluğ Tekin. *İkinci Dünya Savaşında Türk-Alman Ticaretindeki İktisadî Siyaset (A Survey of Economic Policy in Turkish-German Trade Relations During the Second World War).* Ankara: Türk Tarih Kurumu Basımevi, 1961.

Kuyucak, Hazım Atıf. *Memorandum on Exchange Control in Turkey.* Paris: International Institute of International Cooperation, 1939.

Lacoste, Raymond. *La Russie Soviétique et la Question D'Orient: La Poussée Soviétique vers les Mers Chauds—Mediterranée et Golfe Persique (Soviet Rus-*

sia and the Eastern Question: The Soviet Push Toward Warm Waters—The Persian Gulf and the Mediterranean). Paris: Les Éditions Internationales, 1946.

Lall, Arthur. *Modern International Negotiation: Principles and Practice.* New York: Columbia University Press, 1966.

Langer, William and S. Everett Gleason. *The Undeclared War 1940-1941.* New York: Harper & Bros., 1953.

Leahy, William D. *I Was There.* New York: McGraw-Hill Book Co., 1950.

Leites, Nathan. *The Operational Code of the Politburo.* New York: McGraw-Hill Book Co., 1951.

Lenczowski, George. *The Middle East in World Affairs.* Ithaca, N.Y.: Cornell University Press, 1952.

Lerner, Daniel. *The Passing of Traditional Society.* New York: The Free Press of Glencoe, 1958.

Lev, Nikolaevich Ivanov. *Ocherki Mezhdunarodnykh Otnoshenii v Period Vtoroi Mirovoi Voiny, 1939-1945.* Moscow: Adka, Nauk SSSR, 1958.

Levonian, Lutfy. *The Turkish Press: 1932-1936.* Beirut: n.p., 1937.

Lewis, Bernard. *The Emergence of Modern Turkey.* New York: Oxford University Press, 1961.

Lewis, Cleona. *Nazi Europe and World Trade.* Washington, D.C.: The Brookings Institution, 1941.

Lewis, Geoffrey. *Turkey.* New York: Frederick A. Praeger, 1960.

Lindblom, Charles E. and David Braybrooke. *A Strategy of Decision-Making: Policy Evaluation as a Social Process.* New York: The Free Press, 1963.

Long, Gavin. *Greece, Crete and Syria.* Canberra: Australian War Memorial, 1953.

Lyttelton, Oliver (Lord Chandos). *The Memoirs of Lord Chandos: An Unexpected View from the Summit.* New York: The New American Library, 1963.

Macridis, Roy C. (ed.). *Foreign Policy in World Politics.* Englewood Cliffs, N.J.: Prentice-Hall, Inc., 1959.

Mardin, Şerif. *The Genesis of Young Ottoman Thought: A Study in the Modernization of Turkish Political Ideas.* Princeton, N.J.: Princeton University Press, 1962.

Massigli, René. *La Turquie Devant La Guerre: Mission à Ankara 1939-1940* (*Turkey Before the War: Mission to Ankara 1939-1940*). Paris: Librairie Plon, 1964.

McNeill, William Hardy. *America, Britain, and Russia: Their Co-operation and Conflict 1941-1946.* Vol. III. *Survey of International Affairs 1939-1946*, Arnold J. Toynbee (ed.). London: Oxford University Press for the Royal Institute of International Affairs, 1953.

Mears, Eliot Grinnel. *Modern Turkey.* New York: The Macmillan Co., 1924.

Medlicott, William H. *The Economic Blockade*, 2 vols. London: Longmans Green & Co., 1952-1959.

Molotov, V. M. *Foreign Policy of the Soviet Union.* Moscow: Foreign Language Publishing House, 1939. Report by the Chairman of the Council of People's Commissars of the U.S.S.R. and People's Commissar of Foreign Affairs at the Extraordinary Fifth Session of the Supreme Soviet of the U.S.S.R. October 31, 1939.

———. *Soviet Peace Policy.* London: Lawrence and Wishart, 1941.

Montchiloff, N. *Ten Years of Controlled Trade in South-Eastern Europe.* Cambridge, England: Cambridge University Press, 1944.

Moyzisch, L. C. *Operation Cicero.* Constantine Fitzgibbon and Henrich Fraenkel (trans.). New York: Coward-McCann, 1950.

Murphy, Robert. *Diplomat Among Warriors.* Garden City, N.Y.: Doubleday & Co., 1964.

Nadi, Nadir. *Perde Aralığından* (*Through an Opening in the Curtain*). İstanbul: Cumhuriyet Yayınları, 1964.

Neumann, William L. *Making the Peace 1941-1945: The Diplomacy of the Wartime Conferences.* Washington: Foundation for World Affairs, 1950.

Newman, Bernard. *The Captured Archives: The Story of the Nazi-Soviet Documents.* London: Latiner House, 1948.

Ökte, Faik. *Varlık Vergisi Faciası (The Tragedy of the Capital Levy).* İstanbul: Neblioğlu Yayınevi, 1951.

Ortaç, Yusuf Ziya. *İsmet İnönü: 1884-1932.* İstanbul: n.p., 1946.

Papagos, Alexander. *The Battle of Greece 1940-1941.* Athens, Greece: The J. M. Scazikis "Alpha" Editions, 1949.

von Papen, Franz. *Memoirs.* New York: E. P. Dutton and Co., 1953.

Phillips, Ernest. *Hitler's Last Hope: A Factual Survey of the Middle East War-Zone and Turkey's Vital Strategic Position, with a Special Chapter on Turkey's Military Strength by Noel Barber.* London: W. H. Allen & Co., 1942.

Potemkin, Vladimir P. *Histoire de la Diplomatie (History of Diplomacy).* 3 vols. Paris: Librairie de Medicis, 1955.

————. *Politika Umirotvoreniia Agressorov I Borba Sovetkogo Soiuza Za Mir.* Moscow: Gozpolitizdat, 1946.

Ramsaur, E. E. *The Young Turks: Prelude to the Revolution of 1908.* Princeton, N.J.: Princeton University Press, 1957.

Reitzel, William. *The Mediterranean: Its Role in America's Foreign Policy.* New York: Harcourt, Brace & Co., 1948.

Riker, William H. *The Theory of Political Coalitions.* New Haven: Yale University Press, 1962.

Roosevelt, Elliott. *As He Saw It.* New York: Duell, Sloan & Pearce, 1946.

Rosenau, James A. *Public Opinion and Foreign Policy: An Operational Formulation.* New York: Random House, 1961.

Rossi, A. Angelo Tasca. *The Russo-German Alliance August 1939–June 1941.* John and Micheline Cullen (trans.). Boston: Beacon Press, 1951.

Rothstein, Robert L. *Alliance and Small Powers.* New York: Columbia University Press, 1968.

Rozek, Edward J. *Allied Wartime Diplomacy: A Pattern in Poland*. New York: John Wiley & Sons, 1958.

Rustow, Dankwart A. *Philosophers and Kings*. New York: George Braziller, 1970.

Sâbis, Âli İhsan. *Harb Hatıralarım (My War Memoirs)*. Vol. I. İstanbul: İnkılâb Kitabevi, 1943.

Şapolyo, Enver Behnan. *Ziya Gökalp*. İstanbul: Güven Basımevi, 1943.

Schacht, Hjalmar. *Account Settled*. Edward Fitzgerald (trans.). London: Weidenfeld and Nicholson, 1949.

Schmidt, Paul. *Hitler's Interpreter*. R.H.C. Steed (ed.). New York: The Macmillan Co., 1951.

Scott, William Evans. *Alliance Against Hitler: The Origins of the Franco-Soviet Pact*. Durham, N.C.: Duke University Press, 1962.

Sherwood, Robert E. *Roosevelt and Hopkins: An Intimate History*. New York: Harper & Bros., 1948.

Shirer, William L. *The Rise and Fall of the Third Reich: A History of Nazi Germany*. New York: Simon and Schuster, 1960.

Shotwell, James T. (ed.). *Perspectives in Peace 1910-1960*. New York: Frederick A. Praeger for the Carnegie Endowment for International Peace, 1960.

Shotwell, James T. and Francis Deák. *Turkey at the Straits: A Short History*. New York: The Macmillan Co., 1941.

Smith, Elaine Diana. *Turkey: Origins of the Kemalist Movement and the Government of the Grand National Assembly 1919-1923*. Washington, D.C.: Judd and Detweiler, 1959.

Sokolnicki, Michael. *The Turkish Straits*. Beirut, Lebanon: American Press, 1950.

Soku, Şakir Ziya. *İsmet İnönü: Hususî, Askerî, Siyasî Hayatı (İsmet İnönü: His Private, Military and Political Life)*. İstanbul: Ülkü Basımevi, 1939.

Soysal, İsmail. *Türkiye'nin Dış Münasebetleriyle ilgili Başlıca Siyasî Anlaşmaları (Turkey's Main Political Agreements Related to its Foreign Policy)*. Ankara: Türkiye İş Bankası Kültür Yayınları, 1965.

Soysal, Mümtaz. *Dış Politika ve Parlamento: Dış Politika Alanındaki Yasama-Yürütme İlişkileri Üzerinde Karşilaştırmalı Bir İncelemene (Foreign Policy and the Parliament: A Comparative Analysis of the Legislative-Executive Relations in the Field of Foreign Politics)*. Ankara: Ankara Üniversitesi Siyasal Bilgiler Fakültesi Yayınları, No. 183-185, 1964.

' Stettinius, Edward R., Jr. *Roosevelt and the Russians: The Yalta Conference*. Walter Johnson (ed.). Garden City, N.Y.: Doubleday & Co., 1949.

Stimson, Henry L. and McGeorge Bundy. *On Active Service in Peace and War*. New York: Harper & Row, 1948.

Swinton, Philip Cunliffe-Lichtes. *I Remember*. London: Hutchinson and Co., 1948.

Tanor, Bülent and Taner Beygo (eds.). *Türk Anayasaları (Turkish Constitutions)*. İstanbul: Filiz Kitabevi, 1964.

Tarhan, Servet. *La Monnaie Turque Pendant La Deuxième Guerre Mondiale (Turkish Money During the Second World War)*. Neuchâtel: Imprimerie H. Messeiller, 1952.

Tebelen, A. Mennan. *Carnet d'un Diplomate (A Diplomat's Notebook)*. Paris: Denoel, 1951.

Tepedelenlioğlu, Nizamettin Nazif. *Ordu ve Politika (Army and Politics)*. İstanbul: Bedir Yayınevi, 1967.

Tevetoğlu, Fethi. *Türkiye'de Sosyalist ve Komünist Faaliyetler 1910-1960 (Socialist and Communist Activities in Turkey 1910-1960)*. Ankara: Ayyıldız Matbaası, 1967.

Thomas, Lewis V. and Richard N. Frye. *The United States and Turkey and Iran*. Cambridge: Harvard University Press, 1951.

Tobin, Chester M. *Turkey, Key to the East*. New York: G. P. Putnam's Sons, 1944.

Toğan, A. Zeki Velidî. *Bugünkü Türkili (Türkistan) ve Yakın Tarihi (Today's Turkestan and Its Recent History)*. Vol. 1. *Batı ve Kuzey Türkistan (West and North Turkestan)*. İstanbul: Arkadaş İbrahim Horoz ve Güven Basımevleri, 1942.

Tokın, Füruzan Hüsrev. *Basın Ansiklopedisi (Press Encyclopedia)*. İstanbul: n.p., 1963.

Tongas, Gerard. *La Turquie: Centre de Gravité des Balkans et du Proche-Orient*. Paris: Libraire Orientaliste Paul Geuthner, 1939.

Truman, Harry S. *Memoirs*. Vol. 1. *Years of Decisions*. Garden City, N.Y.: Doubleday & Co., 1955.

Tunaya, Tarık Z. *Türkiyede Siyasî Partiler 1859-1952 (Political Parties in Turkey)*. İstanbul: Doğan Kardeş Yayınları, 1952.

Tynlenov, General I. V. *Cherez tri voiny (Through Three Wars)*. Moscow, 1960.

Ülman, A. Halûk. *Türk-Amerikan Diplomatik Münasebetleri 1939-1947: İkinci Cihan Savaşının Başından Truman Doktirinine Kadar (Turkish-American Diplomatic Relations 1939-1947: From the Beginning of the Second World War to the Truman Doctrine)*. Ankara: Ankara Üniversitesi Siyasal Bilgiler Fakültesi Yayınları, No. 128-110, 1961.

Uran, Hilmi. *Hatıralarım (Memoirs)*. Ankara: Ayyıldız Matbaası, 1959.

Váli, Ferenc A. *Bridge Across the Bosporus: The Foreign Policy of Turkey*. Baltimore: The Johns Hopkins Press, 1971.

Ward, Barbara. *Turkey*. London: Oxford University Press, 1942.

Webster, Donald E. *The Turkey of Atatürk*. Philadelphia: The American Academy of Political and Social Science, 1939.

Weinberg, Gerhard L. *Germany and The Soviet Union 1939-1941*. Leiden: E. J. Brill, 1954.

Werth, Alexander. *Russia at War, 1941-1945*. New York: E. P. Dutton and Co., 1964.

Wilmot, Chester. *The Struggle for Europe*. London: Collins, 1952.

Wilson, Henry H. Maitland (Field Marshal Lord Wilson of Libya). *Eight Years Overseas 1939-1947*. London: Hutchinson and Co., 1949.

Winder, R. Bayly (ed.). *Near Eastern Round Table 1967-1968*. New York: New York University Press for the Near East Center and the Center for International Studies, 1969.

Wiskemann, Elizabeth. *The Rome-Berlin Axis: A History of the Relations Between Hitler and Mussolini*. London: Oxford University Press, 1949.

Wolfers, Arnold. *Discord and Collaboration: Essays on International Politics*. Baltimore: The Johns Hopkins Press, 1962.

Yalman, Ahmet Emin. *Turkey In The World*. New Haven: Yale University Press, 1930.

Yücel, Hasan Âli. *Hürriyet Gene Hürriyet (Freedom, Again Freedom)*. Ankara: Türk Tarih Kurumu Basımevi, 1960.

Yücel, Hasan Âli (ed.). *İnönü'nün Söylev ve Demeçleri (İnönü's Speeches and Declarations)*. Vol. 1. İstanbul: Millî Eğitim Basımevi, 1946.

Zartman, I. William. *The Politics of Trade Negotiations between Africa and the European Economic Community: The Weak Confront the Strong*. Princeton, N.J.: Princeton University Press, 1971.

ARTICLES

Açıkalın, Cevat. "Turkey's International Relations," *International Relations*, Vol. xxiii, No. 4 (October 1947), 477-91.

Belge, Burhan. "Moskova Buluşması" (Moscow meeting), *Aylık Siyasî İlimler Mecmuası* (October 1944), Vol. xix, No. 163, 408-13.

Berkes, Niyazi. "Ziya Gökalp, His Contribution to Turkish Nationalism," *Middle East Journal*, viii, 4 (Autumn 1954), 375-90.

Birge, John Kingsley. "Turkey Between Two Wars," *Foreign Policy Reports*, Vol. xx (November 1, 1944), 194-207.

Davidson, Basil. "Can Germany Live on the Balkans?" *Free Europe* (December 29, 1939), pp. 67-69.

Davison, Roderic H. "Turkish Diplomacy from Mudros to Lausanne," Gordon A. Craig and Felix Gilbert (eds.). *The Diplomats: 1919-1939*. Princeton, N.J.: Princeton University Press, 1953, pp. 172-209.

deWilde, John C. "The German Economic Dilemma," *Foreign Policy Reports*, Vol. XIII, No. 1 (March 15, 1937), 2-16.

———. "German Trade Drive in Southeastern Europe," *Foreign Policy Reports*, Vol. XII, No. 17 (November 15, 1936), 214-20.

Doğrul, Ömer R. "Turkish Foreign Policy Since the Revolution," *Pakistan Horizon*, Vol. IV (June 1951), 61-67.

Edwards, A. C. "Impact of the War on Turkey," *International Affairs*, Vol. XXII (July 1946), 389-401.

von Engelmann, H. "Turkey Extending Railroads to Develop Chrome Resources," *Engineering and Mining Journal* (June 29, 1929), pp. 1,037-38.

Eren, Nuri. "Dumbarton Oaks Konferansı," *Aylık Siyasî İlimler Mecmuası*, Vol. XIX, No. 164 (November 1944), 423-44.

Esmer, Ahmet Şükrü. "The Straits: Crux of World Politics," *Foreign Affairs*, Vol. XXV (April 1949), 183-201.

Henderson, Alexander. "The Pan-Turanian Myth in Turkey Today," *Asiatic Review*, N.S. 41, No. 145 (January 1945), 79-90.

Hostler, Charles Warren. "Trends in Pan-Turanism," *Middle Eastern Affairs*, Vol. III, No. 1 (January 1952), 3-13.

Howard, Harry N. "Germany, The Soviet Union, and Turkey During World War II," *Department of State Bulletin*, Vol. XIX, No. 472 (July 18, 1949), 63-78.

———. "The Problem of the Turkish Straits: Principal Treaties and Conventions (1774-1936)," *Department of State Bulletin*, Vol. XV, No. 383 (November 3, 1946), 790-807.

———. "Turkey's Foreign Policy and Hitler's War," *New Europe*, Vol. I (August 1941), 221-24.

————. "The United States and the Problem of the Turkish Straits," *Middle East Journal*, Vol. I (January 1947), 69-72.

İnönü, İsmet. "La Neutralité Turque au cours de la Deuxième Guerre Mondiale" ("Turkish neutrality during the Second World War), *Dictionnaire Diplomatique Internationale*, Vol. IV. Paris: Académie Diplomatique Internationale, 1957.

Kemp, Arthur. "Chromium: A Strategic Material," *Harvard Business Review* (Winter 1942), pp. 199-212.

Kocaeli, Nihat Erim. "The Development of the Anglo-Turkish Alliance," *Asiatic Review*, Vol. XLII (October 1946), 347-51.

Ringwood, Ona K. D. and Louis E. Frechtling. "World Production of Selected Strategic Materials," *Foreign Policy Reports*, Vol. XVIII (June 15, 1942), 90-96.

Russett, Bruce M. "Components of an Operational Theory of International Alliance Formation," *Journal of Conflict Resolution*, Vol. XII, No. 3, 285-301.

Rustow, Dankwart A. "Foreign Policy of the Turkish Republic," Roy C. Macridis (ed.), *Foreign Policy in World Politics*. Englewood Cliffs, N.J.: Prentice-Hall, Inc., 1959, pp. 295-322.

Sadak, Necmettin. "Turkey Faces the Soviets," *Foreign Affairs*, Vol. XXVII (April 1949), 449-61.

Smith, Edward C. "Debates on the Turkish Constitution of 1924," *Ankara Üniversitesi Siyasal Bilgiler Fakültesi Dergisi*, Vol. XIII (September 1958), 82-130.

Towster, Julian. "Russia: Persistent Strategic Demands," *Current History* (July 1951), 1-11.

Türkkan, Reha Oğuz. "The Turkish Press," *Middle Eastern Affairs*, Vol. I, No. 2 (May 1950), 142-49.

DOCUMENTS AND OFFICIAL PUBLICATIONS

Germany. *Reichgezetzblatt*, Vol. II, No. 42 (1941). "Regelung Des Warenverkehrs" (Regulations of Commercial Transactions) (October 9, 1941).

Germany. *Reichgezetzblatt*, Vol. II, No. 29 (1943). "Abkomen Zur Regelung Des Warenverkehrs Zwischen Deutschland und Turkei" (Treaty for the Regulation of Commercial Transactions between Germany and Turkey) (April 18, 1943).

Great Britain. Foreign Office. British and Foreign State Papers. Treaty of Mutual Assistance between His Majesty in respect of the United Kingdom, the President of the French Republic, and the President of the Turkish Republic, Ankara (October 19, 1939), Cmd. 6165 (Treaty Series No. 4), *House of Commons Sessional Papers*, Vol. XII (1940).

Great Britain. Foreign Office. Research Department (Series N, The Near and Middle East) (1941-1945).

Great Britain. Royal Institute of International Affairs. Foreign Research and Press Service. *Review of the Foreign Press* (Series B, Allied Governments, European Neutrals, Southeastern Europe and the Near East) (1941-1945).

Great Britain. Parliament. House of Commons. *The Parliamentary Debates (official reports)* (Fifth Series, 1942-1945).

Great Britain. Export Promotion Department. E. R. Lingeman, *Turkey: Economic and Commercial Conditions in Turkey* (1946).

Great Britain. Royal Institute of International Affairs. *Chronology of the Second World War* (1947).

Great Britain. Foreign Office. *Documents on British Foreign Policy 1919-1939* (Third Series, 1939), E. L. Woodward and Rohan Butler (eds.), Vol. V (1952).

Great Britain. Foreign Office. *Documents on British Foreign Policy 1919-1939* (Third Series, 1939), E. L. Woodward and Rohan Butler (eds.), Vol. VI (1953).

Great Britain. *History of the Second World War.* (United Kingdom Military Series), J.R.M. Butler (ed.), Vol. I, Ian Stanley Ord Playfair, *The Mediterranean and Middle East* (1954).

Great Britain. *History of the Second World War*. (United Kingdom Military Series), J.R.M. Butler (ed.), Vol. v, John Ehrman, *Grand Strategy* (1956).

Great Britain. *The War at Sea 1939-1945*. Vol. III, Stephen W. Roskill, *The Offensive* (1960).

Türkiye Cumhuriyeti Başbakanlık. Neşriyat ve Müdevvenat Genel Müdürlüğü (Office of the Prime Minister of the Turkish Republic. General Directorate of Press and Publications), *Düstur*, Üçüncü Tertip, Vols. XXIII-XXV (*Code of Laws*, Third Format) (1942).

Türkiye Cumhuriyeti Başbakanlık. Neşriyat ve Müdevvenat Genel Müdürlüğü (Office of the Prime Minister of the Turkish Republic. General Directorate of Press and Publications), *Resmî Gazete* (*Official Record*), No. 5255, November 11, 1942 (1942).

Türkiye Büyük Millet Meclis (T.B.M.M.), *Zabıt Ceridesi* (*Tutanak Dergisi*) (The Proceedings of the Turkish Grand National Assembly), Devre VI ve Devre VII (Sixth and Seventh Assemblies) (1942-1946).

Türkiye Cumhuriyeti Başbakanlık. Basın ve Matbuat Genel Müdürlüğü (General Directorate of Press and Publications), *Ayın Tarihi* (*News of the Month*) (1942-1946).

Türkiye Büyük Millet Meclis (T.B.M.M.), Üyeleri için Bastırılmıştır (Publications for the Members of the Grand National Assembly) (*Sicil-i Kavanin*) (*Register of Laws*), Vol. XXIII (1943).

Türkiye Cumhuriyeti Başbakanlık. Basın ve Yayın Umum Müdürlüğü (Office of the Prime Minister of the Turkish Republic. General Directorate of Press and Publications), Kanun No. 4475, "Basın ve Yayın Umum Müdürlüğü Teşkilat, Vazife ve Memurları Hakkinda Kanun" (Law Concerning the Organization, the Function and the Personnel of the General Directorate of Press and Publications, July 23, 1943), *Dışişleri Bakanlığı Mevzuatı ve Yayınla İlgili Hükümler* (*Rulings Concerning the Press and Publications and the Foreign Ministry*), Sadi Kıyak (ed.) (1943).

Türkiye Cumhuriyeti Başbakanlık. Basın ve Yayın Umum Müdürlüğü (Office of the Prime Minister of the Turkish Republic. General Directorate of Press and Publications), *Türkiyede Matbuat İdareleri ve Politikaları* (*Press Directives and Policies in Turkey*), Server İskit (1943).

Türkiye Cumhuriyeti Başbakanlık. Basın ve Yayın Umum Müdürlüğü (Office of the Prime Minister of the Turkish Republic. General Directorate of Press and Publications), *Basın ve Yayınla İlgili Kanun, Kararname, Nizamname, Talimatname ve Tamimler* (*Laws, Decisions, Rules, Instructions and Declarations Concerning Press and Publications*) (1944).

Türkiye Cumhuriyeti Başbakanlık. Basın ve Yayın Umum Müdürlüğü (Office of the Prime Minister of the Turkish Republic. General Directorate of Press and Publications), *Devlet Yıllığı: 1944-1945* (*The State Yearbook: 1944-1945*) (1945).

Türkiye Cumhuriyeti Başbakanlık. Basın ve Yayın Umum Müdürlüğü (Office of the Prime Minister of the Turkish Republic. General Directorate of Press and Publications), *Son Değişikliklere Göre Matbuat Kanunu* (*Press Law with Recent Modifications*) (1946).

Türkiye Cumhuriyeti Başbakanlık. İstatistik Umum Müdürlüğü (General Directorate of Statistics), *İstatistik Yıllığı 1942-1945* (*Statistical Yearbook 1942-1945*), Vol. 15 (1946).

Türkiye Cumhuriyeti Başbakanlık. Maliye Tetkik Kurulu (Financial Research Committee), *Yıllık Bütçe Giderleri 1924-1948* (*Annual Budget Expenditures 1924-1948*) (1948).

Türkiye Cumhuriyeti Başbakanlık. İstatistik Umum Müdürlüğü (General Directorate of Statistics), *Dış Ticaret 1938-1952* (*Foreign Trade 1938-1952*) (1953).

Union of Soviet Socialist Republics. Ministry of Foreign Affairs. *Correspondence Between the Chairman of the*

Council of Ministers of the U.S.S.R. and the Presidents of the U.S.A. and the Prime Ministers of Great Britain During the Great Patriotic War of 1941-1945 (July 15, 1944).

Union of Soviet Socialist Republics. Arkhivnoe Upravlenie Dokumenti Ministerstva Inostrannikh Diel Germanii Soinza SSR. Dokumenti Ministerstva Inostrannikh Diel Germanii, Vipusk II *Germanskai Politika v. Turtsii (1941-1943)*, OGIZ-Gospolitizdat, 1946; translated into French by Madeleine and Michel Eristov, *Documents Secrets du Ministre des Affaires Étrangers d'Allemagne* (Paris: Éditions Paul Dupont, 1946); also *İkinci Dünya Savaşının Gizli Belgeleri: Almanya'nın Türkiye Politikası—Almanya Dışişleri Bakanlığı Arşivinden 1941-1943 (Secret Documents of the Second World War: The Turkish Policy of Germany—from the Archives of the German Foreign Ministry 1941-1942)* (İstanbul: May Yayınları, 1968).

United States. Department of the Interior. Bureau of Mines. Robert L. Ridgeway, "Shifts in Sources of Chromite Supply," *Information Circular 6886* (1936).

United States. Department of Commerce. Bureau of Foreign and Domestic Commerce. S. Goldberg, "Turkey: Basic Economic Position and Recent Changes," *International Reference Service*, Vol. 1, No. 9 (April 1941), 1-4.

United States. Department of Commerce. Bureau of Foreign and Domestic Commerce. "Effect of War on Turkey's Foreign Trade," *Foreign Commerce Weekly* (December 13, 1941), pp. 4-5.

United States. Library of Congress. Legislative Reference Service. *Events Leading Up to World War II: A Chronological History, 1931-1944* (1944).

United States. Department of State. *Twenty-Third Report to Congress on Lend-Lease Operations*, Publication No. 2707 (1945).

United States. International Military Tribunal. Office of Chief of Counsel for Prosecution of Axis Criminality. *Nazi Conspiracy and Aggression*, Vol. III (1947).

United States. Department of State. *Nazi-Soviet Relations 1939-1940: Documents from the Archives of the German Foreign Office*, Raymond James Sontag and James Stuart Beddie (eds.) (1948).

United States. Department of the Army. Office of the Chief of Military History. Richard M. Leighton and Robert W. Coakley, *Global Logistics and Strategy 1940-1943*, Vol. IX (1955).

United States. Department of State. *Foreign Relations of the United States: The Conferences at Malta and Yalta, 1945* (1955).

United States. *Message from the President of the United States Transmitting the Thirty-Sixth Report to Congress on Lend-Lease Operations for the Year Ending December, 1954* (1955).

United States. Department of the Interior. Bureau of Mines. Lotfallah Nahai, "The Mineral Industry of Turkey," *Information Circular 7855* (1958).

United States. Department of State. External Research Staff, Office of Intelligence Research. *Russian Materials on Turkey: A Selective Bibliography*, Rudolf Loewenthal (ed.) (1958).

United States. Department of State. *Foreign Relations of the United States: Diplomatic Papers*, 1940, Vol. III (1958).

United States. Department of State. *Foreign Relations of the United States: Diplomatic Papers*, 1941, Vol. I (1958).

United States. Department of the Army. Office of the Chief of Military History. Maurice Matloff, *Strategic Planning for Coalition Warfare 1943-1944* (1959).

United States. Department of State. *Foreign Relations of the United States: Diplomatic Papers*, 1945, *The Conference of Berlin (The Potsdam Conference)*, Vol. I (1960).

United States. Department of State. *Foreign Relations of the United States: The Conferences at Cairo and Tehran, 1943* (1961).

United States. Department of State. *Documents on German Foreign Policy 1918-1945, The War Years* (Series D), Vol. xii (1962).

United States. Department of State. *Documents on German Foreign Policy 1918-1945, The War Years* (Series D), Vol. xiii (1963).

United States. Department of State. *Foreign Relations of the United States: Diplomatic Papers, 1942*, Vol. iv (1963).

United States. Department of State. *Foreign Relations of the United States: Diplomatic Papers, 1943*, Vol. i (1963).

United States. Department of State. *Foreign Relations of the United States: Diplomatic Papers, 1944*, Vol. v (1965).

United States. Department of State. *Foreign Relations of the United States: Diplomatic Papers, 1944*, Vol. i (1966).

United States. Department of State. *Foreign Relations of the United States: The Conferences at Washington, 1941-1942, and Casablanca, 1943* (1968).

UNPUBLISHED DOCUMENTS

Great Britain. Office of Naval Intelligence. "Fuehrer Conferences on Naval Affairs" (1947) (mimeographed).

United States. Library of Congress, Manuscript Division. *Papers of Laurence A. Steinhardt*, Box 45, "Memorandum," Leo Hochstetter to General Representative (W. H. Britt), United States Office of War Information, İstanbul, September 6, 1944.

United States. National Archives. *Captured Files* (German Embassy in Ankara). Micro-copy, Serial T-120, Roll 2618.

United States. National Archives. *Captured Files* (German Embassy in Ankara). Micro-copy, Serial T-454, Roll 88.

Unpublished Material

Banque de Paris et des Pays-Bas. *Étude* No. 638. "Situation Economique et Financière de la Turquie" (The Economic and Financial Situation of Turkey) (Paris, 1947) (mimeographed).

Frey, Frederick W. "Concepts of Developmental Administration and Strategy Implications for Behavioral Change," Massachusetts Institute of Technology, unpublished monograph, p. 26.

Helseth, William Arthur, "Turkey and the United States: 1784-1945" (Washington, D.C.: Foreign Service Institute, 1957) (mimeographed).

Menemencioğlu, Numan. "Les Détroits vus de la Mediterranée: Aperçus, Études, Souvenirs" (The Straits Seen from the Mediterranean: Glimpses, Studies, Memories) (unpublished manuscript).

Reed, Howard A. "The Destruction of the Janissaries by Mahmud II in June 1826." Unpublished Ph.D. dissertation, Princeton University, 1951.

The Wartime Diary of Michel Sokolnicki and the Private Papers of Irena Sokolnickia.

Weiker, Walter F. "The Free Party of 1930 in Turkey." Unpublished Ph.D. dissertation, Princeton University, 1962.

Newspapers

Great Britain

Daily Mail, 1940-1945
Manchester Guardian, 1940-1945
News Chronicle, 1940-1945
The *Times of London*, 1940-1945

BIBLIOGRAPHY

Turkey

Akşam, 1940-1945
Cumhuriyet, 1940-1945
İkdam, 1940-1945
Son Posta, 1940-1945
Son Telgraf, 1940-1945
Tan, 1940-1945
Tanin, 1940-1945
Tasvir-i Efkâr, 1940-1945
Ulus, 1940-1945
Yeni Sabah, 1940-1945

United States

Chicago Daily Mail, 1940-1945
Christian Science Monitor, 1940-1945
Daily Worker, 1940-1945
The New York Times, 1940-1945

OTHER SOURCES

Etibank, Conjuncture and Statistics Department. *Statistics of Etibank Mining Exploitations 1941-1951.* Ankara, 1954.
Etibank, Conjuncture and Statistics Department. "Principal Characteristics of Government Economic Institutions to which Etibank Belongs." Ankara, 1949 (mimeographed).
International Bank for Reconstruction and Development. Loan Department, Eastern Division. "Statistical Tables on Turkey." Washington, D.C., 1947 (mimeographed).
Irkçılık-Turancılik (Ankara: Türk İnkılâp Enstitüsü Yayını, No. 4, 1944).
Justus Perthes. *Almanach de Gotha: Annuaire Genéalogique, Diplomatique et Statistique,* 1944.
Keesing's Publications, Ltd., *Keesing's Contemporary Archives, 1943-1946.* June 24-July 1, 1944.

359

League of Nations, *Treaty Series*, Vol. cc, No. 4689.

League of Nations, *Treaty Series*, Vol. clxxiii, No. 4015, "Convention regarding the Regime of the Straits, with Annexes and Protocol, signed at Montreux," July 20, 1936.

League of Nations. General Study Conference on Economic Policies in Relation to World Peace. Hazım Atıf Kuyucak, *Memorandum on Exchange Control in Turkey.* Paris: International Institute of International Cooperation, 1939.

Wilson, Henry H. Maitland (Field Marshal Lord Wilson of Libya). *Operations in the Middle East from 16th February 1943 to 8th January 1944.* Supplement to *London Gazette*, November 12, 1946, No. 37,786.

INDEX

Abadan, Yavuz, 313
Abalıoğlu, Yunus Nadi, 77-80
Abdülhamid II, 15-16n, 16
Acheson, Dean, 127
Açıkalın, Cevat, 35, 36n, 39n, 45n,
    47n, 50n, 51n, 86n, 108n, 129n,
    132n, 149, 150n, 151n, 179n,
    180n, 188-89, 205n, 251n, 267n,
    268, 281n, 290; Ambassador in
    Moscow, 143, 176n; at Cairo
    Conference, 203n, 208n; at Cairo
    meeting of Menemencioğlu
    and Eden, 177, 178, 181;
    Secretary-General of Foreign
    Ministry, 54-55; on Turkish
    relations with Britain, 225;
    Vinogradov's interview with,
    189-90n, 329
Adana, 203-204
Adana Conference, 6, 131, 133-45,
    153, 183, 203n, 205, 329, 331,
    332; Churchill's proposals,
    138-39; military supplies,
    agreement on (Adana lists),
    138-39, 207, 209, 332
Adrianople (Edirne), 26-27
Aegean Islands, 163-66, 194, 195,
    203
Afyon Karahisar, 158
Ağralı, Fuat, 58, 88, 231n, 236
agricultural products: prices,
    89-92; sale, compulsory, to
    Bureau of Soil Products, 94;
    tax on (Toprak Mahsulleri
    Vergisi), 95
agriculture, 89
air bases in Turkey, 158, 160-61,
    170, 174, 178-80, 181n, 213
aircraft, British, for Turkey,
    157-58, 170n, 178

Akşam, 81, 147, 226, 309
Albania, 284, 304
Alexander, Sir Harold, 120
Alexandretta, 8
Allen, George V., 127n, 128, 129n
Alling, Paul H., 127n, 178n
Amasya Protocol (1919), 19
Anadolu Ajansı (Anatolian News
    Agency), 75-76
Anatolia, 18
Anatolianism, 18, 19
Ankara: Anglo-Turkish military
    staff conference, 153-56; capital
    established, 18; cost of living in,
    91-92; newspapers, 74
Antalya, 39
Aras, Tevfik Rüştü, 49n
Ardahan, 26, 315
Arıburun, Tekin, 127n
Armaoğlu, Fahir H., 33n, 64, 146,
    150n, 275n
Armenia, 17
Armenians, discrimination
    against, 233
Arnold, A. C., 153
Arnold, Gen. Henry H., 120, 122
Aron, Raymond, 322n
Artunkal, Ali Rıza, 35, 58
Arzık, Nimet, 50-51n
Aşkale, labor camp, 233-35
Atatürk, Kemal (Mustafa
    Kemal), 16n, 38-39, 44, 47,
    55, 248; Anadolu Ajansı
    founded by, 75; foreign policy,
    speech on, 9, 10n; ideology of,
    7-13; Lenin and, 27-28;
    newspaper closed by, 83n; in
    Revolution, 18; on Soviet
    Union, conversation with
    MacArthur, 21, 22; in World

Atatürk, Kemal (cont.)
War I, 27. See also under
Kemalist
Atay, Falih Rıfkı, 77, 81, 83n,
227, 243, 245n, 293n; and
British occupation of Greece,
284, 286
Athens, 284, 285, 301
Atsız, Nihat, 241-43, 255
Atsız (publication), 242
Austria: in Crimean War, 25;
wars with Ottoman Empire,
22n, 23
Axis, see Germany; Italy
Aydemir, Şevket Süreyya, 34,
37-38, 90n, 135, 156n, 185n;
on air bases, 181n; on
Pan-Turanian movement,
244n; on Soviet relations with
Turkey, 198n; on Varlık
Vergisi, 235
Aydınalp, Cemal, 127n
Ayın Tarihi, 141n
Azerbaijan, Turkic people in, 247
Azov, 24

Bahça, Sükrü Enis, 248
Baku, Gen. Mürsel, 248
Baird, Brigadier, 166
Balkan Wars: First, 26-27;
Second, 27
Balkans: Allied campaign in,
proposed, 180n, 207n, 208, 223,
269, 325, 329, 330; Churchill's
plans for, 198-99; federation
proposed, 144-45; independence
of, 184; Soviet sphere of
influence, 289, 291, 304; Yalta
Conference on, 299
Balladur, Nicholas, 234n
Baltic States, 149
Başkırıa, 239
Batalı, Kemal, 144n
Bayazıt, 26

Baydur, Hüseyin Ragıp, 309
Bayülken, Ü. Halûk, 3n
Bayur, Yusuf Hikmet, 69
Bekir Sami Bey, 28
Bele, Refet, 69
Belge, Burhan, 293
Belgrade, 136
Beneş, Eduard, 275-76
Benice, Etem İzzet, 84, 304n
Bessarabia, 24, 25
Beyoğlu, 84, 85
Big Four, see Great Powers
Big Three, 147, 149; Moscow
Conference of Foreign
Ministers, 167-76
Bilge, A. Suat, 33n, 37n, 65, 86n,
268
Birge, John Kingsley, 38n
Birgi, Muharrem Nuri, 48
Bismarck, Otto von, 26
Black Sea: naval battle in World
War I, 27; Russian territory on,
24, 25
Bodrum, 165
Boettiger, Maj. John, 203-204
Bolayır, 155
Bosnia, 15n
Bosphorus, see Straits
Bozkurt, 241
Braybrooke, David, 333
Britain, see Great Britain
Britt, George W.H., 79
Brooke, Gen. Sir Alan, 120, 122n
Bulgaria, 15n, 17, 26-27, 197, 269,
270n; German invasion of, 39;
rail traffic with Turkey, 41n;
Soviet occupation of, 277-84;
in Soviet sphere of influence,
289, 291, 292; Turkish
nonaggression pact with, 41n
Bullitt, William C., 316-17n
Bureau of Soil Products
(Toprak Mahsulleri Ofisi), 94

Cabinet, *see* Council of Ministers
Cadogan, Sir Alexander, 44-45
Cafer, Ahmet Said, 248
Cairo, Eden and Menemencioğlu
    meeting, 176-85
Cairo Conferences, 6, 295; First
    (Roosevelt and Churchill),
    192-94; Second (Roosevelt,
    Churchill, and İnönü), 159,
    191, 201-15, 228, 332
Çakmak, Fevzi, 155, 159n, 251;
    and Pan-Turanian movement,
    247-50
Çakmak (place), 158
Captured Files, 51-52n
Casablanca Agreement, 123-30;
    reactions to, 126-30
Casablanca Conference, 119-23,
    141
Çatalca, 26, 155
Çatalgazi electrical plant, 137
Catherine II, Empress, 24
Caucasus, Turkic people in, 240
Cebesoy, Ali Fuat, 59
Cemal Paşa, 17
Chiang Kai-shek, 193-94
China: in Dumbarton Oaks
    Conference, 295; as Great
    Power, 147; Roosevelt's
    preoccupation with, 203n
CHP, *see* Republican People's
    Party
chrome, 110n
chromite: British purchase of,
    101-103, 105-106, 111-14, 225;
    definition and description of,
    110n; German imports of,
    101-102, 104-105, 107, 112-13;
    shipments to Germany stopped,
    257-60; Turkish production of,
    110-11
chromium, 110n
Churchill, Capt. Randolph, 204
Churchill, Winston, 105, 132,

180n, 228, 268, 304, 318, 320,
    323-25, 326n, 329; Adana
    Conference, 133-45, 153, 183;
    and British occupation of
    Greece, 285, 286; Cairo
    Conference (First), 192-94;
    Cairo Conference (Second),
    191, 201-15; Casablanca
    Agreement, 123-26, 128;
    Casablanca Conference, 119-23;
    and Eden's meeting with
    Menemencioğlu, 181-83; Italy,
    plans on, 151-52; and Moscow
    Conference of Foreign
    Ministers, 168-69, 172-74;
    Roosevelt, meetings with, 151,
    162-63; and Soviet occupation
    of Bulgaria, 280-82; on Soviet
    Union, 148; on Stalin, 135;
    Stalin's communication with,
    139-40, 143, 271; Stalin's
    meeting with (Moscow), 282,
    288-94; strategic plans for war,
    121, 122n, 162-64; Tehran
    Conference, 194-201; Turkish
    entry into war, plans for,
    122-23, 133, 135-38, 140, 146,
    151-53, 162-64, 173n; on Turkish
    military equipment, 136; on
    U.S. failure to support British
    action, 164n; Yalta Conference,
    298-302
Clark, Gen. Mark W., 120
Clodius, Karl: and Pan-Turanian
    movement, 238n; trade
    agreements, 104, 106-109,
    112, 113
coal, 136; transportation of, 157
Comintern, dissolution of, 286
Committee on Union and
    Progress, 16, 17
communist agents in Turkey, 71n
communists in Greece, 285-88
Congress of Berlin (1878), 26

Constitution, Turkish (1876), 15
Constitution, Turkish (1924), 18, 61n, 63; Article 4, 60
Cos, 163, 165
COSSAC, 123
cost of living, rise in, 91-92
Council of Ministers (Cabinet, Bakanlar Kurulu), 33, 50-51, 61-64, 244; policy-making, 54-60
Crimea, 20; Russian-Ottoman wars in, 23-25; in World War II, 66
Crimea Conference, see Yalta Conference
Crimean War, 25
Cripps, Sir Stafford, 53n
Cumhuriyet, 77-81, 251
Cumhuriyet Halk Partisi, see Republican People's Party
Cunningham, Adm. Andrew Brown, 250n
Curzon, Lord, 39, 200
Czechoslovakia, 277, 294; Soviet treaty with, 275-76

Dallin, David, 57n
Damad İbrahim Paşa, 23
Damad Mahmud Celaleddin Paşa, 16
Damaskinos, Archbishop, 287
Dangerfield, Royden, 108-109n
Dār al-Ḥarb (House of War), 12
Dār al-Islam (House of Islam), 12
Dardanelles, 25, 200. See also Straits
Daver, Abidin, 84
Davison, Roderic H., 39
debt, national, 114
defense: expenditures for, 90; Law of National Defense, 93. See also military supplies and equipment
de Gaulle, Charles, 120

Dersan, Kâzım Şinasi, 81
Deutsch, Karl W., 28-29n
Devrin, Şinasi, 69
DeWilde, John C., 99n
Dhimmī, 11-12
Dill, Sir John, 120
Disraeli, Benjamin, 15n
Dodecanese, 195, 287
Doenitz, Adm. Karl, 165n
Doğubayazıt Kazası, 26
Dördüncü, Halil Lûtfi, 81, 83n, 84
Douglas, Sholto, 155, 178, 211-12n
Dumbarton Oaks Conference, 295-97, 311
Duru, Kâzım Nami, 69n

Ebuzziya, Ziyad, 79n, 80
Eckstein, Harry, 62n
economic policy, 88-115; domestic measures, 92-95; inflation, 89-92. See also trade
Eden, Anthony, 51, 53, 124, 133, 146-47, 159, 264, 268, 281, 286, 301, 323, 326n; at Cairo Conference, 206n, 209, 212, 213n; Cairo meeting with Menemencioğlu, 176-85, 329; on Churchill and Roosevelt, 193; Menemencioğlu's antagonism to, 226; at Moscow Conference of Foreign Ministers, 168-70, 172-75; Roosevelt confers with, 149-50, 151n; at Tehran Conference, 200
EDES, 285
Edirne, 26-27
Edwards, A. C., 61, 114
Egypt, war with Ottoman Empire, 25
Eisenhower, Dwight D., 164n
ELAM-ELAS, 285, 286
Emeç, Selim Ragıp, 84

Enver Paşa, 17, 27, 247
Erden, Gen. Ali Fuad, 43n,
   247, 250-52
Eren, Nuri, 296
Erer, Tekin, 36-37n, 81
Erim, Nihat, 267n
Erim, Tevfik K., 49n
Erkilet, Gen. Hüseyn Hüsnü
   Emir, 78, 79n, 247, 250-51
Erkin, Feridun Cemal, 35, 86n,
   87, 119n, 130-32, 142n, 144,
   151n, 161-62, 180n, 267n; at
   Adana Conference, 134; on
   Cairo Conference, 214; on
   passage through Straits, 262,
   264, 265; at San Francisco
   Conference, 309; on Soviet
   policy with Turkey, 198n; on
   Turkish relations with Britain,
   220-21, 230
Erol, Tevfik, 83
Erzincan, 27
Erzurum, 27
Erzurum Conference (1919), 19
Esendal, M. Ş., 69, 273n, 302n
Esin, Şeyfullah, 50
Esmer, Ahmet Şükrü, 33n, 39n,
   42-43n, 58n, 59n, 64, 86n,
   108n, 113n, 143n, 150n,
   161-62, 227n, 251n; Anadolu
   Ajansı criticized, 75-76; on
   Balkan plans, 223n; on Cairo
   meeting of Menemencioğlu
   and Eden, 179n, 180-81, 182n;
   on San Francisco Conference,
   311-12; on Soviet attitude
   toward Turkey, 167-68, 201n;
   on Tehran Conference, 199n;
   with Ulus, 77; on Yalta
   Conference, 298
Ethiopia, Italian campaign, 39
Etibank, 111n
expansionist-revisionism,

Turkish policy opposes, 3, 7,
   9n, 10, 20
exports, 96-97

Fenik, Mümtaz Faık, 307
Fiala, Fritz, 76, 79-80, 81-82n
Fikret, Tevfik, 83n
Finland, 274, 276n, 277
Finletter, Thomas K., 113n
food: Bureau of Soil Products
   policy, 94; hoarding, 94;
   prices, 90-92; rationing, 90
Foreign Ministry, see Ministry of
   Foreign Affairs
Foreign Relations of the United
   States; Diplomatic Papers, 41n
Fox, Annette Baker, 113-14
Fox, William T. R., 8n
France: in Crimean War, 25;
   foreign policy, 44; French
   newspapers in Turkey, 84-85;
   Treaty of Mutual Assistance
   between Turkey, Britain, and
   France (1939), 65, 96-97, 101;
   Turkish trade with, 102
Frey, Frederick, 34, 50, 58n, 68,
   328n
Frye, Richard N., 108n

Gamson, William A., 324
Garoun, 248-49
General Directorate of Press and
   Publications, 73
Georgiev, Kimon, 278, 282, 283,
   304
Gerede, Hüsrev, 247, 250, 253-54
Germany: Aski marks, 99n;
   Captured Files, 51-52n; military
   supplies for Turkey, 105, 109,
   112, 113; Nazi agents in
   Turkey, 71n; New Plan
   (economic), 98-99; newspaper

Germany (*cont.*)
attitudes toward, 76-80, 83-85; newspapers, German, in Turkey, 85; Pan-Turanian movement and, 250-54, 255n; Saar annexed by, 39; *Secret Documents*, 42n; Soviet alliance with, 56, 57n; Soviet occupation of, 294; Straits closed to Axis ships, 261-68; trade relations with Turkey, 95-115. *See also* chromite; Treaty of Territorial Integrity and Friendship (with Turkey, 1941), 41-42n, 104; Turkey declares war on, 302-303; Turkey severs relations with, 268-73; Turkish alliance with, in World War I, 27; Turkish relations with, 22, 39-43, 52-54, 68, 134, 136-37, 161, 184, 257-73; unconditional surrender of, doctrine, 130-32, 151-52n, 319-20; in World War II, 39-40, 43, 66, 69, 165-66, 229

Giraud, Gen. Henri, 85, 120
Gökalp, Ziya, 17
Gönlübol, Mehmet, 311
Gordon, David L., 108-109n
Grand National Assembly (Türkiye Büyük Millet Meclisi), 19, 33, 93, 210; authority, 60-61; policy-making, 60-70; and Turkish declaration of war, 302-303; and Turkish severance of relations with Germany, 272-73; and *Varlık Vergisi*, 231, 233
Great Britain: Adana Conference, 133-45; in Balkan Wars, 27; Cairo Conferences, *see* Cairo; Casablanca Conference and Agreement, 119-30, 141; in Crimean War,

25; in Dumbarton Oaks Conference, 295; economic sanctions against Turkey considered, 258-59; as Great Power, 147, 149; Greece occupied by, 284-88, 293-94, 304; military mission to Turkey, 220-24; military supplies for Turkey, *see* military supplies and equipment; in Moscow Conference of Foreign Ministers, 167-76; policy on Soviet Union, 146-50, 182-84; spheres of influence, 288-94; Treaty of Mutual Assistance between Turkey, Britain, and France (1939), 65, 96-97, 101; Turkish aid to, 165-66; Turkish relations with, 22, 42-45, 52-54, 65, 121-30, 133-66, 186-91, 219-27, 230, 275n, 296-97, 316, summary of, 319-26, 328-32, 334; and Turkish severance of relations with Germany, 268-71; Turkish trade with, 96, 101-14
Great Powers (Big Four), 147, 148, 321-22; spheres of influence, 290-94; Turkish strategy with, 330-33; United Nations Security Council veto, 147, 296, 298, 310-13
Greece, 45, 199, 274, 290, 318; British occupation of, 284-88, 293-94, 304; communists in, 285-88
Greeks in Turkey, discrimination against, 233, 234n
Grey, Sir Edward, 26
Groza, Pietro, 301, 304
Guetzkow, Harold, 327
Günaltay, Şemsettin, 69, 70
Gündüz, Asım, 153, 155, 249

Halifax, Viscount, 100n
Halil Paşa, 252
Ḥarbī, 11-12
HARDIHOOD (operation plan),
153-54, 156-57
Harriman, Averell, 173n, 175-76,
316; policy on Turkey,
recommended, 188n; and
Turkish severance of relations
with Germany, 269, 271-72
Haydar Paşa, 233
Hayter, William, 178n
Helseth, William Arthur, 100n,
103n
Higgins, Trumbull, 160n
Hinsley, F. H., 11n
Hitler, Adolf, 39, 172; letter to
İnönü, 40-41; Turkey, attitude
toward, 57n, 164-65n; Turkish
representatives visit, 251
Hochstetter, Leo D., 76n, 79, 82n,
85n, 246, 254
Hopkins, Harry, 159, 183, 196;
at Cairo Conference, 209, 212,
213
Hostler, Charles Warren, 237n,
238n, 246-47, 249, 255
Howard, Harry N., 261n
Hugessen, see Knatchbull-
Hugessen
Hull, Cordell, 124-26, 190, 222,
225, 268, 290, 291; at Moscow
Conference of Foreign
Ministers, 168, 170-72, 173n,
174-75
Hungary, 23; Soviet conquest of,
274; in Soviet sphere of
influence, 292, 294, 304; Turkish
trade with, 259
Hurewitz, Jacob C., 24

İbrahim Paşa, 25
İğdemir, Uluğ, 59n, 70, 86n

İkdam, 84
Iklé, Fred Charles, 326-27
Illustrious Rescript, 14
Imperial Rescript of the Rose
Chamber, 14
imports, 96-97; prices and, 89-90
İnan, Afet, 70
inflation, 89-92
İnönü, Ismet, 67-69, 75, 86n, 88,
129n, 140n, 143n, 149, 150n,
219, 220, 235n, 257, 266, 290,
302; Adana Conference, 133,
139, 141; Cairo Conference
(Second), 191, 201-15; Çakmak
and, 155n, 249-50; criticism of,
36-37; economic policies, 92-95,
108; Foreign Ministry papers
for, 85-86, 160-61; foreign
policy, changes in, 274-75;
foreign policy summarized,
319-22, 324-26, 329, 332, 334;
and Grand National Assembly,
60, 63-65; Hitler's letter to,
40-41; and Menemencioğlu,
49n, 50, 54, 55; and
Menemencioğlu's resignation,
6, 267, 268; and Özalp, 66;
and Pan-Turanian movement,
246, 247n, 249-52, 254, 255;
Pan-Turanism, speech on,
244-46; policy-making, 33-46;
press controlled by, 73, 77, 78,
80, 83; and Soviet denunciations,
304, 306, 308; and Turkish
entry into war, 180n, 185n;
and Turkish Historical Society,
70-71, 185n
Iran, 277; Tripartite Allied
Declaration on, 275
İskenderun, 8, 158
Islam: orthodoxy, 10; in Ottoman
period, 11-12; sovereignty
incompatible with, 11n
Ismay, Hastings, 120

İstanbul, 136, 138, 329; cost of
living in, 91, 92; newspapers,
74
İstanbul (newspaper), 84-85
Italy, 293, 294; air bases, 170;
Churchill's plans on, 151-52;
Ethiopian campaign, 39;
Turkey threatened by, 39;
Turkish trade with, 97n; U.S.
plans on, 152; Yugoslav forces
in, 301
İzmir, 138, 329
Izvestia, 167, 305, 309

Janissary corps, 13, 23
Japan, 293; Turkey declares war
on, 302-303; Turkey severs
relations with, 296-97
Jews, tax discrimination against,
232-35
Jihād, 8, 12

Kadıköy, 233
Kansu, Sevket Aziz, 71
Kaplan, Rasih, 69
Kara Mustafa, 22
Karabekir, Kâzım, 69
Karacan, Ali Naci, 39n, 81
Karal, Enver Ziya, 34n, 38n, 39n,
70-71, 86n
Karpat, Kemal H., 58n, 59n, 92n,
93n, 95, 242n
Kars, 26, 315
Kartal, 233
Kassel (German vessel), 264, 265
Kavur, Sadi, 48, 177n, 203n
Kâzım, Hüseyin, 83n
Kelley, Robert F., 112, 177n
Kemal Atatürk, see Atatürk,
Kemal
Kemalist government, 4;
established, 18-19; foreign
policy, 9, 10n; ideology, 7-13;
18-20; secularization, 11-12;

Soviet recognition of, 27-28;
Westernization, 13, 18, 19
Kemalist Revolution, 3, 7-10,
18-19
Kemp, Arthur, 110n
King, Adm. Ernest J., 120,
122, 195
Knatchbull-Hugessen, Sir Hughe,
47n, 51n, 100n, 187n, 188, 191,
224, 230; at Ankara staff
conference, 156, 159-60n; at
Cairo Conference, 203n; at
Cairo meeting of Eden and
Menemencioğlu, 176-78, 184-85;
and chromite shipments to
Germany, 257-59; and German
vessels passing through Straits,
263-64, 268; and Turkish
severance of relations with
Germany, 269; and Turkish
trade with Axis, 257-60
Kohler, Foy D., 185n
Konya, 25
Krecker, Lothar, 247, 253-54
Kroll, Hans Anton, 105n
Külçe, Süleyman, 249-50
Kuneralp, Zeki, 34n, 47n, 108n,
111n, 159, 249n, 253, 266n,
302n, 305n
Kuşadası, 165
Kythera, 284

labor: compulsory, 93;
punishment for tax evasion,
232-33, 235
Lacoste, Raymond, 53n
Lall, Arthur, 327
Lausanne Conference (1923), 39
Law of Fundamental
Organization (1921), 19
Law of National Defense (1940),
93
League for Private Initiative
and Decentralization, 16

368

Leahy, Adm. William D.,
125-26, 296
Leathers, Lord, 120
Lenczowski, George, 249
Lend-Lease Act, 109n
Lend-Lease Administration, 126
lend-lease operations, 109n;
Casablanca Agreement on, 124,
126; stopped, 225
Lenin, Nikolai, 27-28
Leninism, 4
Lerner, Daniel, 86
Leros, 163, 165, 174
Lewis, Bernard, 8-9, 11n
Lewis, Geoffrey, 234n
Liberal Republican Party, 68
Lindblom, C. E., 333
Lindsell, Wilfred, 156
Lingeman, E. R., 98n; *Turkey:
Economic and Commercial
Conditions in Turkey*, 88n
Linnell, Air Marshal,
Francis John, 220-22, 224

MacArthur, Gen. Douglas, 21
McCormick, Anne O'Hare, 289
Macedonia, 278, 281, 284
MacMurray, John Van Antwerp,
46n, 54n, 57n
McNeill, William Hardy, 197n,
198n
MacVeagh, Lincoln, 290
Mahmud II, 13
Mahmut, Reşat, 83
Maltepe, 233
Maritza (Meriç) River, 27, 41n;
Bridge, 257
Marshall, Gen. George C., 120,
122, 123, 171n, 188-89n; at
Tehran Conference, 195; and
Turkish severance of relations
with Germany, 270
martial law, 93n
Massigli, René, 47-48n, 57n

Matthews, Herbert L., 157
May, Richard, 127n
Meclis Gurubu, *see* Republican
People's Party, Parliamentary
Group
Medlicott, William H., 37n, 88,
102, 107, 109n, 112
Melamid, Alexander, 89n
Menemencioğlu, Muvaffak, 75
Menemencioğlu, Mme. Nevin, 48n
Menemencioğlu, Numan, 14n,
33, 35, 41n, 57, 59, 62, 63, 67,
119n, 131, 149, 150n, 222-25,
227n, 302, 325, 326, 332; and
Açıkalın, 55; on Adana
Conference, 142n, 143n; British
hostility to, 224-25; and British
military installations, 159n,
174; and British policy, 173,
221; at Cairo Conference, 203n,
204, 206-207n, 209, 211, 212,
213n, 214; Cairo Conference
described, 219-20; in Cairo
with Eden, 176-85, 329; on
Casablanca Agreement, 129-30;
and chromite shipments to
Germany, 257-58n, 259; Eden's
antagonism to, 226; as Foreign
Minister, 46-54; and German
vessels passing through Straits,
264-68; and Pan-Turanian
movement, 238n, 241n, 246,
247n, 254; policies, 51-54, 88,
266-68; resignation, 6, 257,
265-67, 333; Soviet Union,
negotiations with, 143, 228-29,
274; trade negotiations, 102-103,
104n, 108, 111-12, 114; and
Turkish aid to British forces,
166; on Turkish entry into war,
186-88, 190-91; and Turkish
trade with Axis, 258-60; Wilson
confers with, 155-56
Menemencioğlu, Turgut, 48,

Menemencioğlu *(cont.)*
50n, 129n, 144-45, 177n, 178n;
at Cairo Conference, 203n,
213n, 214n; on foreign policy,
266n; on Second Front and
Turkish policy, 223-24n
Menemencioğlu Manuscript, 48n
Meriç (Maritsa) River, 27, 41n,
257
Merritt, Richard L., 28-29n
Mersin, 158
Michael, King of Romania, 276,
301
Midhat Paşa, 15, 15-16n
Milas, 158
military supplies and equipment:
Adana agreement and list,
138-39, 153, 207, 209, 332; from
Britain, 153-61, 206-209;
British and U.S. shipments
ended, 225; Churchill's
comment on Turkish needs,
136; from Germany, 105, 109,
112, 113; Turkish delay in
accepting, 156-61; Turkish
demands from Britain, 220
Ministry of Foreign Affairs,
46-54; papers for İnönü, 85-86,
160-61; political bureaus, 50;
position paper (March 1943), 37
Ministry of the Interior, 244
Molotov, Vyacheslav, 56n, 57, 143,
179, 180, 193, 197, 276, 287;
at Moscow Conference of
Foreign Ministers, 168-70,
172-75; at San Francisco
Conference, 309; Sarper's
conversations with, 315-17; and
Turkish severance of relations
with Germany, 269
money: exchange rate, 90;
purchasing power, 90-91
Mongolia, Turkic people in, 240
Montchiloff, N., 98n

Montreux Convention, 261-68;
revision of, 292, 298, 300, 315
Moscow, Churchill's meeting with
Stalin, 282, 288-94
Moscow Conference of American,
British, and Soviet Foreign
Ministers, 167-76, 182, 323;
secret protocol, 175, 176n
Mountbatten, Lord Louis, 120,
122n
Muğla, 158
Munitions Assignments Board,
126, 128
Münnich, B. C., 23
Muraviev, Constantine, 277-78
Murphy, Robert, 120, 121n
Murray, Wallace, 124
Mussolini, Benito, 39, 57n; fall
of, 162
Mustafa Kemal, *see* Atatürk,
Kemal

Nadi, Nadir, 36, 37n, 46n, 72-73,
76-80, 141, 307-308;
Cumhuriyet, 77-80; on
Pan-Turanian movement,
238-39n; on *Varlık Vergisi*,
232, 233
Nadi, Yunus (Yunus Nadi
Abalıoğlu), 77-80
Namık Kemal, 14, 15, 47
National Pact (1920), 19
nationalism, Turkish, 12-14,
17-18
neutrality: public opinion on,
85-86. *See also* peace
New York Times, 149n, 177n
news agency (Anadolu Ajansı),
75-76
newspapers, 72-85; circulation,
statistics, 74; foreign-language,
84-85; political ideologies in,
76-83
Nicholas I, Czar, 21

Nizam-ı Cedid, 13
Nuri Paşa, 247, 250, 253

Ökmen, M., 312-13
Ökte, Faık, 233
Okyar, Ali Fethi, 65, 66n
Okyar, Osman, 252
Oral, Cavit, 33n, 63, 66n, 283n, 304n
Orhun, 242
Osman I, 11
Ottoman Empire, 11-16; Austrian wars with, 22n, 23; Egyptian war with, 25; ideology, 10-12; Islamic theocracy, 11-12; Russian wars with, 20-27
OVERLORD (operation), Second Front, 162, 171n, 196, 197
Özalp, Kâzım, 33n, 58n, 59n, 250-51n, 273n, 302n; accused of profiteering, 252; in Parliamentary Group, 66
Öztrak, Faık, 66n, 69, 302n, 303

Pan-Islamism, 12, 14
Pan-Slavism, 282-84, 289
Pan-Turanian movement, 5-6n, 17, 27, 43, 59, 80, 237-56, 309; definition of, 237n; government influenced by, 246-56; leaders and ideologies, 239-46; racism in, 241-44; sentences of leaders revoked, 251; suppression of, 230, 237-38, 243-46
Papen, Franz von, 40, 51-52n, 82n, 144n, 207-208n, 227n, 264; Menemencioğlu's statement to, on Casablanca Agreement, 129-30; and Pan-Turanian movement, 247-48, 251n, 254; and Varlık Vergisi, 236
parliament, see Grand National Assembly

Parliamentary Group, see Republican People's Party
Paulus, Gen. von, 119
peace: in Kemalist ideology, 7-8, 10; priority of, in Turkish policy, 3-4
Peker, Recep, 58-59, 69, 313
Pendik, 233
periodicals, 73
Peter the Great, Czar, 23
Peterson, Sir Maurice, 303
Philby, Kim, 284
Piraeus, 284
Ploesti, oil refineries, 163
Poland: German invasion of, 39; Ottoman Empire and, 23; Soviet Union and, 134, 149, 150, 183, 274, 294, 301-302; Yalta Conference agreement on, 298-99
Polar, Abdullah Zeki, 48
Portal, Charles, Marshal, 120
Potsdam Conference, 317, 318
Pound, Adm. Sir Dudley, 120
Pravda, 272, 305-306
President: duties of, in Constitution, 63n; election of, 60
press, 72-85; censorship of, 72-73; laws regulating, 72; political ideologies in, 76-83
Prime Minister, appointment of, 60-61
public opinion, 85-87; on İnönü's policy, 37; on neutrality, 85-86; on Soviet Union, 85-87

Quebec Conference, 151, 162-63

Raymont, Henry, 316n
Refet Paşa, 47
Republican People's Party (Cumhuriyet Halk Partisi,

Republican People's Party *(cont.)*
CHP), 34, 61, 243; Independent
Group (Müstakil Group), 68;
newspapers and, 77, 84; Nine
Principles (1923), 19;
Parliamentary Group (Meclis
Gurubu), 44, 60-64, 66-68, 77;
and Turkish severance of
relations with Germany, 273;
Ulus as official newspaper, 77
Reston, James, 177n
Review of the Foreign Press,
Royal Institute of International
Affairs, 74-75n, 84
Rhodes, 163-65, 196
Ribbentrop, Joachim von, 40, 53,
56n, 253-55
Riker, William H., 323, 324-25n
Rizan, Kadri, 48
Romania, 26; communist-
controlled regime, 301; oil
fields and refineries, 163; Soviet
occupation of, 274, 276, 277;
in Soviet sphere of influence,
289-92, 294; Turkish trade
with, 259-60
Rommel, Gen. Erwin, 119
Roosevelt, Franklin D., 138, 190,
222, 225, 228, 316-17n, 320,
324; Cairo Conference (First),
192-94; Cairo Conference
(Second), 191, 201-15;
Casablanca Agreement, 123-26,
128; Casablanca Conference,
119-20; Churchill, meetings
with, 151, 162-63; Eden
confers with, 149-50, 151n; and
Moscow Conference of Foreign
Ministers, 170, 171-72n, 175-76;
on Rhodes, letter to Churchill,
164n; and spheres of influence,
290, 291n; on Stalin, 206n;
Stalin's communication with,

192-93n; Tehran Conference,
194-201; and Turkish entry
into war, 189n; unconditional
surrender doctrine announced,
130, 319; Yalta Conference,
298-302
Rosen, Steven, 324
Roskill, Capt. Stephen W., 264n
Rothstein, Robert L., 321-22
Rumania, *see* Romania
Rumelia, 20, 24, 26
Russia (before Revolution), 4;
war with Ottoman Empire
planned (1876), 15n; wars with
Ottoman Empire, 20-27; in
World War I, 27. *See also*
Soviet Union
Rustow, Dankwart A., 9n, 10n,
49n

Saar, German annexation of, 39
Sabahaddin Âli, 243
Sabaheddin, Prince, 16
Sâbis, Gen. Âli İhsan, 80, 84, 247,
250, 252; memoirs, 252-53n
Sadak, Necmettin, 81, 82n, 245n,
276n; on British policy, 147,
226-27; on Germany, 294; on
Soviet occupation of Bulgaria,
279, 281n, 282; on spheres of
influence, 292, 294; on United
Nations, 309-10
Sadullah, Mandel and Levy, 234n
Safa, Peyami, 78, 80
Saka, Hasan, 59, 68-69, 273n, 297,
303, 309, 312
Salonicka, 278, 282-83
Samos, 165-66
Sanatescu, Constantine, 276
San Francisco Conference on
United Nations, 68, 301, 303,
304n, 309-14, 316n
Saracoğlu, Cemaleddin, 83

Saracoğlu, Şükrü, 55-57, 59n, 62, 63, 65n, 83, 88, 145, 149n, 150n, 219, 230, 251, 252, 329; at Adana Conference, 134; Atsız' open letters to him, 242-43; becomes Foreign Minister, 265; on foreign trade, 100; and Pan-Turanian movement, 253n, 254; in Soviet Union, 56-57n; Steinhardt's interview with, 275n; on Turkish declaration of war, 302; and Turkish severance of relations with Germany, 269, 272-73; and Varlık Vergisi, 231, 235-36; Wilson confers with, 155-56

Sardinia, 25

Sarper, Selim, 73, 275n, 281n, 289, 298n, 308, 310n; at Cairo Conference, 203n; Molotov's conversations with, 315-17; and Moscow Conference protocol, 176n; and Turko-Soviet Treaty, 305-306

Sawyer, Jack, 327

Saydam, Refik, 55, 65, 78, 235

Schacht, Hjalmar, 98-99

Scobie, Gen. R. M., 285

Second Front, plans for, 168, 171, 195-97, 223-24n

Selim III, 13

Serbia, 15n, 25-27

Sertel, Sabiha, 81, 87

Sertel, Zekeriya, 73, 81, 84, 87, 317n

Şevket, Memduh, 248

Sicily, invasion planned, 122n, 123, 133

Sikorski, Wladyslaw, 150

Siren, Zeki, 177n

Sirmen, Fuat, 62, 93n

Sivas Congress (1919), 19

Sobieski, Jan, 23

Socony-Vacuum Company, 234n

Sökmensüer, Şükrü, 69, 90n

Sokolnicki, Michel, 86, 106n, 182n, 183n

Sokolnickia, Irena, 47n, 86, 106n, 224-25n

Soldarelli, Gen. Massimo, 166

Son Posta, 84

Son Telegraf, 84

Soviet Union: Adana Conference, effect on Turkish policy, 139-40, 143-45; and British occupation of Greece, 286-88; British policy on, 146-50, 182-84; Bulgaria occupied by, 277-84; Churchill's views on policy, 148; communist ideology, 4; Czechoslovak-Soviet Treaty, 275-76; in Dumbarton Oaks Conference, 295-97; German alliance with, 56, 57n; German-Turkish agreements published by, 42n; Germany occupied by, 294; as Great Power, 147, 149; Kemalist government recognized by, 27-28; Menemencioğlu's negotiations with, 143, 228-29; in Moscow Conference of Foreign Ministers, 167-76; newspaper attitudes toward, 81-83, 85; note to Turkey (March 19, 1945), 304-309; Pan-Turanian movement and, 237-41, 245-47, 255-56; Poland and, 134, 149, 150, 183, 274, 294, 301-302; postwar policies, 301-302, 304-309, 315-18; public opinion on, 85-87; Romania occupied by, 274, 276, 277; spheres of influence, 288-94; territory ceded to Germany, 43; as threat, 3-5, 20-29, 52-54,

INDEX

Soviet Union (*cont.*)
66, 86, 128, 131-34, 201-202,
226, 288; Turkey, denunciation
of, 305-309; Turkey, postwar
demands on, 315-18; Turkic
peoples in, 239-40, 255n; and
Turkish entry into war, 168-72,
175, 181, 197, 198n; Turkish
relations with, 43-46, 54n,
56-57, 139-40, 143-45, 182-84,
196-200, 204-205, 210-11, 219-21,
228-29, 267-68, 288-94, 297,
303-309, 315-18, summarized,
319-25; and Turkish severance
of relations with Germany,
271-72; Turkish treaties with,
28, 305-306; in World War II,
43, 45, 66, 69, 119, 274-77
Soyzal, Mümtaz, 62n, 64, 67n,
68, 312
Stainov, Petko, 282, 283n
Stalin, Josef, 131, 146, 167, 205,
276, 319-20; Churchill on, 135;
Churchill's communication
with, 139-40, 143, 271;
Churchill's meeting with
(Moscow), 282, 288-94; invited
to Casablanca, 119-20; policy
on Turkey, 139-40, 145;
Roosevelt's communication
with, 192-93n; Roosevelt's
impression of, 206n; and Soviet
occupation of Bulgaria, 282;
suggests Greek territory be
given to Turkey, 45; Tehran
Conference, 192, 194-201; on
Turkish entry into war, 123; on
Turkish severance of relations
with Germany, 271; Yalta
Conference, 298-302, 316
Stalingrad, 45, 119, 135, 144
Steinhardt, Laurence A., 45, 46n,
58n, 130, 137, 188-90, 202, 221,

222, 225, 268, 297; and chromite
shipments to Germany, 257-59;
Menemencioğlu's statement to,
on entry into war, 186-88;
personal papers, 79; Saracoğlu's
interview with, 275n; and
Turkish trade with Axis, 257-60,
261n; and *Varlık Vergisi*, 232,
233, 234n; on Vyshinsky, 204n
Stimson, Henry L., 162
Straits: Allied ships, passage of,
297; closed to Axis ships,
261-68; Montreux Convention
on, *see* Montreux Convention;
Soviet postwar demands on,
315; Stalin's recommendations
on, 300
Streater, Jasper, 16n
Streater, Nermin, 47n, 49n, 50n,
52n, 55n, 129n, 159n, 181n
Sublime Porte, 22-26
Sudetenland, 39
Sulzberger, C. L., 278n, 290
Sümer, Nurullah Esat, 58, 88
Sweden, air bases, 168
Swinton, Lord, 105, 106n
Syria, 165; British forces in, 161

Talat Paşa, 17
Tan, 81, 85, 87
Tanin, 75, 83
Tanridağ, 242
Tanzimat, 14-15
Tarhan, Ali Râna, 68-69, 231n,
273, 302n
Tass, 278
Tasvir-i-Efkâr, 80-81
taxes, 94-95; on soil products
(*Toprak Mahsulleri Vergisi*),
95; on wealth (*Varlık Vergisi*),
35, 68, 83, 95, 230-36, 333
Tehran, 192, 193
Tehran Conference, 194-201, 295

374

telegraph system, 16n
Tepedelenlioğlu, Nizamettin
Nazif, 250n
Tevetoğlu, Fethi, 241-43n, 250n
Thomas, Lewis V., 108n
Thrace, 278, 281
Times, London, 140, 146, 148,
149n, 151-52n, 177n, 225-28,
233n
Tito, Marshal, 274, 282-84, 301,
304
Toğan, A. Zeki Velidî, 239-40
Togay, Muharrem Feyzi, 78, 79n
Tokın, Füruzan Hüsrev, *Press
Encyclopedia*, 75n
Tolbukhin, Marshal, 278
Toprak Mahsulleri Vergisi (Tax
on Soil Products), 95
Trabzon, 92
trade, Turkish: balance of trade,
114; British-French-Turkish
agreements, 102; with France,
102; with Germany, 95-115;
with Great Britain, 96, 101-14;
with Hungary, 259; with Italy,
97n; preemptive purchasing
program, Anglo-American,
105-13; with Romania, 259-60;
with U.S., 96, 106, 108, 109,
112, 113. *See also* chromite
Transkontinent Press, 76, 79
Transylvania, 23
Treaty of Adrianople (1829), 25
Treaty of Alexandropol or
Leninikan (1920), 28
Treaty of Belgrade (1739), 23-24
Treaty of Bucharest (1812), 25
Treaty of Friendship
(Turkish-Soviet, 1921), 28
Treaty of Hunkâr-Iskelesi
(1833), 25
Treaty of Isaşi (1792), 24-25
Treaty of Karlowitz (1699), 23

Treaty of Küçük Kaynarca
(1774), 24
Treaty of Mutual Assistance
between Turkey, Britain, and
France (Tripartite Agreement,
1939), 65, 96-97, 101
Treaty of Neutrality and
Nonaggression (Turkish-Soviet,
1925), 28, 305-306
Treaty of Paris (1856), 25
Treaty of San Stefano (1878), 26
Treaty of Sivatorok (1606), 22n
Treaty of Territorial Integrity
and Friendship between
Germany and Turkey (1941),
41-42n, 104
Tripartite Allied Declaration
on Iran, 275
Truman, Harry S., 304
Truman Doctrine, 318
Türk Tarih Kurumu, *see* Turkish
Historical Society
Turkestan, Turkic people in,
239, 240
Turkey: before World War I, *see*
Ottoman Empire; Constitution
(1876), 15; Constitution (1924),
18, 60, 61n, 63; economic policy,
see economic policy;
government established, 10n,
18-19; government structure,
60-61; as independent state,
10n, 13, 18, 184; internal policy,
changes in, 230-56; in United
Nations, 299-300, 303, 304n,
309-14; in World War II, *see*
World War II
Türkische Post, 84, 247
Turkish foreign policy: Atatürk's
speech on, 9, 10n; operational
code, 3-5; origins, history of,
7-29; policy-making process,
33-71; revision of, 257-73;

Turkish foreign policy (cont.)
summary analysis of, 319-34;
two principles of, 3
Turkish Historical Society (Türk
Tarih Kurumu, TTK), 33,
70-71, 185n
Turkism, 17-19, 237n
Türkiye Büyük Millet Meclisi
(TBMM), see Grand National
Assembly
Türkkan, Reha Oğuz, 240-41,
242n
Türquie, La, 85
Tynelov, Gen. I. V., 164n
Tzigantes, Col., 166

Ukraine, Turkic people in, 240
Ulukışla, 158
Ulus, 75, 77, 81, 84, 293, 307
unconditional surrender, doctrine
of, 130-32, 151-52n, 319-20
Üner, Celal, 203
United Kingdom Commercial
Corporation, 105
United Nations: Charter, 312-13,
316n; Dumbarton Oaks
Conference on, 295-96, 311;
San Francisco Conference on,
68, 301, 303, 304n, 309-14,
316n; Security Council, Great
Powers and veto, 147, 295-96,
298, 310-13; Turkey in, 299-300,
303, 304n, 309-14; Yalta
Conference decisions on,
299-301
United States: and British
military supplies for Turkey,
158-59, 163; Churchill's views
on, 138, 164n; economic
sanctions against Turkey
considered, 258-59; as Great
Power, 147, 149; Joint Chiefs
of Staff, 170-71, 272; Joint

Strategic Survey Command,
170-71; lend-lease, see
lend-lease operations; State
Department, 258, 291n, 316-17;
Turkish relations with, 22,
188-90, 222, 230, 236, 275n,
296-97, 316-18, summarized,
319-25, 328-32, 334; and
Turkish severance of relations
with Germany, 270, 272;
Turkish trade with, 96, 106,
108, 109, 112, 113; War
Department, 126; in World
War II, 122, 123, 152-53,
162-63, 180n
United States Commercial
Corporation, 106
Uran, Hilmi, 58-59, 69
Us, Asım, 83n, 84, 141, 292-93,
307; and Soviet occupation of
Bulgaria, 277, 281-82; on
United Nations, 310
Uşaklıgil, Ekrem, 84
Uzunçarşılı, Ismail Hakkı, 71

Vakit, 84, 307, 310
Varlık Vergisi (Tax on Wealth),
35, 68, 83, 95, 230-36;
discrimination against
minorities, 232-35; punishment
for evasion, 232-33; repealed,
235n, 236, 333
Vatan, 83, 148, 234-35
Velidî, Zeki, 247
Venice, Republic of, 23
Vergin, Nurretin, 48
Vinogradov, Sergei A., 143,
187-88, 189n, 306, 329; at
Cairo Conference, 203n;
Menemencioğlu's negotiations
with, 228-29
Vyshinsky, Andrei, 203, 204,
271-72, 301

War and the Working Class, 167
Ward, Barbara, 96
Wedemeyer, Gen. Albert C., 120
Weiker, Walter F., 58n
Weizsäcker, Ernst von, 253
Westernization, 15, 16; Kemalist, 13, 18, 19
Wilson, Edwin C., 316
Wilson, Gen. Henry Maitland, 154-56, 158-59, 163, 165; at Cairo Conference, 209; at Cairo meeting of Menemencioğlu and Eden, 178; *Operations in the Middle East*, 154n
Winant, John G., 160n
Wiskemann, Elizabeth, 57n
World War I, Turkey versus Russia, 27
World War II: Allied victories, 119, 274-77; Churchill's strategy, 121, 122n, 162-64; end of, in Europe, 315-16; German annexation of territory, 39-40; Germany versus Soviet, 43, 45, 66, 69; Second Front, plans for, 168, 171, 195-97, 223-24n; Turkey declares war on Germany and Japan, 302-303; Turkish aid to Britain, 165-66; Turkish entry, plans for, 122-23, 133, 135-38, 140, 146, 151-53, 162-64, 167-76, 178-80, 182, 186-88, 195-201, 207n, 213-14, 222-24; Turkish resistance to Allied demands, 185-91; unconditional surrender, doctrine of, 130-32, 151-52n, 319-20; U.S. plans for, 122, 123, 152-53, 162-63, 180n
Wright, Michael, 125

Yalçın, Hüseyin Cahit, 82-83, 252, 284, 297, 302, 306; on British occupation of Greece, 285-88, 293-94; on Dumbarton Oaks Conference, 296; Sertel's dispute with, 317n; on Soviet denunciation of Turkey, 308; on Soviet occupation of Bulgaria, 277, 279-84; on United Nations, 313-14
Yalman, Ahmet Emin, 59n, 73, 80, 81, 82n, 83, 233n, 277; on British policy with Soviet, 148-49; *Varlık Vergisi* criticized, 234-35
Yalman, Rifat, 81
Yalta Conference, 294, 298-302, 316; "Declaration on Liberated Europe," 299, 301; on Turkey, 299-301
Yeni Sabah, 75, 83, 307
Young Ottoman movement (1860s), 14-15
Young Turks (1908), 16-17
Yücel, Hasan Âli, 58, 59n, 243, 244, 245n
Yudenich, Gen. Nikolai, 27
Yugoslavia, 199, 289; Bulgaria and, 282-84; Italian territory occupied, 301; Soviet forces enter, 284; in Soviet sphere of influence, 291, 292

Zartman, I. William, 326n, 327, 330
Zervas, Col. Napoleon, 285
Ziya Paşa, 15
Zonguldak coal field, 136, 157n, 329
Zorlu, Fatin Rüştü, 48

NEW YORK UNIVERSITY
CENTER FOR INTERNATIONAL STUDIES

STUDIES IN PEACEFUL CHANGE

Why Federations Fail: An Inquiry into the Requisites for Successful Federalism. Thomas M. Franck, Gisbert H. Flanz, Herbert J. Spiro, and Frank N. Trager. New York: New York University Press, 1968.

A Free Trade Association. Thomas M. Franck and Edward Weisband, eds. New York: New York University Press, 1968.

Comparative Constitutional Process. Thomas M. Franck. New York: Frederick A. Praeger, Inc.; London: Sweet & Maxwell Ltd., 1968.

The Structure of Impartiality. Thomas M. Franck. New York: The Macmillan Company, 1968.

Agents of Change: A Close Look at the Peace Corps. David Hapgood and Meridan Bennett. Boston: Little, Brown and Company, 1968.

Law, Reason, and Justice: Essays in Legal Philosophy. Graham B. Hughes. New York: New York University Press, 1969.

Microstates and Micronesia: Problems of America's Pacific Islands and Other Minute Territories. Stanley A. de Smith. New York: New York University Press, 1970.

Czechoslovakia: Intervention and Impact. I. William Zartman. New York: New York University Press, 1970.

Sierra Leone: An Experiment in Democracy in an African Nation. Gershon B. O. Collier. New York: New York University Press, 1970.

International Business Negotiations: A Study in India. Ashok Kapoor. New York: New York University Press, 1970.

Foreign Capital for Economic Development: A Korean Case Study. Seung Hee Kim. New York: Frederick A. Praeger, Inc., 1970.

The Politics of Trade Negotiations between African and the European Economic Community: The Weak Confront the Strong. I. William Zartman. Princeton: Princeton University Press, 1971.

Word Politics: Verbal Strategy among the Superpowers. Thomas M. Franck and Edward Weisband. New York: Oxford University Press, 1971.

Developing Democracy. William A. Douglas. Washington, D.C.: Heldref Publications, 1972.

Integration or Fragmentation or International Markets? Commercial Policy Options for the United States in an Age of Controls. Ingo Walter and Robert G. Hawkins, contributors and eds. Boston: D. C. Heath & Co., 1972.